T0274963

ESSAYS ON LANDSCAPE

ESSAYS ON LANDSCAPE

LAURIE OLIN

LIBRARY OF AMERICAN LANDSCAPE HISTORY

AMHERST, MASSACHUSETTS

Library of American Landscape History
P.O. Box 1323
Amherst, MA 01004
www.lalh.org

Printed in the United States of America by Porter Print Group, LLC

Library of Congress Control Number: 2021934454
ISBN: 978-1-952620-30-0

Designed by Jonathan D. Lippincott
Set in Fairfield

Drawings by Laurie Olin

Distributed by
National Book Network
nbnbooks.com

Publication of *Essays on Landscape* is supported by
the Ann Douglass Wilhite Nature and Design Fund.

CONTENTS

PREFACE

The landscape architect Laurie Olin writes the same way he draws—without apparent effort, buoyed by some inner well of curiosity, an urgent desire to understand. In this volume he takes on a great range of topics, sometimes diving beneath the surface of things, and sometimes soaring high above them. Among the most significant landscape practitioners of our era, Olin is also arguably the most prolific, well read, and reflective designer addressing core issues in landscape architecture today.

The essays gathered here were drawn from a much larger body of published work that would have made an impressive but unwieldly volume. We asked Olin himself to take on the difficult task of selecting which pieces to include, putting aside the question of subject altogether. In response, he assembled what he felt were his most important articles, without regard for overall organization, simply letting each essay have its own say.

We settled on a chronological arrangement for the collection, because it illuminates Olin's development as a designer, teacher, and critic over the four decades these writings span. It is quite an amazing tour, as well as a tour de force. We resisted the impulse to illustrate the book except for occasionally slipping in one of Olin's beguiling line drawings or plans.

In a wonderful convergence of spirit and substance, this is the first LALH publication to be supported by the new Ann Douglass Wilhite

Nature and Design Fund. Ann and Laurie knew each other, and Ann was a staunch admirer of his. She regarded Laurie as one of the era's consummate designers of urban parks and one of the field's most important voices. She would have been proud and deeply gratified to see this book in print.

Robin Karson
Executive Director
Library of American Landscape History

ESSAYS ON LANDSCAPE

INTRODUCTION

What prompts a designer to write when their deepest creative impulses lie elsewhere?

For me, as for others in various fields—doctors, philosophers, artists, architects, historians—the answer is that I couldn't find anything satisfactory that addressed a current interest or problem I wanted to solve. So I wrote in hopes of sharing and perhaps enlightening or persuading others (colleagues or the public) about something I learned or speculations I came to believe were important. On occasion, I have been asked to write on a particular topic, and I have agreed to, as well.

I published my first piece in 1963 when I was just two years out of architecture school, a review of a pair of recent books by R. Buckminster Fuller, *No More Secondhand God* and *Education Automation: Comprehensive Learning for Emergent Humanity,* for *Design* magazine in Britain. This was the first of what has been a series of requests to lecture or write about a topic others were engaged in—and often not of particular concern to me at the time.

The earliest pieces I wrote out of my own interest were simple narratives or descriptions of a situation, historic place, or landscape that stimulated me and that I desired to share with others. Some were rejected. In 1969, for instance, I was living on Bainbridge Island, Washington, and had made a series of drawings of tree stumps and forest regrowth. At an exhibition of them, I happened to meet the editor of *Pacific Search,* a journal published by the Pacific Science Center, who suggested an illustrated essay on the topic. I responded with a piece that made some harsh remarks about clear-cutting and the timber industry. It turned out that the journal was underwritten by Weyerhaeuser, the giant timber and pulp producer. I was asked to make some changes. I refused. The article was killed. I sold the drawings, and that was that.

My next effort was *Breath on the Mirror,* a report on life in the Skid Road, Pioneer Square, and Pike Place Market area of Seattle, a small illustrated publication in the tradition of eighteenth-century London pamphleteers. Something of an anti-planning tract aimed at the Seattle City Planning Commission, it came out of my growing interest in urban and civic life, issues of historic preservation, adaptive reuse, and social conflict. I managed to finance and publish it myself, to accompany an exhibition of my drawings in April 1972.

A month later I left Seattle for Europe to study Italian urban life, landscape, and design, and to work on a book about the English landscape. This was to be a collection of linked essays and drawings which would bring together various fields that had little or no apparent awareness of each other: art history, architectural history, geography, ecology, economic and agricultural history. Naively ambitious, I set out to describe the rich result of the interaction of these diverse histories in the making of a particular cultural landscape. The project took many years to reach fruition (*Across the Open Field: Essays Drawn from English Landscapes* was published in 2000), but it set me on the path to landscape architecture and everything I have written since.

Subsequent talks and essays that followed on my return to the States in 1974 were attempts to explain in the simplest terms what I had come to believe landscape architecture and urban design to be—what we actually do or might aspire to. Most of my writing, whether for a professional, scholarly, or general audience, has been in this vein. I have made an effort not to write in an academic mode, and I have often used projects from my own office that I knew well to illustrate my points. I also frequently turned to work by others that is indisputably admirable—designs by Bernini, Frederick Law Olmsted, or Lawrence Halprin, for instance—in my effort to explain and persuade. Along the way I have written out of my exploration of particular topics that I was wrestling with. Central among them has been the problem of expression in the medium of landscape, along with related issues of meaning, memory, and representation. In this I have been encouraged, stimulated, even provoked by my students, friends, and colleagues in practice and academia.

In my first eight years at the University of Pennsylvania I did not write much. Teaching both undergraduates and graduates while starting a professional practice was intense and time-consuming labor. Writing is work, and it takes time. My colleagues were finishing dissertations and publishing articles and reports on methodology and technology for landscape planning and design which were based largely on their research in the natural sciences or anthropology.[1] While enthusiastically following and absorbing their work, I continued to think about the field as an art—albeit a useful one—and about the things that had engaged me when I was abroad: the age-long considerations of the rich issues and unities of form and content in landscape design.

In 1982, I left the University of Pennsylvania to take up a position at Harvard's Graduate School of Design. Almost immediately something I had noticed in my early years in academia became clear: artists, designers, architects, and landscape architects were not respected intellectually by colleagues in the humanities and sciences. We were considered to exist somewhere between cultural ornaments and idiots savants. It was acknowledged that we knew how to make things (somehow), but intellectually we were inferior. We didn't do research or publish papers that were discussed and debated, advancing something called "theory." We were deemed inarticulate and, to a degree, illiterate, despite the fact that we provided considerable material—some of the "art"—that was studied by scholars in the "Arts and Sciences." We generated their content, albeit seemingly unwittingly. The other prevailing attitude that disturbed me was that many of my faculty colleagues in architecture and planning, who were themselves disrespected not only by arts and sciences faculty but also by deans of other graduate schools as well as the provost and the president, in turn looked down on the field of landscape architecture and its practitioners as soft, undisciplined, and wandering about ungrounded by a body of literature and theory.

This situation upset me. It wasn't true. Artists and designers are stuffed with all manner of knowledge, but rarely do they express their thinking verbally. There are exceptions, of course (the New York School painters Robert Motherwell and Fairfield Porter come to mind), but generally artists and designers don't use words to articulate their thoughts or explain the specific intentions embodied in their work. Aside from a few interviews with prominent landscape architects such as Dan Kiley, the only contemporary texts we could point to were Ian McHarg's *Design with Nature,* Kevin Lynch's *Image of the City,* and a few magazine articles by Lawrence Halprin, or essays by Thomas Church and Garrett Eckbo written thirty years earlier. From my time abroad, I knew the writings of English landscape architects—Sylvia Crowe, Geoffrey Jellicoe, and Peter Shepherd, among others—and was familiar as well with several journals published in Europe, notably *Garten und Landschaft.* I had also spent a fair amount of time in the rare books stacks of the American Academy and the Hertziana libraries in Rome, which were filled with texts, folios, prints, and manuscripts on Renaissance and Enlightenment landscape design and theory. There was no dearth of literature and theory from the past.

The ignorance of my colleagues irritated me. Landscape design is easily as ancient a practice as architecture. It is exceedingly complex, difficult, and subject to nuance and subtlety. Along with drawing and music, the activity of landscape design and planning predates writing, science, and philosophy by millennia. There is a body of written history and theory of landscape, its nature, design, and planning that dates to classical antiquity in a number of different cultures but especially in Asia Minor, Europe, and East Asia. My colleagues were simply ignorant of the richness of landscape history. We didn't discuss it and publish the way architects did about architecture. Additionally, I felt that the problem extended into the field itself. Most practitioners, academics, and students of landscape architecture I encountered were poorly informed if not totally unaware of the existing history and theory.

In the early 1980s, there were very few schools where one could study landscape history or that offered a PhD in landscape architecture. Landscape architectural history, such as it was, was taught by practitioners who had taken a course or two, traveled a bit, and used either their own or old slides left behind by other landscape architects. The most common text was Norman Newton's *Design on the Land: The Development of Landscape Architecture,* which, published in 1971, was even then woefully out of date, contained errors, and ignored much of the world.

There was only one solution: start teaching and writing and encouraging others to do the same. Create the courses, articles, and books that were needed. At the GSD, Jorge Silvetti, a young architecture professor, John Whiteman in urban design, and I created an introductory history and theory course for all first-semester students in architecture, landscape architecture, and urban design. In addition to the history of western landscape design and planning, I felt it was critical to include examples from Asia and Latin America. I decided that a prerequisite for anything that might be called landscape architecture theory must be a history and description of what people had made—only then should we consider what had been said about it. I also hoped to have students read. My syllabus included Geoffrey Jellicoe and Susan Jellicoe's *The Landscape of Man* (1964) and Clarence Glacken's *Traces on the Rhodian Shore* (1967).

Contrary to many architects I knew, I believed that theory is developed in retrospect, to account for what had been or was being done in the field, and that it rarely preceded or led creative practice. It was through the act of doing that creative people advanced ideas. This was not to say that creative artists had no ideas or goals before they set to work but rather that it was in the course of working with self-imposed problems and a particular context that they made discoveries and created fresh, often highly complex work. There is general confusion that a hypothesis, such as artists and scientists employ when beginning a project, is theory. Theory is explanation, and should simply present the social and artistic goals and achievements embodied in a work, along with its intellectual context.

Fortunately, at that time there were others in art history, cultural studies, geography, and American studies who were beginning to explore landscape and gardens, along with a small handful of practitioners and academics in landscape architecture who had become interested in history, especially the late Renaissance and the modernist era. Things were beginning to change. At Dumbarton Oaks, Harvard's humanities research center in Georgetown, the art historian Elisabeth MacDougall was appointed to direct the program in landscape architecture studies with the goal of developing it to equal their pre-Columbian and Byzantine studies programs. MacDougall was a pioneer in applying art historical method to the study of gardens. I had met her when I was in Rome and had enjoyed discussions of our research interests and work. Under MacDougall's direction Dumbarton Oaks inaugurated a series of annual symposia and publications, and I soon joined the senior fellows who discussed and appointed visiting scholars. Encouraged by these developments, I decided to relaunch an updated history and theory course, and hired MacDougall to teach in the department.

Other currents were guiding me toward writing as well. In 1983, the architect Peter Eisenman, who was then a visiting professor at the GSD, and I began a twenty-five-year-long collaboration in which, through exploring the relationship of theory, methodology, and practice, we developed an approach to projects that gave equal importance to the building and its surrounding landscape. (Many of our projects, including *Fertilizers: Olin/Eisenman,* a site-specific environmental installation at Penn's Institute of Contemporary Art, were documented in a book of that title, published in 2007.)

Spirited conversations with Peter Rowe, himself a prolific writer, who joined the Urban Planning and Design faculty at GSD in the mid-eighties, about issues of design in relation to culture, history, economics, and sustainability were energizing. In addition, I spent many hours with Harry Cobb, founding partner with I. M. Pei of Pei Cobb Freed & Partners, who was at that time chair of the architecture department. We had long discussions of his interest in the work of Donald Schön, a philosopher and professor in urban planning at MIT. Schön was developing ideas regarding an iterative process he believed self-aware designers engaged in, which he published in 1983 as *The Reflective Practitioner: How Professionals Think in Action.* For Schön, professional growth resulted from a practitioner's turning a critical lens on his or her work—by doubting. In his view, doubt and questioning lead to a different way of thinking that casts situations as problems. The next step was to try out actions and situations that dispel doubt and, through reiterative action, arrive at a set of versions and solutions. Schön maintained that the best practitioners knew more than they could put into words.

This seemed right to me. I recalled an essay from the late sixties by the architectural historian Henry-Russell Hitchcock in which he discussed Michelangelo's design studies for fortifications. Hitchcock advanced the notion of the self-reflexive gesture, suggesting that when Michelangelo made a drawing, he subsequently made another in reaction to it, building and altering a scheme in a sequence of discoveries and inventions on the page. In my view, that, indeed, is the nature of design. Peter Rowe, who joined Cobb's and my conversations, was examining theories of the design process, expanding on Schön's work, which led to his publishing *Design Thinking* in 1987. I was inspired to write as a designer about the things I knew and felt about design and landscape, as both subject and activity.

I was less concerned about methods and instrumentality than I was perturbed by the lack of discussion of art, ideas, and meaning in landscape design. Years earlier, in Rome, I had been captivated by an approach to Renaissance art developed by the English historian Frances Yates and other scholars at the Warburg Institute in the 1960s and 1970s, particularly their interest in iconography. During that period, I was also inspired by the scholarship of several students of Rudolf Wittkower, including Henry Millon and Elisabeth MacDougall, whom I considered mentors. By coincidence, while in Rome I happened upon an article by Lawrence Halprin on the landscape of the High Sierra as the model for his recently completed Portland, Oregon, *Open Space Sequence.* Its representation and abstraction of natural forms and processes were obvious and were a powerful confirmation of what I was learning about visualization and meaning in Italian Renaissance gardens.

This influential strand of art history was in marked contrast, if not opposition, to the stances taken by Eisenman, Silvetti, and others who were under the spell of contemporary French literary theory and philosophy, especially the work of Gilles Deleuze and Jacques Derrida. During my lengthy collaboration with Eisenman, I saw his desire to derive designs from theoretical positions and one or another set of what might be called post-structuralist operations. For a time, the most prominent of these were aspects of fractal geometry as promulgated by Benoit Mandelbrot, then visiting at Harvard. Eisenman was occasionally impatient with my tendency to employ figural gestures and formal strategies linked to historical modernism in painting and architecture as well as allusions to historical tropes. We argued, produced projects, and gave and wrote separate—quite different—lectures and essays on the same projects. One year, for example, at the Rhode Island School of Design, Eisenman gave a lecture titled "The End of the Classical: The End of the Beginning, the End of the End" (published in *Perspecta* in

1984), in which he posited the impossibility today of history informing design. A month later I gave a lecture there on the puzzling continuity of classical landscape types and imagery, arguing that they still had agency, and presented a few of our collaborative projects.

By 1984, I felt the need to find another path between the conflicting poles of critical thinking at the time. Thanks to Whiteman and Rowe, I discovered several philosophers then at Harvard: Nelson Goodman, who was particularly interested in aesthetics and expression, Hilary Putnam, and Stanley Cavell. Conversations with Goodman and diverse reading during my commute between my office in Philadelphia and the GSD each week led me to the American pragmatists, principally Emerson and Thoreau, who had interested me years earlier, and to Cavell. I never did meet him, but I found Cavell's skepticism, aesthetics, and discussions of Emerson, Thoreau, J. L. Austin, and Wittgenstein especially useful. Most appealing in all of this ferment was the idea that one should try to write clearly, simply, in ordinary language, in an effort to discuss basic and important things. I felt strongly that academic jargon and convoluted thought about arcane matters were to be avoided at all costs.

Late in my time at Harvard, 1986 or 1987, Peter Walker, my predecessor as chair of landscape architecture at the GSD, and I decided to invite our students to an evening discussion on the need for designers to write and publish. As different as our approaches are, Walker and I agreed about the desirability of having practitioners articulate their thoughts about design, whether their own or others'—their insights and strategies, beliefs, ambitions, and ideas. We acknowledged that most of us will present what we hoped to have accomplished in terms of purpose and poetics, whether or not others agreed or perceived our intent. We both posited that the majority of writing by academics and journalists was often inadequate and woefully ignorant about what designers actually do or think, and that there is a deep lack of understanding of design, and landscape design in particular.

We also pointed to the architects in the past who used writing as a superb career move—Alberti, Palladio, Colen Campbell, Robert Adam, James Gibbs, and more recently Robert Venturi, Charles Moore, Rem Koolhaas, and Bernard Tschumi. We noted that in the 1950s two landscape architects on the West Coast, Thomas Church and Garrett

Eckbo, had written successfully about their work, but since then, with few exceptions (Lawrence Halprin is one), there had been little else published by active practitioners. And though there was an emerging body of writing about dead designers—Capability Brown, André Le Nôtre, Frederick Law Olmsted—there was virtually nothing about living landscape architects.

As a teacher, I saw that anxieties and insecurity, a seeming dichotomy between an internal private world and the external public one, were common in students, and I told them that possibly the most interesting thing they might ever design was themselves, if they made the effort. Difficult as it might be, they should try writing honestly, even emotionally, as well as intellectually and be prepared to wander somewhat adrift artistically, piecing together incongruous and disparate thoughts and interests. Until they attempted to write about what interested them, they wouldn't find out what they knew and understood or were doing in their own work or valued in the work of others.

Meanwhile, I attempted to follow my own advice. Just before I left Harvard, Anne Whiston Spirn, then assistant director of landscape architecture, was invited to guest edit the fall 1988 issue of *Landscape Journal* devoted to the theme "Nature, Form, and Meaning" and asked me to contribute an article on the work I had undertaken in my theory course. This was an opportunity to clarify things for myself, to do a think piece. The result was my essay "Form, Meaning, and Expression in Landscape Architecture," a corrective to what I saw as the utilitarian emphasis of our curriculum, and the field, at the time. It elicited a set of questioning, even argumentative responses from colleagues and friends on the West Coast. Mark Francis, a respected faculty member at UC Davis, Marc Treib, a prolific writer and teacher at UC Berkeley, and Jane Gillette, also at Berkeley, whose frequent writing and criticism on landscape were widely known and respected, took me to task for my position on representation. John Dixon Hunt, the prominent author, editor, and teacher at Penn, then came to my defense in a subsequent essay. While marked and heated aesthetic differences had emerged in dialogues between architects on the West Coast and their eastern contemporaries in the 1960s and 1970s—the "Whites" in New York, the "Greys" in Philadelphia, and the "Silvers" in Los Angeles—it hadn't occurred to me that there might be a similar philosophical divide in landscape theory and formal attitudes, or that from time to time I had been moving comfortably between one and the other. I was as pleased as I was surprised by their response and public engagement in the topic.

By the end of the eighties, a literature of landscape architecture was beginning to grow, not only in the United States but around the world. My compulsion to fill the perceived void lessened. Since then most of my writing has been at the invitation to lecture or contribute a piece on one or another topic. At times the subject was challenging, if not exactly what I would have chosen to think about—Marc Treib's request that I write about construction documents or hand drawing in the age of digital media, for instance. At other times I was invited to write about the work of individuals such as Frederick Law Olmsted Jr., Frank Lloyd Wright, Lawrence Halprin, and Richard Haag—all heroes of mine— and I took up the project with pleasure.

A few pieces motivated purely by personal interest incubated for some time, but they eventually got done, such as an essay on the Vigna Madama and William Kent, originally conceived as part of my study of the English landscape but not included in it. Another essay was spurred by anger and despair when the garden of the Museum of Modern Art in New York, one of my favorite twentieth-century landscapes, was ruined by its uncomprehending curators, director, trustees, and architects involved in the museum's expansion. Landscape is still a mystery to most people, even otherwise sophisticated ones. I felt that it was critical to say what had happened, what the garden had been, what was lost. (That was two expansions ago. Each successive growth upheaval has exacerbated the damage. The cliché that landscapes are dynamic not stable applies to urban ones as well.)

Despite my doubts about the value of autobiography in this age of selfies and solipsism, in recent years I have indulged myself and written about the environment of my childhood in Alaska at the request of friends who were curious and wanted me to talk about it. There are a number of other topics I still hope to get around to. Principal of these is a response to my "Form, Meaning, and Expression" essay. Years later, I find that some of the ideas that I put forward then have evolved and changed, but the task of tackling the complex issues of form, representation, and meaning as I now see them, to explain my understanding of them clearly and simply, requires more time and effort than I currently can give it. It is a daunting but worthy project that still lies before me.

Throughout all of my endeavors I have had the help and support of many individuals. I especially wish to thank John Dixon Hunt, professor emeritus of landscape architecture at Penn, with whom I shared lectures in a history/theory class for a decade and who inaugurated the Penn Studies in Landscape Architecture series; Marc Treib, professor emeritus of architecture at UC Berkeley and friend, goad, and sometime editor, who continues to present valuable conferences with subsequent publications; Elizabeth Barlow Rogers, president of the Foundation for Landscape Studies, for soliciting my work for *Site/Lines,* and editor Alice Truax for taming it; and Paula Deitz, editor of *The Hudson Review,* who has been a loyal supporter and superb enabler of my efforts. And more recently, Robin Karson, executive director of Library of American Landscape History, who has become a valued, insightful correspondent and editor, and the talented souls she introduced me to: Carol Betsch, Jonathan Lippincott, and encyclopedic, ever-inquiring Mary Bellino.

In addition, I particularly thank my partners at OLIN for their questioning of me and what we are doing as we continually evolve our office, as well as their forbearance for my version of time management. I also owe a debt to my students, who have asked challenging questions that demanded I explain myself. And finally, without Victoria Steiger and her unwavering support, I could not have gotten through it all this far: the practice, the teaching, the travel, the writing, or, simply, life.

FORM, MEANING, AND EXPRESSION
IN LANDSCAPE ARCHITECTURE

(1988)

Historically, landscape design has derived a considerable amount of its social value and artistic strength from three aspects of the endeavor: the richness of the medium in sensual and phenomenological terms; the thematic content concerning the relationship of society and individuals to nature; and the fact that nature is the great metaphor underlying all art.

Human landscapes exhibit a complexity akin to living organisms. They are composed of disparate elements that form entities different from their parts; they inhabit real time and interact with their environment. They can be evolutionary, undergoing morphological change (for example, trees growing and maturing with subsequent visual, spatial, and ecological changes), and can even die, both physically and metaphorically.

Recently, two important and, in my view, incorrect theoretical assumptions have become so ubiquitous that they have seriously weakened landscape architecture as an artistic field, despite its social utility. The first has been to confuse human landscapes and the needs and achievements they embody with natural landscapes and their processes. Students, teachers, and practitioners alike demonstrate a lack of understanding of the relationship between the author/artist/

From *Landscape Journal,* special issue, "Nature, Form, and Meaning," 7.2 (Fall 1988): 149–68.

designer and the medium of expression; also, they fail to understand its limits, range, and potential on the one hand and display an ignorance of the formal issues within the field and an anticultural stance that eschews aesthetic concerns and their history on the other. The second assumption is a new deterministic and doctrinaire view of what is "natural" and "beautiful" that has replaced older, alternative, views that were equally doctrinaire. Couched in a born-again language of fundamentalist ecology, this chilling, close-minded stance of moral certitude is hostile to the vast body of work produced through history, castigating it as "formal" and as representing the dominance of humans over nature.

This failure to appreciate the formal possibilities, typological repertoire, and potential content (allegorical, iconographic, symbolic, emblematic) of the field that have been developed through history is encouraged in part by an anti-intellectual and anti-historical bias that runs deep in American society and the profession, and in part by the wide scattering of the built work in time and space. The difficulties that accompany the amount of travel necessary to visit this diffuse body of work are compounded by the difficulties of describing and recording the phenomenological nature of sites that possess even minimal complexity or subtlety. As long as I can remember, the vast majority of practitioners have espoused a functional and "problem-solving" ethic that, although socially beneficial up to a point, has in effect asserted that mere instrumentality is sufficient in the creation of human environments, eschewing the more difficult issues that are raised if one also aspires to practice at the level of art.

In theory, the range of formal expression in landscape design could be as broad and varied in scope as that of the numerous landscapes, things, and events in the universe, if not more so, since one might presuppose an opportunity for new experiments and combinations of existing phenomena. The things we make might only be limited by the laws of physics, chemistry, and biology. As Buckminster Fuller once remarked, "The opposite of natural is impossible."[1] Yet despite the astonishing number of different landscape designs built since prehistory, there has emerged a finite, even limited, repertoire of favored formal strategies and expressions that have been applied to countless different and particular places through time.

EXPERIMENTATION IN
CONTEMPORARY LANDSCAPE DESIGN

The principal reason for the limitation of formal expression thus far is predominantly cultural, although certain constraints in building materials and physical intervention transcend both art and technology. Water, when unrestrained, runs downhill; plants die when their biological needs are not met. Nevertheless, the choice of materials with which to build—soil, stone, cardboard, tin, and so forth—is determined almost exclusively by social factors (economics, safety) and cultural factors (aesthetics). The stir created by revolutionaries in design is usually brought about by their transgression of what is culturally acceptable regarding the choice of material or form or composition.

Three recent American landscape designs that exemplify such transgression of convention, thereby attracting critical scrutiny, attack, and praise, are Martha Schwartz's Bagel Garden in Boston, SWA's Harlequin Plaza in Denver, designed by George Hargreaves, and SWA's Williams Square at Las Colinas near Dallas, designed by Jim Reeves and Dan Mock. These projects have followed other contemporary art and design fields in an attempt to broaden the range of acceptable (and serious) formal expression from that which is normative in the field. No one does this in the name of program, function, or biophysical imperative except as broadly defined—that is, only if aesthetics and the risk-taking that accompanies inquiry and a craving for change (to see what is around the next bend) are defined as functions. In fact, one of the things that all of these projects have in common is how little they use the most traditional materials and devices of landscape design, specifically plants and reference to natural landscapes. Their shock value derives from this abnegation of "normal" imagery and texture. They are "contrast gainers" that in every likelihood will lose their strength and energy over time as they become members of a new class of landscape designs that eschew dependence on planting or direct reference to natural form for their organization. This is not to say that they do not refer to nature. They do, but indirectly, by reference first to other works of art that were more directly inspired by "nature." As in transmission of energy in other forms and media, there is at each step a loss and a dissipation of that energy.

One dilemma of much recent avant-garde landscape design is that, in the desire to reinvigorate the field, many have turned to devices or strategies that lead away from the central source of its power: nature. In the attempt to avoid banality and transcend imitation, a crisis of abstraction has developed. By adopting strategies borrowed directly from other fields and by referring to work that is itself an abstraction from the referent, many contemporary landscape designers are producing work that is thin, at best a second- or thirdhand emotional or artistic encounter.

Materials

The work of Martha Schwartz (the Bagel Garden and her mother's garden in Philadelphia), of Schwartz and Peter Walker (the Necco field installed temporarily at MIT), and Walker's Tanner Fountain at Harvard University raise the issue of palette. They argue that landscape design can use a host of untried and unconventional materials. Garrett Eckbo and Gabriel Guevrekian pioneered this endeavor earlier in the twentieth century with mixed results. Both experimented with industrial materials as substitutes for traditional materials. One thinks of Eckbo's use of plastic panels (corrugated and otherwise) and various precast elements and shapes in lieu of wood arbors, masonry walls, and screens, his search for new colors, textures, and shadows, and his adoption of shapes from the School of Paris painters; or of Guevrekian, who substituted shiny metal spheres and crystalline polygons for shrubs in his remarkable "Garden of Water and Light" (Jardin d'Eau et de Lumiere) at the 1925 Exposition Internationale des Arts Décoratifs in Paris.

Landscapes throughout history have predominantly been made of natural materials, with the objects and structures placed within them made from processed or manipulated natural materials. In the nineteenth century, iron, concrete, asphalt, and glass were added in the works of Peter Joseph Lenné, Joseph Paxton, Adolphe Alphand, Frederick Law Olmsted, and others. Recent projects by the artist Robert Irwin with ephemeral qualities that are both analogous and complementary to those of plants and the play of light and shade through their structure and surfaces, and the successful mingling of metal and wire with natural elements, should convince any thoughtful person that the problematic effort to expand and invigorate the palette with which we work is a worthy one. On the other hand, when one considers the overwhelming variety of plants and the almost endless variety of patterns that one can achieve with only a few colors and shapes of pavement stones, it is easy to understand why some of the most gifted designers in the field have spent their careers working with a limited palette that was self-imposed, gradually reducing their choices to fewer and fewer elements, thereby producing profoundly poetic works. In fairness, one must further remark that Schwartz and Walker have embarked on a similar reductive regimen and that their exploration of tainted or unexpected materials and formal orders has been carried out with enormous self-control and restraint. The self-conscious, continual referring to contemporary works of art rather than to the world itself, however, is a genuine weakness.

Imagery

Williams Square at Las Colinas, Texas, near the Dallas–Fort Worth airport by Skidmore, Owings & Merrill, SWA, and the sculptor Robert Glen, can be considered to have expanded the range of expression currently practiced by attempting to rescue rhetoric and imagery from the past, specifically that of Baroque aquatic sculpture groups. This is a revisionist (even historicist) piece that makes the assertion that a landscape design composition today can include elements that are figurative or narrative, and that they can be heroic in scale and understandable to laymen of the region. This work of folk imagery—"wild horses"— is raised to a level of civic prominence with violent and illusionistic presentation. The frozen moment of the Hellenist tradition that was revived by Bernini and continued by the Vanvitelli family in works such as Actaeon and his dogs in one of the fountains at the Palace of Caserta come to mind. The little jets that forever record the splash of the hooves are a touch that both the dilettante and connoisseur of the eighteenth century would have liked.

Composition

At Harlequin Plaza, George Hargreaves and his colleagues used old and accepted materials arranged in geometric compositions that were new and startling to landscape design in America. The materials—stone, stucco, soil, plants, metal, and water—can all be found in the Bois de Boulogne and Central Park. What is new and different (and unsettling to many) is the compositional methods and devices employed.

The composition is indebted to strategies developed in painting, especially surrealism. This is a landscape of displacement, distortion, and dislocation. There are echoes of Jan Vermeer and Pieter de Hooch, of Dalí and de Chirico, of Haight-Ashbury, Latin America, and of the School of Paris. Things assume positions or weight that we don't normally expect. The floor, or pavement, which we usually expect to be a fairly neutral ground quietly holding everything in place, not only is a brightly contrasting and active surface, but its orthogonal patterns are skewed and begin to writhe under the comparatively weightless objects that break and interrupt it more than sit upon it. Walls rise and fall, or are pulled apart, the outsides of which are harsh. Inside, between two central walls, things are small, fragile, oddly domestic, and out of place. Regardless of one's personal pleasures and aesthetic preference, this is an effective and moving work. It stimulates and disturbs. It pleases and teases. It winks and talks tough. In this work we can see an old strategy that has led to a succession of design styles in painting and architecture. Style is largely concerned with the development of a set of formal characteristics that are common to a group of objects or works of art (Renaissance, Baroque, Rococo, Picturesque, Gardenesque, Deco, Modern, and so forth). Once such a set of characteristics becomes obvious, at least to the point where a designer can consciously know how to achieve them, then it is only a matter of desire to be able to break from those conventions. Examples of how to break from the conventions of classical, Beaux-Arts, and picturesque design composition lie all about us like beacons in the work of many twentieth-century artists, writers, architects, and musicians. Hargreaves simply stepped over that line and utilized several of the most common devices of our era—principally collage and distortion.

A Critique

I am a little uncomfortable with the results of all of these works, partly because of my own predilections regarding what I wish to make myself, but also because of my skepticism about either the position taken by the designer or the choice of subject or materials. Experimentation with new materials is desirable, and Walker/Schwartz in their emulation of Frank Gehry and numerous sculptors such as Carl Andre are to be applauded. Walker's Tanner Fountain in front of the Science Center at Harvard—

which places a series of handsome glacial boulders within a field of asphalt and water, steam, and an eerie hum—is a remarkable piece. In my opinion, it is stronger than many of Walker/Schwartz's other works because it refers more directly to the material that it abstracts: natural landscapes of violence and erosion. I would have arranged the stones differently—denser to looser and not so uniform and equal in space and stone sizes—and I would have set them within a sea of pebbles and smaller stones. This would, of course, have completely changed the effect and the meaning, which raises an important question: How can changing the spacing of the stones or the simple substitution of what is, after all, only the bottom of a basin (but it isn't really a basin either, which is important) change the meaning?

Because we invest certain patterns and materials with particular ideas and meaning, especially regarding nature and man's works, these patterns are loaded with associations. In this case, the material—asphalt—and the uniformity of position between solid and void have an association in our culture with the mechanistic and artificial, even to the point of abhorrence, whereas stones and water are quintessentially "natural" and are almost universally enjoyed by people, both old and young. This juxtaposition of the abhorrent and the delightful creates a challenge to our expectations of what is normal or proper. Likewise, the mechanical repetition of the near grid and near randomness of the stones, which denies particularity of place and focus, is ironic in its self-denial (it is a particular place and a focal point within its context) and at the same time alludes to the absolute infinity of matter and its extension throughout the universe—a clearly evocative and apt metaphor to find at the doorstep of an academic building devoted to the study of matter.

This is a powerful and successful work, employing traditional artistic devices for the presentation of meaning, some of which are referred to above. There is more here, for those who take the time to consider, about the seasons, the mutability of matter—water, steam, and ice, for instance—the deception of appearances, the energy that comes unbidden from the earth or from the sky, volcanoes and seacoasts, and so on. The piece also raises questions about alternatives to conventional fountains with their cascades, basins and pools, copings, walls, and ornament. Although this design eschews planting, it relies for its success on the circumstantial planting that exists there as its context. The trees and grass of its campus setting form a background, a benign cultural interpretation of "Mother Earth" against which this disruptive and stimulating composition is positioned. Like many so-called site sculptors such as Michael Heizer, Nancy Holt, Mary Miss, or Alice Aycock, who are enormously dependent upon the preexistence of a broad, cohesive, often beautiful natural or cultural setting in which to make their disruptive gestures or to build their mysterious large-scale objects, this fountain (and the early work of Martha Schwartz as well) are gestures that play off and against an environment but are not about nor capable of creating an environment beyond that of an extended object.

Denver's Harlequin Plaza confronts different expectations and raises other questions. How are we to regard a landscape of disorientation and alienation? Is surrealism an acceptable strategy to employ in constructing an ordinary part of the workaday world? Why or why not? Such thoughts first occurred to me upon seeing several projects of Aldo Rossi. These were visually powerful schemes (for housing and education) that were obviously sophisticated works of art. The most apparent source of Rossi's visual schemata is the early work of the Italian painter Giorgio de Chirico, whose haunting work I greatly admire. I balk, however, at its use for the design of everyday environments for family and civic life. I do so because the principal focus of these paintings is on alienation and a hallucinatory and obsessive preoccupation with loneliness, self, and unfulfilled yearning. De Chirico's paintings are among the most poetic works created in the twentieth century, but it is debatable whether such private (even if universal) attitudes regarding alienation can and should be used as a basis for design of environments for dwelling. The other undiscussed aspect of Rossi's work is its familiarity with and nostalgic evocation of the architecture of twentieth-century totalitarianism—especially that of Fascist Italy and Germany. Do I think that Harlequin Plaza is crypto-fascist or perverse? No, but I do think it transgresses the boundary between that which is acceptable and understandable in private and that which is welcome and desirable in public. This does not imply a double standard, but rather that we have different needs as individuals and as a group. What people may indulge in for themselves on private estates may be debatable when proposed for the public realm. My reaction has more to do with the rhetoric of coercion and gratuitous violence than it does with dreamlike distortions of traditional architectural elements. Harlequin Plaza is, nevertheless, a watershed in American landscape composition and imagery. It has opened up possibilities that did not seem to exist before its brash appearance.

The horses of Las Colinas, like the exuberant figure of *Portlandia* that hunkers (or floats?) above the entry to Michael Graves's celebrated bunker in the City of Roses, attempt the retrieval of a distant trope from a society profoundly different from our own. Several questions are raised by this revisionist work. Is any single image—regardless of its merits—adequate for civic contemplation and elevation to heroic scale in an era of so many powerful and multiple images? If the answer is yes, is this the one to be singled out for such an honorific situation? Or is it like so many by Andrew Wyeth, a work that is nostalgic in its emulation of the technique and appearance of authentic work of the past yet lacking the authority of those works, an empty simulacrum of something else? Is it a daring and genuine piece, bursting with disarming energy and innocence? Have its creators simply said that narrative and figurative sculpture used as the centerpiece of a public space is passé only until someone steps forward and dares to attempt it? Is this private plaza in this suburban office sprawl a public place? I am skeptical of this piece, which seems too pat, too sentimental, too much a product of western cowboy commodity art of the sort that fills galleries throughout the Southwest with the kitsch that has devalued the work of Charles Russell and Frederic Remington. The reason to devote attention to this design lies in its attempt to shift the boundary of what is acceptable, to retrieve an artistic strategy that has slipped beyond the grasp of the modernist norm. It is a powerful and evocative work; it has been embraced by the community and has been the recipient of an American Society of Landscape Architects award. It is art regardless of how lasting or great it may turn out to be. What authority it possesses comes from cultural values, and what form it has comes from art, not from nature or any fresh insight or abstraction therefrom.

LANDSCAPE FORM

Everything that exists has form. The words "formal" and "informal" as used in everyday speech are meaningless and an obstacle to a discussion about design, which by definition always contains formal properties of some sort. Where do forms come from? Forms come from forms first. Forms do not come from words. They cannot. Words can describe physical forms, but they do not (or did not) originate them; nor can they perform operations on them. One must be familiar with a repertoire of forms before one can use them or manipulate them. This includes the forms found in nature and the forms of art, our art and that of others— other media, other cultures, and other periods. In nature are all forms. In our imagination is their discernment and abstraction.

Art, and landscape architecture as a subfield of art, proceeds by using a known body of forms, a vocabulary of shapes, and by applying ideas concerning their use and manipulation. Landscape architecture, like other fields, evolves as it finds new ways to perform operations on a particular corpus of forms—reusing, reassembling, distorting, taking apart, transforming, and carrying forward an older set of forms—often quite limited in range, but constantly making new things with new meanings. Occasionally a few new forms will be let in or discovered, but more generally new material consists of the re-presentation or recombination of material that has been forgotten or has been deemed banal or out-of-bounds for some reason.

Once again, where does this repertoire of forms come from? As I have remarked elsewhere in a discussion about places and memory, the only thing that we can ever know for certain about the world is what exists now or has existed in the past. To make something new we must start with what is or has been and change it in some way to make it fresh in some way. To merely repeat or rebuild what has existed is not creative and does not advance the field, eventually devaluing what is repeated. How to make old things new, how to see something common and banal in a new and fresh way, is the central problem in art. Arthur Danto in the essay "Works of Art and Mere Real Things" goes so far as to say that the central activity of art is to transform ordinary (or extraordinary) real things into things that are art, that is, no longer ordinary or mere real things.[2] Examples range from representations of landscapes (say, in Claude Lorrain or George Innes) to Marcel Duchamp's declaring a urinal or bottle rack to be an artwork. The planting of trees in rows, whether good or bad, new or old, is an act of transformation and can under particular circumstances be art of a very high order.

Two of the greatest landscape designers that ever lived are André Le Nôtre and Lancelot Brown. Neither of these artistic giants invented the elements that comprise the parts of their greatest compositions. In the case of Brown, the meadows, clumps, and belts of trees, lakes, dams, classical pavilions, even the positioning strategies, all existed in the landscape gardens of his contemporaries and immediate predecessors. Nevertheless, he produced unique, startlingly fresh, and profoundly influential designs that still possess energy and authority. The elements he used can be found in the works of William Kent, Charles Bridgeman, and Henry Wise and in the villas of Rome, especially the vignas of the Villas Madama and Giulia, but it was his particular assemblage that blended these elements into cohesive and tightly structured (albeit large-scale) compositions that were not episodic or disjointed, but plastic and "whole." The source of cultural authority for these pastoral compositions was literature (from classical verse to the Georgian poets) and graphic art (from Roman frescoes to Claude and the Dutch landscape school, especially Jacob van Ruisdael, Meindert Hobbema, and Aelbert Cuyp). Also, there was a predisposition on the part of his audience to understand and appreciate his constructions, both as sensual environs and as emblematic representations of agrarian social views.

For Le Nôtre, one could say the same thing. Every shape and form he used exists in seventeenth-century pattern books and in the sixteenth-century Italian and French gardens that he knew as a child and young adult. What then is so special and creative about his work? Like Andrea Palladio in his work at Il Redentore in Venice or the Villa Rotunda at Capra, he is working in a tradition, using standard elements, yet the results are more than a skillful or interesting repetition, more than traditional. He was highly original. His invention is one of recombination and transformation, frequently accomplished through a jump in scale, with the simplest of elements and unexpected juxtapositions. Take the Château de Chantilly as an example: every shape—oval, square, circle, rectangle, ramp, parterre, and cascade—can be found in any of a dozen Roman gardens of the sixteenth and seventeenth centuries. Part of the transformation was to take elements originally conceived as furnishings for terraces or small garden rooms adjacent to houses (admittedly villas and palazzi) and to change their scale, enlarging and frequently stretching them, and then to use these new figures to organize and unify entire estates or large tracts of land, reversing the relationship until the building was essentially a furnishing or embellishment of the landscape composition. This is true even when, as was usually the case, the building was the seed about which the enormous garden had grown.

If Vaux-le-Vicomte and Versailles are two of his central and most fundamental creations, Sceaux and Chantilly are possibly his most original. This is largely because of the amount of transformation from prototype and the relegation of the chateau in each case to a peripheral or tangential relationship to the composition, especially in its relationship to the most important water elements, which exist as if for themselves with the parks subservient and organized about them. Here the shape, spirit, and meaning of these axial bodies of water and verdure are transformed from those that preceded them in France and Italy, in his own work as well as that of others. The source of their energy and authority is similar to that of Brown's work: foreign precedent and aesthetic paternity (especially Roman literature, archaeology, and Renaissance masterworks) plus contemporary science, particularly optics. How does one go about doing such things? How did he know to do this? It is hard to say. It is obvious that he had to abstract, perhaps I should even say extract, the forms, the types of basin, terrace, and bosque, from the works he was exposed to, from his practice and immediate experience, and from representations in views, prints, and plans. Then, too, there was probably a certain felicitous amount of chance and direction given by the society, his clients, their budgets, programs, and desires, as well as the capabilities and constraints imposed by the site, the climate, and technology.

If one returns to my opening thesis that the strength of landscape architecture derives from the fulsome sensual properties of the medium, its expression of the relationship of society to nature, and the centrality of nature as the ur-metaphor of art, it is not difficult to understand why the works of Brown and Le Nôtre are among the very greatest in the field. Despite their differences in geometric form and organization, both men worked with the same limited palette, which reduced the elements of their designs to the most basic—earth, trees, turf, stone, water—and arranged them at a scale that dwarfed the individual and created an ambience that, if not resembling any natural scene, by its very extent, diversity, and texture possessed the attributes of one.

It is difficult to exaggerate the impact of their work on one's sensi-

Pantheon and lake in Henry Hoare's Elysium park, Stourhead, England, 1974

bilities when on the spot, moving through their compositions. Artificial as they may be, ecologically simplified as they are, the effect is that of being in a landscape larger than oneself and beyond the immediate comprehension or control of oneself, of many of the feelings one has in a "natural" landscape—of light and space, of amplitude and generosity. Although two generations apart, both men produced work that responded to a particular moment in the economy and social structure of their society, that could not be sustained beyond their own life and career, and that was impossible to imitate or extend. Both refer to agriculture—whether pastoral herds or forest plantations, irrigation, and drainage schemes—the larger organization of the cosmos, and whether it is knowable or not. Both were masters of the simple detail and the subtle, complex, large design, thereby rendering their work truly analogous to the natural landscape. Redundancy and profligacy do not appear to have been a concern or issue, another natural analog. Neither ever designed or built a composition that visually or formally imitated nature; both abstracted their forms from nature, farming, and art. The lakes at Blenheim and Stowe, at Vaux-le-Vicomte and Versailles all were, in part, responses to an abundance of rainfall, surface water, and poorly drained soils. Each one expanded or drowned the work of a predecessor with an uncanny sense of organic logic. Until one has actually seen these works, on foot with one's own eyes, one cannot appreciate their character, achievement, or worth. Students who know this work only from slides or plans in books have no idea what they are like. In this way they also resemble natural environments of great scale, beauty, and cohesion.

All of this may be true enough and still one might ask, where did the prototypes Le Nôtre found in the sixteenth-century Italian gardens come from? In large measure they derived from the villa gardens of ancient Rome, especially as codified in the great landscape villas of the first century CE. These in turn seem to have been derived from earlier eastern Mediterranean prototypes brought by Syrian and Greek architects working in the new western centers of power and industry. If one examines these remote works and their formal repertoire, one finds a host of venerable and familiar geometric and organic shapes. Nearly every Bronze Age culture shows a predilection for compositions made up of prime geometric shapes, often elaborated into surfaces of intricate textures of lines, whorls, and abstractions of powerful ambiguity—circles, squares, triangles, and their elaboration, recombination, and distortion. Knowledge, power, and the religious beliefs of these peoples were often embodied in such images and diagrams. The evolution of social authority and power was coincidental with the development of theories of reality and technology. The elementary shapes found in nature and abstracted by humans were, for many centuries, both sacred symbols and the building blocks of secular analytical methods.

Today, spheres and cubes, triangles and cones are not as charged with meaning as they once were. Nevertheless, their ancient lineage and indisputable primacy in the vocabulary of formal structures are still sources of considerable authority. In a world consisting of small towns, irregular construction, straw roofs, and few paved streets, surrounded by farms and wilderness, overlooking broad plains and vast oceans, and dwarfed by mountains, the perfection of a sphere or cube and the order of geometric symmetries were powerful inventions of the human imagination. Today, as an urban culture, housed continuously in a world of crisp Euclidian geometries and surrounded by a surfeit of machined surfaces extending in Descartean order to the limits of the horizon, it is the biomorphic shapes of nature, the blurry, unclear, compound and complex forms of natural processes that intrigue us with their mystery, promise, and atavistic energy. Perfection, regularity, and ancient geometries, especially those of classical Greece and Rome, have been drained of their energy through overuse and exposure. Despite recent developments in postmodern architectural endeavors they remain empty to us of their original meanings. Once great abstractions of nature itself, today they only refer to former leaps of imagination. They have become too far removed from their original source and inspiration to be anything but derivative and banal to us. An echo of their former power still occurs, however, when small children take these platonic solids in their hands and stacking them one atop another construct their first imaginary worlds, miniature structures that invoke and reflect aspects of their known and imagined world.

Even the most casual examination of forms used in Roman garden design and ornament reveals a direct and rich tradition of natural forms and abstractions from nature as well as representational images that assume the stature of figures. By *figure* I intend the meaning as defined by Alan Colquhoun, who has differentiated the words *form* and *figure* approximately thus: *form* applies to "a configuration with natural meaning or none at all," where "natural meaning" signifies meaning without the overlay of an intervening interpretive scheme of a culture; *figure* applies to a "configuration whose meaning is given by culture."[3] This distinction implies that the synthetic invention of a figure organizes ideas and thus is both expressive and didactic. There are therefore two traditions, the formal and the figurative, which are almost never totally separated, indeed are often inextricable. Each one, from time to time, seems to have more or less importance or dominance in a work and its intentions and success. Much of twentieth-century art could be said to have been interested to varying degrees in abstract formalism and its possibilities (or limits). Recently, considerable interest in a renascent figural exploration has been evident in all of the arts, including architecture and landscape design. The three examples of so-called postmodern landscape experimentation with which I began are part of this renewed interest in the "figural" aspect of the landscape medium.

LANDSCAPES AND MEANING

The subject of meaning in human expressions of all sorts is a daunting one with an enormous literature. It is the province of numerous philosophers of widely opposed views (Husserl and Wittgenstein, for instance, or Kant and Hegel, Plato and Popper). Husserl seems useful as a starting point in this matter. In his first logical investigation he says, "each expression not merely says something, but says it *of* something; it not only has a meaning, but refers to certain *objects*. . . . But the object never coincides with the meaning."[4] Immediately we are confronted with a thicket of words, definitions, and problems. Suffice it to say we are interested in *nonverbal* expressions, those of landscape design and what they can mean. As Nelson Goodman put it in his stimulating discussion of style in *Ways of Worldmaking*, "Architecture and nonobjective painting and most of music have no subject. Their style cannot be a matter of how they say something, for they do not literally *say* anything; they do other things, they mean in other ways."[5]

Despite the frequent use of the analogy of language and linguistic structures and operations (my own use of the concept "vocabulary of forms" above, for example), landscapes are not verbal constructions. They can express certain things, can possess symbols and refer to ideas, events, and objects extrinsic to their own elements and locus, and in certain circumstances can be didactic and/or highly poetic. How they do this is not well understood. That they do is. Recent issues of various art history journals or the publications of papers delivered at Dumbarton Oaks symposia are rich with examples of sympathetic and recondite readings of the meanings, iconography, and imagery contained in various landscapes, from classical antiquity to the modern era, in both the West and the East. Particularly well known examples are those of sixteenth-century Italy and Japan (Villa Lante, Villa d'Este, Ryoan-ji, Katsura, etc.).[6]

The fundamental questions concerning meaning in landscape design are probably the following:

What sort of meaning can landscapes convey or hold?

How do they convey or embody these meanings?

What, if any, correlation or relationship is there between the intent of the designer of a landscape regarding devices intended for meaning and the subsequent interpretation, reception, and understanding of this or other meaning by a viewer, user, or recipient of the landscape?

Concerning the first two of these questions, there seem to be two kinds of meaning or large categories that landscapes possess (in Colquhoun's terms, all of these are figural to a greater or lesser degree). The first kind is a "natural" or "evolutionary" meaning given to a landscape in the past or recent times. (I regret using the word "natural" but have no better term at hand, as I hope will become clear.) Generally, these relate to aspects of the landscape as a setting for society and have been developed as a reflection or expression of hopes and fears for survival and social perpetuation. They often relate to particular places or features that are (or have been) sources of sustenance and danger, safety, and play, of stimulus and rest. The second category are those that I will refer to as synthetic or "invented" meanings. They encompass most of the works of landscape design and represent our art. Often, however, these works refer to aspects or examples of the former non-designed, although culturally freighted, group of landscapes and their meanings. I don't mean to imply in this distinction that I think those in the first category are not products of human activity and imagination. It is, after all, people who project ideas on nature, who create values, systems, and structures of thought, not the other way around. Whatever meaning occurs in any landscape, natural or otherwise, is only that which has been created by society. This we have seen when cultures are in conflict, so tragically demonstrated when European invaders desecrated the sacred lands of the Native American peoples. In the mining of metals in the Black Hills of South Dakota one can see how invisible these powerful and elaborate meanings can be to those not of that society and its beliefs.

Archetypal settings developed in one culture and place after another have contributed to the repertoire of forms and meanings used as foundations or structural elements of subsequent synthetic, designed landscapes. These include landscapes of work, mysticism and worship, dwelling (both individually and as group settings), authority, pleasure, and death. Work settings have included pastoral and arable farms as well as piazzas, streets, and roads. Patterns and structures of simplicity and elaboration associated with agriculture have a powerful resonance in this category. Religious and mystical settings are frequently centered around unusual and dramatic landforms, large or prominent features that dominate regions, or sources of water and secret or inaccessible sites. Group settings related to dwelling and community have often included the piazza or forum type of enclave, clearings, commons, and partially bounded spaces. These become transformed into places invested with authority when combined with approaches, avenues, frontality for presentation, and distortions in scale. Places most associated with pleasure have been those that approximate or have inspired gardens or areas of floral and natural beauty and delight—grottoes, pools, cascades and streams, bizarre and stimulating formations of rocks, landforms, plants, and water. Consistently these landscapes have induced feelings of fascination, awe, fear, contemplation, amusement, and delight—in short, visual and sensory interest and stimulations of all sorts.

Among the oldest and incontestably most meaningful landscapes are those that I would term "sacred" landscapes, those associated with spiritual values and especially those of the origin myths of ancient peoples: Ise and Itsukushima in Japan; Delos and Delphi, or Mount Ida and Olympus in Greece; Clitumnus, Cumae, and Avernus in Italy; Yosemite and Shasta in California; and so forth. Other sites have become special because of events that have transpired there or persons who have been associated with them.

Battlefields and the scenes of natural or human disasters are one example. These range from the ruins of ancient imperial pleasure grounds (Hadrian's Villa at Tivoli), through bucolic farms turned battle-field (Gettysburg, Pennsylvania), to sites not remarkable in themselves, such as Walden Pond, which come to be shrines for those who have embraced a set of ideas associated with the place. In this last case ideas associated with freedom of the individual, contact with nature and its processes, self-reliance, and traditions of civil disobedience and tran-scendentalist literature in America and England are all conjured up to the initiated by this scruffy glacial pond and its setting. Nothing of the sort is possible, though, for those unfamiliar with the writings of Thoreau.

In many cases the meaning assigned to these sites was not originally intended or anticipated. In others, particularly those dedicated to gods or believed to be the ancestral home of a people, it has been imposed or in some way intended toward the site, invested and cultivated through human action and designation. A recent example of such intentions with success (of sorts) has been the creation of the National Park system in the United States. Consider Yosemite, Niagara Falls, Yellowstone, the Grand Canyon, and the great peaks of the West, which were originally the sacred sites of Native Americans and have become so to us who, in the hundreds of thousands, annually make our pilgrimages to them. Other countries which have followed our lead do so with recreation and ecological values in mind, but probably not with the quasi-religious motives of those involved in the creation of our parks, especially the great western preserves that initiated the system. John Muir, Freder-ick Law Olmsted, and others involved in their creation shared a tran-scendentalist point of view and an urge to establish natural sanctuaries (sanctuary in the full sense of its meaning) for the consideration and reverence of nature and the American landscape in its most original, wild, and dramatic state. This was in part a reaction to the rapid urban-ization and industrialization of the country and partly an urge to forge a creation myth for the rebirth of the nation after the horror of the recent civil war that had very nearly destroyed it. The strength and beauty perceived in these landscapes, their scale and character, were seen to be uniquely American and un-European; their association with native peoples as sacred or treasured sites also contributed to their being chosen. They were a balm and a stimulus. They were pure and innocent of human order. Protecting them from exploitation became a cause for intellectuals, liberals, and upper-class members of the ruling establishment. Yosemite came first; other sites were added later: Niagara Falls, the Grand Canyon, Glacier, and more. This history is well known but rarely considered. These landscapes still have a number of meanings that can be read and articulated by some (but not all) members of our society and represent what I have referred to awkwardly as "natural" or "evolutionary" meaning in landscapes, whether of human construction or not.

Now let us turn to those landscapes that are constructed and for which we might consider meaning to be invested or synthetic as a part or product of our art. The methods of injecting meaning into a designed landscape range from creating tableaus with recognizable creatures and figures to abstract references implied by the structure or arrangement of nonrepresentational elements totally unrelated to those to which the design refers. The content or "meaning" of many of the most famous landscape designs of the past often was established through the use of works of sculpture and architecture that already carried associations with or recognizable references to particular ideas and other works of art, literature, landscape, or society. The iconographic program of the Villa Lante or the Villa Aldobrandini, with their classical figures and fountains expressing Neoplatonic concepts, and suggesting or recalling passages from Ovid's *Metamorphoses* and other works of classical mythology while referring to the patron, his family, and works, are familiar to today's student of landscape history. The study of iconography in Renaissance art and architecture established by Irwin Panofsky and Rudolf Wittkower has introduced the theory that a work can contain at least three levels of content:

1. The subject of the work—what is present or constructed (denoted); in other words, it is a park, a garden, or a piazza, just as a painting presents a subject, say, a bowl of apples or a Roman soldier with arrows sticking into him.

2. The reference of the work to things not present but invoked (connoted); for example, a range of mountains that one cares for, the mar-

tyrdom of a saint, a time or moment that has passed. The things that are connoted can be numerous, all at once; there can be multiple layers of reference within any particular image or composition, and oftentimes the higher the art, the more such connotations there are.

3. A mood or feeling about these two previous things that is developed through *expression or style*. A garden, like a painting, can be somber or gay, witty or matter-of-fact. This is an issue that produces considerable confusion and hostility, for this aspect of design is the one that has the most to do with matters of change in taste and fashion, although the previous one is more closely related to the recent changes that attempt to reinvigorate the boundaries of the field of landscape architecture.

Goodman and Danto disagree in some respects concerning the effectiveness of meaning that can be intended. Some of the meanings that landscape designs of the classical tradition have carried include thoughts about duty and love for family and country (Stowe, Stourhead, Rousham), or have combined attitudes toward classical learning and the duties of the Christian church (Villas Lante and d'Este), or have explored themes of passion and love, of mental disorder and analogous forces in nature (the Villa Farnesina and the Sacro Bosco). Themes such as metamorphosis and transfiguration recur frequently, as do those of a hero overcoming a variety of obstacles, whether historic in Neoplatonic Christian overlays on pagan tales, as in the choice between virtues of Hercules in the Pantheon at Stourhead, England, or contemporary themes such as the Calvinist rocky path to the Temple of Apollo (representing wisdom), also at Stourhead. The tradition of depicting and pointing out through the use of recognizable and symbolic elements, combined with the emotive and connotative device of naming things or places to ensure the desired association or "reading" of landscape compositions, continued from the Renaissance until near the end of the nineteenth century. Consider an example. At the end of a long and stately mall of elms in Central Park—the principal geometric figure within the entire park—at a place where the most important pedestrian promenade intersects the principal carriage drive, at an overlook to a carefully contrived lake with a "natural" backdrop of a skillfully reforested hillside (now known as "the Ramble"), the designers placed a remarkable fountain, piazza, stairway, and boat landing. The entire ensemble is presided over by a graceful angel, created in Rome by Emma Stebbins. The name given to this place is Bethesda Fountain.

To the public today the name is not particularly emotive, but to the Christian, Bible-reading population of the years after the Civil War, the reference was a particularly meaningful one. Bethesda was the name of a basin in ancient Jerusalem that had five entryways. Its waters were considered to possess healing powers, and many who were ill, crippled, or in physical or mental distress came to bathe in it. The Apostle John related that one of Christ's miracles took place on this spot on a Sabbath, when a man too crippled to enter the basin on his own lay languishing beside it (John 5:2). Christ told him to pick up his quilt and walk, whereupon he was able to do so. The result, of course, was to get Jesus in further trouble with the authorities for attending the sick on a holy day and for giving vent to the people's excitability, stirring up their expectations by this action. The representation of a source of cleansing, healing, and recovery was both personally (to Olmsted) and publicly an emotional and welcome message to be understood and appreciated at the time by the citizenry regardless of class—not necessarily regardless of faith, of course. Additionally, parks were seen by Olmsted as performing a cleansing or purifying role within cities, an association of great lineage. Alberti and the ancients all have asserted the relative importance of nature as a therapeutic device. The central symbol of Central Park, therefore, is one of healing and purification.

This sort of representational and symbolic narrative was not, however, to continue much longer in landscape design—at least in the most advanced design—in fact not even in Olmsted's own work. Just as in the work of Capability Brown, there was a rapid evolution toward a more pure formal abstraction utilizing landscape structures to connote landscape imagery. This can be observed as early as Brooklyn's Prospect Park and becomes more noticeable after Olmsted's separation from Calvert Vaux and the team of designers and craftsmen associated with the New York practice who exemplify many of the aesthetic propositions of John Ruskin and Augustus Pugin. I refer to the more transcendental and abstract tendencies of Olmsted that are revealed in his proposals for Mount Royal in Montreal, Quebec, the Fenway and Muddy River designs for Boston, and the quasi-southern marsh landscape he proposed for the south lakeshore of Chicago, which became such an inspiration for Jens Jensen.

Let us consider some of the imagery of Prospect Park and its formal structure. Although much has been added and destroyed in this park to blur the original meaning and intent, I believe it can still be read and understood. Unlike Central Park, Prospect Park is not a patchwork quilt of objects and entertainments stitched together in a rectangular setting or frame—episodic and jumbled. Instead, it has a purposeful and plastic structure derived from the landform (Calvert Vaux was the genius here), which has been developed with only a few major features and themes, each of which was then furnished to the degree appropriate to its use and purpose, with a careful eye to mood and thematic unity. The principal parts are the long meadow and woodland belts that define it; the broad lake and its shore; and a tumbled rocky set of ravines, ledges, and highlands that both separate and connect these first two. Within this wilder and more "natural" portion stands an enormous, crude, and puzzling structure. It is a bridge carrying a pedestrian trail over a stream and bridle path, unlike anything produced by the Olmsted consortium up until then. Its rude form should not be mistaken for accident, poverty, or lack of sophistication, for nearby stands the music terrace, a feature analogous to Bethesda Terrace, replete with elaborately conceived and carved walls, piers, and sculpture with ornament derived from native American flora and geology similar to that at the US Capitol in Washington, DC, and Central Park. This sophisticated place, with its busts of composers such as Beethoven, faces west, out across the water of the lake, to receive the full reflection of the late-afternoon and setting sun.

Returning to the comparatively paleolithic structure of Boulder Bridge, we are faced with a problem of meaning and intention. What are we to make of it? Crude things go with wild places? In a way, yes, but much more than that. Earlier in Central Park, the same office had produced one elegant and delicate bridge after another, with details of resplendent and enthusiastic character, bursting with life and references to nature and its processes, especially vegetation, with floral motifs, rosettes, entwined branches, and so on. The relationship to William Morris and Ruskin, to the roots of Art Nouveau, is everywhere evident. But in this park all of the bridges are different in mood or expression from those of Central Park, as are all of the landforms. Larger, simpler, more robust, several of the bridges are made of heavy industrial members, evocative of railways, ships, boilers, and the new heroic machines of the day. They are, however, touched with a few grace notes of a particular sort of ornament—the sort one associates with Frank Furness and Louis Sullivan, of singular floral motifs, often only in one place, and low down near the pressure point, the contact area between the engineered object and the earth. The machine devoted to human and social purpose is portrayed as an outgrowth of man and as a creature of nature. Earlier there had been a few hints, as in the partial step cut into a rock ledge at the Ramble, of an attitude of man in nature as co-worker, making minimal gestures, and of nature completing the art. Later Olmsted even wrote in his Montreal report: "When an artist puts a stick in the ground, and nature in time makes it a tree, art and nature are not to be seen apart in the result. . . . The highest art consists, under such circumstances, in making the least practicable disturbance of nature; the highest refinement in a refined abstinence of effort; in the least work, the most simple and the least fussy and pottering."[7]

In my view, Prospect Park is a meditation on post–Civil War America. It presents Olmsted's renewed inspiration drawn from the scenery of the Far West and his emotional transcendentalism—the grandeur and roughness of the landscape on the one hand and yearnings for peace and prosperity, for agriculture and industry to serve the needs of the nation and to produce graceful, livable cities on the other. Boulder Bridge does not stand for any one thing. It is a contributing element to a larger fabric, a mysteriously geological and noncultural detail, ambiguous and heavy, the metamorphosis of boulders into the semblance of a bridge. In this fashion his later works can be seen as poetic and emblematic in much the same way as those of Brown and Humphry Repton were. Unlike Kent and Henry Hoare, or other earlier connoisseur-designers whose work presented its meaning through a series of tableaux of silent assemblages of pavilions, inscriptions, evocative sculpture, and titles, Olmsted moved to a more abstract and sophisticated presentation. This is partly because the ideas to be presented made reference to other landscapes and to their meaning for society, not to stories about gods or patrons, and had more to do with general concepts of the medium, the expression of physical properties, and the manipulation of them as part of the presentation (the denotation) and as an embodiment in these works of the formal ideas that were contained within the earlier and more anecdotal narrative landscapes. In this development, he had retraced the evolution of the strategy of presentation and analogous content of the Japanese stroll gardens (which he never saw).

RHETORIC AND METAPHOR IN LANDSCAPE DESIGN

Regarding expression, one must address "rhetoric" and "metaphor" in landscape design. If works of design can be considered to refer to things that are not present and can do so while establishing a particular mood or feeling, then those devices that are used to suggest, persuade, or lead an audience to the desired conclusion are what has been called rhetoric. A rhetorical question is used to make a statement not by stating it, but rather by leading the listener to complete the thought, to reach what might at the time or in the situation created by the author appear to be the obvious or "natural" conclusion. Aristotle, who understood such things as well as anyone ever will, believed that rhetoric consisted of those effects that seek to arouse certain attitudes toward whatever is being presented (he was mostly referring to verbal structures). In his view rhetoricians must have a sufficient understanding of human sensibility and emotion so that they can characterize an action or an object sufficiently to induce the desired response in their audience: anger, sympathy, distress, patriotism, and so forth. As Danto writes, "It is not enough for a rhetorician to demonstrate that a certain feeling ought to be felt, or that you—his audience—would be justified were you to feel it and perhaps unjustified in not feeling it: he is only worth his salt if he *gets you to have that emotion* and does not just tell you what you should be feeling."[8] The devices and strategies that designers use to manipulate a setting and its furnishings to produce responses are many and normally involve a remarkable amount of craft and learning. As in every other art, a certain amount of feeling and instinct for the medium and its devices are necessary. To this one must then add a level of performance ability before one can begin to manipulate or discuss style, expression, and meaning.

Consider the phenomenon of rhetoric in the art of building design. Many critics, historians, and philosophers have commented on the "verticality" of Gothic cathedrals, and the fact that this expression of the idea of verticality, this property that has been invested into the inert materials through the manipulation of form, structure, and detail, gives these buildings a property that is not possessed by other buildings. Furthermore, in some ways this "vertical" characteristic that we read in these buildings is linked to metaphors for soaring, rising up from and leaving the earth in some manner similar to ideas held by the people of the religion that built them and that were associated with the progress of the human soul after death as well as the assumption of the resurrected Christ and his mother into Heaven, which was poetically considered to be away from the earth, up above the clouds in the sky or heavens.

The piety and yearning for release from life on earth were embodied in these structures through numerous strategies of design related to the suppression of architectural motifs that normally connote mass or weight, and emphasized verticality over horizontality through distortion, stretched proportions, segmenting of structural masses into what appear to be bundles of tall, thin elements, and the like. That the arrangement of parts and their articulation and shape can change more than a building's appearance is an established theory of architectural practice and analysis of our time. Alan Colquhoun, Kenneth Frampton, Anthony Vidler, Robert Venturi, Peter Eisenman, and Jorge Silvetti have written eloquently and at considerable length about the rhetoric and devices of twentieth-century architecture and its predecessors. Very little has been written about the rhetorical devices employed in landscape architecture, especially by its greatest practitioners. Hamilton Hazlehurst and Kenneth Woodbridge are among the few who have tried. Even less has been written about such matters in contemporary practice. The entire effort is clouded by the nature of the medium. The fact that natural materials, some of them alive, are frequently used to represent aspects of nature and landscape (i.e., the referent and referee may be made of the same substance) greatly complicates matters. This is especially so when one turns to the most powerful rhetorical device—metaphor.

The most common and persuasive poetic device used in all fields of art is the metaphor; indeed, metaphor seems to be almost synonymous with art. Metaphor is commonly described as a figure of speech in which a name or descriptive term is transferred to some object to which it is not properly applicable. There must, therefore, be an untrue equation. It is the describing or presentation of one thing in terms of another.

It is not literally true at all, but there is a discovered truth or insight that does in some way make sense and gives us a new understanding of the world or some aspect of it, whether small or large, funny or tragic. The old clichés that use a river as a metaphor for time or life are examples; Shakespeare's phrase "all the world's a stage" is another; or Kenneth Koch's student who in error penned the masterpiece "a swan of bees." Danto in a chapter of *The Transfiguration of the Commonplace* describes at great length the mechanisms of metaphor and its centrality to the creation, meaning, and understanding of all art. It would be foolish either to attempt a synopsis or to paraphrase this remarkable essay. I refer readers to it.[9] In his view one thing essential to the workings of metaphor is a phenomenon of incompleteness and correlation to which the audience must react for the metaphor to work. In important ways this is related to and partially derived from the "rhetoric" employed by the artist/designer. It is also conditioned by the education, experience, and attitudes of the audience. Therefore, as education, experience, and beliefs change, metaphors can die, lose their potency, become clichés or stale figures of speech, design, or art.

It is also through the evolution of society and education, knowledge and values, especially as stimulated by historians, critics, and artists, that dead or lost metaphors can be revived. It seems, therefore, that there is a guaranteed tension between the nature of art (its processes of renewal, or evolutionary transformation, and the potency of its metaphors) and the accessibility or immediacy of its meanings in a changing society. This process has intensified in recent decades. As Clement Greenberg has commented, "modernization" in art has largely consisted of discarding expendable conventions.[10] As long as conventions survive and can be identified, they will be attacked. This will continue until the resultant work begins to deny its own essence or can no longer be understood to be art in the form or medium as previously intended. In the view of many people, painting and music have come to a halt, for now, in terms of formal invention and revision and can only retrace various aspects, nooks, and crannies of their historical corpus—appearing to have reached the limits of their recognizability and validity. The same cannot yet be said for the architecture of landscapes and buildings.

Often the most "advanced" artists do not set out to be revolutionary or advanced, but rather to be good. The "advance" comes from an emulation of those qualities that they admire in previous work. As a rule, having digested the major art from the preceding period or periods, the young artist or designer looks for alternative ones in order to break away from overpowering precedents. In landscape design it would appear that a moment has arrived when many practitioners and students are looking for alternatives to conventions that are perceived to be empty and used up. Some (as I have remarked earlier) have turned to the conventions of art. This, however, is to place oneself in a secondary or derivative relationship to the fundamental source of form and imagery in the field, that is, the world of nature, natural processes, and the cultural land-scapes of the past, whether sacred, agricultural, or ornamental.

Several of America's most original and powerful landscape design-ers of the twentieth century appear to have drawn upon these primary sources. Richard Haag, A. E. Bye, and Lawrence Halprin have all pro-duced direct fresh abstractions of natural phenomena. Thomas Church and Dan Kiley have done the same with particular landscapes and gar-dens of the past. All of these individuals have understood the need to abstract and distill formal essences without imitating or building min-iature encapsulated versions of the source of their inspiration. Their work represents the first truly fresh development (both stylistically and formally) since the late eighteenth century.

A. E. Bye has produced some of the most abstract work, for instance, the Soros garden in Southampton on Long Island, which looks neither like a painting, nor a garden, nor a natural landscape. It is truly a com-position that could only exist in the landscape medium. It is pared down and yet deeply sensual. Its subject matter is the earth and its surface is delineated by light, the texture of plants and water in all of its forms—mist, water, and snow.

Haag, too, has plumbed the depths of our urban and rural psyches, maneuvering the city of Seattle into leaving the monstrous heart of a gas refinery as a colossal memento mori in the center of a park on Lake Union. Despite a citizenry that wanted to build a pseudo-sylvan realm, Haag subverted the plan into an archaeological playground of genuine meaning and poetry. This park now exists and may come to be a fine one, in a conventional sense, in terms of its verdure and facilities. But it also has a sculpture many times more powerful than all the site artists in America could make, one that speaks to us about our past in ways that only the broken aqueducts and fallen columns of ruined temples can. There is no foolishness, no sentiment, no false note. There is also no other urban park quite like it.

Elsewhere, in the woods of Seattle's Bainbridge Island on Prentice Bloedel's estate, Haag quietly labored for over fifteen years on another highly personal and startlingly fresh series of landscape studies. Linked to each other and to the place, they constitute an extended essay on the making of landscape compositions. Most are produced by a strategy of subtracting from the second-growth forest. Several examine traditional devices of the Far East—moss gardens and miniature abstractions that dwarf the adjacent larger landscape, the stroll sequence of views; or Western conventions—the reflecting ponds, hedges, and geometrics of the Renaissance, the invented naturalism of the eighteenth century (in this case a natural-seeming pond created to attract blackbirds for the pleasure to be had in their song), and so on. I know of no other person who could so cunningly create a garden room in the forest presided over by a haunting collection of moss-covered stumps that stand as gaunt reminders of the primeval forest that once stood there on what is now the estate of one of America's wealthiest timber barons.

Haag's work, like that of an old Zen monk (which he often resembles), confounds us with its apparent directness and deep subtleties. Like Sung dynasty scrolls or an old koan, it seems to grow directly from experience and the forces of nature. The artist has somehow stepped back out of the picture. It seems simple, yet contradictory. What had been a swimming pool and terrace have disappeared. In their place a great mound of white marble chips has appeared, next to a hole in the ground—also of the white stone chips. This act of quiet displacement sits within a green sea of grass. The terrace itself has been sawn into bits, some of which remain drifting about in this lawn. Like fragments of a shattered planet they move away from the center of the space and appear to orbit the haunting white pyramid. This in turn is encircled by planted mounds, which in their color and texture appear like distant mountains. Beyond these, the light filters through clearings and deep vistas that Haag arranged far off into the woods of Agate Point. This composition demonstrates a mastery that grows out of a lifetime of developing abstract representations. Haag's Bloedel designs are among the most powerful works of this century in their exploration of the relation of gardens to nature. It is only to be lamented that the University of Washington has recently destroyed and mutilated several portions of his unfinished masterpiece.

Almost as the alter ego to this quiet work executed *in medias rus* stands the exuberant and equally inspired work of Halprin, which burst forth in the heart of numerous American cities in the 1960s and 1970s, most notably Portland and Seattle. Long after this one-man theater-workshop, circus, and human dynamo is gone, the work will remain, the best of it superior to all its imitations around the world. It is no surprise to those who know of the many years of residences (e.g., McIntyre in California) and suburban shopping centers (e.g., NorthPark Center in Dallas) that Halprin cranked out that his work is genuinely intended for the pleasure and use of people. His celebrated fountains (several of which derive much of their character from the sensibility and intelligence of Angela Danadjieva, who worked on them under his direction) are both an extension of the European Baroque public-fountain tradition and a departure from it, conditioned by their American context. Halprin himself has been quite articulate about the sources of form and imagery in this work: the High Sierras and their glaciated valleys, boulders, torrents, and meadows; the carved cliffs and headlands of the Pacific coast from California to the Northwest; the overwhelming human creations and devastation of granite quarries; and a couple of the great Italian fountains, especially the central passage of the water organ of the Villa d'Este at Tivoli. The Portland Auditorium Forecourt Fountain and the one built over a freeway in Seattle are not pastiches of this source material, however, but deeply organic and plastic creations. Echoes of the sources of their inspiration reverberate through the massing and even the shape and batter of the monoliths, plinths, and buttress shapes over and down which the water cascades. Nowhere does this work really imitate or literally represent, or even look like, its antecedents, either natural or cultural. Halprin, like Bye, Haag, and Kiley, adamantly rejects the possibility that one can or should imitate nature. One should be inspired by it, emulate its logic, generosity, processes, and forms, but eschew attempts or desires to copy it; all of them have said this in their words and affirmed it in their work.

The largest and most radical break from the past in our time has been our attitude toward composition—the conventions of order. Traditionally, in European art there has been a strong tendency to bring diverse elements of any work into a balanced composition, replete with harmony and symmetry (often in several dimensions), to complete a whole that reaches a degree of resolution and finality. This can be done with exuberance and considerable movement and formal complexity, as in the great Baroque works, or with a calm, quiet restraint of form and shape approaching near stasis, as in certain neoclassical gardens and buildings. In a statement admired and quoted by Olmsted, the French landscape architect Édouard André notes, "The first law of a work of art, either on canvas or on the earth, is to be a whole."[11] Although that may still be true enough, the criteria of what is an acceptable whole is probably very different today than in his time. Twentieth-century art has opened new possibilities that have become part of our mental equipment, significantly altering our visual sensibilities. Cubism, for instance, introduced the now commonplace idea that multiple points of view can exist within a single work of visual art and that apparent conflicts between them do not need to be resolved. Collage has introduced further study of the relationship between representation and illusion and between the fragment or part and the whole, while utilizing a combination of mass-produced images and handmade or preindustrial craft gestures as raw materials for representation. The results have been the recombination of shattered or dislocated fragments into something other than that of their origin. This use of real rather than rendered material, when translated into the use of ready-made industrial items or the use of things that are meant to be absent yet referred to, but are in fact present, has a direct bearing on landscape architecture.

This ironic position when taken toward the tradition of representation and the surplus of images in our society has only begun to filter into the field. Fletcher Steele, Gabriel Guevrekian, and Garrett Eckbo certainly have broken some ground here, but only recently have Walker, Schwartz, Hargreaves, Michael Van Valkenburgh, Lee Weintraub, and a new generation, especially on the West Coast, begun to mine this rich vein of ideas. Fragmentation, dislocation, displacement, and distortion have all become acceptable strategies for design manipulation of traditional material and imagery, and are central in efforts currently under way as the field renews itself. The schools are full of students experimenting with these strategies, and we will likely be awash in work, much of it not very good, that attempts to put it into practice. Nevertheless, it is probably for the best. Inevitably this will lead some back to a reexamination of the plant palette, landform, and natural process. The forms available to cast this material into compositions, however, may partake of the new structures revealed through the telescope and microscope, ranging from those of recombinant DNA to the most archaic constructions of the Bronze Age and tomorrow's computer technology.

The subject matter or meanings that I believe are being dealt with in the most thoughtful landscape designs today—beyond the programmatic and instrumental—are the following:

1. Ideas of order.

2. Ideas of nature, including a critique of past views as provoked by knowledge of ecology.

3. Ideas about the arrangement of cities and thereby society and its desires (as well as needs).

4. Ideas about the medium as an expressive one (the landscape as medium), revealing something about our methods and its processes.

5. Considerations about the history of art and landscape design, and the history of places—their archaeology.

In these, the design expression is often a critique of past designs and landscapes. Many of the best works of the moment are inquiries into the validity of past expressions and their extension into the present, as well as being new and healthy creations of their own. One need only think of Richard Haag's Gas Works Park and Bloedel Reserve gardens in Seattle to realize the validity of this statement. In works like these one sees that the sensual properties of the medium are undiminished, that it continues to carry an expression of our ideas about nature and our place in the scheme of things. Finally we see the power of fresh abstractions and how futile are the attempts to replicate nature—in fragment or in toto—as a design method or a goal.

REGIONALISM AND THE PRACTICE
OF HANNA/OLIN, LTD.

(1995)

This essay will examine the question of regionalism and the degree to which it informs and affects the work of a contemporary landscape architectural design practice, and when it does, what forms and expressions such considerations take. To answer this question, the following must be considered: What is generally meant by the term "regionalism," ecologically and culturally? What is meant by the term "regionalism" in design? Definitions and examples are given, first for architecture, and then for landscape architecture. With these criteria and definitions established, one can then turn to the body of work executed by the firm of Hanna/Olin, Ltd., in the fifteen-year span from 1976 to 1991, to determine to what degree these projects exhibit an interest in or understanding of their regional situation, and which strategies are employed to make them regional or not. Of further interest, and possibly more important, to what purpose is this done? Several examples of deeply regional, highly particularized schemes are given, along with examples of more universal, generalist (potentially "placeless") schemes and those with elements that merely refer to their regional situation. This leads to an examination of the strategies employed in those deemed more regional. These include elements that are both biological and cultural. Among the latter are references to the history of the region and place,

From *Regional Garden Design in the United States,* ed. Therese O'Malley and Marc Treib (Washington, DC: Dumbarton Oaks Research Library and Collection, 1995), 243–70.

Playa Vista . Nov 3 . 1989 .   Neighborhood Park .

Neighborhood park sketch, Playa Vista, Los Angeles, 1989

formal and stylistic traditions, notions and theories of predecessors, earlier designers, heroes, myths, and cultural norms. Finally, what conclusions are reached by a practitioner after such self-examination and critical reflection? What is (or was) the purpose of the intention to invest work with regional properties? Should it have been attempted, and why? The conclusion for the moment is both cautionary and optimistic.

ON REGIONALISM

What is a region? Generally, *region* is a term used to connote a geographic area of considerable extent, indefinite in size and shape, that despite considerable diversity within its parts exhibits some overall commonality or possesses a set of shared properties that render it distinct from other areas and their general properties, which are in some way(s) different. An example of the ambiguity and specificity of such a term may be found in one of the opening paragraphs of Victor Shelford's landmark work, *The Ecology of North America,* where he writes:

> The temperate deciduous forest, or the *oak-deer-maple-biome,* occupies North America from the center of the Great Lakes region south to the Gulf of Mexico. It covers the northern two-thirds of the Florida Peninsula and extends west beyond the Mississippi River to the Ozark Mountains. The chief characteristic of the temperate deciduous forest is the predominance of trees with broad leaves which are shed each autumn. An understory of small trees and shrubs is usually also deciduous. The shedding of the leaves brings a striking change in light conditions and shelter for animals. The forest floor is covered with a dense layer of leaves in various stages of decay. The extreme southern part of the forest also contains evergreen species. The white oak, white-tailed deer, and turkey are important throughout practically all of the biome.[1]

He then goes on for the next seventy-one pages to explain the constituent elements that make up this forest biome, its variety and consistency, identifying three large subdivisions or regions: northern and upland forests; southern and lowland forests; and stream-skirting forests.[2] Each of these he further subdivides. For instance, the northern and upland regions usually have beech and sugar maple in climax stands and wapiti and deer as permanent dominant animals. There are five regions: the tulip-oak region, oak-chestnut region, maple-basswood-birch region, maple-beech-hemlock region, and maple-basswood region. Each of these has its particular soils, climate, animals, and plant community.

Of particular interest is the concept that each region grades off into the next and is a constellation of various factors having to do with dynamic communities within a physiographic setting. Shelford's work is a masterpiece of observation, data gathering, description, and synthesis. Similar works by cultural anthropologists and ethnographers have attempted to do the same for human settlements, community, and ecology. Here, however, several differences creep in. Henry Glassie in his early work *Pattern in the Material Folk Culture of the Eastern United States* observes: "In general, folk material exhibits major variation over space and minor variation through time, while the products of popular or academic culture exhibit minor variation over space and major variation through time. The natural divisions of folk material are, then, spatial, where the natural divisions of popular material are temporal; that is, a search for patterns in folk material yields regions, where a search for patterns in popular material yields periods."[3]

Glassie asserts that folk or vernacular artifacts are different in kind and purpose from those of popular culture, and he places works of art, those products that are intended to please aesthetically, together with popular products of the dominant culture in a regionless, placeless continuum. Interestingly enough, this is consonant with the prevailing use of the terms "regional" and "regionalism." These terms have been used to characterize and enfold a wide array of work that has been generally considered in some way separate from or counter to the mainstream of contemporary culture. "Regional" development in broader movements often was (and still is) motivated by the desire of some local group to express their own identity and to resist being overrun by the personality or expression of others or from distant centers of power of influence—Los Angeles and New York, for example. The geographic isolation and contiguity of each region, likewise, gives it its identity. A further connotation implied in Glassie's study and listed as a specific characteristic of folk culture is that it is conservative, backward-looking, and resistant to change. The dilemma that modernity has posed to those involved in regional movements has been discussed at length by several authors. (See, for example, the essays by Friedrich Achleitner, Alena Kabova and Guy Ballange, and François Burkhardt in *Jože Plečnik, Architect: 1872–1957.*)[4] Put simply, regionalism in the arts connotes some sort of localized tradition that is inevitably in conflict with many forces of change, especially those of international modernism.

If regions in natural science are characterized by physical and geographic characteristics, cultural regions are also spatially defined. They may, however, cross or subdivide physiographic boundaries (e.g., German and French development of the Rhine River Valley; or the Athabascan Indians and later European settlers on the Pacific Coast, who colonized both the Pacific Littoral with its distinctive physiography, climate, and biota, and the eastern area between the Coast Range and the Rocky Mountains). In this second case, not so surprisingly, the people, their settlements, art, and politics turned out to be quite different on each side of the mountains after several centuries. In all of this one must be careful about notions of causality and determinism. The chance results of human variability and individual personality have been easily as powerful as the natural environment. Think of Joseph Smith and his Mormons, of Frémont's expedition, Sutter's Mill, or Chief Joseph and Chief Seattle, or why the Pacific Northwest is neither a Russian- nor a Spanish-speaking country or colony such as Mexico.

The differences in physiographic regions, therefore, are most pronounced in terms of geology (landform) and plant and animal ecology, which have to do with soil and climate as well. The differences in cultural regions have largely to do with language, land development practices (primarily agricultural and the habits of property division, inheritance, and management), the religious beliefs and ethical system that underpin the economy and development pattern, and the art and architecture created by and for the group. Often this art and architecture have evolved in direct response to the opportunities and constraints posed by the physical environment.

WHAT IS REGIONALISM IN ARCHITECTURE?

Regionalist work inevitably looks in two directions simultaneously: back to a past tradition and to aspects of the vernacular and folk culture on the one hand; and forward to new forces, ideas, and styles emanating from elsewhere that must be dealt with lest they overwhelm whatever traditions and regional character may remain on the other. Central to the concept of regionalism is the notion of giving a particular version, a "regional" variation to some thing, force, or activity that is widespread. Thus, regional schools of painting and writing are known for the particular flavor or distinctive stylistic characteristics that their otherwise ordinary, ubiquitous work might have, especially in relation to that which is seen as more central, original, or dominant. For example, Siennese painting in the Cinquecento is a regionalist school compared to that of Rome or Florence (which were the norm and presumed dominant standard of Italian Renaissance painting at the time). In architecture the characteristics of regionalism most noticeably include the conscious use and adaptation of aspects of vernacular building characteristics, especially those related to climate and indigenous building materials, combined with more general and accepted methods of design and composition common to broader national or international practice.

Good examples of this in architecture range from the remarkably flat and prismatic buildings built in England in the early seventeenth century to those of the American prairie school or Pueblo Deco buildings of this century. Among the first of these examples are Kirby Hall and Montacute House, clearly Renaissance buildings of sophistication that, despite having all of the compositional elements of similar buildings in Italy of the same and previous generation, look nothing like them. So too, one would have to say that the buildings of Frank Lloyd Wright built between 1900 and 1910 in Oak Park, Illinois—which launched an entire stylistic movement and are touchstones of modernism in both America and abroad—exhibit many of the characteristic elements, materials, and concerns of the contemporary Arts and Crafts movement and of late Victorian/Edwardian building elsewhere, such as the work of Greene & Greene or Gustav Stickley, none of which look the same at all. As is often the case, Wright's work was the combined product of his conscious selection of elements and motifs found around him in the

Midwest and of his unconscious handwriting and compositional traits. His later work in California and the Arizona desert shows further evolution and experiment with highly regionalist notions.

Even more pointedly one can consider the KiMo Theatre in Albuquerque, New Mexico, the Ahwahnee Hotel in Yosemite Park, California, or Union Station in Los Angeles and conclude that they are very cunning and self-conscious attempts to transform particular generic building types of their era (theater, hotel, train station) into particular and localized civic and public monuments.[5] Careful effort is employed to "ground" them in time and space so as to take banal, universal building programs and make them "local heroes" architecturally. The attempt is both to create a regional imagery, not unrelated to mythmaking, and to personalize an impersonal program, a highly poetic activity.

To summarize, the difference between the merely vernacular and the regional is one of intent, expression, and self-consciousness. Regionalist works are self-conscious in the face of alternatives and resistant to the pressure to conform to someone else's aesthetic, proffering instead a countercultural artifice that combines carefully selected elements that are intended to relate a building to regional traditions in some way. The motive can be aesthetic or political, and often is both. Phoebe Cutler has written on this aspect of regionalism with regard to Harold Ickes and Franklin D. Roosevelt: she discusses their agenda regarding American public life, the land, and the regionalist images employed by their designers across the country from 1934 to 1944 in the parks and structures of the Interior Department and Works Progress Administration.[6]

Strategies of Regionalism in Architecture

Using the KiMo Theatre as a regional work of high degree, what are the strategies employed that convey its regionality?[7] These may be summarized as comprising overall form or shape; fabric, that is, the material and technique employed for its structure and materials; details and ornament, which include those that are merely applied rather than integral; and finally narrative devices that convey messages. In this case, the overall form is derived from the profile and general shape of the Taos pueblo. In terms of the fabric, here the adobe and timber infill themes derive from the mission churches of Las Trampas and, particularly, San Esteban at Acoma pueblo. The fabric, thick walls, small openings, beam ends, flat roof, stucco finish, texture, and color are particularly consonant with the first image, that of a pueblo. Third, the details are all subjected to the theme of Native religious devices and are selected/invented to evoke this world. Indian shields, ceremonial staffs, and beam ends with carved ornaments are all applied to surface. Finally, representative narrative paintings are added that firmly place the building within the tradition of these earlier vernacular buildings. The similarity of this device to the paintings of Antonio Tempesta in the Villa Lante and of Paolo Veronese at the Villa Barbaro is striking. At the same time, the arrangement of elements, the design and pattern for the windows, and the choice of decorative motifs and materials are very much in the Art Deco mode, an international movement within the design fields between the two world wars concerning compositional strategies, formal structure, and the relationship between flat surface and decoration, particularly shallow relief and patterning.

The magnificent railroad station in Los Angeles designed by Donald and John Parkinson, with W. E. Markas as chief draftsman, between 1937 and 1939 is a similar distillation and adaptation of the Spanish Colonial mission churches with their simple basilica halls, campanile, and cloisters. Again, southwest Indian motifs are used here in the paving, and mission-derived ornament is used throughout the fabric, mixed with Spanish Baroque and Deco ornament.

WHAT IS REGIONALISM
IN LANDSCAPE ARCHITECTURE?

Regionalism in landscape architecture is the very same thing described above in architecture; however, as is common when discussing the two fields, it must be said that the means are somewhat different, and the results often unrecognizably different. (The medium leads to different concerns and perspective.) The first implication of difference is that of physiographic determinants of location; secondarily one considers cultural traditions. The medium (the physical material of the landscape), and especially the living palette of plants, does indeed offer an opportunity to declare a particularity not afforded to architecture. On the other hand, plants alone rarely constitute the full complement of design elements in a landscape, nor can they fulfill all of the cultural and social needs or responses in a human landscape. As in the architecture of buildings, designed, self-conscious landscapes can and often are intended to derive strength and instrumental devices from the vernacular, in this case the landscapes, indigenous settlement patterns, and agriculture, as well as natural physiographic and ecological conditions of particular regions.

Also, as in architecture, the twin poles of design—ideas and technique—come into play: values (religious, ethical, and commercial) on the one hand, and working practices (artistic and technological) on the other. Furthermore, the central purpose of regionalism, the resistance to homogenizing and leveling tendencies coming from distant or dominant groups, is, if anything, stronger in landscape design. For centuries the precept "consult the genius of the place" (to use Alexander Pope's phrase) has been a central tenet of landscape design. Although most commonly applied to immediate sites, this principle of ascertaining the underlying order and processes of larger areas that at times do have a genuine regional nature and of shaping one's plans and design so that they do indeed respect, preserve, and enhance these preexisting qualities is fundamental to the concept of regionalism.

This was an underlying belief propelling Ian McHarg's *Design with Nature*. Certainly at the gross planning level presented in his book, the rhetoric and studies offer an attempt to orchestrate a modernist regionalism in landscape planning.[8] In a quasi-scientific manner, the studies in this work authored by McHarg, Narendra Juneja, and others, as in the architectural examples given above, look backward and forward simultaneously: backward to land unspoiled by human settlement and a set of interrelated physiographic and ecological phenomena, and forward to a landscape of development and change. One of the principal criticisms of this work has been its scale of operations and the lack of demonstration of its methods at smaller, site-specific scales. The desire for rational, non-nostalgic methods to use in the production of critically regional work at a more normal project scale has not been met—not by McHarg, but also not by anyone else in the field.

Nevertheless, despite the lack of theoretical texts, there is a body of work that one can point to in the field that is truly regional. Bernard Maybeck, Horace W. S. Cleveland, Jens Jensen, and Thomas Church and their work are exemplars of regionalism. To these one could also add Roberto Burle Marx, Luis Barragán, Dimitris Pikionis, Florence Yoch, and Richard Haag,[9] each of whom found their own way to relate to the broad forces of modernism and, in some ways, was a proponent of it while simultaneously producing work that was quintessentially regional and personal. Two of these designers, Burle Marx and Haag, are deeply knowledgeable about plants, their work largely grounded in native flora. Two others, Barragán and Pikionis, were both architects who managed to produce remarkable and deeply regional landscape spaces and ensembles with a minimum of plants. Their work, while considered exclusively modern, was also tied to the vernacular in terms of building, forms, technics, and materials. Florence Yoch, conversely, mastered the eclectic palette of exotic, imported plants and Mediterranean Revival architectural elements that have come to be so characteristic of Southern California.

Strategies in the Production of Regional Landscapes

Highly pragmatic and heavily constrained developments over long periods of time in agriculture and diet have played a significant role in shaping the cultural regions of the world. So much so, in fact, that much of modern industrialization in agriculture has had to do with questions of how to grow more of the traditional produce faster and cheaper and not with changing what might be grown. At the same time, this practice has led to a universalization or homogenization of what is produced and, as a side effect, an increasing standardization and loss of regional differences of the lands affected. Historically, farms have been our largest cultural artifact and have been the predominant formal structures in our landscapes, giving each region its particular character. One has only to consider the different character of landscapes such as that of southwest Britain, the Île-de-France, Holland, or the American Midwest to acknowledge this.

While I have argued elsewhere that one of the greatest sources of form and ideas for landscape designers has been nature and its processes, it also can be argued that agriculture has been, as well, one of the other great sources of material for the design of parks, gardens, and public space. One obvious example of this is the pastoral parks of the eighteenth and nineteenth centuries, based directly on the pasturage of livestock in Greece and Italy and subsequent associations with classical life, literature, and late Renaissance art, which in themselves became emblematic pastoral icons for Western society. Another is the Moorish and Hispanic use of Mediterranean orchards, groves, and small market gardens for the basic structure, materials, and details (primarily irrigation and water conservation devices) for their famous, highly poetic gardens. André Le Nôtre's great parks, adaptations of Italian gardens and parks to the flat, poorly drained sites of the Île-de-France, are more redolent of the agricultural boundaries, hedgerows, and windrows along roads, canals, and rivers, and of forest plantations for timber (one of the oldest of Mediterranean harvest crops) than they are of the small country estates and gardens in the hills surrounding Rome. The most common and obvious strategy used in such work has been to seize on one or two key elements without which the countryside or agricultural type would not be recognizable, or to isolate and refine it, presenting it, as on a platter, to the viewer or user of the new design for their pleasure and contemplation. In the case of Moorish gardens, the key elements are the runnel of water (the *jube* of Middle Eastern agriculture) and the tank or well, a bosquet (the grove of fruit trees—oranges, dates, etc.), and an assortment of potted plants (the fruit, herbs, and flowers of every farm, nursery, and souk from Spain to India). Taken out of context, burnished and re-presented, these elements fill our senses and imaginations. Entering the Alhambra or Madrid's Royal Botanic Garden, one is overwhelmed by a presentation of the familiar that is as reductive as it is generous. Like recombinant DNA, new aesthetic organisms have been fashioned from ordinary bits that have existed for ages in the everyday, working world.

Thus it is that Barragán's work seems so fresh and new, so old yet familiar. It partakes equally of the vernacular painted adobe of Mexican haciendas and villages and of the modernism descending from De Stijl, Adolf Loos, and the Bauhaus. The jazzy counterpoint of his colored volumes is both forward- and backward-looking, referring to high and low art. The walls and windows, horse troughs, and exercise yards are literally agricultural elements as old as the work of the Roman agronomists Columella, Cato, and Varro. Their form and color are rooted in Latin American culture and its traditions from before as well as after the arrival of Europeans. Other examples abound: Olmsted's hacienda/mission-cum-botanic garden for Leland Stanford and Richard Haag's moss garden with its stumps on Bainbridge Island in Washington State. The list can be expanded to great length.

Another common strategy is to identify key natural forms and processes (in addition to vegetation) and, as in regionalist architecture, isolate their form and structural properties. In such cases, vegetation is
used as an ornamental addition to reinforce the forms and give more
specificity. Probably the most obvious example of this strategy has been
the work of Lawrence Halprin done in the American West during the
late 1960s and throughout the 1970s.[10] The waterfall and plaza structures, choice of material, color and texture, local forms, and planting
of the projects executed in Portland, Oregon, Seattle, and Denver all
demonstrate these ideas at work.

As in the production of regionalist architecture, one can summarize
that those elements or operations that offer the most toward attempts
to create regional work are the structure and overall form; the fabric
of this structure; the elements and technics of the structure; and the
details and ornament, whether integral to the form and structure or
applied. This last issue, ornament and structure, poses a particular and
unresolved problem in all modern work. Are the patterns of a tree's
branching or a bridge truss ornament or merely structure? Another
structure would have a different pattern. Is ornament only an applied
and extraneous phenomenon, as Adolf Loos asserted, or can it be integral with form and elements of the fabric and "deep structure" as Louis
Sullivan, Christopher Alexander, and Thomas Beeby propose?[11] Finally,
there is narrative. Of all of these, narrative has been the least attempted
and exploited in twentieth-century landscape design until very recently.
(See the work of Ian Hamilton Finlay, Bernard Lassus, and Pamela Burton for recent developments in this area. Their work does not necessarily promote regional attitudes, with the exception of Lassus. Exceptions
such as Carol Johnson's early work in Chelsea, Massachusetts, and
SWA's Plaza at Las Colinas in Dallas come to mind as examples that
have, however.)

EXAMPLES OF REGIONAL ELEMENTS
OR STRATEGIES IN HANNA/OLIN'S WORK

Few elements so immediately connote place and regionality as do key
indicator species of plants. As mentioned earlier, this is one of the most

common and important aspects of ecological description and analysis. One has only to conjure up the pines of Rome, the maples of Japan, the rows of poplars lining canals and plane trees along the country roads of France, or the lindens of Berlin and the chestnuts of the parks in Paris to realize that cultural landscapes, even the most urban places, have such particular possibilities. Two of America's most characteristic species, the chestnut and elm, have vanished from our cities in this century, leaving them poignantly barren and bereft of what had been one of their essential regional place-making elements. Nevertheless, many other specific plants and humble vernacular elements can be drawn upon in the different regions of America. In our work, plants and materials have often played an important role in the establishment of place and region. One such example is the use of paper birches, white pines, kinnikinnick (bearberry), and herbaceous material such as wigelia, Solomons seal, and duetzia associated with traditional domestic gardens, and a very Yankee wood fence of white dowels and urns on a granite base that unmistakably locate one project in Maine. Another example is the Codex Corporation headquarters in Canton, Massachusetts. Here brilliant sugar maples, dry-laid fieldstone walls, mill ponds, and a granite-trimmed knot garden of herbs with painted trellis and lattice place this project also in New England, but farther south. Even the winter garden with its small lawn, baby's tears, palms, and small tank of water plants evokes a memory of Isabella Stewart Gardner's fantasy in the Back Bay Fens of Boston and a yearning after warmer climes on the part of this frequently icebound population.

Robert Frost's remark that good fences make good neighbors was literally followed by us on a small rocky hill at the Pitney Bowes headquarters in Stamford, Connecticut. Covered with a scrap of native second-growth woodland that we took great pains to edit—removing invasive non-native material, nursing the forest back into health—this hill became the centerpiece for the entire composition. Once we had restored the basic structure, we were able to add numerous native understory plants and reinforce the edges. This project was as much a meditation on the stony outcrops, ledges, and generations of shifting them about by settlers as it is about planting or shaping of spaces.

The Playa Vista project in Los Angeles is in many ways a more ambitious project. We are re-creating wetland and a riparian habitat complete with 240 acres of estuary with native plants, fluvial processes, and animal habitat restoration, along with two miles of streambed and plant and animal habitats. It also includes miles of streets with street trees, some native and many naturalized exotics, albeit linked to the cultural history of city and region—for example, the palms, pines, and flowering trees of Beverly Hills, Santa Monica, Santa Barbara, Pasadena, and numerous other towns and smaller cities of the region. The identity of this American coastal community is linked to Mediterranean and tropical vegetation in countless images from orange crates to motion pictures. Today part of the genius of the Los Angeles region lies in this profusion of lush imported vegetation.

The projects referred to above display a marked absence or low volume of rhetoric with little or no persuasion beyond that of "being there." Whatever argument they contain, it is not so much about regionalism (their place in a particular region is assumed); these projects are more concerned about the relationships between public and private realms and the creation of socially useful and aesthetically rewarding spaces. As these examples may indicate, it is hard to limit landscape design to matters of planting indigenous, or even native, species. To understand and operate effectively, regardless of point of view, one must also consider purely cultural elements. Certainly as one shifts the focus of consideration and work from rural, suburban and small-town settings to more urban ones, the cultural, built artifacts become more strident and dominant than vegetation. (This is not to say that vegetation is no longer important; in some senses it becomes even more so, for all of its scarcity.) In the context of cities, the devices that give particularity, place, and regional character range from the general urban structure, streets, squares, and building types, with the particular dimensions, scale, and grain of the parcels and block sizes (200′ × 200′ in Portland, Oregon, to the 300′ × 600′ east–west oriented blocks of midtown Manhattan), to the habits of public infrastructure, street furnishings, selection of building materials, and architectural styles that predominated when particular districts and significant public institutions were built. These many separate and interrelated variables combine to form urban ensembles that are unique and memorable. One has only to think of the French Quarter in New Orleans, or midtown Manhattan, the nineteenth-century expansion district in Barcelona, the West End and Mayfair in London, or Haussmann's Paris to realize how clear and distinct these collective works can be. Steen Eiler Rasmussen's study *London: The Unique City,* Donald Olsen's recent book *The City as a Work of Art,* and Carl Schorske's study of Vienna all elaborate this theme.[12]

In our practice, therefore, we have consciously pursued what we perceived to be the "genius of the place" in urban works, employing several of the strategies listed earlier. For projects in New York, London, and Los Angeles, we have consciously perused the ordinary properties of streets, buildings, and open spaces and proposed either extending or creating new districts in the spirit of the patterns we observed. In no case, however, were these direct copies or literal extensions, but rather exercises done in the manner of what we perceived. None of the blocks in Manhattan's Battery Park City are really the same or typical of each other or the adjacent city, although they are perceived as such. The principal square at Canary Wharf in London, although surrounded by enormous buildings that are quite different from those around the well-known squares of Westminster, is bathed in light due to the proportions and strategies used in cornice heights, arcades, and materials. The fabric of Playa Vista, although it includes no single-family detached houses, will join other districts of the city as a familiar and attractive set of streets and buildings with a decided ambience of Los Angeles not seen elsewhere. Urban structure, the proportion and length of streets and blocks and the very pattern of the city, not just the detail, is one of the key elements in the creation of urban regionalism. The ignorance and open disregard for such knowledge and values lie at the heart of the suburban sprawl so ubiquitous today, with the result being the placelessness and regional devastation so often commented upon, but so rarely confronted or countered with the alternative just discussed.[13] (There are rural equivalents popularized by Tony Hiss in his book *The Experience of Place,* which is one of the most accessible examples.) The short-term financial gains and greed that are often cited as the root cause are only possible once one dispenses with a sense of value in the existing structure, landscape, and ecology, which often can be demonstrated to generate more and longer-term profits for developers—that is, ignorance of net long-term value drives these short-term goals.

At the other extreme, street furnishings are among the most common, often banal, and yet conclusive indicators of place. One has only to consider the elements of a street in Paris or London to see how they reveal the results of evolution of particular elements through industry, governance, use, and an aesthetic (that can be every bit as idiosyncratic as it may also represent any gestalt). The result of such processes can be a highly particular set of ordinary details that are an eloquent expression of "place." At Battery Park City, therefore, we chose to forgo the pleasures of invention and instead dipped into the array of furnishings developed for public spaces in New York City, selecting and modifying several that we felt had become part of the anonymous background to life in the city. It was our belief that these furnishings would give familiarity and continuity to this enormous project that was to be created almost overnight and would help to weave it into the existing fabric of the city, adding—as it were—a new link to the chain of parks and open spaces begun in the nineteenth century by Olmsted and expanded so dramatically by Robert Moses, New York City park commissioner for three decades ending in the 1960s. We have been publicly attacked by our peers and elders for doing this. Paul Friedberg at a Harvard symposium and Richard Haag in comments made while on an American Society of Landscape Architects design award jury have seen our decision not to make these elements new and personal as a failure of artistic vision.

Our counter view is that this is precisely the best use of modern machine tool production, and that like automobiles, light bulbs, and ready-to-wear clothing, there are valid and important uses for off-the-shelf manufactured goods in the creation of places. The point of the public spaces at Battery Park City was to open the city out to the river and to provide places to walk, sit, and stand—to partake of the broader context and social intercourse. It was our intent to produce an environment that would not call attention to itself, but rather one that would direct one's consideration elsewhere. We hoped to produce an environment so quintessentially "New York" that it would unconsciously become part of peoples' lives as well as an armature for works of art and future developments by others. All of which have happened. In an interesting reversal, the hexagonal asphalt paving, B-pole lamp from Central Park, Belgian blocks, standard New York Parks railings, and ready-made benches are now as much identified in the public's mind with Battery Park City as they are with our sources of inspiration.

Playa Vista · 4 November 1989 ·   Bay Street · Looking South ·

Boulevard sketch, Playa Vista, 1989

A different approach to such key details is to make, of the most humble elements, something radically new, self-conscious, and imbued with meaning. In two projects, the Sixteenth Street Transitway Mall in Denver and Westlake Park, Seattle, we chose to reexamine paving, the most common element in terms of its geographic area, extent, and normal expectations regarding its material properties, and used it as the principal design intervention. In both cases, we transformed the ground surface, ordinarily made of moderately durable, albeit cheap and not particularly attractive materials such as concrete or asphalt, into extensive polychrome stone carpets. Although there were numerous reasons for doing so, especially to achieve our particular social or artistic goals (maximize the apparent size and extent of the spaces, unify disparate, episodic, or far-flung spatial portions, create a statement of social importance and an assertion of civic worth and pride, create a unique sense of location and place within the labyrinth of the city, etc.), from the perspective of this discussion it should be noted which patterns we chose to use and their effect on the appearance, success, and potential meaning of each project.

During the design stages of both the Denver and Seattle projects, numerous options for pattern, color, and material were considered. In Denver, because the public space under design was eighty feet wide and twelve blocks long, analogies to a carpet runner came to mind almost immediately. At one point I discovered that both Henry Cobb, the partner of I. M. Pei who was leading the project, and I were studying nineteenth-century Navajo blankets. The pattern finally developed with a progression from large, separate, geometric figures in the center to continuously linked ones in the bus lanes to a diffusion at the edges, each responding to a particular zone of movement, refuge, or commercial activity. The pattern is strongest under the trees, less dense in the busway, and of less force and insistence as one moves toward the shop windows, where the eye should be redirected from this public show of generosity and spirit to that of the private entrepreneur. I will also confess to thinking of the pattern of rattle-snake skins, which were being sold as belts and souvenirs at a shop at one end of the street on my initial site visit. Whether the citizens of Denver and tourists to the mall realize these sources of form or not, I do not know. I only know we would not, and could not, have come up with such a pattern somewhere else. To me it is deeply regional and particular to its place and condition.

At Westlake Park in Seattle, after a series of pattern studies, my partner, Robert Hanna, and I determined that we could not utilize a bounded figure with variable density and directionality as at Denver, but needed instead an allover field of uniform density. What pattern to use? Again, after considerable study and trial and error, Bob began experimenting with a particular pattern of an obscure Salish basket that we found in a book I had bought on the subject of Northwest Indian basketry. This particular geometric structure, although containing elements common to Athabascan design from the desert southwest to Alaska, turned out to work remarkably well with the proportions and shape of the triangular piece of land designated for the park. In our final design this pattern has been greatly enlarged. The change of scale has freed the pattern from its original material—grass, bark, and roots—and allowed each twist of fiber to be transformed into a large paving block. No longer evocative of these soft baskets, despite some recall of weaving and blankets, the patterned stone surface becomes a remarkable "ground" for both public events and ordinary business and respite. It at once declares a unique condition in the city. The main ornament of the space is the very surface of the space itself. Its pattern comes from the oldest known people of the region. It has not been applied or added to a structure, but rather is the structure and base for everything that can take place there, providing a ground for trees, pavilions, sculpture, and people. Although there are other elements, such as a fountain made of large sheets of water, a speaker's platform and arch, benches, and trees, it is this lithic surface that dominates. There are embellishments that in their literal representation comment on and enhance this surface. These consist of planting pots and carved capitals employing references to the Art Deco buildings that surround the square, whose ornament itself refers to the vegetation and marine life of the region.

Even in projects of ours that have been labeled avant-garde, deconstructionist, and postmodern, we have pursued both local and regional properties, seeking to imbue our work with a considered and deep sense of place. Over the last ten years, we have collaborated on nine projects with Peter Eisenman, a well-known and controversial architectural theorist. To date, Peter and I have only managed to get one of our collaborations built, the Wexner Center for the Visual Arts at Ohio State University in Columbus. We have produced a work that could be in no other place. It is a highly personal work on the part of both of us. It is also rooted in place through an open appeal to memory, specifically the demolition of the old Armory building that once stood on the site and is evoked in our scheme by fragments of architecture and several landscape features; that is, a small garden contained within a partial re-creation of fragments of its structure, and the outline of the former building traced in the ground. Regional issues are raised in the overall site strategy and by the landscape structure, fabric, detail, and metaphor. Again, without presenting the whole project, the logic of its artistic gestures in relation to the campus context, town and gown, the dilemmas of an architectural stance of uncertainty versus that of classical revival, modern attitudes toward spatial organization, and tendencies toward hierarchy and centrality in western architectural tradition that this project deliberately questions and confronts, let me present two aspects that relate to the topic of regionalism. If anything, the other issues raised by this project only reinforce my earlier assertion that regionalist concerns are strategies employed in confronting broad international or universalist design practices and theories.

In 1967, I executed a number of illustrations for Sibyl Moholy-Nagy's book *Matrix of Man,* an extended discussion of environmental design. One depicted the Jeffersonian survey grid as applied to the eastern portion of the state of Ohio in the first decades of the nineteenth century. When Peter and I decided to extend the Wexner's building program throughout the entire site offered by the university and to intertwine the building and landscape so as to make each become portions of the other, it was this Cartesian, abstract, and placeless grid—which oddly enough has come to characterize the settlement pattern, agriculture, and towns, the very look and feel of the Midwest and Great Plains— that became our first organizing device. At the same time, I became obsessed with the notion of growing prairie grasses and flowers over, across, and through this grid and buildings. Despite long opposition from the university, which wanted instead the conventional ground covers and shrubs found in commercial nurseries (another industry partially responsible for the loss of place and the homogenization of America's regions and cities), I persevered and finally persuaded a new generation of physical plant administrators to let me use a selection of ornamental grasses and flowers. The effect is very much a suggestion and abstraction of prairie fragments without replicating or pretending to be one. The restlessness of the tilted and heaved planes of earth and grass is in stark and seemingly violent contrast to the marked flatness of the site and entire surrounding region. One result is that everyone becomes acutely aware of the surface of the earth, its color, texture, and seasonal change. As in Seattle, it looks like nothing else around, could not be called contextual, does not come from some immediate or even distant design tradition (except perhaps the Ohio River mound builders of pre-Columbian times), yet like the KiMo Theatre, it is in my view deeply regional in its purpose and essence. Like Westlake Park in Seattle, it appears to have developed a strong popular appeal to those who experience it and seems to be well on the way to being taken up as a local landmark of meaning and significance.

Failure and Success in Courting the Regional

Working with I. M. Pei & Partners on a project for a particularly dramatic hilltop in Westchester County, north of New York City, I became particularly interested in producing a landscape that would provide a regional setting for a series of quintessentially modern buildings. The buildings were to be a series of highly abstract white prisms, loosely grouped about on the mountaintop, connected by tenuous covered walks and surrounded by large areas of parking. My attempts to get Pei's office to group the buildings more closely together, similar to a village or college, were rebuffed. No buildings could be less regional, except from the point of view that they were very much in an American 1980s high-tech corporate office style, with metal panels, continuous ribbon windows, and pyramidal atriums with angled shapes jutting out toward various points of the compass. As one moves about the country and sees the dissemination of these forms, materials, and building topology, one can only speculate that a new industrial vernacular has emerged, on the one hand placeless and mechanical, on the other deeply American and of the moment.

I decided that I would attempt to create a quintessential Upstate New York landscape to bind these buildings to the site and yoke them together into a more cohesive and tempered whole. To do so I proposed filling the entire set of open spaces between the buildings with apple orchards. Then I planned to reach out to the north and south with two large meadows, similar to the old fields one sees in farms throughout the region, fragments of which existed on the site before we began. Along the sides of these meadows, I proposed planting alleys of deciduous trees similar to old farm lanes. Finally I began layering each parking lot with brushy hedgerows of native species, through which the employees would have to pass on arriving and leaving each day. The allées of trees were to serve as lanes for employees to walk or jog on their breaks, at lunch, or after work, as well as to aid the many deer on the site to move up to the orchards to feed and return to the woods without having to move across clearings. Detention basins needed to control stormwater runoff and for firefighting were to be made of puddled clay similar to farm ponds. The decision on my part to focus on and create this evocative and fulsome middle-ground landscape was partly informed by the surrounding forests, mountains, farms, and villages that formed a background and by the client's expressed intent to eschew the foreground. For reasons of economy, project politics, and aesthetic consistency, there were to be virtually no fine details or site furnishings around or near the buildings. They were in the country, not the suburbs, and the imagery was rural, not suburban. The inspiration and subject matter of the landscape design was that of the declining agricultural landscape of the Hudson River Valley. I was as aware of nineteenth-century American landscape painting as I was of the current state of affairs, having an affection for both and finding strong cultural support for my intent in both.

In my opinion, this approach was never fully appreciated by the architects or the owner and client and was badly mangled in the construction process. Simple and clear as the concept appeared at the time, it now seems to me that it was too pure and remote from the expectations and techniques of the owner, contractors, and architects.[14] It is my greatest and saddest defeat in professional practice to date, for it seemed to be among the most spiritual and fundamental of all our projects in terms of a landscape concept that was as timeless as it was regional and particular, as ecological as it was cultural, as economical in means as it was generous in spirit.

Are such attempts to reach directly into the structure of a region and to use primary elements to give character and order to modern endeavors inevitably doomed? I do not think so, but I do think that the methods to achieve such goals cannot be those of modern fast-track, large-scale construction but rather must proceed at slower pace and with more care. On the other hand, it does not require preindustrial handcraft methods either, merely people who have a sympathy and understanding for this sort of construction, something we have recently found on a project in central Ohio.

Wexner Estate, New Albany, Ohio

Again working in a lovely agricultural region, this time the Midwest, I turned once more to agricultural traditions for clues and materials with which to fashion several private estates. This time sympathetic owners and superb contractors have understood the spirit of our proposals. Although it is still under construction, the orchards, meadows, hedgerows, ponds, canals, lakes, roads, hills, gardens, and architectural elements are deeply American. It remains to be seen whether it will also end up truly regional as discussed above.

If asked why, despite some of its quite derivative European-inspired elements, I think this project is American in feeling, not English or French, I would start out by saying "because it was built here, and we cannot help thinking and building in an American way." From the brick architecture—a reverie on tidewater Georgian, that particular moment of American palladianism that has left a deep imprint on our nation's public and private institutions and country retreats—to the white wooden fences, whether horse fences or those of the dependencies and gardens, the flood of memories that they evoke of bluegrass pastures, New England villages, Tom Sawyer, and every midwestern town is so strong as to clearly position this work in the American heartland. Interestingly enough, the particular combination of elements employed also rules out New England and the South, either of which might possess some, but not all, of these elements, commonly found together between the Appalachians and the Mississippi. There is a subtlety in the use and inflection of these materials akin to local accents in language that probably only an American would perceive or care about.

As in many of the works of Lancelot Brown in England, the entire ensemble can be taken as an emblematic construction, not as one of

Stream and habitat design sketch, Playa Vista, 1989

symbolism or prone to iconography. It is what it purports to be: a country estate that demonstrates its owner's and designers' awareness of the tradition of country estates at home and abroad. The Wexner estate, now known locally as Abigail House, exhibits a series of architectural and landscape elements that possess a rambling order and loosely formal set of relationships to each other, to the site and surrounding landscape. Each part—roads, gatehouse, drive, barn, main house and dependencies, tennis and pool pavilions, paddocks, pastures, lakes, canals, basins, stable, riding ring, guest pavilion (a rotunda with gardens), the rides and allées, meadows, orchards, kennels, gardens, and woods—demonstrates that the designers and client are historically informed and working within a tradition. Despite a modicum of atavism in both buildings and landscape, the ensemble also seems to succeed in reaching a degree of regionalism not found today in the bulk of the design work executed by major commercial landscape architecture design firms, or the estate work done by prominent society garden designers.

CONCLUSION

Several issues have been raised by the foregoing that should be considered directly:

> Given the roles of the owner, builder, and designer and the nature of practice and the landscape industry today, what effect do these have upon regionalism, if any?

> Having worked in urban, suburban, and rural situations, can one draw any conclusions from this? Are there differences that result from the nature of place, clients, or projects? Do any lend themselves to considerations of regionalism more or less, etc.?

> What is the degree of influence exerted by earlier designers and their work? Does it help or hinder?

> Despite a generally accepted belief that there are several different and distinct regions in the United States, could one see the

whole of America as a region in much the same way that France and England have come to be? What is the relationship between regionalism and nationalism?

Despite my attempt to discuss our work in terms of the theme of regionalism, are not many of the things that have been presented more properly local and place-specific as much or more so than they are truly regional?

Finally, one should consider Henry James's three questions: What was the author trying to do? How well did he succeed? Was it worth it?

To start with the first issue, what are the effects on regional expression of the changing nature of practice and clients? As the Westchester corporate example suggests, many modern clients are international in nature and go to great lengths to create a recognizable image for their facilities that is openly opposed to regionally responsive design solutions. Fast-food franchises and corporations are not alone in behaving this way. Government agencies, sophisticated developers, private individuals, and all kinds of people and institutions are "worldly" and chary of what they consider "provincial." Contractors and builders, whom one would expect to be locally or regionally based, frequently are when small- or medium-scale in their operations. However, many of the construction management firms that we work with in Los Angeles we also work with in New York and Philadelphia. The firm that built the Codex Corporation headquarters in the Boston area is also working on two of our Los Angeles projects in addition to having produced two of our works in Philadelphia earlier. A construction firm that we are now working with in Barcelona and London also executed work for us in New York. Small subcontractors may still be local, but stone that is quarried in Africa, Spain, or India is shipped to Italy for cutting before being sent to Ohio, London, or New York for our projects. The trees we are planting at Canary Wharf in London are coming from a nursery in Hamburg, Germany, which grew them up from lining-out stock supplied from Oregon.

At a certain scale of operation, the construction industry today is one of the most international of all our businesses. Methods are becoming so standardized and schedules so compressed that designers concerned with craft are tearing out their hair. The small, private garden is, of course, a haven from this, which partly accounts for its current appeal to designers of all sorts. Firms like ours that attempt to use native plants, concern themselves with ecology, and look for local materials and methods are swimming upstream. At Ohio State University, when I decided to use native red sandstone for the walls of the sliced planes of the grass terraces, I discovered that all of the local quarries in Indiana and Ohio were played out. Only rubble was available. Recent restorations of nineteenth-century American red sandstone buildings had to import it from England, Germany, or India. Thus we used German sandstone in Columbus to achieve the "sense" of a native stone. This does not bother me, since artifice lies at the heart of all design. The pressure to conform and make everything the same does, however, bother me.

Are rural settings more resistant to this deadening homogeneity and sameness of expression than urban ones? I do not think so. The pressures on modern farming to become one vast business network with a reduced number of common products, the continuing adoption of horrendous and deadening highway standards throughout the country, the ubiquitous foundation planting, lawns, and limited palette of commercially produced trees have rendered our rural countryside and highway corridors remarkably similar and placeless. The urban scene is equally banal in large part. Nonetheless, most cities still have a flavor that is unique. So do most truly rural areas. The suburban areas in between are the most intractable. Certainly the work we have done in the suburbs—because it has been primarily corporate (Johnson & Johnson, IBM, Pitney Bowes, Nestlé, AT&T, etc.)—has been most commonly in what could be called American Pastoralism and is regional to the degree that America may be considered a region (as opposed to Europe). Despite our attempts to "ground" them, locally they are, in general, fairly consistent and uniform in both their ideas and handling.

In my memory, I cannot remember any client or owner ever saying to us that they were interested in regional expression. Local character or "appropriateness" are ideas they have mentioned. Leslie Wexner and Jack Kessler in Columbus have talked to us and to their builders and contractors at considerable length about their desire to "build a house in the country" and that the estates and other structures we are creating for them should be "country," not suburban. The form such instincts take is usually to question our ability to know local flora, for most people still think that landscape architects merely plant things. Horticulturalists, on the other hand, think that as a group we are fairly ignorant about plants. One client after another has wondered why or how a landscape architect from another region can solve their problems and has challenged us on the subject. Sometimes we satisfy their insecurity by associating with a local landscape architect who purportedly will know more about the local soils, climate, plants, and the nursery business, which in fact they often do. In the process, we have made many close friendships and learned a lot from these other professionals. At times, clients have worried that we would bring inappropriate cultural (and thereby inappropriate formal) attitudes to their situation. The most skeptical critics of our working in other regions have been European civil servants and journalists; both groups are extremely chauvinistic and resentful of what they perceive to be American imperialism. Since I have not presented our European work to any extent, I will not dwell on the point. They, too, remain skeptical of our understanding their particular ecological conditions. My only comment here would be that as outsiders we have probably been far more sensitive to the cultural traditions and ecology than most of the professionals we have met who are practicing there.

As we have seen in the case of H. W. S. Cleveland and Olmsted, the cultural agenda of a designer can be one of the strongest influences on his form and material expression. The committee that awarded us the commission for Westlake Park in Seattle expressed concern that we might be too formal and stiff in our response to their needs and character. In the repartee of the interview, it became clear to us that they had visions of themselves as relaxed, fun-loving folks and considered us a bit too serious. They also expressed a desire for quintessentially suburban elements—lawns, flowers, and "informal" spaces—for example, biomorphic, curving, or asymmetrical forms. In many other commissions we have found clients who have believed and hoped that the "landscape," which to them is trees and bushes, would be used to "soften" or "humanize" the urban quality of some project. They intended our work to counteract some basically unwelcome characteristics of the architecture that they were commissioning.

The continuing American anti-urban bias that began as an agrarian, political, and economic stance has been transformed into a suburban, consumer stance. Americans did not like and trust cities when most people did not live in them, and now that most people do, they still do not like them. This may have a lot to do with the absence of "sense of place" in our urban scene, but should not necessarily be so. In fact, it could as easily lead to highly or pseudo-rustic expressions. Instead, however, a dreadful suburban homogenization has spread in both directions to country and city. This in fact is what much of the regional and situational strategies that have been employed by us and others have been intended to counteract.

The question of whether regional cultural differences can survive current universalizing forces is a question with no clear answer. Biophysical differences will certainly persist. To the degree that society ignores them, there will be problems, at times of great consequence, such as those of water shortage, pollution, and famine. In many cases, however, such problems will not occur or be so severe. What, therefore, is the motive to seek and produce a regional character in a work of landscape architecture, especially at a moment when travel, contact, dialogue, and interchange—commercial, social, intellectual, scientific, artistic—are taking place throughout the world? The answer must be that this movement of goods, ideas, and images that began as an outgrowth of the centuries-old quest for more personal freedom and self-realization—a struggle for economic and religious opportunity as well—has not been seen as necessarily leading to better societies. The same forces that are so beguiling to Third World countries urgently seeking to improve their quality of life and to join the prosperous nations of the world are also the same that are leading to a pronounced loss of self and place there and in the most industrialized regions. The ubiquitous homogenization of culture and environment, the rapacious consumption of the products of art and heritage, the proliferation and rapid debasing of the accumulation of works of architecture and art through mass industry, marketing, and consumption, and the substitution of images and simulacra for real objects or places of historic achievement that are ideologically or aesthetically laden with meaning for particular societies have led to a revulsion for such facile and exploitive devices on the part of many practitioners and academics in design. As a counter strategy to mainstream, postmodern architectural design, which has largely been coopted by the most banal and rapacious aspects of international commerce and development, at least three different strategies have emerged.

One, following architects of the early decades of this century, such as the Vesnin brothers and El Lissitzky, proposes a radical agenda that asks architecture to refer only to itself, to transcend or eschew function, even construction (building), and to propose designs that critique the institutions that call them into being.[15] This approach asks for architecture that resists any attempt to pin it down, except as being architecture. It dreams of permanent and continual revolution in its break with the past and tradition. Needless to say, this strategy to resist mainstream materialism and conformity is incompatible with the procedures of regionalism outlined above.

A second, related strategy also attempts to return to portions of early modernism, picking up certain dropped threads but not others. This approach pursues its resistance and meaning through techniques borrowed from twentieth-century art, literature, criticism, and scientific theory. Equally distrustful of the mechanisms of the marketplace and programmatic determinism, it rejects Hegelian and Kantian progressive theories and notions of historic continuity and formal evolution.[16] Using devices of fragmentation, dislocation, and collage, and borrowing metaphors and theory from structuralism and surrealism, this work is dependent on the conventional and historic world of signs and images for the raw material of its productions. This strategy can and has produced significant designs and built works that have had a marked effect on mainstream practice, but have also, at the same time, largely succeeded in their resistance to cooption, retaining much of their potency. It is not a strategy generally thought of as conducive to regionalist concerns (think of George Hargreaves's Harlequin Plaza in Denver, for example), although I would assert that Peter Eisenman and I have in fact shown that the two are not necessarily exclusive in the Ohio State University Wexner Center project.

The third strategy, which has come to be called "critical regionalism" by Kenneth Frampton and Jürgen Habermas, has also been around since the turn of the century and has been used by several designers responsible for works considered to be masterpieces of the modern movement, as well as by others who, until recently, have been ignored by history and criticism. Examples include work by Frank Lloyd Wright, Greene & Greene, Dimitris Pikionis, Sigurd Lewerentz, Jože Plečnik, Alvar Aalto, Ralph Cornell, Thomas Church, A. E. Bye, and Richard Haag.[17] This strategy opposes cooption by a rapacious, image-hungry market through the production of works that are so grounded in a particular time and place that neither their image nor their particular formal organization can be copied or repeated elsewhere with success. Although this is also a goal of the two previous strategies, their methods are intended to be used wherever one finds oneself; that is, the strategies are conceived as somewhat universalist, while the product is intended to be unique. In the so-called critical-regionalist strategy, it is possible to vary the technique from place to place while striving for results that are more familiar and tied to tradition.

Our practice, Hanna/Olin, Ltd., has never been interested in the first of these strategies: that of endless revolution, the rejection of history, and a hermetic discourse of architectural theory sans object. We have a strong urge to build and would rather make mistakes and produce flawed experiments than merely talk about things. Thus we have on several occasions participated in schemes of the second sort, but we have succeeded in getting very few built because of client or public resistance to their unorthodox appearance and organization. To date I have collaborated on nine projects with Peter Eisenman, every one of which has had elements as particular to their geographic location as the Wexner Center at Ohio State, but have succeeded in getting only one built. Other such projects done on our own or with others in London, Florida, and California have also foundered and remain unbuilt. Apparently, therefore, there is a strong normative ethos expected by the viewer (owner, client) in works that contain regional devices. For this reason most of the work we have executed that could be termed regional or regionalist has been highly conventional or "ordinary" in many or most of its properties.

Our motive to create these works stems from the fact that we are deeply troubled by the loss of identity, the despoliation of land and cities by late twentieth-century commerce, and the exploitive use of imagery and heritage by widely divergent sectors of our economy ranging from perfume and clothing manufacturers to real estate and entertainment organizations—all of which blend together in our urban centers and our daily lives. Many of our clients have been part of this spectrum of modern commerce and institutions. They have sought us out (not the other way around), presumably for our skills in fulfilling programmatic needs while bringing other contributions to the situation. What these seem to be are both an ability to understand this Orwellian pressure to wield imagery laden with secondary, desirable meanings to their advantage (i.e., to lend them legitimacy, pedigree, quality, and concern for traditional social and landscape values) and an intuition that we will in some way resist this, producing something of worth on its own terms that remains aloof from their goals and manipulations, that speaks directly to the region and setting that surrounds them spatially, that precedes and succeeds them in time.

Although we have been attacked from the left and accused of manipulating and exploiting images of traditional landscapes for the benefit of a capitalist consumer apparatus that parasitically feeds on the people, places, and history it coopts and destroys, it is my view that the devices, concerns, and strategies I have presented above are part of a conscious effort on our part, while working within the mainstream of modern (contemporary) practice, frequently for large and powerful developers, corporations, and institutions, to resist their unconscious (and conscious) desires to coopt, dominate, and destroy the various local and regional societies and landscape they engage. I often feel that the people who hire us silently count on our knowledge and sensibility to do this for them. Our quiet lobbying and scheming to accommodate and contribute to the experience and life of the common man, their employees, passersby, as well as to the board and executives who pay our bills, is something that they more than tolerate, but hope for and count on. Concerning issues of regionalism, here too our clients expect their designers to solve them, to know what is appropriate and what will work, and to contribute positively to their property and society. How we choose to work it out really is our problem, no one else's, and there is no clear path to follow. In fact, outside of particular courses in a small handful of universities such issues are rarely discussed. It is with great pleasure and curiosity, therefore, that I share these thoughts on a subject that has played such a central role in our work.

WILLIAM KENT, THE VIGNA MADAMA, AND LANDSCAPE PARKS

(1997)

It is a commonly held belief among laymen, scholars, and design practitioners that the landscape park with its trees, grass, undulating landforms, and bodies of water originated in England in the eighteenth
century. Although Lancelot "Capability" Brown may be the best known
designer of the landscape park, William Kent is generally credited with
having invented it. Kent's imaginative innovations in garden and landscape design are rightfully considered revolutionary; his work at Carlton House, Chiswick, Stowe, Rousham, Esher, Claremont, Holkham,
and Euston greatly influenced the changes in form and taste that
occurred in England between 1725 and 1745.

Over the course of the past fifty years, there has been considerable discussion regarding the sources of the architectural and sculptural elements found in eighteenth-century English landscape parks.
Although Kent's influential role in introducing most of the elements and
imagery of the landscape park to England and northern Europe is not
in question, in fact he did not invent them. One can find the sources
of the architecture, sculpture, and ornament used in his gardens, as
well as the progenitors of his landforms and planting, in sixteenth- and
seventeenth-century Italy.

In Italy most of the landscape constructions and parklike places that

From *Form, Modernism, and History*, ed. Alexander von Hoffman (Cambridge, MA: Graduate School of Design, Harvard University, 1997), 125–50.

served as models for English parks were located on private estates, commonly referred to as *vigne*.[1] One of the most influential of these was the Vigna Madama outside Rome. This particular "park" was well known; it was visited by many tourists and depicted in drawings and paintings in the sixteenth, seventeenth, and eighteenth centuries. The most important record of the principal landscape elements of the Vigna Madama are those made in the 1630s and 1640s by the French expatriate painter Claude Lorrain. In a series of extraordinary sketches made within this "park," Claude reproduced the essential elements of Kent's landscape repertoire.

How these particular Roman landscape features were used to create what has come to be seen as a uniquely English contribution to cultural history, and how little is known about the landscape settings of late Renaissance villas, is now clear. The thicket of misinformation to be cleared away is substantial, however.

From the time of Joseph Addison, Horace Walpole, and Alexander Pope onward, there has been a long list of writers who have argued that such parks are an English invention, repeating like parrots that it all began with William Kent who "leapt the garden wall." No less an authority than Nikolaus Pevsner asserted in a sweeping statement that remains largely uncorrected:

> The landscape garden is the most influential of all English innovations in art. Its effects can be studied all over the Continent and from the United States to Russia. . . . Any account of landscape gardening must start from the English climate. . . . The English Garden, the *Jardin Anglais,* the *Englischer Garten,* is asymmetrical, informal, varied and made of such parts as the serpentine lake, the winding drive and winding path, the trees grouped in clumps, and smooth lawn (mown or cropped by sheep). . . . The English Garden is English in a number of profoundly significant ways. . . . First the simplest way: formally the winding path and the serpentine lake are the equivalent of Hogarth's Line of Beauty, that long, gentle, double curve which dominates one kind of English art from the Decorated style in architecture to William Blake and beyond.[2]

Furthermore, many have argued that Kent and his successors based their work on the *paintings* of Claude and Poussin.[3] H. F. Clark, who along with Christopher Hussey could be considered one of the fathers of modern scholarship on the English landscape and garden, wrote in 1948:

> From Claude English gardeners inherited the quest of an ideal, as well as the associations which were so important for their appreciation. Claude was a product of the Italian Renaissance and the Italians were the first among modern peoples to feel, and to transcribe into an art form, their love of nature. . . . From this appreciation of the beauty of nature came the desire to copy these subtle effects in gardens. . . . Nature herself had less obvious charms to display to those with an eye trained to see them, trained by the study of pictures, and with a memory of the gardens seen on the Grand Tour in Italy and France.[4] . . . Henceforward gardens were to be judged as worthy of the connoisseur's attention if the prospects were pleasing, and if it happened to be "an Albano landskip," a reflection of that vision of nature seen by Claude among the Alban hills a century before.[5] . . . The English had invented a new environment.[6]

Distinguished scholars such as Kenneth Woodbridge and Christopher Hussey pass along this Anglo-chauvinism.[7]

The truth as usual is a bit more messy and interesting. In her essay "The Genesis of the English Landscape Garden," Susan Lang revises the standard view espoused by Hussey, Clark, Pevsner, and Miles Hadfield.[8] She asserts that "the theory most prevalent, that the English landscape garden was modeled on paintings by Claude or Gaspard or Salvator Rosa, cannot be reconciled with an assumption of a slow development towards the fully fledged landscape garden."[9] Nobody before Walpole, it appears, even mentions Claude in connection with gardening. It is true that later in the eighteenth century, after Kent's death, one can find visual quotations from Claude's paintings in actual gardens. The most famous of these can be seen at Stourhead and was executed after 1754.[10] Lang surveys developments in both gardening and theory regarding art, gardens, and politics from the seventeenth century on, discussing Addison, Pope, Walpole and the derivation of their ideas from classical, Renaissance, and earlier English thinkers. Disputing the view that the English landscape garden was adapted somehow from the rural scenery of England, she remarks, "Nor can one truthfully say that the landscape garden, looks like the English landscape. To the beholder of the English countryside any present or former landscape garden stands out quite clearly. The types of trees, their arrangement and the general planting within the garden are strikingly different from the countryside without."[11]

Lang and others have recognized that several instances of features and settings in gardens by William Kent appear to derive from specific precedents in Italian villa gardens, namely a pavilion and set of radiating walks at Chiswick, the cascade at Rousham, and the Temple of British Worthies at Stowe. (She suggests the Teatro Olimpico in Vicenza, the Villa Barbarigo at Valsanzibio, and the Villa Mattei in Rome, all of which we know Kent visited.) "Generally speaking, Italian gardens of the seventeenth century were more leafy than the contemporary English gardens, the trees feathery and parts of the gardens were always 'irregular,' 'wild' and 'natural.' England had borrowed so much from Italy, why not their gardens?"[12]

Nevertheless, Lang concludes that it was the theater which was the most influential force on the development of William Kent's ideas and methods, suggesting links to theater sets and designs of Inigo Jones and Filippo Juvarra. Today there is no question that Kent was influenced by the theater, and that he was one of the last masque designers of sorts.[13] However, it is incumbent on us to understand his considerable knowledge of Italian landscapes and gardens themselves, for they were the most basic source for his subsequent work.

Both John Dixon Hunt and Sir Roy Strong in recent books have presented in great depth the richness of seventeenth-century garden activity and thought in England, establishing beyond doubt the many precursors and forerunners to the landscape gardens of the eighteenth century.[14] One can now add the missing transition a few years later in the career of Kent, his experience and borrowings, as well as knowledge of his sources—parks and landscapes around Rome— and their conditions in the years between 1630 and 1720, particularly as depicted in many drawings and paintings of Claude, Poussin, and others.

Kent's varied experiences make him a fascinating figure. Sent to Rome to study the art and craft of painting in order to learn how to decorate English country houses, he stayed there for ten years, from 1709 to 1719. In that time Kent did indeed become a painter of some accomplishment, but he also studied and traveled with numerous architects and tourists who were seeking antiquities, art, and general cultural enrichment. He became a purchasing agent for several individuals, a cicerone for English lords, and a companion to many artists and designers of various nationalities while in Italy.

With the exception of a journal kept on portions of his travels and occasional letters, very little is known about Kent's movements and life in Rome. Upon his return to England, Kent became a favorite of Lord Burlington and successfully executed numerous interior designs, frescoes, and wall paintings. Due to the interest of his friends and patrons, Kent gradually became more involved with architecture and the design of gardens. While associated with the Palladian movement in architecture, his furniture and interior designs were highly original and astonishingly varied in their composition, ranging from Rococo and Baroque to Gothic Revival.

Kent himself left no measured drawings or plans for garden designs. Instead, he made sketches of the elements and effects that he imagined would create a certain view or scene. In almost all his projects, Kent worked with other people who were trained as draftsmen, engineers, or horticulturists. Sometimes others were already on the scene directing the sitework and planting, such as at Rousham, where Kent collaborated with William White, the clerk of the works. Since Kent took up garden design almost by accident, there is no early record of his preparation for his landscape undertakings. Except for the few villas and gardens that he mentions he visited with Lords Coke and Burlington, we have no records about where Kent went and what he saw while in Italy or Rome.

On the other hand, we can infer a great deal about his exposure to landscape imagery in Italy. There is a well-known series of buildings and gardens in and around Rome that tourists have visited consistently from the seventeenth century to the present day. As the lifelong companion and collaborator of Burlington, Kent would have been familiar with books and drawings of Claude Lorrain and Giovanni Battista Falda, whose images he occasionally reproduced in his landscape designs.

Except for specific architectural inspirations and quotes—the most obvious and frequently discussed being the circus, obelisk, hemicycle, and pyramid from the Villa Mattei and the rusticated cascades of the Villa Aldobrandini—it is likely that after ten years in residence Kent was so well imbued with Roman gardens and the landscape of the Campagna that he could conjure up whole passages of them from memory. What is also not well understood by recent scholars is that many of the landscape drawings and paintings emanating from Rome in the seventeenth century that were so avidly collected by foreigners (and the English *milordi* in particular), while somewhat idealized, were largely based on real landscapes and scenery that they had visited.

In an age before photography and postcards, prints and paintings served as mementos of places visited and memorialized the ruins and artistic achievements of classical antiquity as well as the recent art and architecture of the Renaissance. In the case of Kent, there is every reason to believe that he would have been familiar with virtually every scene that Claude drew and painted, sites so commonplace that there was no reason to record his visits to them.

One important such site—immediately accessible and unquestionably known to him—was that of the Vigna Madama. This suburban estate was the location of the Villa Madama, which contained a spectacular loggia executed by Raphael, Giulio Romano, and Giovanni da Udine. While many people have commented on the fact that Kent was sent off to become the "second Raphael" and the subsequent disappointment when he failed to paint portraits or scenes with anything like the skill of the original, few have noted how closely he studied and successfully absorbed the decorative work of Raphael and his shop, particularly as executed at the Villa Farnesina, the Vatican, and Villa Madama.[15] That he also absorbed the park and garden settings of this decorative work has been even less noticed.

In their day, and for over two hundred years, both the Villa and Vigna Madama were famous and accessible, frequented by tourists and Romans alike. Sometime after Easter 1581, for example, while in Rome, Michel de Montaigne wrote in his *Travel Journal*:

There is nothing so hostile to my health as boredom and idleness; here I had always some occupation, . . . like visiting the antiquities and the vineyards, which are gardens and pleasure spots of singular beauty, and where I learned how aptly art can make use of a rugged, hilly and uneven spot; for here they derive from them charms that cannot be duplicated in our level places, and very artfully take advantage of this diversity. Among the most beautiful vineyards are those of the cardinals d'Este at Monte Cavallo, Farnese on the Palatine, Orsini, Sforza, Medici; that of Pope Julius, *that of Madama* [the Duchess of Parma, daughter of Charles V]; the gardens of Farnese and of Cardinal Riario at Trastevere, and of Cesio outside the Porta del Popolo. These are beauties open to anyone who wants to enjoy them, and for whatever purpose, even to sleep there, even in company if the masters are not there, and they do not like to go there much.[16]

This is an interesting remark, partly because it points out how much more there was to the landscape of Italian villas than the architectural terraces for which they are best known.[17]

Although the Villa Madama itself was restored in 1928 by Count Dentice di Frasso and has again recently been *in restauro* by the Italian government for several years, hardly anything of the Vigna remains today. In fact, from 1850 and the years thereafter, when we first see it depicted in early photographs, it had been dismembered and turned into an industrial suburb. The pastoral views recorded by Claude and visiting Flemish and English artists between 1630 and 1750 have been totally ruined. Standing on the terrace today, one sees a vast panorama of suburban sprawl accompanied by the snarl of traffic rushing along the highways and bridges below. The foreground immediately beneath the villa is filled with a huge sports complex begun by Mussolini and expanded for the 1960 Olympic games.[18] In the distance one can barely make out the rebuilt fragments of the Ponte Molle dwarfed by the new highway bridge of the Via Flaminia. Monte Soracte, the more distant Sabine hills and Apennine ridges, so familiar from several generations of sketches from this spot, are usually lost in the smog. The partially restored villa building is a mere fragment of its intended structure. Moreover, it has been difficult to visit since it became a government

facility for receptions and dignitaries during the Mussolini era. No wonder the Villa Madama has nearly dropped off the map of landscape
memory and history.

Nevertheless, if one visits the Villa Madama on a clear winter day,
there are still panoramic views of Rome and the Tiber valley. One can
easily see the ancient river crossing of the Via Flaminia. Of the two
means of approach to the villa available in earlier times, today only
the southern one leading to the Viale Angelico in the Prati remains.
A lengthy drive built in the sixteenth century, it connects the villa to
a modern street that follows an ancient route. Leading from the Porta
Angelica of the Vatican fortifications, a country lane, the Via Angelica,
crossed the farm fields of this floodplain known as the Prati in the time
of Cardinal Giulio de' Medici, providing easy access to his villa once he
became pope. The hillside above and along the entry drive supports a
young forest of oaks and pines, largely grown up since World War II. The
terrace immediately adjacent to the loggia, while attractively neglected,
is planted in a pattern similar to that of earlier times. Below and close to
the villa on a rumpled hillside is a collection of trees, largely oaks, pines,
cypresses, and olives, planted singly and in clumps typical of municipal
parks around the world. Farther down and beyond are enormous stadi-
ums, athletic buildings, parking lots, roads, and flood-control barriers
that have engulfed the former estate.

Immediately north of the enclosed villa terrace lies a garden laid out
in this century consisting of a series of allées of cypresses, hedges, and
urns in a hippodrome-shaped plateau. From here one can take a path
that leads around a small shoulder of the hill to the northwest, where
the upper end of a small ravine extends and opens out into a broader
valley, meeting the lower grounds of the river. Within the upper end of
this small ravine is a nymphaeum attributed to either Antonio da Sangallo the Younger or Giovanni da Udine, both of whom worked on other
aspects of the villa. In any case, it has been altered and reconstructed
at least once since. Here at the head of this small valley, even today in
midsummer when the city is swarming with tourists and choked with
smog, one can rest surrounded by trees, bathed in dappled light, and
refreshed by the cool drip of water from a spring. The sprawling twentieth-century city below disappears. The loudest things one hears are a
chorus of birdcalls and wind in the trees. In this refuge, one can begin

Buckland House deer park, Oxfordshire, England, 1970

to understand how this park was for generations a favorite sanctuary for powerful ecclesiastics and poetic painters.

HISTORY OF THE VILLA

The property of the Villa and Vigna Madama occupies land that, until it was built, had remained largely undeveloped since classical times. The high ground, where Giulio de' Medici elected to build, was on a wooded slope of Monte Mario, the Clivus Cinnae of ancient Rome. The floodplain below constituted the northern extent of the Prati Vaticanus. Together they formed a part of a vast imperial park, the Horti Domitiae. Subject to frequent floods, the Prati was scorned by the ancients. The poet Martial compared its wine to vinegar, and Juvenal wrote that it produced bad pottery.[19]

Two roads of some age existed here when the Circus of Gaius and Nero and Hadrian's tomb were erected in the first and second centuries. One, the Via Triumphalis, led north and up around the back or western side of Monte Mario and thence to the Via Cassia. The other, now called the Viale Angelico, running almost due north across the middle of the Prati, was a secondary route to the northern end of the Pons Milvius or Milvian Bridge (the Ponte Molle of postclassical times) and gave access to the Via Flaminia. Both exist today with almost no change in their alignment since the second century.[20]

The Ponte Molle stands one mile north of the Villa Madama and just under two miles from the Porta del Popolo. It was fortified in medieval times, redesigned by the French, blown up by Garibaldi, and rebuilt again in the nineteenth century. A frequent and prominent feature in the drawings and paintings of Claude, this bridge also appears in views made by scores of artists from the seventeenth through nineteenth centuries. This is partly due to its location and picturesque character, and partly because of its association with Constantine and his conversion to Christianity. It was from this bridge that Maxentius was hurled into the Tiber and drowned after his defeat by his co-emperor near the village of Saxa Rubra, a few miles upstream, in 312 CE.[21]

Although St. Peter's and the Vatican had become the focus for Christendom by the ninth century, much of the area that had been incorporated in the former imperial city lay abandoned to fields and wilderness. On the west bank of the Tiber, the entire Prati, from the small community that huddled about the walls of the papal fortress north to the Ponte Molle, lay in farm fields from this period until the late nineteenth century.[22] (Aside from agricultural drainage works, the only improvement in this area between the time of Gregory and the speculative subdivisions of Victor Emmanuel's day occurred in the 1660s when Alexander VII planted continuous rows of trees along each side of the Viale Angelico as part of his scheme of grand avenues for the city of Rome.)[23] In 1518, when Cardinal Giulio de' Medici (who became Pope Clement VII in 1523) began to plan his retreat on the slopes of Monte Mario, it was a rural and attractive site with panoramic views of the Tiber valley and Sabine hills, the city of Rome, and the Vatican. Contemporary drawings indicate that the hill was almost completely covered with trees, and that the plain below was largely open, with meadows and scattered trees.[24]

The Villa Madama has been much considered and studied in architectural history because of the tantalizing drawings and exquisite, though unfinished, villa begun by Raphael for Cardinal Giulio de' Medici.[25] Because the sad story of this building may not be familiar to the reader, I will briefly outline its history. Sometime around 1518 Cardinal Giulio de' Medici and his artist/designer, Raphael, began work on a villa just to the north of the Vatican on the eastern slopes of Monte Mario. Raphael died two years later, in 1520, but the project continued under the direction of two of his assistants, Giulio Romano and Giovanni da Udine. They quarreled about the design so much (and so publicly) as to require an intermediary, who considered them both to be "madmen."

After 1520 Antonio da Sangallo the Younger made a series of drawings of an ambitious group of gardens and stables as well as the villa, which still seemed to follow the parti initiated by Raphael. This building was to be biaxially organized, with a large circular court at its center, a semicircular hillside theater behind it against the hill, a triple arched loggia opening out to an enclosed terrace on the north, with a great hall, stair, and entry court opening to the south and the approach drive. All of this was to be erected on a masonry terrace atop an imposing cryptoporticus, on the flank of the hill. It is a most informed Roman build-

Buckland House deer park, 1970

ing, clearly influenced by the ruins of the Basilica of Maxentius, the Golden House (Domus Aurea) of Nero, and the Theater of Maxentius. The decoration was (and is) exquisite, rivaling—and in the opinion of some, surpassing—that of the loggia of the Vatican by the same group of designers. (Whether the idea was that of Raphael or his protégés, the architecture as begun and projected in the Uffizi drawings would have given physical form to the palatial sequence of spaces presented in Raphael's painting of the School of Athens in the Stanze of the Vatican.)

Part of the importance of this building and garden lies in the fact that following Donato Bramante's scheme for the Belvedere Cortile at the Vatican, this was the first integrated axial scheme for villa and garden of the sixteenth century, introducing to Rome ideas of interrelationships between interior and exterior space, villa and garden, which earlier had been developed more modestly in the villas of Tuscany, particularly those of the Medici. The drawings of Sangallo the Younger are tantalizing in their implication of a revised organization. They reveal the possibility of a different entry sequence to be developed from the river, proceeding up the hill axially, at a right angle to the principal facade, as was done later at the Villa Farnese in Caprarola and the Villa Aldobrandini in Frascati. They also suggest substantial additions to the gardens, including a hippodrome, filled with pines and chestnuts, below which was to be a grove of oranges. Next was to come stables and below them more walled gardens for food and flowers.

Despite the obstreperousness of the design team, construction of the Villa Madama was well under way when political events stopped it. The part that was built consisted of one wing of state rooms with a magnificent triple arched loggia opening onto a sunny garden and wall fountains, part of the curved wall of the circular court, and a lower fish tank with monumental arches of a cryptoporticus.

Then in 1527 the troops of Cardinal Colonna attacked Rome and set fire to the structure, almost half-built by then. At the Vatican, Giulio de' Medici, now Pope Clement VII, watched as smoke ascended from his precious villa. Traumatized by the sack of Rome, many intellectuals and artists fled—Michelangelo to Florence, Giulio Romano to Mantua—not to return for a generation. Building in the Campagna ceased due to insecurity. Rome shut down as an artistic center, not awakening again until nearly the 1560s when Pirro Ligorio, Giacomo Barozzi da Vignola, and Giacomo del Duca embarked on the series of villas so renowned today: the Villas Lante, d'Este, Mattei, and Giulia, the Villa Farnese and Villino at Caprarola, the Villa Pia, the Sacro Bosco in Bomarzo, and the Orti Farnesiani on the Palatine in Rome. In the background behind them all lies Bramante and this particular structure of Raphael's, the Villa Madama.[26]

When Clement VII died, the property passed to Alessandro de' Medici. Upon the second marriage of his wife, Margaret of Austria, daughter of Charles V, to Ottavio Farnese, Duke of Parma, it descended through Elisabetta Farnese to the Bourbon kings of Naples, whence it entered a limbo of social and physical neglect for several generations. Its name, "Madama," derives from the period of Margaret's ownership, when it still was a venue for sparkling social engagements, refined artistic gatherings, and memorable feasts. Even in its unfinished state, this fragment of a villa was indeed a *locus amoenus*.

Despite the interest and amount of scholarship devoted to the villa, the park (or vigna) has hardly been considered at all.[27] Only one terrace was completed, that adjacent to the loggia. Like other Medici villas of the period in the north, it was walled and contained evergreen shrubs cut into hedges in a geometric pattern, with a quantity of large potted plants, primarily citrus and flowers. Set into the back wall against the hill were three niches with fountains, the central one containing the celebrated Elephant Fountain by Giovanni da Udine. Below this terrace a giant tank for fish was also completed. In addition, beyond to the north earth was moved and graded to create another terrace that resembled a hippodrome and was guarded by giant figures created by the sculptor Baccio Bandinelli.

None of the other site features indicated in the various plans were executed, however, except for the aforementioned nymphaeum, which nestles into the head of a small ravine just north of the hippodrome site. This declivity leads down to the Tiber, opening out into a miniature valley until it disappears in the broad floodplain along the river. Drawings by Sangallo the Younger exist for the nymphaeum, but again this doesn't appear to have been executed as drawn. Some sort of retreat and water feature taking advantage of hillside springs was built, however, and has been remodeled at least once since.

For the rest we have a good, albeit generalized, idea of what existed in the park, thanks to a series of drawings made at or near the site for the next several generations. From the time of the cessation of construction until the late nineteenth century, the slopes and top of Monte Mario above and behind the villa were wooded with oaks and pines; the ravine was also cloaked with them. The hillside immediately below the villa was largely cleared and kept in meadow or pasture. Farther down where the sports facilities now stand, numerous freestanding deciduous and evergreen trees were scattered in open fields. The banks of the river were almost continuously lined with trees (poplars, willows, and elms from the look of the drawings) and coarse, water-loving plants such as reeds, rushes, and cattails. A few rustic agricultural buildings stood in this area near the old road from the Porta Angelica to Ponte Molle and on the hill below and to the north of the villa at the edge of the trees.

While the Villa Madama was used for various social events and as a retreat by its owners, few or no improvements were made to the grounds or the vigna between 1524 and 1624. There is a drawing by Maerten van Heemskerck from the 1530s that depicts Bandinelli's giants flanking the gate that leads from the enclosed terrace garden to the vigna. In it one can see the already overgrown and disheveled state the gardens had reached within ten years of the end of construction.[28]

CLAUDE'S DRAWINGS OF THE VIGNA MADAMA

Our understanding of the landscape sources of Kent's vision is dependent on knowing what those sources actually looked like. The key to analyzing Kent's vision, then, is to find adequate representations of the landscapes he viewed. It so happens that they have been in plain sight and on exhibition for centuries, most notably in the drawings of Claude Lorrain. By good fortune, this French expatriate artist, indisputably one of the greatest draftsmen and painters of the landscape in western history, lived and worked in Rome from 1623 to 1682.[29] From 1626 until his death in 1682, Claude lived near the base of the Spanish Steps, a few minutes' walk from the Porta del Popolo.[30] He is well known to have frequently drawn out of doors, sometimes in the company of other artists. One account states that he also occasionally even painted out of doors in his earlier years, producing among other works a large painting in the Vigna Madama, which he "would never part with, as he constantly used it for reference in his painting of trees in the studio."[31]

Claude's corpus of surviving work includes a large and varied body of drawings executed in the field. Among these are scenes of Civitavecchia to the northwest, Tivoli to the east, various parts of the Roman Campagna, and numerous sites about the city of Rome. Drawn from nature, these are exercises in observation, representation, and composition. They utilize different methods, some laborious and painstaking, some rapid and gestural. These drawings focus on particular things found in the landscape—trees of different species, plants, rocks and landforms, water in varying states, specific views, different effects of light—and include novel graphic and notational devices to record these objects and phenomena.

The Roman sketches of Claude include many done over several years in and around the Vigna Madama. Ranging in date from approximately 1630 to 1640, some are signed and dated with their locations noted. Others can be identified by their subject matter and topography.

One particular location in the vigna—a slope on the hill immediately north and just a little below the Villa—provided Claude with a view looking north up the Tiber valley, with the Ponte Molle in the distance, a hill (the northern slope of Monte Mario) on the left, and sometimes another coulisse on the right (the southern side of the small valley mentioned above) and large trees in the foreground. It became one of his favorite places to draw, providing motifs for numerous studio paintings. Most of the drawings made in the grounds of the vigna are detail studies and fragments of this particular locale. At least twenty-nine drawings done by Claude here or elsewhere within the grounds of the villa survive, as well as eight of the immediate environs, such as the banks of the Tiber or the Ponte Molle. One of the most famous is that of the river valley with its trees and Mount Soracte.[32]

The collection includes twelve views in and around the ravine, four more at its lower end where it opens out into the meadow, three done out in the open meadow between hill and river, six of bosques or within the woods, a couple executed at the riverbank looking north, and two miscellaneous ones that appear to be made on the would-be hippodrome site near the enclosing wall of the terrace garden.[33] Of the sketches made in the vicinity, there are four of the Ponte Molle, seen from both upstream and down from the east side of the river. (Although numerous other unidentified drawings depicting generic subjects such as individual portraits of different tree species, paths in the woods, and so on might have been made here, they could also have been made in any number of other places on his various walks and expeditions.)[34]

In addition, there are also four drawings of the Tiber, its banks and situation. Three are made along the riverside path located between the Porta del Popolo and the Ponte Molle (later known as Poussin's walk) looking upstream, across toward the Vigna Madama, and from Acqua Acetosa toward the curve of the river above the Ponte Molle.[35] He also made a drawing of St. Peter's from the Villa Pamphili on the Janiculum to the south that clearly depicts the wooded nature of Monte Mario and its southeastern slope at the time.[36]

The use of artistic material for the study of topographic history raises the question: how accurate are Claude's sketches? The answer is that these studies of nature are accurate and reliable. This can be determined partly by his numerous studies of the Ponte Molle, which are consistent with each other, with drawings and paintings by other artists, with nineteenth-century photographs, and with the existing reconstruction. Their verisimilitude is also supported by his patient search for appropriate graphic notations to represent particular qualities of light and species of vegetation. In this period of his career, Claude was concerned with developing methods for the accurate representation of particular visual effects. The techniques he developed for the graphic representation of leaves, for the recession of features in the landscape, and of the effects of sunlight on clouds and water were to influence and inspire painters of the landscape for the next two hundred years, from Caspar Friedrich and J. M. W. Turner to Frederic Church and George Innes.

Careful examination of Claude's sketches and drawings shows that at times he did move things together for effect, and that he collapsed several things into closer proximity than was the real situation. Everyone who draws does this at times. It is a natural result of trying to present just a bit too much of the vast panorama of our visual field on the limited page of a sketchbook. If, however, we set aside those drawings where he puts fictional temples and people into fragments of real landscape, or the drawings that are imaginative constructs, one must conclude that among his nature sketches, these sketches from the Vigna Madama are exercises in factual representation of the highest order.

Drawings and paintings by his contemporaries only confirm what Claude recorded. A painting by Cornelius Bloemart II depicts the Villa and Vigna Madama as seen from farther to the north, looking back toward the city.[37] It clearly presents the villa and valley of the Tiber looking south from the opposite side of the ravine so often depicted by Claude. In it one sees the wooded hillsides, the clearing below the villa, the meadows in the floodplain with scattered trees, the vegetation along the riverbank, and both the large ravine between the villa and the next adjacent hill to the north with the smaller one that contains the nymphaeum, with even the path that connects it to the hippodrome terrace and gate to the garden and villa. It is a meticulous topographic representation as only a Flemish painter of the day influenced by Claude could have made. With it one can locate with confidence the major landscape features depicted by Claude in the studies listed above.

The few drawings of this same subject matter by Nicolas Poussin also tell us a great amount. There have been speculations and assertions since the seventeenth century that Claude and Poussin not only knew each other's work but on occasion visited the countryside together, possibly sketching together. There is no way to tell from the drawings if this is so, but it is clear that they visited the same locations and sketched similar subjects. Three Poussin drawings in particular prove this. One is a careful pen-and-brush drawing made from the hillside above the ravine immediately north of the Villa Madama with a view of the Ponte Molle and Tiber valley. Another depicts the river and banks looking north from the east between the Porta del Popolo and the Ponte Molle. The third is a study of five trees done in the lower meadow of the vigna, seemingly of some of the same trees that Claude sketched several times. Other sketches, such as one by Poussin of the Aventine, reveal what a fine topographical draftsman he could be when sketching from nature. So while there are differences in the style and technique of representation related to each artist's personality, there is concurrence regarding what is represented.

The Vigna Madama very much resembled what later generations, especially the English, came to think of as a park. There were woods and groves of trees—deciduous, evergreen, and conifers. Although there were some shrubs, the grazing of animals had cleared out most of the understory, allowing for light and vision through the trees. There were paths, slopes, uneven ground, and a curving valley that led down to an open meadow with freestanding specimens and clumps of trees in grass. This lower area was bounded by a curving body of water (the river), partially lined with vegetation but affording views to a distant picturesque fortified bridge. Some of the Claude sketches depict works of sculpture within a grove of pines and rustic structures at the foot of the hill in the edge of the trees. Bloemart's sketch and others confirm the presence of these smaller agricultural structures. Poussin's view confirms the strong visual presence of the Ponte Molle from favored places within the vigna—that it, the river, and distant scene had become integral parts of the ensemble.

Several questions remain. If the vigna was accessible to visitors, as both Montaigne and these painters indicate, why are there no drawings of the villa or nymphaeum by Claude or his contemporaries? Claude did make drawings of other villas, ruins, and buildings in and around Rome.[38] Were the building and nymphaeum fenced? Perhaps we just have not yet recognized the sketches that depict parts of them. The most likely reason, however, is that at the time this part of the estate was private and walled or fenced off. Therefore, unlike the vigna itself or the lower, current park and sports complex, entry to it was difficult, as it still is today.

THE VIGNA AFTER CLAUDE, 1660–1760

There is a lovely drawing by Gaspar Van Witel of 1681, looking out across Rome from the street linking Trinità dei Monti and the Villa Medici, which clearly shows the heavy vegetation of Monte Mario and the vale north of the Villa Madama. A companion sketch of the same period depicting the Ponte Molle shows open fields and partially cleared slopes on the hills west of the river just north of the Vigna Madama.[39] There is another such lovely drawing made over a hundred years later, in 1806–7, from nearly the identical spot looking out past the Villa Medici by an equally meticulous draftsman, Ingres. Even more clearly one sees the Villa Madama on Monte Mario surrounded by pines and oaks. The vale to the north stands out as still wooded, while the slope below the villa is partially cleared toward the river.[40]

Only a few years later, in 1826, Corot produced a drawing from the hill above Acqua Acetosa looking west across the Tiber to the land immediately beyond the Ponte Molle, confirming that this area had hardly changed in the 175 years since Claude's expeditions. While there are a few more structures than before, once more one sees the same farms and small clearings extending up the valleys with pines and oaks on the sides and tops that characterized the land from the Ponte Molle to the Villa Madama in 1630.[41]

The riverside walk that was so popular in the seventeenth century from the Porta del Popolo along the east bank of the Tiber had deteriorated considerably by then, however, and was nearly devoid of trees by the nineteenth century. Corot and others render the river, its banks, and the distant hills with affection, as much for their associations with Claude and Poussin as for their picturesque attributes. In the background and to the left, however, the hillsides between the Ponte Molle and Madama remain constant. Comparison of Corot's studies with sketches of Poussin and Claude made in virtually the same spot point out how obvious were the coulisses that come to form such an essential part of their pictorial equipment and of pastoral landscape design. These erosion forms so characteristic of riverbanks around the world were all swept away by the flood-protection embankments built along both sides later in the century.[42]

One of the most specific representations of the conditions of the villa itself in the eighteenth century is a watercolor drawing by John Robert Cozens. Here one sees the villa from the area once proposed to be a hippodrome, looking south to the wall of the upper terrace. Above the villa, forest trees stand as they had for three hundred years. Below, the trees have been cleared to maintain the panoramic view. The foreground is covered with seedling oaks moving in among a scattering of tall, wild cypresses, threatening to take over this still undeveloped terrace.[43]

That the villa and grounds were in a state of deshabille by this time seems to be confirmed by the highly romantic view of it made by Hubert Robert sometime prior to 1778. Inspired by Piranesi's vedute, Robert has obviously sped up the deterioration of Raphael's loggia and taken some license with the insertion of a group of peasant washerwomen camped out in the area of the fish tank to create a picturesque study of *vanitas*. Despite his obvious pleasure in the presentation of heroic splendor and abandoned grandeur, he indicates the same pines above the villa as does everyone else, and an overgrown cypress on the terrace facing the loggia.[44]

A diversity of other eighteenth-century views exist that help to confirm the conditions of the estate at the time. One, now in the Los Angeles County Museum of Art, is an anonymous aerial view of Rome looking north, rendered in mosaic, which depicts the Prati and the Vigna Madama in detail. An avenue of trees lines the Via Angelica, passing beneath the villa. A full stand of mature trees, apparently pines, covers the hill to the north and above the villa, extending beyond, across the small valley and onto the next hill. To the south and below the villa a large pasture has been cleared, although numerous clumps of trees are dotted on the slope immediately between the villa and the river. From the villa north to the Ponte Molle lies open country and farms similar to the area between the Via Angelica and the Tiber. The eastern bank from Porta del Popolo to the Ponte Molle is also largely open farm fields, except for a few clumps and one large stand of trees at the big bend in the Tiber along Poussin's walk.[45]

This little-known view is supported by a better known (and better drawn as well) similar aerial view of Rome issued in 1765 by Giuseppe Vasi.[46] One can see within the Vigna Madama similar locations and stands of trees. The architectural features agree closely with the Los Angeles mosaic.

Final confirmation of the character of the riverbanks, water meadows, the shape and disposition of the hillside, and their vegetation comes from a view made by the German artist Jacob Philipp Hackert four years later, looking back in the other direction from the Ponte Molle.[47] Oaks, poplars, and other broad-leafed trees nearly continuously line the soft banks of the river. A large pasture or meadow sweeps from the villa around and down past the Via Angelica to the trees along the river. Not very many of the familiar pines and cypress climb the ravine beside and the hill behind the villa any longer. Additional confirmation of the maturity of the trees and their parklike informal disposition below the villa and of the survival of the wooded ravine and hilltop comes from several drawings in the Ashby collection now in the Vatican. An 1803 sketch by Susan Percy made from the Pincio looking across the valley over the Piazza del Popolo and its church toward Monte Mario clearly depicts every structure there, including Villa Madama. The same cypresses seen in Cozens's sketch have grown to maturity. A more detailed and closer view by "Gimelly" made twelve years earlier leaves no doubt that above Madama a continuous live oak forest stretched to the top of the mount and the Villa Mellini. Below, however, one sees deciduous trees and a large clearing or meadow stretching down to the floodplain. A moonlit sketch by Richard Wilson of the view from the Ponte Molle nearly forty years earlier in 1754, however, shows more growth and neglect, more trees in this same hillside area.[48]

WILLIAM KENT IN ROME AND AFTER

It is one thing to establish what the conditions of this park were in the years between Claude's death in 1682 and William Kent's departure from Rome in 1720. It is another to say what Kent saw and knew, or to say that what he saw inspired him to create work derived from it several years later in England. Nevertheless, we can establish several things. First, William Kent, the chief innovator in the sudden development of what has come to be known as the English Landscape Garden, lived for nearly ten years in the same neighborhood near the Spanish Steps that Claude, Poussin, and numerous other northern artists had inhabited in the previous century. Nearby lay the Porta del Popolo, the promenade along the Tiber opposite the Vigna Madama, and other large parks, those of the Villas Giulia and Borghese. He had ample time and access to know them all well. We know for a fact that he knew and borrowed from gardens farther afield, such as those of the Villa Mattei on the Caelian Hill in Rome and the Villa Aldobrandini at Frascati.[49] Why not those near his home? Second, he was apprenticed to a painter, studying decorative painting as well as portraits and more ambitious easel works. One of the most common subjects of minor architectural decoration of the period (above doorways and mantels and on cupboards in palazzi and villas) was that of landscape scenery, particularly that of the Campagna with Roman ruins, and pastoral tableaus. We know that he would have visited many interiors of the great palazzi in Rome and seen not only this work but also the paintings, such as those of Claude in the Palazzo Doria on the Corso. We also know that within a few years of his arrival he had become a respected guide to the sites of Rome, leading English noblemen on tours of the sites, indoors and out.[50]

One of the styles of decoration that he introduced to England on his return is derived from the grotesque decoration of the school of Raphael, which in turn is derived from first-century Roman work known in the Domus Aurea of Nero near the Coliseum. While it is probable that Kent knew this original source, it is more than likely that he also would have seen and considered at length the two most famous examples of its revival by Raphael, those of the Vatican corridors and the Villa Madama. He was, after all, encouraged by one of his sponsors to become a "Second Raphael." In the course of visiting the latter site, he would have traversed the Vigna Madama both going and coming each time.

Finally, there is his knowledge of Claude's drawings and paintings that recorded and gave nearly iconic stature to the spaces of the vigna. How well did William Kent know Claude's drawings? In particular, did he know those that depict the Vigna Madama? Several scholars have commented recently on the relationship between his drawings and those of Claude, noting the change in his drawing style after 1725 that corresponded with the arrival of the *Liber Veritatis* and other sketches into the collection of the Duke of Devonshire, a neighbor and friend of Kent's patron and long-term host, the Earl of Burlington.[51] In Kent's own collection of Roman landscapes, mostly from the previous century, were three drawings by Claude. While it would be nice to believe that he also knew some of the most evocative drawings done in the Vigna (now lodged in the British Museum), it appears that he never did, for the bulk of them came as a gift in the bequest of Richard Payne Knight in 1824, and had been only just recently purchased from a Spanish collection that Kent didn't know. Instead it is to the memory of the vigna itself and other real places and the generalized evocation of them in Claude's paintings and in the *Liber Veritatis* of several in particular— one of which was that of the Vigna Madama—that we must attribute his inspiration.

It would have been a simple matter for Kent to have visited the Vigna

Madama. Although in later years he became somewhat corpulent and apparently less active, he was young and vigorous while in Rome. To test the possibilities, the author recently set out on foot from the Piazza del Popolo and walked first to the Ponte Molle along the Via Flaminia, and then having crossed the river walked back through what is now the Foro Olimpico to the hillside frequented by Claude. Despite modern traffic and the jumble of intersections, the walk from Porta del Popolo to the Ponte Molle took only thirty-five minutes, and from the bridge to the Vigna Madama only ten. Since one of the pleasures of Rome has always been strolling and walking its streets and terrain, one can only assume that this route outside the gate was a popular walk, especially in its more rambling form on Poussin's walk, along the bank of the river. It is and was a relatively easy and pleasant stroll. If one were to hire a carriage or ride, it would have been even quicker and easier.

That one could easily gain access to the portion of the vigna utilized by Claude is demonstrated by the continuing series of studies, sketches, and paintings made here by a variety of artists until well past Kent's lifetime. That there are no drawings made by him within the vigna is of no consequence. Little of anything is known to survive from his long stay in Rome except for letters and partial journals. There are no drawings of architecture, nor of furniture or paintings, subjects that he later demonstrates extraordinary skill and facility in designing, and of which many examples were clearly inspired and derived from particular models in Rome and elsewhere in Italy.[52]

William Kent's landscape designs have been well documented, and it has been convincingly demonstrated that many of the architectural features of his more constrained or "poetic" garden schemes were derived from Italian villas such as those of the Mattei, Ludovisi, and Aldobrandini villas, as well as several others in the Veneto, including Valsanzibio and Barbaro.[53] It is now clear, also, that Kent's "broad style" of landscape park design, which formed much of the basis for the work of his successors in the next generation, was derived directly from contemporary Roman landscape in general, and from the vigne of the Villa Giulia and the Villa Madama in particular. This influence can be seen in both his drawings and built work. Kent's first exercises in garden design date from between 1727 and 1730, with work executed at Carlton House and Chiswick. In addition to references and quotes from the

villas mentioned above, his earliest work shows a multitude of influences, not the least of which is the lovely drawings from the previous
century for masque scenery made by Inigo Jones, then in the possession
of Kent's patron, Lord Burlington.[54]

His greatest surviving landscape work, Rousham, develops architectural and iconographic themes introduced earlier in his own work at
Stowe and Chiswick.[55] This later garden incorporates a new handling of
landscape form, water, and vegetation. At Stowe, where he is known to
have supplied the design for at least two of the garden structures, Kent
met the young Lancelot Brown. What their relationship may have been
is unknown. Kent was his senior and the social companion of many of
the friends of Brown's employer. In the ten years that Brown resided at
Stowe, he taught himself to draw and acquired considerable knowledge
of architecture and design. While the manner is very much Kent's, it was
Brown and his patron, Lord Cobham, who softened and tore up large
portions of the Baroque work of John Vanbrugh and Charles Bridgeman
at Stowe, creating the Grecian valley, Elysian fields, woodland edges,
great lawn, and lake with its bridges and pavilions. The handling of
landforms and vegetation, which appeared so fresh and novel to his
English contemporaries, would have seemed quite familiar to anyone
acquainted with the Roman Campagna and suburban estates such as
the Vigna Madama.

While it is probably true that the earliest garden work completed by
1724 at Chiswick—the trident of paths terminating in pavilions—was
conceived and directed by Burlington with Bridgeman as the nursery-
man and clerk of the works, there is also no doubt that the central allée
(circus) with its exedra of hedges and Roman figures, the transformation of Bridgeman's canal into a soft body of water with islands, rock-
work cascade, and the far meadow with its clumps of trees, the forest
with lanes and obelisk are the work of Kent. All of these features are
recorded in a series of marvelous sketches that Kent executed in ink
and wash. Whatever triggered such an outburst of effort is not known,
but it instantly propelled Kent into the forefront of landscape design in
England, where he remained until his death in 1748.

Many observers have noted the sources of Kent's architectural contributions, such as the cascade and circus, but apparently no one has
commented on the setting itself, the composition of trees, the form of

the water, or the shaping and regrading of the land. Bridgeman's rectangular pond was transformed into a representation of a river, its terminus in the woods obscured by an island, a device which was to become a stock in trade of Lancelot "Capability" Brown and the English landscape school. Its edges are contrived to appear as soft natural banks with grass sloping down to them and trees standing in clumps and irregular groups.

At its southern end, in a strip of land between the rustic cascade and the entry drive leading to Burlington's Rotunda, Kent had the earth reshaped into several undulating mounds, pronounced enough to form a miniature vale opening out toward the lawn and water. This he planted with trees, some of which were firs with their branches limbed up. Elsewhere, in both sketches and executed work, he planted trees with the lower branches trimmed off so as to provide a relatively open veil of trunks between foreground spaces and those beyond. As a review of Kent's sketches reveals, this is a technique he subsequently employed throughout his career.

Although there is no attempt at Chiswick to represent any particular landscape from Rome, these devices and two of his less-discussed architectural compositions there—the obelisk, with arch and *rond-point*, and the aviary—cohere into an echo or memory of the walk from Piazza del Popolo out along the Tiber past the Villa Giulia to the Villa Madama. The scale and topography at Chiswick are all wrong for it to be a representation. It is rather more like a reverie, or nostalgia for a set of conditions.

The Piazza del Popolo in Rome, of course, contains an ancient Egyptian obelisk erected at just such an intersection of three streets opposite the Porta del Popolo, an arched city gate adjacent to the quarter frequented by northern European visitors. All those who had spent time in Rome and had walked out toward the Ponte Molle would have recognized the reference of a gateway (designed by Inigo Jones and brought from Somerset House) paired with an obelisk at the intersection of radiating paths. Furthermore, Kent's whimsical aviary scheme employs a device that he suggested to clients as often as he did that of a cascade based on the Villa Aldobrandini cascade, employed here and in different versions at Rousham and elsewhere. This is the use of herms as columns in an arcade for a small garden pavilion or grotto.

His source or inspiration for the aviary structure was obviously the sub-terranean grotto in the nymphaeum of the Villa Giulia by Bartolomeo Ammannati. Like its park and gardens, this exquisite pavilion was easily accessible a short distance beyond the Porta del Popolo, halfway to the Ponte Molle and located even closer to Kent's lodgings than the Vigna Madama.[56]

While no design sketches or proposals by Kent for site development at Stowe survive—if he ever made them—numerous drawings for unused architectural features proposed for Chiswick and eventually executed at Stowe do exist.[57] There are, moreover, drawings of consider-able interest regarding the site development for Claremont, Esher, and Rousham.[58] Each of these schemes contains a variation on the elements of the Vigna Madama. For each Kent made drawings of hillsides sloping down to bodies of water, which were fashioned to resemble winding rivers. In each the trees are dense on the hill at the top, thinning out as they border the vales and clearing of the hillslopes, opening out to a meadow with scattered trees and clumps at the bottom. All have one or more classical structures or pavilions in the woods on the upper level, usually with arches. For both Rousham and Claremont he invents or rusticates bridges for the river below, which he locates off to the left in the distance.

Particularly striking is the treatment of the slopes leading down to the river at Rousham in the Venus Vale, his reworking of the Cherwell itself, and the gothicizing of the mill and bridge in the distance. Despite his borrowing from the Aldobrandini cascade, one can see a clear and distinct evocation of the Vigna Madama as it was in fact and in Claude's various representations of it. Both Kent's sketches and the built garden at Rousham present a strong image of Madama's groves of pines, the trimmed and browsed oaks and elms of the vigna and earlier sketches of them. This accounts for one of the most markedly mannered aspects of Kent's drawings and landscape constructions: his unprecedented (in England) planting of so many conifers and practice of limbing them and other trees up to a great height, especially as they lined a descending vale or stood before a body of water. Not only do the vales at Clare-mont and Rousham conform to the physical characteristics of the vale at the Vigna Madama so frequented by Claude, but also Kent populates the riverside meadow of one of the Claremont sketches with cattle and goats straight out of the vigna as Claude recorded it. On the water he places a boat of the sort used at the time on the Tiber River.[59]

Despite William Kent's great interest in theater, his early work in painting, architectural ornament, and decoration, and his great facility in the design of buildings and furniture, it is for landscape design that he is most famous today. Twenty years ago, Susan Lang attacked the idea that Kent's landscape gardens were derived from paintings and two-dimensional images, especially those of Claude and Poussin. She asked why Kent's landscapes might not be derived from gardens. The answer seems to be that in significant parts, they were. While it appears that several locales were available to provide such an influence, one most certainly was the very park which also inspired many of Claude's images, that of the Vigna Madama on Monte Mario.

THE MUSEUM OF MODERN ART GARDEN

The Rise and Fall of a Modernist Landscape

(1997)

It is not altogether unusual in the history of art and design for someone to carry on and develop the work, ideas, and aesthetic agenda of someone else, most often those of a master or predecessor whose work is not only admired but also passionately taken up as a cause or mission. The pleasure garden in England at Stourhead, Wiltshire, created by the banker Henry Hoare and the architectural draftsman Henry Flitcroft, formerly an assistant to Lord Burlington and William Kent, can be seen as a culmination of Kent's career, or even as one of his greatest achievements, although he was never involved. In a similar manner, Philip Johnson in his design for the Museum of Modern Art garden and its subsequent expansion not only applied principles and ideas put forward by his preferred master, Ludwig Mies van der Rohe, but also literally built a masterpiece in a genre never realized by Mies despite the latter's own drawings and thoughts on the subject.

Much has been written about Johnson and his relationship with and to Mies, especially between 1932 and 1953, a good deal of it by Johnson himself. Unlike, say, the relationship between Robert Craft and Igor Stravinsky, Johnson—the pupil, curator, critic turned assistant, and interpreter—was eventually to break away and go off in search of his own career, identity, and creative works. After Johnson opened his own office in 1953 in Manhattan, one of the very first projects done under

From *Journal of Garden History* 17.2 (Summer 1997): 140–62.

his own name was the garden for MOMA. In it he showed himself to be a remarkably deep student of Mies's work and thought, so thoroughly involved with his entire oeuvre and its influences that he accomplished a work for which virtually no precedent had been built. On the other hand, many aspects of the garden as designed can be found or suggested in Mies's unrealized work of the 1930s and 1940s.

It would be a fallacy to say that Johnson was capable of thinking like Mies, or that the MOMA garden is what Mies would have done if he had been given the commission, or even to make assertions about what Johnson himself may have thought or intended. On the other hand, without the precedents and deep involvement in Mies's career on Johnson's part, could this particular garden have come into being? Finally, it is (or was) one of the two or three best examples of Miesian thought and architectural accomplishment regarding exterior space, its design, and the relationship between buildings and landscape that was ever realized. If one were to take the German National Pavilion of 1929 (the "Barcelona Pavilion"), the Illinois Institute of Technology (IIT) campus in Chicago, the Farnsworth House on the Fox River in Illinois, and the Lake Shore Drive Apartments in Chicago as representing the key built works by Mies in the realm of site planning, buildings in space, and the relationships between the two, one would have to add the MOMA garden as the best (and only) example of his extended studies of courtyard space. Unfortunately much of what made it both quintessentially Miesian and a masterpiece has recently been destroyed, probably beyond retrieval, by the unfortunate additions of César Pelli. Whether the fault for this lies with Pelli or his client is considered below.

As a scholar and protégé of Mies, Johnson came to know and understand his work probably better than anyone, with the single exception, of course, of Mies himself. In the course of such scrutiny and familiarity Johnson developed an uncanny ability to draw on the full range of his master's work and thought. Few projects by Johnson (with the notable exception of his own residential complex in New Canaan, Connecticut) draw so deeply on as many diverse projects and periods of Mies's work or assemble the parts so seamlessly to produce a unique environment as the MOMA garden project. At the same time it should be noted that the synthesis is totally successful. There is never a sense of pastiche, of quoting, or of an inferior or derivative work. The garden is (or was) whole, robust, and deceptively calm, seemingly effortless.

Elements that make this scheme so Miesian range from underlying spatial concepts and the arrangement of parts and their influence on circulation and vision to the parts themselves, their shapes, material, and details. Johnson adopted Mies's favorite unit, the rectangle, for each of the overlain parts at every scale—the overall shape, the raised terraces, the basins, the bridges, the pavement, the walls, their openings, even the bricks. These he proceeded to use in two directions, nearly always with the change of direction coinciding with a change in plane vertically.

"THE PLAN IS THE THING: MODERN ARCHITECTURE IS BASED ON PLANNING. THE ARCHITECT BUILDS TO KEEP THE PLAN INVIOLATE."[1]

From his early brick houses of 1922–23 through the campus plans for IIT of 1939–40, Mies used orthogonal plans with rectangles of varying sizes and direction, but always composed in a shifting, dynamic manner, pinwheeling about one or more centers. The walls, steps, platforms, roofs, pools, and screens used to create such swirling spatial compositions often differed from each other in some way—height, material, or situation (under a roof, in the open, against a pool or partially so)—so that one was not overly conscious of repeated, parallel, and secondary gestures that completed the forms or reoriented and resolved this endless rotation. As Johnson has pointed out, this compositional method was most immediately derived from that of the Dutch De Stijl movement and is markedly noticeable in the work of contemporaries such as Walter Gropius and Adolf Meyer in their buildings for the Bauhaus in Dessau, Germany.

Theo van Doesburg, who created a stir during his brief tenure at the Bauhaus while Mies was there, wrote in his six-point manifesto: "The new architecture is anti-cubic, that is to say, it does not try to freeze the different functional space cells in one closed cube. Rather, it throws the functional space cells (as well as the overhanging planes, balcony volumes, etc.) centrifugally from the core of the cube. . . . In this way architecture acquires a more or less floating aspect that, so to speak, works against the gravitational forces of nature."[2] If one examines the most famous residential-scale structures of Mies that Johnson knew exhaustively, the Barcelona Pavilion and the Farnsworth House, it is immediately clear that both begin with a simple rectangle in plan, roughly in the proportion of a Golden Section. Both then undergo a series of operations and elaborations best described as subdivision, shifting, and dislocation. In each case the original rectangle receives additions above (or below) of other rectangles that modify the original. Freestanding planes or screens are added, blocking movement and vision, determining circulation, and directing one's view or path out away from the center to the periphery, where it is met by another element that turns and directs one back around the periphery or toward the interior. In each case one cannot actually enter or stand at the absolute center or linchpin of the composition. Near it, *yes*, but actually occupy the center or static place, *no*.

In the book that Johnson wrote on Mies, published six years before his design for the MOMA garden of 1953, he wrote enthusiastically about the Barcelona Pavilion: "The design is simultaneously simple and complex: its ingredients are . . . disposed in such a way that space is channeled rather than confined—it is never stopped, but allowed to flow continuously. The only decorative elements besides the richness of materials are two rectangular pools and a statue by Georg Kolbe, and they are inseparable components of the composition."[3] Later, reflecting on this and on what he had written about this aspect of Mies and his work, Johnson said: "I didn't discuss the influence of cubism and the connections to Expressionism were a mystery to me. These are two things I would go into now. The de Stijl influence is clear enough—in fact he did it better than de Stijl ever did."[4] With these descriptions of the 1929 Exposition pavilion, Johnson, whether consciously or not, wrote the program brief for the MOMA garden. His first garden scheme of 1953 began as a simple rectangle that was shifted slightly to the northeast and down from an implied first position immediately adjacent to the museum lobby and a café terrace. This rectangle consists of a taut sheet of gray-and-white Vermont marble pavement, also of rectangles laid in a stacked bond pattern, a Miesian note that keeps the surface neutral vis-à-vis "grain" or direction, thus countering the motion set up by other devices. It is a calming device that would seem stiff in a different composition, such as an axial or bilaterally symmetrical one.

Next, a long rectangular basin of water was placed off-center in the lower terrace. It is subdivided near the center; the two resultant segments are shifted and pulled apart, away from each other in two directions, thereby dividing the whole terrace into four rectangles of different sizes that rotate about the area of dislocation, alternating in size—big, little, fat, thin—and providing a remarkable variety if one were to move through them sequentially. Next come the bridges, also thin slabs of marble of rectangular shape, seemingly possessing a modular relationship to some other aspect of the composition. To the visitor it is not clear whether they are of the same dimension as the basins, only lifted and rotated, or some multiple of the paving units, or of the planter, or of all of these. In any case, as in Greek and Roman classical architecture, there is a perceived relatedness of elements, in both dimension and proportion. As in the first move with the basins, these two bridges are carefully placed off-center, thus creating a larger and smaller portion of water on each side. Later placement of sculpture would take advantage of these relationships to increase focus and concentration on some pieces and to give breathing space to others. Most obviously, a circular motion was set up for visitors to progress through each of the spaces—in effect, outdoor gallery rooms. That they can be called rooms within the overall garden enclosure results from the next element added to the composition: trees.

Despite the fundamental importance of paving, walls, and steps and the modernist architectural pedigree of the spatial organization, it is nevertheless a *garden* and not a piazza or courtyard. Toward this end Johnson consulted two landscape architects at different times, each of whom made important contributions to its character. While Johnson's sensibility and the spirit of Mies's compositional ideas can largely be considered the informing "genius of the place," the knowledge and selection of plants of these two landscape architects have been central to its success—literally so in the case of one change made in the 1963 revision and expansion. It must be noted, however, that their role in this project has been that of consultants to Johnson and MOMA rather than as equal collaborators or coauthors. The first was James Fanning in the 1950s; the second was Robert Zion in the 1960s. Both were involved in the selection and situation, technically and aesthetically, of the planting. Fanning, a little-known figure from Johnson's milieu in

For all of his faults- Philip Johnson is still a brilliant planner- and sometimes architect. study the following plans for example: Museum of Modern Art Garden

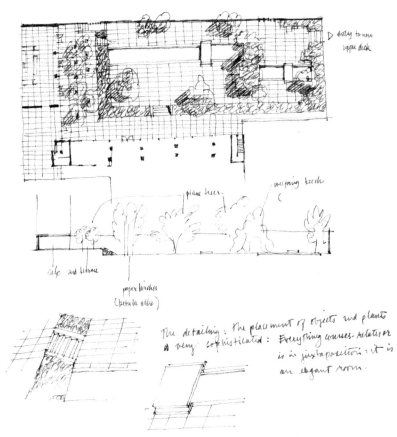

entry to new upper deck

weeping beech

plane trees.

café and terrace

paper birches
(betula alba)

The detailing: The placement of objects and plants is very sophisticated: Everything courses-relates or is in juxtaposition: it is an elegant room.

Museum of Modern Art Garden, New York, sketchbook notes, 1974

New Canaan who had earlier worked on projects in Washington, DC, and the Carolinas, assisted him on the first scheme, experimenting with several plants that were unfamiliar and not in common use at the time. Utilizing a refined palette of evergreens, the black-and-white weeping birches, river birches, a weeping beech, hornbeams, plane trees, and a large variety of ground covers, he complemented Johnson's scheme. This first planting emphasized variety and was somewhat innovative for an urban garden at the time. In the center island of planting between the shifted water basins, or "canals" as Johnson preferred to call them, Fanning planted a group of hinoki, or *Chamaecyparis obtusa,* a Japanese evergreen tree related to the redwood and cypress. He also used rhodo-dendron and the azalea, understandably hoping for the lush masses of leaves and flowers so fondly grown in the gardens of many of MOMA's patrons. Although rarely mentioned, Fanning's role as a major contrib-utor to the garden design was acknowledged during the opening party. While Johnson squired board members and guests about the galleries he had renovated and created, Fanning conducted tours of the garden.

Johnson and Fanning consciously and effectively used plants in two ways. First as screens, exactly as Mies would have used glass, stone, or brick to make planes, filters, and edges, to direct and shape space, vision, and movement; and second as sculptural, sensual, irregular organic objects to be seen and enjoyed for themselves. The central and most important group, originally a clump of hinoki, was located between, and in planar opposition to, the two basins. London plane trees were placed inside and along the 54th Street boundary wall. Cho-sen for their tall, open, coarse habit, which effectively screens the mix of row houses and apartments across the street, only the dappled trunks are left below in front of the wall, on which the series of four bronze backs by Henri Matisse were mounted. Two groups of birches, selected for their delicate, veil-like transparency, white trunks, black twigs, and small, finely cut leaves, were placed on the upper L-shaped entry terrace and principal lower garden. To the east and west, plants were chosen for background roles. European hornbeams were drifted in an irregular pattern across the café terrace. This slow-growing tree is renowned for its dark foliage, dense shade, and ability to provide overhead canopy. It is commonly clipped or pruned heavily in Europe, and it may even have been thought that this group could be pleached or sheared into an overhead plane. If so it never happened, and would have been in conflict with the sensibility toward plants that Mies consistently displayed in his work, treating them in sketch and project alike as irregular, organic, and romantic figures set off and distinct from the tight, regular, and tectonic fabric of his buildings. Ground cover, however, was used as a planar surface with a contrasting color and texture to the stone and water. It was also used to resolve the vertical transition from upper to lower terraces, which is not made explicit or worked out architecturally. Evergreen shrubs and trees on the east end, originally conceived as a terminus to the view, especially in winter from the western café terrace, had to be rethought and changed in 1964 when Johnson was able to expand the garden in this direction.

"THERE CAN BE NO SPACE WITHOUT ENCLOSURE"[5]

An important aspect of this work and its debt to Mies at the most fundamental level is that of the enclosed garden court and the nature of the making of that enclosure. Put simply, the garden sat within a rectangular box of a space made of absolutely level, uniformly gray masonry walls on two sides, and large floor-to-ceiling glass walls consisting of windows and doors on the other two sides. While it is true that gardens have been built in courtyards for centuries, it was Mies who introduced them into the modernist vocabulary of building types, studying particular aspects of their application. As someone who had been in Mies's office in Germany for several years in the early 1930s, and had access to his drawings while working on the MOMA monograph, Johnson was very familiar with, and had published and discussed, a series of unrealized courtyard houses that had engaged Mies off and on from 1931 to 1938.[6] He discusses the particular characteristics of the walls of these schemes, noting the proportions and placement of openings as well as the general character and relationship between the interior and exterior volumes. The dynamic but balanced effect of these decisions and the enormous efforts to produce these few seemingly simple yet deeply considered rectangles in plan and elevation have a deep correspondence in Japanese architecture, a subject that both Mies and Johnson—or for that matter Frank Lloyd Wright—have always been cagey about discussing, probably because they could appreciate the affinity but were ambivalent in their attitude, realizing that they had arrived at their formal expression from a different basis and would rather not have to address it.[7]

The kinship with certain Asian prototypes is not merely one of transcending the static framed view, but rather of relationships, contrasts, and physical movement. In all of Mies's projects relevant to this scheme, care was taken to ensure that the different elements usually denoting boundary and "frame" did not coincide in the same place. Instead at least two, and usually three, occur at different locations: the floor extends beyond the glass, a roof or wall extends beyond the floor, or part of one extends past the other, and so on. Just where the enclosure truly stops is not clear, except for a distant wall across the space, but even this usually has at least one opening sufficient to render it a screen or a plane. Peter Eisenman observes that "Mies, according to Johnson, thought of his houses as anything but volumes, as screens connecting inside and outside."[8] Like many other modernists, Johnson has always acknowledged that the person who led Western architecture in this direction was Wright: "It was he, don't forget, who made roofs, walls, wainscoting and floor all independent of each other—independent elements of design."[9]

The Wasmuth editions of Wright's early Oak Park period of work that were published in Europe in 1910 and 1911 were studied carefully in architectural circles there and occupy a central position in the revolution that was to follow. Mies's country house schemes of 1923 and after and the Barcelona Pavilion of 1929 are heavily indebted to principles extracted from this work. In the courtyard houses, however, Wright offered no help. Mies had to tackle on his own the problem of how to apply some of these principles to a confined urban situation. Later he pursued these ideas in terms of a self-contained ensemble, even when located in the countryside. This idea of utilizing the same spatial devices, pioneered by Wright (and himself) in rural settings where horizontal extension and an unfettered and implied infinite perspective were key strategies for the integration of building and site instead of where an absolutely bounded and contained composition was inevitable, is more than interesting. This is a design problem of great difficulty and led to a fresh architectural result that was to be taken up by a generation of residential designers in America after the Second World War, most notably Eliot Noyes, Edward Larrabee Barnes, Craig Ellwood, Johnson, and Mies's contemporary and fellow exile Marcel Breuer. If there is a common quality to all Mies's courtyard houses, it is his attempt and success in breaking down the frontal, planar qualities of the architectural enclosure, and of working within an absolute box and breaking down the sense of limits.[10] In addition to using planes sliding past each other overhead and underfoot, invariably he shifts space and the structure of that space obliquely, creating places "around the corner" from each other, often with L-shaped spaces.

The MOMA garden presented Johnson with several problems in this regard. The site was absolutely prescribed by boundaries on 54th Street to the north, adjoining properties on the east and west, and the tight, flat window wall of the existing museum built by Edward Durell Stone and Philip L. Goodwin in 1939.[11] Nevertheless, by unifying and extending the museum's floor surface out onto an upper L-shaped terrace, placing a clump of trees on axis with the entry and shifting the stairs off axis, placing service gates to the left and right in the opposite wall, and creating a cafeteria room at a right angle to the entry axis and thus obliquely, more in the manner of a building fragment or a pavilion, he was able to evoke the spirit of one of Mies's courtyards. Eleven years later Johnson was able to improve the principal entry and relationship between the interior and exterior spaces dramatically by gutting the old lobby and producing a truly Miesian space of classical calm and proportions that flowed effortlessly and directly out to his upper L-shaped terrace. This space and relationship have since been destroyed by the incongruous and unfortunate placement of escalators across it by César Pelli, blocking the view and access and, worse, eliminating this important upper terrace.

Johnson's understanding of Mies's attitude toward spatial relations, despite and because of the large glass walls, the oblique movement, the L-shaped space, the shift of the main terrace, the taut paved surface, and the brick walls with their shifted openings, was clearly derived from the unrealized courtyard houses of the 1930s. Yet there is another aspect of the garden that is a hallmark of its Mies-ness and of Johnson's achievement. This is its success programmatically and its essence of *luxe*. Johnson may well have been *the* American architect of the past generation, with the most refined sensibility, keenest eye, and sharpest tongue. Despite his later sarcastic remarks concerning functionalism—"architecture can be decorated with toilets" is one such bon mot—in his early writings he praised European modernists for their functionally stripped-down and programmatically responsive works. Additionally, however, he also pointed out that there were aesthetic qualities in their work that transcended such issues and had nothing to do with accommodation. He has said that he was attracted to Mies's work as early as 1930 (before going to Europe) because it "seemed less factory-like, more classical."[12] Discussing Mies's Farnsworth House, he noted that "this structural purity is contrasted with the sumptuous materials used throughout the house: floors of Italian travertine, raw silk curtains and primavera wood cabinets."[13] Anyone who has visited the Barcelona Pavilion knows exactly what he means—the heavy red velvet drapery against sumptuous marble panels and floor, stainless steel and leather chaise and settees, their precise forms, generous quantities, and voluptuous textures exude a sense of luxury. Specifically thinking about Mies's studies for a "Museum for a small city" of 1942, Johnson says: "In order that the arrangement of the museum may be as flexible as possible, the structure is reduced to its simplest terms: floor slab, columns, roof plate, freestanding partitions and exterior walls, which, being of glass, scarcely function visibly as walls. The relative *absence of architecture* intensifies the individuality of each work of art and at the same time incorporates it into the entire design."[14]

The few architectural and spatial moves made by Johnson were executed with remarkable care in the selection of materials—in their colors, textures, and quality. The pavement is a beautiful light-gray-and-white Vermont marble; the walls are a light-gray brick; the pools are dark, of infinite depth, with shimmering and reflective water; the plants are lustrous, each chosen for its particular quality: sculptural shape, delicate leaves, dappled bark, dense shade, black twigs, white bark, and so forth. Finally, there were (and are) the sculptures. Here Johnson had to work with objects already in the museum's collection, and with the curators and director. Nevertheless, photos of the garden as first installed, and as this author first knew it in 1964, confirm that several particular pieces were placed in locations where they remain today, virtually becoming parts of the design in exactly the sense conveyed by Johnson in his discussion of Mies's 1942 museum project.

Specifically, there are the Elie Nadelman figure, a reclining nude by Aristide Maillol, the Matisse backs, Auguste Rodin's *Balzac,* and a Henry Moore. Other pieces have had long tenures in particular places and are now missed, such as the Picasso goat, a Gaston Lachaise figure, and a George Rickey (on the uppermost terrace, discussed below). In recent years Barnett Newman's *Broken Obelisk* and a Hector Guimard Metro sign have also become fixtures. As Mildred Schmertz, the former editor of *Architectural Record,* pointed out in an article on the Pelli addition, the recent loss of the upper terraces added by Johnson in 1964 and a normal acquisitiveness and desire to display as much as possible have recently resulted in crowding too many disparate pieces into the garden, with a resultant loss of relative importance, focus, and quality in the aesthetic experience of both garden and sculpture.[15] Anyone who visited the garden between 1954 and 1982, however, was treated to an experience of clarity and intensity. Each sculpture could be seen separately and in conjunction with another that helped to illuminate the particular qualities of both. An example of this that can still be seen is Nadelman's sophisticated little man, leaning on his staff (or is it Quixote and his lance? a picador? a gondolier or sailor?), gazing off into space toward Maillol's enormous woman, who is floating (or falling, or reclining) by the basin against the curtain of beech leaves. He is vertical, she is horizontal; both are figurative and bronze. They occupy space and our imaginations so differently. It is hard to conceive of the garden without them, for they have become part of its structure.

In the 1960s this space also had two figures by Lachaise staring across the garden at cross purposes and at right angles to the Nadelman and Maillol pieces. One, a giantess standing with arms akimbo atop the L-shaped entry terrace, has now disappeared along with the terrace. The other, a familiar floating figure, smaller, more mysterious, with legs trailing off to the side like a mermaid's tail, was placed against the 54th Street wall at the base of the steps from the café terrace looking back toward the garden entry. The tight and provocative arrangement of these four figures was even improved by shifting the Maillol figure in the 1964 revision to the position where it is now. So too, other sculptures became more than artistic objects in space. They helped to shape portions of the garden, giving it particular character and foci, meaning and purpose.

THE ADDITION OF 1964

A decade later, MOMA's trustees decided to expand the galleries to the east on the site of several more townhouses acquired by the Rocke-fellers. Johnson received the architectural commission. In the course of producing this work he also reorganized and redesigned the entire ground floor and entry area. At the same time he added a new eastern extension to the garden behind a new wing of the museum. Just as the initial garden of 1939 had extended east beyond the actual gallery build-ing, occupying space behind adjoining buildings that were in Rockefel-ler ownership, so too did this new garden extension go beyond the new gallery wing to the east. A formal design problem posed by this new extension dovetailed neatly with a functional and programmatic desire of the museum, namely how to create as much gallery and service space as possible (indoors and out) within the relatively narrow site without crowding the garden and view from some of the upper-level gallery spaces. The garden was so nearly perfect in its parts and composition that it was hard to imagine expanding it in some fundamental way. For reasons already explained, the garden was a set piece with each part contributing to a strong and integrated composition. It seemed difficult to add or subtract sculptures, to have temporary exhibitions, or to show some of the newer and larger works that sculptors were beginning to make more commonly out of doors.

At the same time, a review of Johnson's work in the early 1960s also reveals that despite his continuing belief that Mies was the great-est living architect, he was also slowly but steadily moving out from under his direct influence and exploring other design strategies and concerns. Several of the sources of his new development were in fact those architects who had been of great influence on Mies in his own development, such as Wright and Karl Friedrich Schinkel. Others were contemporaries whose work was getting a lot of press and with whom Johnson rubbed shoulders while teaching at Yale and the University of

Pennsylvania, such as Louis Kahn and Paul Rudolph, or in his Manhattan social and professional life, such as Eero Saarinen and Edward Larrabee Barnes. Johnson was growing and changing; so too was MOMA, and again a felicitous match was made. In conjunction with the addition of a new wing to the east, he solved the problem of how to add space to both museum and garden in one stroke: he raised the addition in two levels—first, to the level of the entry and café terrace, and second, a full (gallery) story above. In so doing he also solved a problem of the first scheme, and that was the somewhat static east boundary with its thin wall of green. This had always been a bit of a fudge, not as clearly "correct" in a Miesian sense as the rest of the composition.

Now too, Johnson could also remove the conifers between the pools that seemed a little too heavy, bristly, and incongruous, and replace them with a marvelous screen of beeches. Over time, several of Fanning's experiments proved unsuccessful. The conifers did not thrive in their urban situation; they also became leggy, allowing too much visual transparency, failing in their role as a screen wall. The ericaceous shrubs planted beneath the hinoki were likewise not as happy as those on Long Island or Connecticut, and when seen in isolation at such close quarters were too coarse and discordant. Fanning had settled into obscurity by the time Johnson was asked to expand the museum galleries and garden, and it had become clear that the existing planting needed editing, revision, and fine-tuning. A new landscape consultant of some sort was needed to help with this aspect of the garden.

In 1961 Robert Zion was hired to consult with Johnson on the expansion.[16] He has been on an annual retainer to MOMA ever since as an advisor on matters to do with the garden. Zion was an apt choice; the chemistry between the two was good and they subsequently worked together on numerous public and private commissions. Today, Zion is well known as one of America's leading landscape architects of the past thirty years, with a large body of public and private work to his credit. At that time, however, he was breaking into the New York scene with more energy and talent than portfolio. Like Johnson, he had a degree from Harvard's Graduate School of Design and had been imbued with a refined sense of modernism. Also like Johnson, he has throughout his career demonstrated a sensibility and instinct for elegance, clear structural organization, and a feeling and subtlety in the use of materials. Put simply, he has a fine eye and sharp, incisive design sense. Also to the point here, he was deeply interested in horticulture and landscape construction technology. His *Trees for Architecture and the Landscape*, published four years after the new garden was complete, demonstrates his comprehensive grasp of the craft and technical issues of urban planting, and it is replete with examples of his research and innovations that date from this period.[17]

Even though his role was constrained—Johnson was to remain the lead designer and sought only limited help regarding plants—Zion's contribution was significant. Several of the planting areas of the earlier scheme were completely replaced with different material in new arrangements, while heavy editing and a reduction of the variety of plants occurred, as well as the creation of new areas of planting associated with the expansion. The importance of the relatively few plants cannot be overemphasized. For a space that is almost entirely paved and bounded by masonry, it feels more like a small park than a piazza or atrium. This combination of planting usually associated with gardens, green parks, or squares (in the London sense) with a thoroughly modern masonry environment was to lead the way to the next generation of American public plazas by Lawrence Halprin, M. Paul Friedberg, Daniel Kiley, and Zion himself.[18]

Zion's principal contribution was to rip out Fanning's hinoki that occupied the all-important center position and replace them with a group of weeping European beeches, underplanted with Japanese andromeda (*Pieris japonica*)—entirely changing and improving the composition. These trees, deciduous in winter, form a pendulous veil of smooth gray stems, branches, and trunks that is particularly harmonious in color and texture with the walls and pavement, while contrasting sharply in their highly nervous linear silhouette with the calm planes and rectangles of the masonry. In summer their dark-green leaves form an absolutely opaque planar screen that supports the De Stijl organization of space. Next, his use of European weeping birches in ground cover on the east between the original lower terrace and the new, raised upper extension turned what had been an isolated event (the other birches of Fanning) into a major, recurrent theme, giving a slipped mirror quality to the planting and a subtle reinforcement to Johnson's strategies. Finally, Zion chose to use the tallest trees possible to end the upper terrace—Lombardy poplars—again, not bothering to try (as Fanning had) to use evergreen material, or to attempt to screen out buildings that would always make their presence felt one way or the other. Instead, he chose to put something dynamic in front of them as a screen, to attract one's attention to its surface, color, and texture, even though one could see through, beyond, or above if one chose to.

In addition to Zion's revision of the original planting scheme, Johnson also modified one of the basic architectural elements, adding an extra four feet to the height of the 54th Street boundary wall. Rarely today do architects have the privilege of such fine-tuning of the proportions in their built work. Clearly the combination of the wall and plane trees was not considered entirely successful in screening the bustling street and variety of row houses beyond. Raising the wall from ten to fourteen feet, however, did produce an absolutely effective "roofless room," as Johnson has often referred to it.

Again, as in the original garden, a sculpture—that of a coiled snake of stone—has become associated with the birch grove, and is just as much a key part of the ensemble as the Nadelman at the opposite end. As in the case of the other peripheral screens of vegetation, now there was a raised space behind the new birch grove—a rectangle positioned at ninety degrees to the rest of the garden. This new space was a different size, orientation, and character from the other four pinwheeling spaces. Better still, in its size and openness it was the inverse of the raised café terrace with its irregular plantation of hornbeams at the other end. In a sense, however, these two now provided the missing balance and counterpoint to the four shifted spaces of the main lower terrace.

Finally, Johnson made a move not appreciated by many, including, it seems, the museum's own leaders and personnel, and certainly not, as we will see, by César Pelli and Mildred Schmertz. Johnson created a grand and handsome stairway against the eastern end (side wall) of this new terrace and connected it to another new upper terrace that was the largest and most open of all. One and a half stories above the street he ended the sequence of spaces with a wall of green toward St. Thomas's church and the buildings of Fifth Avenue. Together with the curators he placed a marvelous kinetic sculpture by Rickey in the corner above the entry landing and bottom of the stair. These two oscillating vertical shafts ("lines") were the tallest work in the garden collection and were placed on the highest point in conjunction with a visitor's vertical ascent. Climbing to this terrace one could encounter the latest sculpture or work to have been acquired or on loan, often a behemoth. From this elevated spot one could turn and look back on the entire garden and trace the path of one's progress through it. As in eighteenth-century landscape gardens such as Stourhead, where one makes a circuit to an eminence and returns, particularly as in the descent from the Temple of Apollo, one saw things in a new and different light. It was tempting to make a circuit of the lower garden again. Some saw this last terrace as a cul-de-sac; others saw it as a fulfilling journey's end with an ever-changing perspective. For a brief period the museum allowed visitors to move in and out of a door from the gallery adjacent to this uppermost terrace, and people had the convenience and pleasure of finding an alternative way back through the galleries. Or, vice versa, they could come out at this upper terrace and wind their way down to the lobby through the garden. Additionally, during the Wednesday evening summer garden concerts of the 1960s and 1970s, this upper terrace was a particularly favorable spot.[19]

In a sense Johnson had found a way out of Mies's box. Like William Kent he had leapt the garden fence, and like Kent his solution was willful, almost awkward, and successful. As he wrote in his 1965 article "Whence and Whither," he had become more and more concerned about aspects of the processional in architecture:

> The problem was to make possible bigger crowds than before. It was approached as a problem of procession. Confine the crowds as little as possible. The design result is almost Beaux-Arts axial. A clear main axial view into the garden from the street. A cross axis leading to the galleries right and left. . . . In the garden we had more luck with the vertical. We took space enough for STAIRS in the old sense. We hope people will climb stairs, an experience lost in modern architecture, the ramps of the great Le Corbusier being the noble exception. In our garden about two domestic stories are climbed by many who would never go to the attic of a suburban house without complaining. It is the experience of the change of direction of what one sees as one rises.

The speed of ascent (slow in the Museum stairs) is crucial. Time to look around, to feel the change that a rise gives. The curiosity of what is on top, the question: What will I see from up there? The comfort of slow, obvious, and wide ascent. All of these considerations are more important than the "looks" of the stairway. Architecture is motion.[20]

Later in the same essay he went on to say:

I purposely exaggerate the processional aspects, which in reality are not obvious to the casual visitor. But then what is obvious to a visitor about the qualities of architecture? . . . The whence and whither is primary. Now almost secondary is all our ordinary work, our work on forms, our plans, our elevations. What we should do is to proceed on foot again and again through our imagined buildings. Then after months of approaching and reapproaching, and looking and turning, then only draw them up for the builder. We should constantly ask ourselves: Am I lost? Did I enjoy that corner I just took? What is overhead? How long to get to the end? What if I turn my eyes back? Will opening and closing, vertical and horizontal, depress me or inspire me?[21]

For all of the spatial manipulation and subtlety in Mies's architecture, there was also a certain hermetic, self-contained quality. This is especially true in his most accomplished and paradigmatic works. Johnson was looking for threads that would lead out of this maze toward some destination, whether it be epiphany or caprice. The desire for a satisfactory termination to movement and the creation of worthy goals at the end of rich journeys permeates his work at this time.[22]

I can no longer build glass boxes. . . . We live in another era. Like the old Beaux Arts men in my youth, yearning for their *partis* and *entourages,* I now look back with pleasure, and yes, even some nostalgia, on the days in the twenties when the battle line was clear, the modern versus the eclectic, the dreams of universal panaceas, standards, types, norms, that would "solve" architecture. Now we know that we cannot "solve" anything. The only principle that I can conceive of believing is the Principle of Uncertainty. . . . I cannot find any shapes to copy, and forms like the good old Malevich or Mondrian 1920 ones to fit in.[23]

Accompanying this statement of 1961 was his scheme for the Sheldon Memorial Art Gallery in Lincoln, Nebraska, which, when combined with the material on Karl Friedrich Schinkel delivered in his talk in Berlin the same year, makes clear that the model for this museum, despite his allusion to paintings by Robert Delaunay or the Gothic arcade of the church of Saint-Séverin in Paris, is a variation and distortion of the Altes Museum in Berlin. At the same moment of his declaration of apostasy, however, he also published the scheme for his scaled-down folly, a pavilion he was in the process of building in the pond at his New Canaan estate. Here, more than ever, he presented the pinwheeling squares and rectangles of early modernism, clothed in references to Moorish pavilions (Alhambra) and mosques (Cordoba) and to the moon-viewing platforms and pavilions of China and Japan. It is a rare instance of his acknowledging the parallel results, if not inspiration, of Far Eastern architecture, garden connoisseurship, and aesthetics with his aristocratic and refined modernism.[24] As in his first garden design, several rectangular planes spiral about a center, here occupied by a basin and jet that sends water out in all directions through runnels that divide and subdivide the surfaces, reinforcing and playing against the division of space suggested by columns and roofs in syncopation with the floor.

At MOMA, the high marble wall at the end of the revised garden, with the great climbing stair and its two uneven runs of steps leading to a large open stone platform with art rather than an altar, is ironically closer to aspects of an early Schinkelesque project of Mies than to his later work, and clearly relates directly to the more atavistic and classical tendencies in his work. Grand stairs that ascend to exhibition space (and enlightenment) have a long association with cultural settings in general, and to museums in particular since their establishment in the nineteenth century. Consider those in Munich and Berlin by Leo von Klenze and Schinkel, Robert Smirke's British Museum in London, Richard Morris Hunt and McKim, Mead & White's Metropolitan in New York, etc. Even more to the point are the palaces, villa gardens, and classical sites of the Mediterranean and the many stately stairs that rise, pause, turn, and rise again. From the Minoan palace at Knossos and the Acropolis in Athens to the Villa Lante and Palazzo Farnese, from the interior circulation of the Bishop's Palace in Würzburg to the pilgrim's path at the Basilika Vierzehnheiligen in Bavaria, Western architecture, whether sacred or secular, contains a vast repertory of ascending paths and stair compositions. One of the figures that Johnson has acknowledged being particularly attracted to at this time of the addition was that of the early nineteenth-century neoclassicist Schinkel.[25] As in Johnson's Roofless Church in New Harmony, Indiana, and several other projects of this period, he was particularly courting comparison and consciously evoking religious settings of antiquity. It was direct, simple-seeming, and abstract. It was there for those who saw it. In addition, this revision—an addition, really—resolved a psychological problem of closure and perpetual motion in his first iteration of the garden. It also allowed the museum and its visitors to see and enjoy large and temporary installations not possible in the earlier garden. It was fully integrated into the exhibition scheme and cultural agenda of the museum physically, didactically, and aesthetically.

THE CÉSAR PELLI ADDITION OF 1984

Marcel Duchamp once said that paintings only live for about thirty years and after that they die.[26] With the exception of a few masterpieces it is a rare work of art that works continuously for each successive generation. Many are rediscovered and subsequently revered, or continuously honored, but rarely can they mean to later generations what they meant to those who made them. Because gardens tend to outlive their authors, they often are revered or merely liked for reasons quite different or only partly related to their original intentions and qualities. Likewise, because they are so fragile, so little understood, and subject to rapid physical change, including growth, erosion, and decline, they are frequently altered beyond recognition or destroyed within one generation of their creation. It is partly for this reason that we treasure those few Renaissance gardens or the handful of Colonial estates that come down to us intact and have not been dismembered.

It is not surprising to report, therefore, that as the founding generation at MOMA passed on, or lost their focus and interest, and as the art
world changed and the museum became less the center of new and progressive events and drifted into the position of keeper of the flame of a
particular brand of modernism, now a historic period, while remaining
the locus of a social scene for the middle class and an old-guard segment
of New York, the new generation of trustees and administrators would
wish to expand and consolidate the collection and physical premises. In
the late 1970s a fundraising venture was launched to ensure financial
security for the future. Ambitious plans were made for the creation of a
revenue-producing mid-block residential tower, new galleries, additional
storage and work space, and enlarged members' club, shops, and cafés.
This time Johnson was not asked to do the work, for he was now a fellow
trustee and enormously busy with his ever-burgeoning practice. After
a feasibility study by Richard Weinstein and a set of attractive preliminary design studies by Jaquelin T. Robertson and a gifted assistant,
Thierry Despont, the project was launched.[27] On receiving planning
approvals, César Pelli, then dean of the Yale School of Architecture,
was given the commission to carry out the work. This discussion will be
concerned only with the effects on the garden and will not attempt to
deal with the merits of the tower or other new facilities except as they
affect the garden and Johnson's earlier work related to it.

Put simply, the additions of 1984 not only truncated the garden but
also encroached on it in several ways that have changed its character,
meaning, function, and quality. The result has been the nearly complete destruction of what Johnson had achieved. To be sure, several of
the terraces, trees, and sculptures remain physically. To the ignorant
and uninformed it presents an attractive picture, but a masterpiece has
been ruined forever. Since the additions of 1984 were executed by a
world-famous architect and have been praised in the *New York Times*
and architectural journals, what is the basis for the charge that it has
been altered for the worse and is beyond repair?

The 1984 additions have been presented as improvements that pre-
served the garden.[28] It is true that the tall residential tower was skillfully kept to the southwest, on the 53rd Street side of the block, leaving
the old Whitney Museum by Auguste Noel, itself a handsome Miesian
structure, terminating the garden on the west. The café adjacent to the

small, raised west terrace, however, has been turned into a temporary exhibition gallery, with no particular relationship to the garden, changing the use, purpose, pedestrian movement, and relationships at this end. More drastic is the elimination of the entire upper terrace and stair on the east, which terminated the garden of 1964 and gave it the release and overview described above. In its place a two-story structure—public café on the ground floor and a private members' restaurant and dining balcony above—has been constructed. This has had several effects on the scheme: first, the loss of a terrace and its vertical dimension (not to mention what the terrace had accomplished); second, it has turned the marvelous mid-level terrace on the east, which was one of the most delightful spaces for exhibition with its north–south orientation and position between the upper and lower spaces, into a large dining terrace and terminus; third, whatever advantages the balcony overlook from the members' lounge retains from the scheme of Johnson, this space has been removed from the general public and the experience of gallery visitation or circulation.

There is no question, therefore, that it is no longer an integral part of the museum's pedagogical and artistic agenda. At most it is of little import beyond the enhancement of dining. The garden, its design, and the collection of sculpture have been reduced to the role of decoration or of Muzak for the eyes. The selling of food and the social activity associated with the two cafés are now considered to be far more important than the quality, extent, and scope of the sculpture collection. Finally, this new structure facing back toward the old Whitney and its former café room and terrace reveals a design sensibility and imagination with different standards, ideals, and habits, which if not ignorant of the aesthetics and subtleties of Johnson's scheme in particular and that of Mies in general, surely disagrees with them, for the designer has placed little value on them. The placement of this restaurant building, which in its frontality toward the garden forms a book-end twin to the former café framing the garden symmetrically, absolutely crushes the quiet and sophisticated series of diagonal shifts, the openness and the light touch that had prevailed before. The Beaux-Arts formal strategies that Johnson and his generation so adroitly escaped have returned to destroy one of his most sophisticated works.

The last, and possibly most disastrous, encroachment of Pelli's is

that of the so-called new Garden Hall. The name itself is a verbal trav-
esty worthy of the US military. Part of the design strategy of Johnson's
1964 masterpiece was to open up the flow of circulation between the
lobby and the original L-shaped upper garden walk and terrace. The
strategic placement of a clump of trees both signaled the garden just
beyond the doorway without allowing a clear view into it and modified
the direction of the circulation, shifting the axial movement diagonally
down into the garden to the right, or around it to the left, albeit out of
doors within the garden space. Johnson had spent a lot of time thinking
about movement and studying classical, as well as eighteenth- and nineteenth-century, sites between his first garden scheme and the second.
As Peter Eisenman has remarked about him at this period, "Entry—the
problem of the door in the wall and the approach to the wall—is fundamental to the nature of Johnson's architecture."[29]

Coinciding with his abiding interest in corners and glass, with their
duality of transparency and reflection, between completion of his first
garden scheme and the second, Johnson began to move away from fron-
talism, developing instead an abiding affection for, and continuous use
and reference to, oblique movement and approach. He has written eloquently on the subject, putting forward a notion that others as different as Theo van Doesburg, Louis Kahn, and Christian Norberg-Schulz
have also expressed, namely that architecture is not really the design of
space, but rather the organization of procession, that it exists in *time*.[30]
Interestingly enough, Pelli has also given lectures and written about the
issues of transparency, reflection, and procession, and these phenomena
have played a role in many of his most interesting works, such as the
Pacific Design Center in Los Angeles, the Winter Garden in Niagara
Falls, the Commons in Columbus, Indiana, and at MOMA. Movement
and the flow of large crowds were a central issue, driving much of Pelli's
reworking of the museum's interior and its additions. Unfortunately, his
principal device to accommodate and reorganize the vertical movement
of visitors came at the expense of Johnson's garden and its relationship
to the building both visually and physically.

Pelli appropriated the narrow upper peripheral terrace, which had
functioned as both landing and threshold within the garden, and placed
a massive set of escalators up and down outside the former wall of the
Stone and Goodwin building. He then draped a glass tent over it that

climbs up, back, and over the other original building terraces and roofs. Having then removed a significant part of the garden by moving the building out into it and eliminating the oblique relationship of the main floor to the central garden pavement and with it the vegetated bank, steps, and screen of trees originally seen from the entryway on 53rd Street, and also by having moved the garden doors to the east to get them out of the way of large crowds now using the escalators, Pelli had created a problem of how to enter the truncated garden. An expedient solution was adopted. A new landing was shoved out into the garden immediately adjacent to the central screen of weeping beech trees. This landing consisted of a symmetrical pair of steps to the left and right with a clumsy parapet directly opposite the doors. Considering the layout and circulation of the original garden, this is a most unfortunate entry location. The stair was so ugly and awkward to use that it has since been altered, but to no better result. It is simply a bad thing in the wrong place.

It would be hard to imagine a more clumsy or destructive set of architectural gestures in what was once one of the most sophisticated, intimate, and quiet spaces in New York City or urban America. The entire weight of the building with all its additions now crashes down hard against the entire length of the south side of the garden, with hordes of staring people riding up and down on escalators, and a ham-fisted stair resembling a bunker in the alleyway that has been produced. Few single gestures could have been so destructive to the character and structure of the garden. To say "the garden is still there, lovely as ever," as was written when it was reopened in 1984, indicates how little people who write for architectural magazines know or understand about design in general and landscape design in particular.[31]

WHAT DOES IT MATTER?

> The role of the critic is to test a work of art from the point of view of significance and value. To do this, however, the critic must first understand the work of art. . . . True criticism must always serve a set of values.[32]

The physical destruction of Johnson's garden is relatively easy to document. The equal transformation and erosion of its meaning and purpose

are possibly more difficult to demonstrate, but are just as real and unfortunate. To do so one must ask why the museum and Johnson chose
to build the garden as they did at one particular time, and then why
at a later date the administration chose to change it as they did. To
answer the first, one must address what the sculpture garden was for,
and what point of view or thesis served. Here one must also speculate
on Johnson's ideas concerning landscape gardens, sculpture, and the
relationship between architecture and nature on the one hand and connoisseurship on the other. In doing so one must reflect on the attitudes
toward all of these issues on the part of Alfred Barr, the director of the
museum, of the Rockefeller family, who were the principal patrons of
the institution in its various building ventures, and of Mies, the spiritual
mentor of Johnson at the time.

A great deal can be learned about Johnson's evolution from Harvard student to architectural critic and curator, to architectural student,
apprentice to a master, to architect in his own right, and finally to arbiter
of taste and architectural guru, by reading the texts and commentary in
the collection of his writings edited by Robert Stern.[33] Although much
of it is self-serving and by now is seriously incomplete, as it stops fifteen
years ago, nevertheless one can develop answers to several of the questions posed above. Namely, like Cole Porter and numerous notables of
his generation, Johnson, the son of a well-to-do family in the Midwest,
was launched on a trajectory toward self-fulfillment and a search for
refinement that was to become a lifelong endeavor. Formative teachers
at Harvard and its art history department at the Fogg, plus a period of
time spent in Europe between the two world wars, helped to shape his
instincts for elegance and matters of style. Moving with the demimonde
and patronized by the wealthy who were interested in art and the avant-
garde, he found it easy to embrace the traditional urban sophisticate's
attitude toward rural retreat and nature, which from Augustan Rome to
the present might be characterized as Virgilian pastoralism. It is not an
accident, but extremely deliberate and meaningful, that one of the two
works of art displayed for contemplation in his rural glass pavilion in
Connecticut, overlooking a pond and a folly of his making, is one of two
versions of *The Burial of Phocion* by Nicolas Poussin. A quintessentially
stoic, pastoral painting executed in Rome in the 1640s, it depicts the
body of a general who for his defiance of a corrupt government was exe-

cuted and refused burial within the ancient city of Athens. His corpse is shown being carried out into a romantic landscape of great beauty, largely based on the Roman Campagna immediately north of the Porta del Popolo, along the Tiber. In his own manner and career Johnson has comported himself as one of the last of the Roman patricians, disdaining the popular, the easy way, and cheapness and sloppiness in any sphere.

The more recent and controversial work of his architectural practice is of no concern here, but even in this, what may pass for a pose of audacity or cynicism is in many ways an outgrowth of a self-confidence in his own intellect and values that comes across in the leveling atmosphere of egalitarian America today as hauteur. In terms of landscape design it would seem that he holds many of the views of the eighteenth-century landed gentry, but unlike them he lives in the twentieth century and is deeply informed of everything that has transpired since, especially in architecture. Also like the artists, architects, and patrons of earlier eras, and unlike most contemporary professionals, he was well traveled, broadly educated, and knew the best gardens, courts, terraces, and buildings, public and private, in Europe and America firsthand when he entered practice. His choice of Mies as his architectural role model rather than Wright, Le Corbusier, or Gropius seems easy to understand. Mies was the most ascetic and controlled of the great twentieth-century architects. His work was very sophisticated, and in its systematic elimination of excess and resultant classical restraint, calm, resolution, and strength it was for Johnson (and many others) by far the most spiritual and sensual model. It was functional, and beyond function. It was rich, but in a sophisticate's cool manner. It was more of an acquired taste and in many ways more private, another appealing aspect. It was both intellectual and hedonistic. It was for snobs, yet was obviously better than the work of many who were more liked. Mies's colors were muted and clear; his structures and forms were also. It was never loud, jumpy, busy, fussy, or muddled, and never, ever, bourgeois.

It is difficult to say with absolute certainty what were all the factors that led to the change in sensibility on the part of the museum and its leaders that allowed Pelli's drastic transformation of the garden. Unquestionably the most important was the change in leadership and the aging of the institution. Alfred Barr, who helped create the first garden for the museum in the late 1930s and was director when Johnson created its successors, was a champion of modern art, especially that of prewar Europe and of American artists who pioneered abstraction and developed out of this tradition after the war. For him MOMA was a cause, an educational mission, and all its activities, buildings, and acquisitions were part of a continuous and integrated didactic program: the presentation of modern art. The sculpture gardens were clearly seen as an integral part of the curatorial and exhibition realm. They were not merely social spaces. Johnson's two garden schemes fit beautifully into Barr's vision of the museum.

As for the Rockefellers and other board members, many had been lifelong gardeners and converts to modern art under the tutelage of people like Barr, and were avid collectors of paintings, sculpture, and architecture. The estates, country houses, and art these people owned were expressions of their adherence to the patrician traditions of collecting, connoisseurship, urban sophistication, and Virgilian pastoralism that I have attributed to Johnson. The collective energy and zeal of this group in its presentation of things modern, in particular European art and design, seems to have run its course by the mid-1970s. The work of artists such as Picasso, Miró, and Matisse, of Pollack, Kline, and de Kooning, of architects such as Gropius, Mies, and Wright, was so generally accepted in America by then that the museum, along with the commercial galleries, was scrambling to find new and pioneering work. In architecture a backlash had set in, leading to postmodernism and deconstruction. New figural work of several varieties had emerged along with conceptual and site art. The museum found itself in the same situation as that of older museums when it had begun. It was a rambling institution in possession of a large body of historic artifacts that no longer had the novelty of being new, different, or particularly contemporary.

At the same time, a whole generation had been raised believing in the centrality of MOMA in the cultural life of New York. It was enormously popular and had become a social scene for the middle class as well as for its patrons and socialites. Like the museums and parks of Paris in the nineteenth century, it had lost its edge as an innovative force but played a role in the social life of the upper and middle classes, largely as a place to go, to socialize, and—like the club it had become—

to eat, drink, and gossip. During this same period, large temporary exhibitions that attracted enormous crowds and generated vast sums of money became common in the museum world. These "blockbuster" exhibitions changed the character and management habits of many museums around the world. At MOMA a new generation of curators emerged. A new director was named. Board members retired and were replaced. New additions to handle the crowds, to get them in and out, move them up and downstairs quickly and in large volumes—both in the galleries and for food and drink—and the revenue-producing tower project moved ahead. The sheer weight of numbers and the desire to pack them in probably would have wrecked the garden and altered the museum for the worse as an aesthetic experience no matter who the architect was or whatever their scheme. We will never know what the alternatives might have been. Certainly the carefully constructed sculpture garden, where each piece could be seen quietly and in a particular relationship to the others and as part of an exhibition regime, went by the board.

Finally one must ask, why was MOMA's garden important as a work of art and landscape design? The answer is because it was so good and so original. It became an inspiring example to other designers, and has rarely, if ever, been surpassed. It was—and even in its fragmentary state still is—beautiful. It was one of the very best modernist outdoor spaces ever made, using a few clear principles and strategies, an economy of means, and a limited palette of elegant materials. It is a lesson in sophistication.

How original was it really? Although one can point to a handful of modernist landscape designs done in the United States prior to the Second World War, by 1953 very little survived, and with the exception of Thomas Church and Garrett Eckbo on the West Coast no one was doing anything like this. The domestic work of James Rose, Garrett Eckbo, and others was formed in conjunction with problems of changing social settings in suburbia, new low-cost materials, and formal gestures derived from School of Paris abstraction and late surrealist paintings. Johnson singlehandedly introduced the Miesian mode to landscape design in the United States,[34] in this case within the difficult problem of urban development and the architectural room, a genre that had been explored by Mies but remained unrealized. Mies's studies also contained other ideas of spatial structure and arrangement that play out in his work from the earliest houses through the IIT campus plan studies. It was only after this well-known, much-visited garden by Johnson was created that a whole generation of landscape architects in America embarked on a series of designs that utilize similar De Stijl, Bauhaus, and Miesian organizational strategies. Most notably these are the work of Daniel Kiley (the Miller and Hamilton Houses, the Oakland Museum of Art, and the Ford Foundation headquarters), M. Paul Friedberg (Jacob Riis Plaza Playground; Pershing Park in Washington, DC), and Lawrence Halprin (McIntyre Garden; the Portland fountains and squares).

While one must always be cautious about ascribing influences of one project or person to others, the fact remains that people are influenced by the things they see and ideas that are in the air. Built works of quality, spirit, and freshness are inspiring, and give other professionals the courage of their convictions, often showing them a way out of their own current situation. Few projects, if any, by this particular generation of landscape architects directly resemble the MOMA garden. In fact, very few are as good. Certainly almost none were built with such fine materials and with such a fine degree of proportion and elegance— trademarks of nearly all of Johnson's early work. There is, however, an absolute devotion to the dynamic, pinwheeling spatial structure, constructed of overlapping and intersecting rectangles of space, of shifted volumes and pure forms, that characterize the work of one project after another of these men and others. It must be noted that many leaders of the postwar generation of landscape architects (Halprin, Kiley, Zion, Hideo Sasaki, Richard Haag) had all been associated with Harvard's Graduate School of Design during the same era, or just after Johnson was there.[35] Of all of them, it was Johnson who first put the principles expounded by Gropius, Christopher Tunnard, Serge Chermayeff, and other faculty critics of the GSD into practice in the making of a thoroughly modern and successful urban space.

Henry James once remarked that there are three questions that a critic or historian should ask of any artist: What was he trying to do? How well did he succeed? Was it worth the effort? Hopefully, the preceding discussion has addressed the first two of these. In answer to the last, which implies judgments of quality and achievement, the answer is affirmative. Johnson's garden was an excellent work. I challenge the reader to name a single urban outdoor space created since the Second World War that is better qualitatively. Several of the spaces that came later, and which set out to accomplish other goals, may be as good despite being totally different. Halprin's Auditorium Forecourt Fountain in Portland, now known as the Ira Keller Fountain, or Freeway Park in Seattle, Zion's Paley Park, and one or two courtyard gardens by Isamu Noguchi compare well, but it would be hard to demonstrate that they are more successful on any level, whether it be formal, aesthetic, programmatic, or that of craft. The MOMA garden is, or was before being truncated, a masterpiece, both timeless and absolutely modern, up to the minute. It was—and is, despite serious architectural blunders that changed its situation, spatial organization, and meaning—beautiful to look at, to move about and be within. It should be considered one of the few landscape-design masterpieces of the modern movement, and a contribution by Ludwig Mies van der Rohe and Philip Johnson to the evolution of landscape design and urbanism.

WHAT I DO WHEN I CAN DO IT

Representation in Recent Work

(1999)

I am a practicing landscape architect and am, therefore, an heir to the legacy of ideas, conventions, and practices of earlier eras in both Western Europe and Asia as well as the United States. There are several points to make before offering examples of how recent work of my office might embody such a concept (or phenomenon) as that of the *immediate garden and the larger landscape.* The first is that as often as not we do not consciously consider such things when at work; that is, much of the activity and product of contemporary landscape design is not intentionally laden with ideas or invested with devices of representation, but rather has as its expressed purpose that of solving technical, physical, social, and functional problems, with some modicum of aesthetic consideration. To a degree, also, landscape architects (including ourselves) commonly act on received theories and intentions that are current and fashionable in their time. As one wag has put it, "If you say you are not interested in theory, you are probably acting upon someone else's theory." The second point is that even when contemporary designers do consider the possibility of representation and of positioning their work in the hope that it might be seen as a work of art (for better or worse) and that it might communicate some particular (or general) meaning, for many today (including myself) there is a tendency to abstraction

From *Studies in the History of Gardens & Designed Landscapes,* special issue, "The Immediate Garden and the Larger Landscape," 19.1 (1999): 102–21.

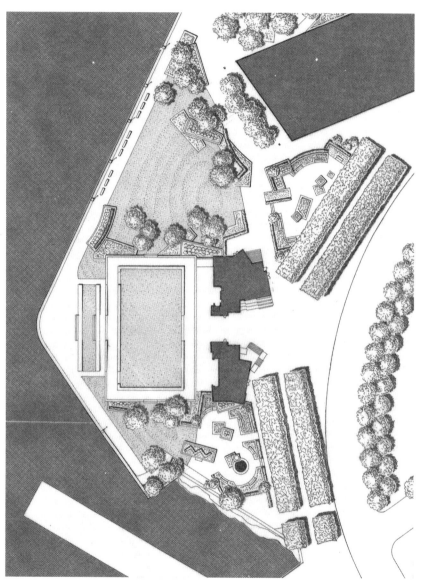

Final plan for Robert Wagner Jr. Park, Battery Park City, New York, 1993

and formal concerns that eschew some of the most traditional devices of representation and iconography, namely the use of words or quotations and symbolic figures or allegorical sculpture. Also, because gardens, landscapes, and their common elements—plants, masonry, earth, water—are not parts of speech or language, they do not literally speak or say anything. That they can convey ideas through their evocation of other places, things, or experiences, through their structure, arrangement of parts, and selection of elements, however, is well established. As in other human endeavors, they may express some things the author intends as well as others that are subconscious or not intended.

To see the two projects I wish to present in context, a general understanding of contemporary professional practices, in particular the work of our office, may be useful. We design and administer the construction of gardens, parks, campuses, estates, and portions of cities. We do not actually build them, as we are not contractors, nurserymen, or gardeners, any more than architects are bricklayers, manufacturers, or contractors. Mostly we go to meetings, visit sites, draw and make studies of what might be, what one could do or build, write technical and legal specifications, and draw up contract documents for construction. We visit nurseries in search of decent plants, write letters, answer the phone, and tear out our hair. Although things *are* busy in the spring and autumn planting seasons in the American Northeast, since our clients are located all over the country and the work consists of urban design and structures, pavements, roads, water features, and earthworks, as well as the selection and use of plants, we are busy at all times of the year, not just seasonally.

Our office has been blessed with an interesting and diverse list of clients, only a handful of whom might actually have been interested in the potential of representation and meaning in the environment. The work executed over the past twenty years has been wide-ranging in kind, size, and ambition. A sampling would include: contained gardens, such as one done to accompany a historic house renovation on Pacific Heights in San Francisco, literally a large backyard; gardens and parks in broader settings, such as Bryant Park in midtown Manhattan and Pershing Square in Los Angeles; urban rescue and rehabilitation projects; estates and residential developments in the Midwest, the Southeast, and Florida; as well as the creation of settings or broader urban fabric, such as Battery Park City in lower Manhattan, which amounts to the creation of an open space system, development guidelines, and execution of portions of the system—other examples of which are the Siedlung Goldstein social housing complex in Frankfurt, Germany, which included reworking a local planning authority's plan and execution of the scheme with all of its public and private spaces; Mission Bay, a 250-acre urban redevelopment on San Francisco Bay; and Playa Vista, a 1,000-acre urban development scheme in Los Angeles with 240 acres of reconstructed wetlands, a three-mile riparian corridor and stream, neighborhood parks, streets, and squares.[1]

Two of the most traditional topics that landscapes or gardens may embody through their design are "ideas of place" and "ideas of order." Ideas of place usually involve the allusion or reference to distant landscapes, real or imaginary, that have some cultural significance to their author or owner—historic, mythic, heroic, nostalgic, and so on. Ideas of order are those that present attitudes or concepts of nature and the cosmos, or our interest in and re-creations of its forms and structures as we characterize and understand them at a particular time.

Examples of both can be found as early as the first century BCE in Roman villa gardens. A few days after the assassination of Julius Caesar in 44 BCE, the central conspirator, Brutus, went into hiding at his villa at Lanuvium.[2] We can never know what his thoughts were then, but we do know some of the objects of his contemplation, for Cicero gives us a brief description.[3] Among other features in a parklike garden were a portico and a stream named Eurotas. The portico was an evocation of a memorial called the Persian Stoa, or porch, which contained trophies and had been erected in Sparta to commemorate the desperate victory of the Greeks over the Persians in the early fifth century BCE; Eurotas is the name of a major river passing through the region of Laconia in southern Greece, which is the central landscape feature of the valley where Sparta lay. Far from being mere Hellenistic conceits or the sort of affectation criticized by some contemporary Romans (as characterized by Atticus in Cicero's *De legibus*, for example), these topographical references reflect Brutus's attraction to the content of Greek thought, especially Stoicism, and his fondness for both the austere landscape and the lifestyle of Sparta. A stern political credo can be read into the few simple elements of Brutus's idyllic scenery. To a receptive viewer of the period, such references to the Greek past would have caused reflection on contemporary life and problems of governance in Rome. This sort of association of ideas through the evocation of a real but distant (in time or space) landscape has recurred in subsequent periods of gardening and high literary imagination, most notably in Renaissance Italy and eighteenth-century England and Japan.

Equally compelling were gardens of Rome of the first century CE that took nature and the human condition within it as their theme. Examples range from Imperial gardens that presented tableaus such as the adventures of Odysseus and his struggles against the forces of wild and dark nature (the blinding of the Cyclops Polyphemus and the death of his helmsman in the tentacles of the monster Scylla) at the seaside establishment of Tiberius at Sperlonga, or the representation of a sweet and bucolic nature such as that created by Pliny the Younger at his villa in Tuscany.[4] Pliny tells us that his gardeners had built a miniature wilderness in the center of a hippodrome, a concoction of artificial scenery interrupting the regular hedges, paths, and architecture of the villa, created for contrast, thereby establishing what is by now the overfamiliar antinomy between the supposed orderly works of man and the irregular, wild, and negligent activity of nature. Although this has been one of the most worked-over topics in the history of landscape and garden design, each generation seems compelled to take a turn to see what it can yield anew.

I make no great claims regarding the two examples I offer from my recent work, but use them only to demonstrate the fundamental and by now almost unconscious way that designers employ these devices. The first example concerns ideas of place; the second, ideas of order.

US EMBASSY (BERLIN, GERMANY) AND IDEAS OF PLACE

> Those who need myths are indeed poor. Here the gods serve as beds or resting places as the day races across the sky. I describe and say: "This is red, this blue, this green. This is the sea, the mountain, the flowers."
>
> —Albert Camus, "Nuptials at Tipasa"

Last year we were part of a design team that won a limited competition for a new US embassy in Berlin. The competition between the lead architects for the building was stiff; it included several who are quite famous and well established—Michael McKinnell, Robert Venturi, Peter Bohlin, Robert Stern, César Pelli, and lesser-known figures such as our colleagues Buzz Yudell and John Ruble of Santa Monica, California. Since each of the buildings proposed was extremely thoughtful and all had been adequately developed to meet the program requirements and budget, I am certain that at least some part of our success was due to our invocation of the American landscape through what amounted to a sort of sequential landscape narrative. I took as a starting point the peculiar but common custom of thinking of embassy grounds as being foreign territory, that is, that the physical space of an embassy is by custom and law not really a part of the host country, but by gift and permission of the host it is extraterritorial, an extension or fragment of the land of the ambassador, and therefore subject to the laws of the ambassador's nation, an adult version of the child's "King's X," or of being "safe" by standing on a "base." For this reason embassies around the world have often been used as refuges by those seeking political asylum. In this case, although everything we might propose to plant would have to survive the specific rigor of Berlin's climate, for practical and metaphorical purposes it could be thought of as being in North America, not Germany.

Located in the former eastern sector adjacent to the now-vanished Berlin Wall, the site of the embassy faces the Tiergarten immediately adjacent to the Brandenburg Gate on Pariser Platz at the beginning of Unter den Linden; this is where the original US embassy had stood before its destruction during the fall of Berlin in 1945. The basic size and limits of the embassy were carefully prescribed by Berlin planning regulations, State Department requirements, and the competition program. The building as developed by Yudell and Ruble is an attractive modern structure that shows an appreciation of its context and the work of Berlin's greatest architect, Karl Friedrich Schinkel. Likewise, partly in memory of the close collaboration of Schinkel and Germany's greatest landscape architect, Peter Joseph Lenné, and their work on the palaces and parks at Klein Glienicke and Sanssouci, and partly in direct response to the character (or idea) of the embassy, within and upon this structure I proposed a series of gardens to evoke different portions, periods, and aspects of the American landscape. I did not, however, propose to create any literal portraits of particular places or scenes. This is to be a *broad representation* of character, not an imitation.

The sequence of gardens begins with a large enclosed space seen from the entry and viewed from several floors of offices surrounding it. A cool, shady space, it is to be filled with tall conifers—coast redwoods, native to California, and deciduous bald cypress. A path (a street or road) leads through the trees to a building the size of a house standing at the end of the street. Although it actually connects the two sides of the taller embassy wings, it appears as a separate structure and has been dubbed by my architectural colleagues as "the lodge." The ensemble is evocative of the American experience of dwelling in the wilderness, of cabins in the forest and national parks on the one hand, and of single-family houses on tree-lined streets so ubiquitous to American settlement on the other. Yet it resembles none of them. The trees, although found in nurseries in Germany and Belgium, are indigenous to North America and are characteristic of vast forests that still extend along its West and Gulf coasts. Virginia creeper and Boston ivy will climb the walls and columns. In runnels alongside the stone-paved avenue are iris, a beloved plant common to much of North America. Ericaceous shrubs such as mountain laurel, rhododendron, and azalea, also native to America, introduced and avidly grown in Western Europe for the past two hundred years, are found beneath the trees.

Cool and shady in summer, the deciduous trees shed their leaves in winter, letting in light to the courtyard and office windows, deemphasizing the parallel rows of the avenue while revealing that the conifers are planted in a circle. These alternating and ephemeral structures revealed by the cycle of seasons serve to remind the reflective visitor or government employee of the simultaneous phenomena of continuity and change within our pluralist society, and of the relationship between (and need for) structure and order on the one hand and the raw energy and diverse purposes and ambitions of those within it on the other. I do not expect many to notice how the dialectic between competing values and ideas that prevail and displace each other from time to time in our society is suggested by the opposing formal structures that ebb and flow in this simple space and garden, any more than I expect the majority to dwell on it in their daily affairs. The building utilizes words and has quotations from some of our most important documents and leaders engraved on portions of it in the most fundamental manner of such signification, but not everything needs to be spelled out all the time, at least not for everyone. If this is a bit too subtle for some, the next episode certainly is not.

The lodge is a split-level dining facility and lounge (known in the consular corps as the canteen) for various employees and officials of the chancery and embassy as well as their guests. It also functions as a bridge on several levels, linking the two sides of the courtyard. Not surprisingly, inside the lodge one finds house plants. In this case, however, they are large and memorable desert plants such as saguaro cactus, ocotillo, agaves, yucca, barrel cactus, and prickly pear. Startling in their scale and form, they are as American as cowboys and Indians. They are also evocative of the American experience, whether of pioneer struggles or of John Ford "Westerns." I am certain that nearly every European knows where they are from and could conjure some sort of image of our West from such powerful and particular stimuli.

The lodge opens out on the south into a raised back garden. Here a patio and barbecue are situated in a "backyard" complete with lawn, shrubs, and trees. More characteristic American natives are employed here: paper birches, maples, and dogwood—all as American as Levittown or Nantucket, the sort of plants and garden that could be found anywhere from Portland, Maine, to Portland, Oregon. While it looks like no one suburban garden in particular, it represents them all. I can envision the American staff having Friday happy hour here, or celebrating the Fourth of July with a large and smoky feast of pulled pork, ribs, and jambalaya.

Above these spaces, overlooking the skyline and the Tiergarten, the ambassador's suite for entertaining and private study opens out to a roof garden. Here a parterre of gravel walks, prairie grasses, and wildflowers stretches toward the horizon. The Quadriga (the winged victory, chariot, and horses) atop the Brandenburg Gate, looking oddly like a pioneer woman with her wagon of goods headed west, glides atop the waving stripes of plants with a big sky above. Here in the midst of Berlin one finds a surreal echo of the Great Plains. Sunflowers and Indian paintbrush, coreopsis and daylilies, daisies and chicory—emblems of the prairie, of the roadside ditch, of the way west, of the open road, of Lewis and Clark, Walt Whitman and Hart Crane, of Frances Parkman and John Steinbeck, Chief Joseph and Harriet Tubman—these flowers and weeds are as persistent as the wind and as hardy, as eternal as the sunlight on the glistening grasses, as the wide horizon and big sky one will see from here above the city.

While it was not on my mind at the time, it has since been pointed out to me that this ensemble falls within a tradition of rooftop gardens that have exploited the use of collage, extension, and appropriation, from Le Corbusier in Paris and his visual pun on the Arc de Triomphe to Giacomo Vignola's sixteenth-century scheme for the Farnese gardens on the Palatine in Rome.

This terrace is generally a quiet and a private space; nevertheless, it is also shared at times with the most important visitors, family members, and key staff. In its simplicity, openness, and humble plants it speaks to those who care for freedom and the effort that maintaining it entails. It is an American situation: a mixture of the old and new world in unexpected ways.

While no words have been spoken, no labels or artwork added to tell a story, the landscape design of this new government building, through an arrangement of its parts and the selection of particular plants, presents a reverie, humorous at times for those with the eyes to see it, regarding the American experience of landscape, while representing places thousands of miles away across the ocean.

WAGNER PARK (BATTERY PARK CITY, NEW YORK) AND IDEAS OF ORDER

> A moment always comes when one has looked too long at a landscape, just as it is a long time before one sees enough of it. Mountains, the sky, the sea are like faces whose barrenness or splendor we discover by looking rather than seeing. But in order to be eloquent every face must be seen anew.
>
> —Albert Camus, "Nuptials at Tipasa"

If the landscape of the Berlin embassy primarily evokes the larger natural and suburban landscape of America, our work at Battery Park City refers to the larger urban landscape of Manhattan, while it grows from and extends it. Wagner Park is the last portion of public open space to be designed and built as part of this 100-acre urban development on a landfill in the Hudson River just west of the Wall Street district of New York City. The 1979 master plan on which I worked with a group of architects and planners put forward several ideas regarding the public landscape. First, it was to extend the character of New York and lower Manhattan into this district, to be recognized as an extension of the streets and buildings with the better, most exciting and humane aspects of the existing urban fabric. This led us to study the proportions, dimensions, and materials of streets and the smaller successful parks in New York such as Gramercy and Carl Schurz Parks, the Brooklyn Heights Promenade above the Brooklyn-Queens Expressway, and the earlier parks that had been created nearby at Bowling Green and the Battery. We consciously chose to utilize certain elements and furnishings that we deemed successful and particular to New York—the World's Fair benches, hexagonal paving blocks, and cast-iron lamp poles associated with parks elsewhere in the city created during the Frederick Law Olmsted and Robert Moses eras—thus extending their work while offering familiarity and identity, a particular sense of "place," or "New Yorkishness," to this de novo portion of the city.

Wallace Stevens may have been one of the toughest and at times most despairing of modern American poets, despite his undeserved reputation for sweetness. In one poem after another he wrestled with the difficulties we all have in imagining and conjuring a world, whole and not partial. Contrasting the two Wordsworthian orders of mind and actuality in "The Idea of Order at Key West," the protagonist encounters a woman walking on the beach who essentially re-creates the world through the act of her own singing against the wind. The energy of the wind and sea are confronted and transformed (and transfigured) by the intensity of her voice, through her song and our listening and imagination. The artist's imagination is one of Stevens's favorite subjects, yet what he returns to over and over is the remarkable physicality of things and their continued independent, inhuman, forceful lives. As some critics have pointed out, this poem could just as easily have been titled "Ideas of Disorder," for one of the central points of this and other works of his at the time was to present the dangers of single-minded dogmatism and of order imposed by certainty.[5] Stevens remarked to his publisher that he feared this work might really comprise nothing more than another version of the pastoral—or a social arrangement of Nature that might appear inevitable and unchanging.[6]

An American deeply imbued with classical literature, especially Shakespeare, Milton, and Keats, Stevens writes his way out of Europe and into America, knowing that his (and our) world cannot be that of his exemplars. In "Anecdote of the Jar" he reflects on Keats's "Ode on a Grecian Urn" and produces a powerful and disturbing piece, declaring in essence—and in fewer words than I am taking to discuss it— that such a world of refinement and aestheticism (that of Keats or of the ancient Greek vase painter) can neither be produced nor survive in America today. Helen Vendler has pointed out that Stevens presents the predicament of the American artist, who cannot feel confidently the possessor, as Keats felt, of the Western cultural tradition. "Where Keats had London, the British Museum, and an Hellenic urn, the American poet has Tennessee, a slovenly wilderness, and a gray stoneware jar."[7] Yet art reshapes that world anew. In some important ways Stevens is correct; in others, his own persistent example argues against accepting this conclusion. This very same problem faced us standing on the open landfill site on the Hudson River looking toward the straggling New Jersey shore in 1992.

As part of the overall plan, we proposed a continuous public walkway along the edge of the property on the Hudson with a series of special places along the way. The esplanade and streets would create continuity and unity, and the individual parks, squares, and coves along the way would offer variety and opportunities for individual expression. To date, Rockefeller Park, North Cove, Rector Park, and South Cove, with their varying styles of expression, artworks, distinct furniture, and architectural elements, have indeed done just that. Wagner Park is the last of this sequence to be designed and built. Its functional role is to mark the beginning or end of this sequence of spaces and public promenade, to be a gateway to this new urban district, and to provide an amenity for the residents and workers of this publicly sponsored project and the nearby area of lower Manhattan. Beyond that it was up to us, the designers, to suggest exactly what to do, which facilities to program, budget, and build. The clients made it known that they desired a green park with trees, grass, and flowers, and that they expected it to be some-how special. Because of its proximity to the Statue of Liberty and Ellis Island in the harbor, and the large number of tourists wandering about in the vicinity, it immediately became clear that the design for this site must recognize both this view and these memorials, and the unique geographic situation on the edge both of the island of Manhattan and of America.

An earlier scheme by Jennifer Bartlett, a prominent painter, and Alexander Cooper, one of the original planners and architects of the entire development, which attempted to represent the history of gardens in a manner reminiscent of early botanic gardens, had led to several years of controversy and had been abandoned. Both the public and the Battery Park City Authority concluded that the meaning and physical forms of their scheme were inappropriate. The design was seen as being too constricted, internalized, and naive in terms of the current state of landscape design and public open space. Critics justly assailed this plan for its compartmentalization, inappropriate planting proposals, and lack of adequate circulation for the public or a clear relationship to the river and its monuments. There was a wall around the garden, even on the Hudson edge. If one were to describe it in terms of a notion of order, it was one that was too orderly, too predictable, controlled, and intro-verted. With such a clear example of what not to do, the new design team assembled by the Battery Park City Authority set to work.

I began with memories of Claude Lorrain's dreamy paintings of clas-sical harbors, of their implied arrivals and departures, of sunset across the water and boats, of pavilions and classical architecture, a terrace or paved landing stage of some sort, and vegetation. My architectural colleagues, who were technically and contractually our consultants but in fact our friends and collaborators, began also with ideas of the loss of the classical past and the end of an architecture based on that of Greece and Rome and of ruins, partly stimulated by surreal notions of the Statue of Liberty as a goddess figure who once stood in a ruined temple on the park site and had recently walked out into the harbor. After a year of private and public design study, meetings, presentations, revisions, changes, budget exercises, more study, and documentation, the final scheme emerged.

While in the process of design, another consultant, a horticulturist who had restored the herbaceous planting of the Conservatory Garden of Central Park and who hoped to create one or more spaces particularly devoted to flowers, began to lobby for separate areas devoted to such plants in some sort of neoclassical arrangement. Knowing that this would result in a disastrous compartmentalization and fragmentation of what is a very small park, I resisted the notion of their formal self-containment and argued for a more integrated and contemporary solution. Since it was no longer the sixteenth century, I saw no reason to create a sixteenth-century layout. This had been part of what was wrong with the earlier proposal of Bartlett's. The world was different now from that of seventeenth- and nineteenth-century gardens; it was New York at the end of the twentieth century, and a lot had changed. In a search for ways to break up the static classical forms and in response to the need for unifying the elements of the plan, I seized on the Renaissance Revival plan of the Conservatory Garden from the 1930s and set to work transforming it and pulling it apart, rearranging the pieces, metaphorically spilling them from the land out toward the water. Simultaneously this led to a transition of plants from exotic and tender species inland to hardier and more native and maritime species next to the harbor, with its harsh winds and salt spray, and from smaller architectural forms and a tighter arrangement to larger, looser ones.

At the same time, the architects continued to pursue our mutual interest in the death of the gods and decay of classical authority and architecture, while accommodating a small café I was insisting on, public toilets, service facilities, and a handicapped-accessible public overlook. This was achieved through the use of material and forms pointedly reminiscent of Flavian brickwork as seen in the ruins at Ostia Antica, such as at the House of Diana, and throughout Rome, most noticeably in Trajan's market and Domitian's palace, on the one hand, and on the other hand through the suggestion of an anthropomorphic transformation of the structures into a buried and deracinated head of a colossus gazing fixedly out into the harbor toward the goddess figure with a torch.

As in other parts of Battery Park City, and especially along the esplanade, one can literally step out of the city into the space of the Hudson. Here in this small park at the end of lower Manhattan we were presented with unique opportunities to frame and present views

Robert Wagner Jr. Park, concept sketch, 1992

to the Statue of Liberty, Ellis Island, New York harbor, and the New Jersey shore and its broad horizon with the rest of America beyond to the west and to the towers of Wall Street and lower Manhattan in the other direction. Our design response was to create allées, partially framed gardens, pavilions, terraces, ramps, steps, walks, and an esplanade offering one gateway, frame, threshold, and opening after another. Beginning at the street on the landward side in a strict geometric arrangement of parts, many of the elements of the park do not appear stable, but instead seem as if moving about, shifting in their arrangement, only to break apart, rising and falling out toward the harbor with its ceremonial and evocative objects, as though responding to the river, the sea, and the tide. Fragments of classical garden and architectural forms appear marooned and partially buried, suggesting a loss of familiar historic structures and aesthetic authority. Other, modern compositions and arrangements are substituted, reminiscent of the New York skyline with its jostling, competing buildings and interests, as evocative of jazz as they are of cubism and surrealism. Structures of granite and brick are presented as animated, shifting, overlapping, and impermanent. Ordinary things such as rows of trees, flowerbeds, and brick walls are first presented in conventional (even neoclassical) ways and then are re-presented in what appear to be new, different, and unexpected situations.

Even to the most casual visitor it must be evident that more is going on here than mere accommodation of leisure behavior. The pavilions and park appear to be both flying or falling apart and coming together at the same time. While almost anyone can feel and experience the energy of the agitated forms, a careful observer will see analogies to natural processes such as geological plate tectonics, bedrock faulting, erosion, dispersion, and deposition, leaves and ice floes, organic and crystalline growth, with their formal structures on the one hand and the anthropomorphic tales and representations of these processes devised in antiquity on the other hand. While the park may be a series of spaces for viewing, strolling, picnicking, sitting, eating, napping, it is also a place to notice the conditions of one's situation on the edge of the island, of the continent, the crust of the earth, or of one's own future. While many people still think of nature as wild, unpredictable, unfathomable, and threatening, there is through it all a logic, an order, a calm and steady ordering of events, of structure—as manifest in growth as in erosion, in life as in death. Things develop purpose: a plant, an animal, a park.

Wagner Park is a public space named for Robert F. Wagner Jr., the son of one of New York City's greater liberal reform mayors of the twentieth century, himself a consummate politician, instrumental behind the scenes and in public office for many years, also an effective liberal who loved his city and fought tirelessly for the public realm and the public good. My colleagues and I have tried to face squarely the dilemmas of what can be accomplished through design today, in a small space in America, between the giant towers of Wall Street and an enormous harbor invested with the vast horizon of the American West and the Statue of Liberty, one of the most potent images of freedom and hope in the world. If ever there was a site where one might despair of producing something worthy, this could be it. Nevertheless, we set out to find a solution that would deal with not only the physical and formal problems posed by the site (of scale and geometry), but also those issues of meaning posed by its place and time. As in Stevens, our solution presents an ambivalence. It looks to the past and acknowledges that one cannot go back or re-create its form successfully. It looks at the world as it seems, finds things falling apart, yet rather than merely presenting chaos as what is and therefore what you get, as being adequate, it reorders the fragments into new and coherent composition, one that is basically calm and generous in those elements that lie at the center. While employing contemporary compositional devices associated with collage and deconstruction, this is not a celebration of chaos, an embrace of things falling apart. Unlike Yeats's falcon, for whom the center "cannot hold," here it most certainly does, reasserting itself emphatically.

While these two projects may be seen as perfectly reasonable and ordinary responses to functional and programmatic requirements presented by two governmental clients, and both consist of a series of spaces sufficient to accommodate the social activities for which they are intended, each in its own way presents thoughts and suggestions through devices of representation of other things or thoughts that neither are present on the site nor have any basis in their functional requirements. There is a parallel to paintings and other works of art wherein the "content" of the work is not limited to the objects depicted or the materials used. Rather, what is presented acts as a springboard for further thoughts, for things not present but evoked in one way or another. In this way the two projects I have presented may be seen as contemporary examples of what is implied by *the immediate garden and the larger landscape.*

Poppies and wheat field, Buckland, Oxfordshire, 1970

MORE THAN WRIGGLING YOUR WRIST
(OR YOUR MOUSE)

Thinking, Seeing, and Drawing

(2008)

DRAWING AND EXPERIENCE

I love to draw. I have drawn as long as I can remember. I draw more than a lot of people, even in my profession. I draw because I like to. I draw to learn. Why? Because drawing is a way of thinking while acting, or of thinking through acting. It really isn't a parlor trick, or some low-intensity athletic activity, or a wriggling of the wrist. Drawing is about seeing and visualizing. It's about memory and finding a sequence of marks that engage observation and thought. In the act of drawing a lot happens in a very short period of time, often almost instantaneously. Watching a person draw is like watching an internal combustion engine power an automobile. You can't see the inner workings, the fire and explosions, the air sucking and fluids circulating, the movement of the parts. All you see are the wheels turning and the pencil moving on the page.

Our society privileges verbal skill and intelligence to the point that by the time they reach middle school, most people abandon other forms of mental imagination and expression such as mathematics, music, or drawing. If these alternative methods of comprehension and expression had a generally perceived social utility, they would be pursued beyond puberty by more than the minority that does persist. Those who continue to draw as they approach adulthood, more often than not, gravitate toward fields where drawing still has value and is either useful or

From *Drawing/Thinking: Confronting an Electronic Age*, ed. Marc Treib (New York: Taylor & Francis, 2008), 82–99.

needed to perform well. While many today in the so-called fine arts have moved away from traditional visual skills in search of conceptual methods that don't require the hand of an author or graphic representation, the fields of architecture and landscape architecture continue to employ visual representation in their design processes, and for marketing and communication within their disciplines and to the world. The recent proliferation of computer-generated imagery may bring an end to the long tradition of drawing skills in these fields as well, but it is not clear that this will completely or ever really happen. The issue of computers versus hand drawing has become a tedious subject, which I will leave to others.

One of the peculiarities of drawing that resembles language, despite their many differences, concerns how it is learned. After decades of teaching I can say with confidence that drawing can't be taught—but it can be learned. By this I mean that you can put people in a situation where they can figure it out through practice, but you can't make them "get it." This is a characteristic shared with language. We all learn to speak the language of our social group before we learn to read. We learn a vocabulary and a series of complex structural rules, exceptions, and inflections, and a particular accent, all before attending school. We do so by constant practice and a striving for understanding. Hour after hour, day after day, year after year, we listen to others, copy them, try things. We listen in order to build a repertoire of noises and associations until it finally clicks, with our brain and mouth working together in a lightning-fast but accomplished way.

Paul Goodman once noted that if we tried to learn our parent language in a modern school setting—studying it only for an hour or two in a day broken up by bells, with competing material and only desultory homework—we would be a nation of stutterers. As it is, as toddlers we work at acquiring language constantly with enormous attention, seeing it as the way to obtain food, love, and the things we can't reach, much less understand. While nearly everyone learns to speak, only a few go on to use language in an elevated manner as artists, as poets, writers, and critics. Yet there is general acceptance that there is a connection between language and our ability to think and conceptualize.

Learning to draw is almost as demanding—but equally possible—and it often takes years, but also in many ways it is just as rewarding. Those of us who have been somewhat successful "teaching" drawing have done so by immersing our students in its practice, with lengthy sessions, tons of assignments, hours of practice with criticism, trips to sketch in interesting places (zoos, parks, museums, the city), and lots of exercises with fundamentals (still lifes, setups of various objects, plaster casts) and of great interest (life drawing both clothed and not). We make our students do quick sketches (thirty seconds, one minute, two minutes, five minutes) as well as mechanically constructed perspectives of increasing difficulty. We show them all sorts of drawings by famous artists from history to help them see how others have solved some of the problems they themselves are now facing. We make them draw from slides and produce copies of Old Master and modernist drawings. In short, we make them do what infants do when they learn a verbal language. In the end some begin to draw well, often in their own way. Others never succeed—largely, I believe, because they do not really care enough and haven't made the time commitment or necessary mental investment.

Because every individual must learn to draw from scratch, there is no such thing as an analog to culture or historical progress in drawing. People in one era don't draw better than those of another. Differently, yes; but better, no. Despite changes in society, material culture, economics, the environment, and beliefs that constitute the perpetual flow of changes we call history, drawings over the past twenty thousand years trace a recurring number of individual achievements of heightened sensibility and ability. Does Delacroix draw a lion worse than Rembrandt? Of course not. Is it better? Again, no. How about Rubens? Does Constable draw a tree better or worse than Claude Lorrain? There is no answer, since each is the result of a particular moment of concentration, acute perception, and succinct expression. Good drawings are records of being alive, of seeing something intensely at a particular moment, in a particular way, and of getting some compelling record, an insight or feeling, down in graphic form.

Proof of this phenomenon can be had in many places, most conveniently in any of the great museums. A 2005 exhibition of Van Gogh drawings at the Metropolitan Museum of Art in New York stunned the crowds that came—and justifiably so. As I left the exhibition I wandered through a gallery of other nineteenth-century artists and past some fifth-century BCE Greek vases that were no less observant and successful in presenting glimpses of life as it was lived and experienced at other times and places. Another humbling yet inspiring encounter with drawing from another era resulted from a visit I made two years ago to the Rouffignac Cave in the Dordogne region of France. Nearly a mile from the mouth of the cave, deep underground, were a series of beautifully executed drawings of wild animals made over thirteen thousand years ago that were full of life. Made with an economy and deftness that Matisse would envy, and deeply observant of the anatomy and movement of these creatures, the drawings are as good as any ever produced. Whoever made them was certainly as conscious of being alive and of capturing an aspect of his world as anyone ever. Here was something seen, studied carefully, known and felt, experienced, and clearly recorded through drawing.

Consider, too, drawings by an early beholder of this Paleolithic art, Abbé Henri Breuil. Despairing of photographing them, he simply recorded the spectacular drawings of the Lascaux cave by making copies of them himself with pastel crayons. Some cultural anthropologists have written that these early graphic adventures were key events in the formation of humanity, in our socialization and spiritual development. In any case they offer further proof that there is no such thing as "progress" in art, or at least in drawing. There are only some moments when individuals rise to a state of heightened awareness and skill, becoming able to express their vision and feeling for life with great clarity and intensity. We can only hope to become as observant and sensitive to life and its events, issues, creatures, and objects as others who have come before us.

A LIFE OF ITS OWN: DRAWING AND THE REFLEXIVE GESTURE

Many things happen when drawing without any accord to a prior plan or preconceived visual result. As soon as one puts several marks down on the page, the brain reacts to them; from a lifetime of visual associations, feelings about composition, balance, and movement, unexpected thoughts occur about where or how to make the next ones. Drawings often develop "a life of their own," we say. Some would ascribe this to intuition, which in this case is actually thinking so rapidly that we don't perceive it.

Most people forget that our eyes are composed of a complex of ingenious light-sensitive cells that are portions of the nervous apparatus of the brain bulging slightly through two holes in our skull. We like to think of them as separate organs, but they are literally extensions of the brain and, as such, provide an enormous amount of the material our mind processes. Sensitive to an almost infinite amount of detail and nuance, they are in turn tied to several levels of conscious and unconscious activity of the brain. People who have spent a lot of time feeding visual material to their brain become adept at manipulating the elements and processes that go into drawing, much like writers who have become attuned to language, words, and diction. If, on the one hand, as Emerson says, "As I am, so I see," so too, as we see, we interact with what we see, and begin to manipulate it. The architect Michael Graves put it thus:

> While it is probably not possible to make a drawing without a conscious intention, the drawing does possess a life of its own, an insistence, a meaning, that is fundamental to its existence. That a certain set of marks on a field can play back in the mind, and consequently bring forth further elaboration, is the nature of this quite marvelous language. Good drawing, by virtue of this intrinsic reciprocity between mind and act, goes beyond simple information, allowing one to fully participate in its significance, its life.[1]

IDEAS AND INTENTIONS: DRAWINGS AS EXPLORATION, DISCOVERY, AND RESEARCH

Most of us today are comfortable with the concept of inventors and scientists in various technical fields performing investigations and research, testing hypotheses through various applications and observing the results, of trying things out, varying the process and learning from the experiments. This is part of the story of humanity and the development of our world. Around such activities we have organized fields of special endeavor called disciplines, sciences, and professions. When the results can be quantified we call them "hard" science. In some fields, especially those that rely on evolving technology, there has been a cumulative series of developments, of one theory and principle, or one gadget or technique, after another, building on and adding to those that came before. This phenomenon, linked with the discovery of biological evolution, helped produce a view of human endeavor that was linear and thought to be "progressive." Although change and additive events are easy to document in fields such as metallurgy, medicine, and physics, one cannot make such a case in the arts—or especially with drawing. One could even say that to some degree all artists are forced to recapitulate the history of art in some way in their own lives and work, with the hope of rising to an elevated level of understanding and expression such as has been achieved in the past. It is also the case that many in the arts, including myself, conduct research and investigations, invent problems, study them, and try out solutions in and through drawing.

We learn an enormous amount about various things, not the least of which might be a series of unquantifiable, but speculatively knowable, things: the nature of various places, the quality of light at different times, the manner of other people (or ourselves), the beauty of things—vegetation, animals, youth, human bodies—the pathos of age, destruction, death, and so on. We learn through seeing, thinking about what we see, studying, and recording it in various ways by drawing.

ART LEARNS FROM ART;
ART LEARNS FROM EXPERIENCE

Like most people who continued to draw after childhood, I have moved through a series of stages in my interest in drawing, as well as a progression of levels of skill. A considerable mixture of artistic or graphic models interested me. From kindergarten through fifth grade the most readily available were comic strips and magazine and book illustrations. Favorites were Harold Foster's *Prince Valiant*, Milton Caniff's *Terry and the Pirates*, Al Capp's *Li'l Abner*, and most of the work of Walt Disney. These were superbly drawn, and I scrutinized and copied them assiduously. There also were Ernest Thompson Seton's ink drawings in his adventure and animal stories, Holling C. Holling's remarkable illustrated books, Tenniel's illustrations for *Alice* and *Through the Looking-Glass*, and E. H. Shepard's illustrations in *Winnie-the-Pooh*. Locally there was a famous Eskimo illustrator, George Agapuk, from Shishmaref in my home state of Alaska, whose work I loved. I scrutinized reproductions in art books and pamphlets either given to me by my parents and friends or purchased myself. I scrupulously avoided art classes all four years of high school while utilizing their materials and equipment to make posters and sets for nearly all of the school dramatic and musical productions. Walt Kelly's *Pogo* and *New Yorker* cartoons were often brilliantly drawn. So too were the pen-and-ink illustrations in *Scientific American* of this period. Sketches and letters by the cowboy artist Charlie Russell, color reproductions of watercolors by Winslow Homer, John Singer Sargent, Edward Hopper, and Thomas Eakins I found in books. Drawings by Auguste Rodin accompanying a translation of Rainer Maria Rilke's essay about the sculptor, which a teacher gave me, added to the mix. It was a thorough stew of really good stuff.

From high school through college, unlike my classmates and friends, I drew what was around me—the people, the animals, and the places. I was concerned with producing a "likeness" and experimented with fountain pen, felt pen, soft pencil, and watercolor. I drew in class and on my own time through winter and summer, learning by looking at and scrutinizing the work of people I admired and knew only through books and reproductions. There were no art museums where I lived in Alaska at the time.

My technical knowledge of drawing grew considerably when I left Alaska and the study of civil engineering and transferred into architecture at the University of Washington. There I found myself in a studio culture. I drew nearly every day for the next four years. We drew freehand, learned and practiced mechanical perspective, and were drilled in Beaux-Arts *analytique* wash-rendering techniques with sketch problems every Wednesday We drew from plaster casts of the Parthenon frieze. We drew from life. We drew indoors in the winter and outdoors in spring. We drew in class and out. We were required to take at least one semester of watercolor painting in the art department. Standards were high, and a considerable number of students dropped out along the way. Like music students in a conservatory, we practiced and were drilled in technique and composition for years. Drawing was seen as fundamental for designers. As an outlet I let off steam as the principal cartoonist for the campus humor magazine, which was banned by the administration after my first year of participation.

After a hitch in the army, during which I continued to draw wherever I was stationed, and several years of architectural apprenticeship, I left architecture. For two years, 1967–68, I retreated from the city, drawing, painting, and reading in a small cabin near Amagansett on the eastern end of Long Island or in an apartment on the edge of Spanish Harlem. For several months I tried not to make elegant or lovely drawings. I had faced prejudice from those in the New York architectural community educated in Ivy League schools with a deep suspicion of excellent draftsmanship. Their education had revolved around theory, not craft. Many I knew at the time had a distrust of elegant drawing, considering it to be related to advertising and deception, implying that a handsome drawing was too much a thing of its own, standing between the viewer and whatever was being drawn. I still encounter this attitude from time to time in the field, especially among some academics removed from practice.

In between painting sessions I attempted to make drawings that eschewed elegance. I used a stick and tried to make lines that were "dumb," that resembled strings dipped in ink then dropped and trailed around the sheet of paper. It didn't do much for me. Next came a series of "dumb" brush drawings—a dreamy set that dealt with the issue of the loss of American wilderness and the suburbanization of the West. Ghost herds of various creatures came pouring out of carports; the spray from lawn sprinklers resembled antlers. They really weren't very good. I needed to try something else. One day in the cabin I turned to pencil on clay-coated paper, starting over, this time trying to be very careful. Over that summer, between paintings, I filled a sketchbook with studies from life, odd drawings in some ways, that were filled with minutia and detail, often of extremely ordinary things, or of things seen more out of the corner of the eye: quiet drawings. Returning to the cabin the following year, I set out to make a series of large-format, sharply focused, but for me quite experimental drawings. Mixing modes of representation—precise rendering with values and tones combined with linear contour drawing, pattern, and saturation of the visual field with empty areas—I began to see what I could leave out. They became rather fevered and intense. Outside, the world was truly blowing up: war in the Middle East; trouble in Eastern Europe; Vietnam spiraling beyond control; civil rights strife; confrontation and riots across America. Who was not disturbed at the time? Some of the drawings became truly obsessive, with all manner of things that were strange, puzzling, wonderful, and disturbing—sex being only one of them. It was exhilarating, however, to make these drawings. Although they began in my mind as a series of preparatory studies for paintings, as so often happens in art they took on an unexpected life of their own. I showed them to a few galleries and museum curators, but they were profoundly out of fashion in New York at the time. It didn't matter. I was doing them as an experiment for myself.

The following year, back on the West Coast, I moved into another cabin, this one in the woods above a beach on Bainbridge Island in Puget Sound. I settled down to draw for the next year and a half. The first product was a small book of sequential pen-and-ink drawings I made as a distillation of part of the trip. While it appears to be a sketchbook, it was actually a carefully composed set of drawings. Each page had two images with some relationship to each other, but which convey a fair amount of tension, graphically and thematically. The drawings were made using a triple-zero Rapidograph drafting pen on a cold-press manila paper. Almost immediately I began another suite of drawings, also in the format of a small book. Made with terrible, cheap, rough oatmeal-colored paper, it was unfortunately highly perishable due to the sulfite it contained. The challenge (difficulty) of drawing on it with an extremely fine drafting pen amused me. This book I filled with drawings of my surroundings: the beach, the trees, the rocks, the waves, and the plants. In both of these projects the influence of music, with its themes, variations, and development, its flow, beginning, middle, and end, or of film with its constantly changing sequence of images, shots, and narrative, were undoubtedly an influence—as they must be for all visual artists of my generation. But drawings are not music or film.

I continued to draw there on the island, working with a trove of Japanese paper brought to a painter friend in Seattle by a Pan American Airways pilot. On sheets of rice and mulberry paper, the size of the drawings grew and the focus narrowed to the forest floor and the surface of the beach itself. I produced a series of mushroom studies and another of ancient stumps sprouting with regenerative plants of various sorts. Next came a group devoted to small, unremarkable, hardly noticeable native flowers and another of the detritus along the tide line. There is no question that years of looking at Japanese prints and Chinese ink drawings had left their sediment in whatever part of my brain makes decisions about how things might fall on the page.

Returning to the city once more I turned my attention to Seattle's Skid Road community. Again, the question of how to draw this new material forced a change in manner and technique. The size and shape of the page as well as the viewpoint altered. I stepped back, looked more broadly from a medium distance, and drew in a looser manner. An almost neoclassical contour technique resulted. I suppose my admiration for many of the pen-and-ink studies of Picasso and Matisse is as clear as is their admiration for the timeless drawings of Ingres, Delacroix, and Degas. Now I was searching for overall gesture combined with a few key details—the crumpled shape of a person and their eyes, a worn shoe and a sagging body.

My work in architecture and planning, and my discoveries among the lives of the poor, led me to an engagement in the politics of urban design and an exhausting and successful fight to save Seattle's Pike Place Market from demolition. In counterpoint to these ink drawings, I made trips with friends to the Cascade Mountains; impatient with both the slow, controlled, and laborious pen-and-ink drawings of Agate Point and the human dilemmas of Skid Road, I shifted to a softer medium and larger format. This time I used Conté crayons on high-quality rag paper. Throughout all of these experiments with drawing was an engagement with what might be termed "thingness," a concern that runs through a particular tradition of modern American poetry and art, namely close study and representation of the physical presence of something, its imminence and being. From Ezra Pound through William Carlos Williams and Wallace Stevens to Charles Simic, this concern for "the thing itself, not ideas about the thing" has led many in the arts to engage particular aspects of the world, to move through sight and feeling into an understanding beyond appearance, and to strive to reach the essence of things: mountains, stones, trees, blossoms, clouds—things separate from the observer. While this may suggest pathetic fallacies or Zen exercises, it is literally what many people who draw seriously are up to.

Rocks in water had become my new problem. I had been drawing them since my days in New York. I felt comfortable with rocks and their infinite shapes; it was the water that was the problem. It would be several years before I came upon the many studies that Claude Lorrain had made in the seventeenth century of a stream and small rapids below one of the cascades at Tivoli, in which one sees him struggling with the problem. There is a dilemma posed by the brain's ability to shift the focus and depth of field of our eyes from one place to another, and the improbability of conveying it adequately in graphic form. We can clearly see an object, say, a stone, above the surface of water. Then we can shift our focus to see that portion of the stone below the water. Finally, we can see the surface of the water with its reflections and light as well. But we cannot really see all of these aspects at the same time, even while knowing they exist simultaneously. There didn't seem to be a way to draw such a perception or knowledge adequately; and that bothered me.

This problem led me to Lake Whatcom in northwest Washington, where standing in a stream at the bottom of a waterfall I made sketch after sketch: studies of an island and the memory of several other islands, which could as easily have been merely rocks or clouds, each representing a class of objects. In Chan (Zen) Buddhism one must concentrate on an external object—say, a mountain—until it ceases to be that thing, becoming nothing (and everything). The awakening that follows returns consciousness to the original object. Now, one sees it as it is, as part of the great flow of existence—but with greater knowledge of its essence. It would be pretentious to say that I reached some sort of enlightenment, but I did produce work unlike anything I had made before. Such concentration is also not far removed from an obsessive concern for particularity and essential gesture that leads to abstraction, and back to absolutely fundamental concerns regarding harmony versus contrast—an issue that Stravinsky noted was a central problem in art, or at least for him in music.

I had again become impatient with my tools. Thinking back several years, I remembered the reed drawings of Van Gogh and Rembrandt and the brush drawings of China and Japan. I put aside pen, pencils, and brushes, and for several months drew only with sticks that I cut from shrubs in the woods about me. Immediately there was a freedom and clarity. The lines that resulted were highly variable and expressive, unlike those produced by the pens I'd been using until then. The stick held very little ink, forcing me to stop and dip it in the bottle quite often. The drawings were made a few lines at a time, built up with each stroke and squiggle. I had to slow down in order to be more free, but going slow felt like going fast. Once more a sequence of studies developed, often portraits of friends and acquaintances drawn from memory. But these drawings are as much about fluid lines as they are of the people. I went against the grain in several, testing and fighting with the ease I'd developed, in some stuffing the drawing with texture as I had in the earlier Amagansett dream sequence, but in an entirely different way that enmeshed figures in their context on the page.

This period ended as I went to Rome, returning to design, becoming a landscape architect. Now drawing had a different purpose and changed again. Seen as art, my next drawings were regressive. They were in service to other purposes. Drawing once more was a tool for recording, for observing sites and places, for note taking. For the next several years I used drawing to study environments, structures, details, behavior, and form. I produced some truly miserable sketches in Rome but didn't really care because in the act of making them I was learning an enormous amount about many things and how they had been made. I was looking keenly.

The study of the English countryside and landscape garden began while visiting a friend near Oxford. I was deeply moved by the beauty of the setting and thought maybe I would do some drawing. I embarked on a week of walking and sketching, but couldn't find a method that seemed to suit the place or my mood. I explored charcoal, pencil, ink wash, and even oil sketches. All seemed inadequate. There was a calm about the place that was both expansive and pellucid. There were great sweeping skies full of activity, and exquisite details and textures close at hand. It all hung together, yet my drawings seemed to be keeping it at arm's distance. They weren't engaging the place at its various scales, nor with clarity and focus. One day I cut a large piece of heavy manila stock into several sheets the size of a tall narrow book page and set off for the fields with a fine drafting pen that I'd used for several years for architectural work. I went back to a spot where I'd made several unsatisfactory drawings.

This time it clicked. I remember the poet Theodore Roethke telling me that Yeats once remarked that when he finally completed a poem it snapped shut like a box. Intuitively I had returned to the scheme used for the southwest road trip several years before—a vertical diptych of near and far aspects of the same place. The floating elements and a page of this shape had a world of precedents, of course. One has only to think of nineteenth-century Japanese woodblock prints like Hiroshige's popular views of Mount Fuji. Characteristically careful detail of a closely observed thing, often objects in the foreground, coupled with a completely different technique of representation in the distance—dots, dashes, and various shorthand gestures and notations. The mountain frequently appears only as a distant reminder of the excuse for the drawing.

I drew outdoors avidly nearly every day for the rest of the summer. Two years later, on returning to Europe, I picked up where I had left off, experimenting once more with how to engage the page. One example, tall and full, was of a tree up close and absolutely centered on the page. The next drawing was nearly empty, leading the eye to race fast and far into the distance into deep space past the distant village lying low on the page. Putting them together as a horizontal diptych assumed the banality of a normal view. This sort of exercise went on for quite a while, producing literally bags full of ink drawings. By now I was selecting subjects around an unfolding ecological and historical narrative while continuing to experiment with working the page: how to run up or down the sheet, how to shift from close focus to distant, with a recurring interest in seeing what and how much I could leave out. I was fascinated by parallel structures and analogies, for instance, in shifting and redundant forms: cows in a field, clouds in the sky, trees on the horizon, roofs in the village, happenstance patterns and significant form. In one way the book I eventually published containing many of these drawings, *Across the Open Field,* is a complete failure because it has text. Most people today, including many of my visually unsophisticated if not illiterate friends, regard the drawings as illustrations of the text. The truth is the opposite. For me the drawings came first. The text illustrates them. I should have published the drawings alone in a separate folio with the text as a companion volume and then instructed people to spend an equal time with each page regardless of the volume.

Since returning to America in 1974 I have devoted my efforts to the medium of landscape itself and the exploration of its design. My drawing has atrophied. Used in the service of something else—as a tool for analysis, for studying situations and speculating about changes and inventions in the environment—my drawing just isn't as involved with itself as it had been in earlier years. My drawings now often verge on becoming cartoons or merely illustrative diagrams. As a visual person, it is easier for me to produce analytical work in graphic form rather than verbal or mathematical. Sketching is a natural method for me to explore and speculate about design, and for me even doodles are charged with three-dimensional implications. While some of my architect friends, like Frank Gehry, use models to sketch and study ideas, it is through drawing that my partners and staff communicate with each other: how we pin down problems, figure out how to build things, and explain them to clients, other professionals, or the public. A discussion of drawing in our practice would be an essay in its own, easily as long as this has been, and must be left to another time. Until I decide to step away from my practice and teaching for substantial periods of time I will not be able to draw again seriously. I will continue instead in the modest way I have for the past thirty years, mostly while traveling or on vacation.

Finally, let me point out that I have yet to see anyone make a sketch from nature with a computer. I honestly don't see how anyone, while typing on a keyboard or wriggling a mouse, can ever really develop a spatial sensibility or a feeling for form, materials, structure, and weight—whether of a landscape, a building, plants, or other life forms. These are things that drawing can do well, and has done for me. Along with shaping the environment, building things, writing books, and having children, drawing may also be about leaving something that outlives one's perishable and imperfect self. It is one of the ways humans attempt to capture moments, to stop time, to hold the sunlight on the garden, to preserve seed heads and ripe fruit, the tipped bell, to record animals moving along in the deep grass, clouds blowing past high above the trees swaying in the cool wind—in all, to leave a record that we have been alive, and have been there.

POSTSCRIPT

This has been intended to be an essay on drawing, not art. Although drawing has been involved in the development of art for many thousands of years, art often has had little or nothing to do with drawing, and there are aspects and some uses of drawing that have little to do with art, or amount to bad or failed art. My interest in drawing has led me to write about it on several earlier occasions. These can be found in "Drawings at Work," in Marc Treib, ed., *Representing Landscape Architecture* (Abingdon, UK: Routledge, 2007), 140–59; "On Drawing" and "Why Sketchbooks?" in *Transforming the Common/Place: Selections from Laurie Olin's Sketchbooks* (Cambridge, MA: Harvard Graduate School of Design, 1996), 5–8; "As the Twig Is Bent" and "On Buckland and Drawing" in *Across the Open Field: Essays Drawn from English Landscapes* (Philadelphia: University of Pennsylvania Press, 2000), 19–21, 28–62; "Place: Memory, Poetry, and Drawing," *Places* 2.3 (Winter 1985): 33, 34; statement in the exhibition catalog *On Site: Travel Sketches by Architects* (New York: Bertha & Karl Leubsdorf Art Gallery, Hunter College of the City University of New York, April 2000); and "Techno-madness, or Dilbert Does Design," in the essay "A Vast and Mercurial Subject: Thoughts from 37,000 Feet," *GSD News*, Fall 1996, 6. Numerous scattered remarks and thoughts about drawing may also be found between the lines in various articles, reviews, and essays, such as *Breath on the Mirror: Seattle's Skid Road Community* (1972) and "Frank Lloyd Wright: Architect—Reflections on the Recent Retrospective Exhibition at the Museum of Modern Art," *Landscape Journal* 14.1 (Spring 1995): 138–55.

About art, although I have blurted out many things from time to time, whenever I hear academicians or critics on the topic, I feel they are telling me that I am really not qualified to write about it. They make it quite clear that those of us who actually make the stuff, who stick our necks out and perform the psychological and artistic equivalent of standing naked in public, are some sort of idiots savants who don't know what we are doing, lack sufficient theory, and are hopelessly limited in our philosophical and aesthetic notions. Personally, I have always found what artists write to be very engaging, and in some cases the most enlightening and profound utterances on the subject of art. Examples range from Robert Motherwell and Fairfield Porter to John Ashbery and Anthony Hecht. Then there are Delacroix, Valéry, Constable, Olmsted, etc. Charles Simic may be one of the most important poets in America today. His essays, criticism, appreciations, and interviews are among the very best things I know being written today about life and art.

THE LESS SAID . . .

(2009)

Reflections on inscriptions and their absence in landscape presented in honor of John Dixon Hunt in gratitude for many long years of collaboration and friendship

Evelyn Waugh once remarked, "Some people think in pictures, some in ideas. I think entirely in words."[1]

For about two decades John Dixon Hunt and I have poked at each other gently, but somewhat seriously, about the use of words in the form of inscriptions, mottoes, or labels in landscape and garden design. As he has pointed out in several of his works, this is an ancient device, in some ways as old as the creation of gardens. The use of words and phrases to suggest to a visitor events or literary associations, whether fictional or historical, that give additional meaning or pleasure to their experience in a garden or landscape beyond what may be derived from the physical elements and properties of a site design has been well established and discussed for centuries. This tradition, however, like that of classical architecture with its elaborate conventions, elements, and details—or rules, as they became in later neoclassical styles and periods—which became despised and rejected by modernist architects in the early twentieth century, became anathema to early modernist

Originally delivered at a retirement gathering for John Dixon Hunt at the University of Pennsylvania in 2009. The text printed here was revised and updated in 2020.

landscape designers as well. In both Europe and America, along with the dismissal of Victorian bedding plants and neoclassical parterres, urns, and statuary, so too, inscriptions, poetic or otherwise, were banished. Emphasis, as in modern painting in New York in the 1940s and 1950s, shifted to the medium and materials employed and to formal exploration. Partly under the influence of modern architects and Christopher Tunnard's teaching and writing, and reinforced by the work of various abstract painters such as Mondrian and Picasso and sculptors such as Henry Moore, Jean Arp, and Naum Gabo, landscape architects (especially those who wrote or taught) from 1950 on talked about space, form, movement, social use, sensual properties, and direct experience. An interest in Japanese design and gardens, along with an atavistic urge and envy of Bronze Age earthworks and primitive art, also occurred. The use of classical tropes, such as inscriptions, was not only undesirable, it just wasn't done. One can look in vain in the work of Fletcher Steele, Pietro Porcinai, Russell Page, Sylvia Crowe, Roberto Burle Marx, Daniel Kiley, Thomas Church, James Rose, Garrett Eckbo, Robert Royston, Hideo Sasaki, Robert Zion, even Lawrence Halprin, and the rest in the period from the 1930s to the early 1960s and not find a single inscription.

As Hunt points out in his book *Greater Perfections,* two recent landscape designers, Lawrence Halprin and Ian Hamilton Finlay, in the last quarter of the twentieth century retrieved the application of words in the form of inscriptions, mottoes, labels, and texts from the dustbin of styles and unloved works.[2] These designers could hardly have been more dissimilar than any two artists or individuals in the world. Their work is dramatically different. So, too, is their choice of words and manner of application. Finlay, a sometime "concrete" poet, relies on classical allusion and radical (at times violently Jacobin) sentiment, and even what might be termed visual puns, in the manner of seventeenth-century wit such as one finds in the English metaphysical poets.[3] Conversely, Halprin's principal use of words has been honorific, as at his Franklin Delano Roosevelt Memorial in Washington, DC.[4] Finlay uses literary suggestion and double entendre that reference a scene or objects to allude to ideas and actions that are contradictory to their actual situation or being, while drawing out or emphasizing qualities and characteristics that are very much present. Halprin, however, used well-known remarks of a charismatic political figure to reinforce or invoke memories and achievements of exceedingly troubled times and his inspired leadership. Finlay's use is provocative, at times irreverent or amusing; Halprin's is to engender respect and reflection, at times sentimental but always intended to be moving. Both, however, use words in landscape design as a filter through which visitors are meant to see a place or design in a particular way their author (artist/designer) intended.

Their words are both a guide and blinders. While they add a surplus of meaning to the physical ensemble, in so doing they also suppress or are antagonistic to other readings, meanings, or thoughts that a viewer might have or could have developed instead.

John and I have talked around this issue some, but with neither conclusion nor outright argument. He rehearses several points of view regarding the differences and results of visual and verbal structures in the landscape in a chapter in *Greater Perfections* titled "Word and Image in the Garden," acknowledging the strengths and limitations of a range of devices using examples from antiquity to the present. Beyond the common difficulty of communication between two human beings (a topic of modern philosophy and literature), there is the fact that he and I approach this subject from very different perspectives. Aware of the breadth of his knowledge and worldly experience, part of which has been to edit the journals *Word and Image* and *Studies in the History of Gardens & Designed Landscapes* for many years, I can attest that although Hunt may be a refugee from the study and profession of English literature, which is surely an empire of word and diction, he is neither a visual illiterate nor a snob toward those who make visual and physical works of art, and has spent years looking at and thinking about gardens, landscapes, and their design.

Central to his discussion is the nearly universal use of *names* for gardens, places, or portions thereof, and the use of language to describe thoughts, ideas, and feelings about visual and physical creations. Our fundamental difference or disagreement revolves around my feeling that a landscape can be as deeply evocative and freighted with meanings for a sensitive and educated visitor *solely* as a result of its physical form, elements, materials, spatial order, and expression as one that relies on the use of words implanted within it. John, on the other hand, has for as long as I have known him been suspicious, when not openly disdainful, of those modernists he believes are too enamored of form and what in his view are overly "formalist" schemes, which for him, if not empty of meaning, are generally shallower than schemes containing language, or words. This is not a contest that can have a winner, especially if one compares designs of equal weight and importance. A *paragone* (a type of artistic debate that dates to the Renaissance, and one of Hunt's favorite strategies) of sorts is called for nonetheless.

In 2008 Hunt published *Nature Over Again: The Garden Art of Ian Hamilton Finlay,* which returns to this topic and, along with considerable discussion of the long tradition and rich potential of inscriptions in his earlier *The Afterlife of Gardens,* expresses his thoughts on the subject. I will not try to reprise his already clear and deeply considered prose, except to agree with his portrayal of the ability of words to project and conjure thought. About a particular example of Finlay's he writes in *The Afterlife of Gardens,* "Finlay uses words, as we have noted earlier garden-makers did, to signal to his visitors the wide range of political, cultural and intellectual ideas and impulses that inform gardens." He goes on to remark that the best work of landscape architects "involves—because they draw upon—a whole nexus of human concerns and activities: these include ideas of the physical world (nature), philosophy and metaphysics, politics and economics, notions of sacred or privileged spaces, social customs and rituals, and play, performance and fantasy. Within this cluster of human resources, words are central to their articulation and understanding, as Vitruvius long ago realized."[5]

John acknowledges by implication in this discussion that landscape architecture, despite its burden (and strength) in being, similarly to architecture, what is thought of as a "useful" art, unlike painting or music, can be a high form of art. He further states that it gains additional depth when words (in the West) or characters (in Asia) are also present.

My position has been, ever since entering the field, that landscape designs can be as rich and poetic, as moving, complex, and evocative of the many things he invokes in the quote above without resort to words or inscription when done brilliantly. Multilayered nuance, historic reference, and social criticism, wit and humor, nostalgia and memory have all been embodied in landscape designs without resort to literary support. Part of the inspiration for my desire to become a landscape architect came from works that accomplished this very thing, namely, a series of landscape gardens from eighteenth-century England—Buckland, Stowe, Rousham, and Stourhead—along with my knowledge of Asian, particularly Japanese, gardens that I knew mostly from photographs, and Olmsted and Vaux's first masterpiece, Central Park. Later, my encounter with seventeenth-century French gardens and sixteenth-century Italian villas and gardens led to my own early research and writing on these topics. Whether one considers Kent's Elysian Fields production at Stowe (which Hunt discusses in several places) or the sequence of fountains and creatures at Villa Lante, both of which are dripping with layers of meaning and allusion, wit and politics, there is no question that they demand an educated, well-read audience. Even so, they do it in pantomime, silently, sans verbal devices.

One example from Stowe may suffice to make this point. There are no words either on a mock-ruined temple or on another perfectly sound one, both designed with their settings by William Kent. The intact structure, the Temple of Ancient Virtue, inspired by the so-called Sybil's Temple at Tivoli (actually a Temple of Vesta), was seen by William Temple (the owner) and his friends to represent the political stance and moral principles of the Whigs as opposed to the perceived corruption of the Tory government and especially William Pitt, the prime minister at the time, while the crumbling ruin was known sarcastically as the "Temple of Modern Virtue"—another pointed commentary on the state of English morals. This landscape tableau was discussed at the time, as it still is today, without any need for plaque or quotations. Admittedly, the owner and his guests referred to both structures by names—Ancient and Modern Virtue, respectively—but nowhere do these names appear. A pastoral river scene that forms the setting for the temples is a clear reference to the Tiber and the Roman Campagna as recorded by Claude Lorrain and other painters in the seventeenth and eighteenth centuries. This landscape therefore evoked references to the historic past, to Stoic and other ancient and modern virtues, as well as happy memories of travel, worldly involvement, and the presentation of an English rural landscape as one of beauty and plenitude, as well as a tribute to the family owner and the nation, among other connotations.

Examples of such wordless achievement abound. Consider the design by Gunnar Asplund and Sigurd Lewerentz for the Woodland Cemetery,

Chapel, and Crematorium in Stockholm, and Richard Haag's work at the Bloedel Reserve on Bainbridge Island in Washington State.

The Woodland Cemetery project and its diverse elements have elicited a range of responses, including books, articles, and lectures in several languages as well as pilgrimages on the part of architects and landscape architects from around the world. It is a truly evocative ensemble of elements, forms, and iconographic symbols and images that draw on a number of ancient sources—Christian, pagan, classical, Nordic—from Bronze Age barrows and emblematic Roman executions, from sacred processional routes to romantic imagery of Gothicized forest graves and crypts. Nowhere, however, did the designers feel a need to advise the visitor or enhance the experience with inscriptions or labels. They were simply unnecessary.[6]

Likewise, Haag's highly poetic masterpiece in the woods on Bainbridge Island is a pure landscape construction that makes its points and prompts to our imagination solely through the forms, materials, and devices of the landscape medium—with moss, stones, plants, stumps, earth forms, and water, with light, space, and movement. Again, absent inscriptions or imposed narrative, it has been inspirational to a steady stream of visitors, a number of whom have written about the various metaphoric and metaphysical suggestions the ensemble offered them.[7]

And then there are even several wordless pieces of wit by Ian Hamilton Finlay, Hunt's favorite exemplar for the recent use of inscription. At Little Sparta, Finlay's home in the hills south of Edinburgh in Scotland, there are two particular installations—one can't really call them landscapes, as they are actually insertions of sculptural elements into a manipulated landscape—that to some degree help to make my point. One is a small sculpture resembling a modern aircraft carrier that is elevated off the ground. On the flat surface representing the deck of this miniature, somewhat cartoonish warship Finlay would spread seeds. Subsequently ground-feeding birds of the sort that are often fed by bird lovers on trays in their gardens would arrive for a free meal. Their frequent landing and taking off from the flight deck of the small warship in his garden couldn't be more amusing or thought provoking. Much of Finlay's work concerns the devastating machinations of modern society. A less jolly and more mordant example also at this garden is a small pond, barely more than a basin in a meadow, containing a polished stone object that bears a striking resemblance to the conning tower of a nuclear submarine. This sinister tableau (named, unnecessarily in my view, *Nuclear Sail*) suggesting the presence of a partially submerged warship in the middle of a blatantly pastoral scene was (is) an unsubtle comment on the controversial presence of American submarines armed with nuclear missiles that were parked for many years in fjords along the Scottish coast facing toward the open sea and Russia. At the same time, as with much of Finlay's work there is a distinct echo of Nicolas Poussin's famous painting *Et in Arcadia Ego,* which shows shepherds encountering a tomb with that inscription, making the point (among others) that even in an earthly paradise such as Arcadia, death is present and inevitable.[8]

My point is that the communication of layered ideas in these landscapes is successful without a word of inscription.

What and how landscapes communicate without resort to language is of course different from what is conveyed in words. Landscapes *mean* in a different way from literature. What they are, what they do, and how they do it is very different from written works of art, or any form of verbal construction. This is what brings together for me the issue of the medium and my appreciation of and ambivalence toward the use of inscriptions. The philosopher Nelson Goodman, in *Ways of Worldmaking,* argues that arts like architecture and nonrepresentational painting do not have a subject and thus do not "say" anything; rather, "they mean in other ways."[9] While I don't agree that landscapes cannot have a "subject," I do acknowledge that they aren't verbal constructions. It was, and still is, my view they are capable of symbolism and can infer and allude to ideas, events, and places elsewhere in time and space, historic and imaginary.

Concomitant with different forms of meaning is the fact that there are different forms of *knowing* as well. One is so fundamental we scarcely sense its continuous presence, namely our physical/spatial/ muscular knowing: our body (and presumably this happens in particular regions of our brain) learns and feels or knows the dimensions and position of things in space, from new environments to those we're familiar with— furniture in our homes, the rhythm and proportions of stairways—to the degree that we can traverse them without consciously looking, or in the dark. Other forms of knowledge include sonic (musical), mathematical, visual, and spatial. Knowledge utilizes information and experience to produce both understanding and the ability to consider and think, to intuit, and act in complex situations. What we call feelings, many of which are tied to emotional states, represent a body of information and knowledge that is acquired from a lifetime's combination of experience and thought. This is a fundamental aspect of all arts, each of which works with different material and devices. The philosopher Susanne Langer has pointed out that "the arts that we live with—our picture books and stories and the music we hear—actually form our emotive experience. . . . The result is an impregnation of ordinary reality with the significance of created form."[10] Landscape, because of its wealth of materials, colors, forms, textures, cultural and natural elements, its legacy of form and historic development, presents an incomparable palette for the presentation of experience and hence suggestion of feeling. Wallace Stevens went so far as to state that "there is, in fact, a world of poetry indistinguishable from the world in which we live."[11] Each of the arts has particular properties that tend to circumscribe the range and character of the knowledge, meanings, and feelings we can derive from them, a certain amount of which cannot be translated, paraphrased, or rendered in another art or through language.

In 2009 I delivered a talk at the CELA conference in Tucson, Arizona, titled "What Did I Mean Then or Now?," a response, if not riposte, to criticism I'd received on my essay "Form, Meaning, and Expression in Landscape Architecture" of 1988.[12] I made it clear that I felt I'd "muddied the waters" with some of my earlier thoughts regarding the embodiment of meaning in landscape designs. I acknowledged an overdependence on a form of hermeneutics or explication currently in use within distinguished institutions and in the work of prominent art historians of the 1970s and '80s. This talk was written while I was still at Harvard, before returning to the University of Pennsylvania, and John Dixon Hunt had joined the faculty at Penn. His earlier historical research in collaboration with Peter Willis and subsequently on his own was very much concerned with the "art" of landscape and garden design, particularly with its literary and visual, historic, and political references and its interpretation in the seventeenth, eighteenth, and early nineteenth centuries. As John and I interacted, first at Dumbarton Oaks and next at Penn as colleagues in the classroom, in conversation and as I followed his evolving work, particularly in *Greater Perfections: The Practice of Garden Theory* (2004), *The Afterlife of Gardens* (2004), and later *Historical Ground* (2014) and *Site, Sight, Insight* (2016), what became the most important aspect of his work—at least to me—was his move away from some aspects of traditional art historical analysis and a growing avoidance of more recently fashionable theoretical methods based on post-structuralism. Instead he was developing insights into the realm of user or participant experience as a way to deduce multiple meanings and valid experience-based interpretations of landscape and perception of public space without discarding his deep well of historical understanding. While to a degree this might be seen as an outgrowth of postmodern or deconstruction theory, in Hunt's case it was with a continuing care for the art and the ideas of the artist behind the work as well as with its reception on the part of others.

Having pointed out above that I am an advocate for landscape "sans parole," that I am more fond of and devoted to landscape design that makes its ideas and possibilities manifest without need or use of words or text, I must say in fairness that this is not a criticism or an attack on Hunt or his thought. In one publication after another he has shown a remarkable and deep ability to explicate landscape and garden designs from multiple approaches and with keen insight having nothing to do with this discussion of inscriptions. In *Greater Perfections* he noted, "But the visual comes before the verbal in landscape architecture. Indeed, an imaginative design will require that we see in wholly new ways. . . . Visual imagery in garden design should be a much less contentious topic than the role of the verbal."[13] Subsequently, in *Historical Ground* Hunt examined at length the role of history in a consideration of meaning in contemporary landscape design, remarking that references and the memory of Roman, particularly Flavian, architecture in pavilions designed by friends of mine in Robert Wagner Jr. Park in New York City may be understood by the designers, but were unlikely to be perceived by public visitors and those using the park. He deftly acknowledged the employment of geography, topography, weather, memory, ruins, and inventions, even fictive histories, as capable of engendering meaning in the hands of skillful designers, giving examples of each. Even so, he ends this book with a photo and quotation in raised lettering on a wall in a work of Lawrence Halprin intended to be read by those who come to stand next to it at an

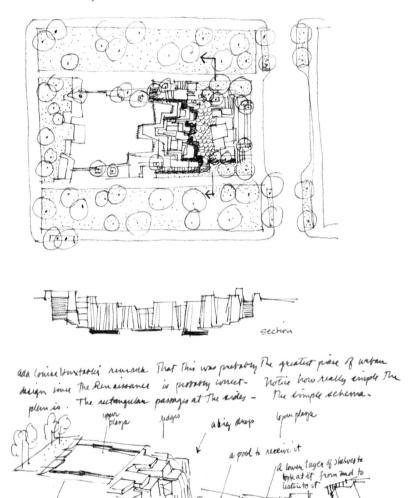

Halprins waterfall in portland Piazza - although seemingly architectonic and Baroque in
influence - is clearly derived from his long and careful study of the water courses in
the high sierras - one of his favorite summer spots - see his sketches and early
articles on the subject.

section

Ada Louise Huxtables remark that this was probably the greatest piece of urban
design since the Renaissance is probably correct - Notice how really simple the
plan is. The rectangular passages at the sides - the simple schema.

upper
plaza   ledges   a big drop   lower plaza

a pool to receive it

a lower layer of shelves to
look at it from and to
listen to it

a plateau as 2 water
sources or streams

a series of shelving
ledges

the water gushes out of the ledges. rather
than actually falling on them.

Lawrence Halprin's Ira Keller Fountain, Portland, Oregon, sketchbook notes, 1973

overlook in his design for Heritage Park in Fort Worth, Texas, above the Trinity River. Hunt writes that it "was designed for visitors to ponder the significance of the old fort (its ground plan is inscribed on another wall) and its situation over the river then and now." The text inscribed on the wall reads "Embrace the spirit and preserve the freedom which inspired those of vision and courage to shape our heritage."[14]

In *The Making of Place: Modern and Contemporary Gardens*, published a year later, Hunt surveyed an enormous range of late twentieth-century landscape, park, and garden design from Europe and North America by topic and typology, teasing out and explicating their ideas, techniques, material, and formal strategies with impressive precision, appreciatively, even at times lovingly. This volume is the best example of a compendium of different landscapes that achieve a variety of purposes and meanings without the need for narrative text, inscription, and labels (with the exception of a few examples of Finlay). One cannot and should not attempt to claim influence on another's thought or work, especially of a colleague so erudite, so independent, and as creative and critically self-inventive as the historian and theoretician John Dixon Hunt. However, our exploring contemporary practice and design together over a number of years, with students continually questioning and hoping we would make things more clear and help them understand what we were talking to each other about in front of them, while not softening either of us particularly, certainly gave us both more to think about and go look at. Likely more important, in that decade Hunt had considerable contact and dialogue with a number of prominent designers and historians in Europe, especially France. Despite his great interest in literary influences and responses to landscape designs, in these several works Hunt clearly presents important landscape designs without words or inscriptions, which he explicates superbly. However, he became troubled in the course of his years teaching and writing about a growing commentary on the notion of "meaning" in landscape designs and how it may or may not be present, perceived, or discussed, whether on my part or that of others.

In *Site, Sight, Insight* Hunt returned to earlier interests in eighteenth- and nineteenth-century writers and gardens, along with further twentieth-century garden reflections. In "Stourhead Revisited and the Pursuit of Meaning in Gardens" he first considers the strong criticism leveled by Jane Gillette of an early essay of mine on Henry Hoare's Elysium at Stourhead in England; Gillette had quarreled with my attempt to record perceptions and thoughts regarding meaning in that park's design and argued further that landscapes and gardens in general were incapable of conveying meaning.[15] After a lengthy explication of the reactions and statements made (visually and verbally) by a number of different visitors to this garden from the eighteenth century to the present, Hunt commented, "It is part of the challenge in reading gardens; working out how to best get the balance right between what we can know historically and what we feel phenomenologically." He went on to say, "So where does this leave 'meaning'—in Stourhead, or indeed in other gardens? I believe that in many cases the word would be best abandoned altogether (being too contaminated by misuse), or at least refined by the occasional substitution of 'significance' or 'experience' for encounters that seem low in 'cognitive content' but otherwise seem important."[16]

As is commonly understood by Hunt and many others, including myself, landscapes are extremely complex, composed as they are of a plethora of elements engaging our bodies and senses physically, as well as our minds visually and suggestively as we move through them. In my view this makes landscape design one of the most difficult and sophisticated of the arts, which is exacerbated by our historic paucity of adequate vocabulary and generally understood conceptual apparatus to discuss them well. In part this explains why some of the most admired designers of the past half-century have been concerned with greatly reducing or limiting their palette of materials and forms in an effort to produce work that is clear and not overly diffuse or ambiguous.

The question behind all of the recent discussion and debate is simply this: can a designer today invest a site with particular meaning through the physical design of its elements, materials, form, and composition, while eschewing the use of an overt narrative, inscriptions, or verbal prompts? And if so, why, how, or when?

Thirty years ago my answer was, and still is, yes and no—depending.

One of the best projects I can think of to explain my current position is the Memorial to the Murdered Jews of Europe in Berlin. It is a powerful work and a landscape intended from the outset to have meaning. It was created purposefully for interaction and experience with a minimum of prompts and no verbal cues or explanation. It needed to memorialize without trivializing or descending to banality or cliché. It needed to be something that would not become merely urban furniture through familiarity, as have so many historic monuments, especially representational and figurative works. An invited competition sponsored by the German government and carried out by a ministry of culture, it was a deeply important project for the nation and unsurprisingly became highly contentious. A number of distinguished international architectural figures were invited to compete. The architect Peter Eisenman, a friend with whom I'd collaborated on numerous projects, was one of those invited. He in turn invited a friend, the sculptor Richard Serra, to join him. They set to work and came up with a concept, which eventually became the winning scheme.

It was both monumental and abstract—something that I believe allowed it to avoid the pitfalls of so many recent memorials. In the course of the competition they ran into numerous difficulties regarding how to realize it, along with questions and challenges from the German authorities. Peter asked me for help.

My memories of World War II are particularly vivid because I was in elementary school living with refugees in Canada at the time. Horrific reports, photographs, and film of the Nazi death camps that appeared later and the many close Jewish friends, classmates, colleagues, and clients I have had through life, more than a few of whom had parents who'd either fled Europe or were survivors of the camps, added a personal sense of purpose in participating. Plus, the scheme as it was developing struck me as particularly promising in its potential power and numbing character, engaging as it does background and foreground—the ordinary and non-striving shapes versus their assertive, attention-getting scale and extent. It would be grim and unforgettable.

Consisting of a field of several thousand concrete prisms—"plinths" or "steles" as Peter called them—uniformly distributed across an area of several acres in the heart of Berlin, the memorial was to be sited only a few blocks away from the Reichstag, the home of the German parliament. It was adjacent to the Brandenburg Gate and on the very site of Hermann Goering's bunker and a portion of the Third Reich's Chancellery, designed by Albert Speer. Serra and Eisenman envisioned that the plinths or steles would all be uniform in plan and section, but that the ground on which they sat would be undulating and descend to such a depth that they would tower over a visitor like ancient megaliths. They also began to consider having them not all be vertical, but to have many of them wandering and tilting so as to appear unstable, leaning about in such a way as to be threatening.

As Eisenman and Serra worked on the scheme, problems arose: what to do about drainage and groundwater; how to make the ground plane; the choice of material; the finish and dimensions of the steles and their spacing; how to engage the surrounding streets; the probable problem of buses of visitors; municipal codes and regulations regarding safety and accessibility; and finally there was a request for a visitor center and possibly even a method for searching a database for family or individual names. A subcommittee of the German senate became involved. Although the scheme was deemed to be the favorite of the chancellor, questions, concerns, and demands, as well as political maneuvers by other disfavored and jealous competitors, had to be dealt with. To me most of the problems were fairly common ones of landscape poesis and praxis: a search for expression appropriate to the concept and strategy, the sort of things I have faced in every significant project in my career.

Serra, however, upset that what he'd envisioned as a pure sculpture was becoming a work of architecture, stormed out and refused to continue working on the project. To him it wasn't pure; it wasn't art anymore. The research and data facility, which he feared would become a building on the site, we put below ground in a profoundly disturbing and effective tomblike situation with scarcely a ripple above grade, invisible throughout the site until one comes upon its stairway among the plinths. From my point of view, we managed to resolve all of the material and technical issues, leaving the scheme strengthened and intact. We managed to get it built. Consider the result.

Watching people interact with it at different times of day, in different seasons, and in different weather, as I have, has been of great interest and relief to me. One sees many different behaviors, from play and picnicking to guided tours and outdoor classes—presumably about the Holocaust or some aspects of social history, politics, and tragedy—to contemplation, clear expressions of sorrow, pilgrimage, and memorialization (leaving flowers, stones, *objets de mémoire*). Clearly part of what sets this disparate thought and behavior into motion are the thousands of concrete objects composing the "field" of the memorial, with the connotations that the word "field" suggests, especially that of crops such as grain which is cut down. It cannot be denied that this array of concrete boxlike shapes that are identical in two dimensions, but not in three, also oddly recalls ancient Jewish cemeteries in North Africa in the midst of Islamic cities such as in Fez and Tangier, or early sections of the Mount of Olives cemetery in Jerusalem, and elsewhere, with their rows of identical, mute, rectangular coffin-sized forms of stone and plaster, slightly raised above the ground with an absence of head-stones, names or inscriptions lost in time.

And yet . . . the transformation of an ordinary, rational grid, a device used since classical antiquity to give order and structure to cities, gardens, cemeteries, data, and research, into a crazed, irrational, and crushing field with no apparent beginning or end is one of the obvious suggestions offered. The allusion to atavistic tomb structures and death, to an endless, mindless repetition, to being swallowed up and crushed, is present as well. And then the absence of individual names or faces, the erasure of any trace of humanity, is there as well. Aware of the way materials affect expression, along with a fear of suggesting conventional gravestones and historic memorials, we carefully resisted the use of stone for the plinths, knowing that its natural texture and color are inherently pleasing in ways not always understood by laymen. I'm certain there are numerous other possible associations that one might have. A great part of the memorial's power, I believe, is in its abstract quality and *the lack of words and inscriptions*. A visitor must work and supply the thought, the feelings, the facts, the memory, the fear, the nightmare that was a Holocaust, *The Holocaust*.

I am aware that presenting these thoughts of mine is not in any way a guarantee of persuasion to others. There is no question, however, in my mind that the memorial is not meaningless. Hunt's perception-theory attitude would strongly suggest how such topics might be presented and how visitors might come to reflect on them. I believe he would insist that each visitor must construct his or her own view, ideas, and attitude to such a place and the possible referents. This phenomenon was brought home to me dramatically during the development of the design. I was concerned about the relationship between the monument and the busy street that lay between it and the Tiergarten opposite, and I suggested that the pedestrian walk alongside should be absolutely normal, made with the materials, dimensions, and layout that had become standard in postwar West Berlin. Then I proposed a thin scrim of evergreen trees, forming neither a wall nor an allée but spaced to allow views and ways into the memorial. I was concerned about transition from the everyday world to the dead zone of the memorial. I thought of conifers because of the forests of Poland, and of Central and Eastern Europe where so much of the killing had occurred, and of their perpetual dark green, how they would appear nearly black in the gray climate of Berlin. To my surprise and dismay, at least one German senator and several other committee members were upset by the suggestion of these trees and opposed their inclusion. They told us they invoked *Tannenbaume,* or Christmas trees, a Christian and to them deeply German family symbol.[17] My association of the snow and horror of Auschwitz, Treblinka, Birkenau, and the other camps, with their bleak and oppressive forest settings away from observation and settlement, wasn't shared. What better example could one find that meaning and interpretation lie with the beholder?

There is no escaping that this landscape is a memorial and that the event memorialized is *death*—death on a scale difficult to conceive, impossible to understand or forgive, and today fading into the past. It is a reminder for us and subsequent generations of what horrors human society is capable of, now that even those who survived the horrific Nazi factories of killing and their staggering volume of identical dehumanized corpses and mountains of ash, and those alive at the time as witnesses, are also disappearing, that the bureaucracy of the Nazi regime behind this obscene apparatus was located at this very spot.

No one is told what to think. There are no inscriptions, legends, keys, mottoes. There are no statues or narrative figures. There are none of the devices used successfully by Finlay or Halprin in several of their major works. The Memorial to the Murdered Jews of Europe consists only of blank, smooth, unlovable concrete forms, an undulating and depressed (literally) obdurate paved topography. There is a handful of plants sparsely edging into one side opposite a lush and beloved historic park. What others think it means, and how it makes them feel, I do not know. It must, of course, mean something, probably many things.

For me as a landscape architect it is a case of "The less said, the better."

WHAT DID I MEAN THEN OR NOW?

Reflections on "Form, Meaning, and Expression in Landscape Architecture"

(2011)

meaning *n.* 1. That which is intended to be, or actually is, expressed or indicated; signification; import: *the three meanings of a word.* 2. the end, purpose, or significance of something: *What is the meaning of life? What is the meaning of this intrusion?*[1]

Some time ago, in fact twenty years ago—almost longer than I can believe—I published "Form, Meaning, and Expression in Landscape Architecture" in *Landscape Journal.*[2] It was largely derived from lectures I'd been giving at Harvard's Graduate School of Design. It was heartfelt, and I hoped at the time for it to be an overdue correction to what I perceived as a prevailing view in the field, namely that landscape architecture was or should be primarily a field of problem solving, largely based on applied sociology and ecology. Against my better instinct, my first partner had written into an early office brochure that we didn't believe in "art for art's sake" in landscape design.[3] At that time only a handful of practitioners not related to or involved in academia, or the training and education of landscape architects, believed or acted on the premise that it was or could be examined as art.

The impact of land art and the anti-museum, anti-object, out-of-the-gallery-and-studio, out-of-bounds sculpture movements of the 1970s

From *Meaning in Landscape Architecture and Gardening: Four Essays / Four Commentaries,* ed. Marc Treib (London and New York: Routledge, 2011), 72–81.

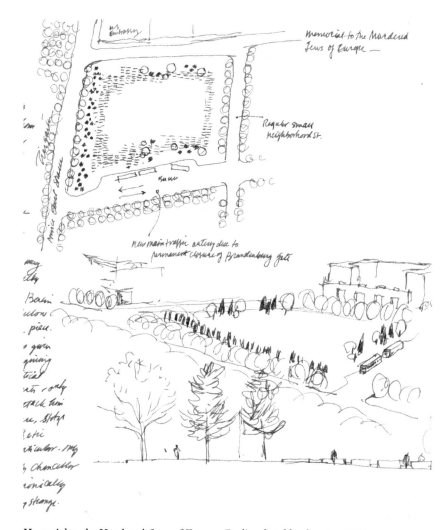

Memorial to the Murdered Jews of Europe, Berlin, sketchbook notes, 1995

was a shock and wake-up call. It announced to the profession that in terms of expression one could do much more with a piece of land than merely solve technical and functional problems. It was not a surprise, however, to those who knew much about the history of landscape and garden design. A general anti-intellectual attitude and ignorance of the history of architecture, art, and landscape—due to the preponderance of landscape architects who had arrived in the field via what was largely a horticultural or architectural background—had exacerbated the situation. To some of us, however, site sculpture was clearly art and subject to the sort of debate, criticism, and interpretation previously devoted mostly to works of painting, sculpture, and occasionally architecture. Even so, these highly promoted, site-specific creations were not the same as landscape architecture in that they didn't bear the same burdens and responsibilities, nor the great potential of landscape architecture when it solves and transcends its utilitarian purposes through artistic expression.

I consciously wrote the article in a manner parallel to those in which my colleagues at Harvard were presenting architecture at the time, in an attempt to regain some of the high ground of previous eras and ambition in our field. As a person who is primarily a practitioner, I was concerned that I not betray the sort of envy expressed by Steven Krog in his provocative articles a few years earlier—"Is It Art?" and "Creative Risk-Taking"—albeit while being very sympathetic to what he was saying.[4] I hoped to encourage a deeper look into the potential of our medium for expression and content. My thesis was that the range of landscape design forms derives, directly or indirectly, from nature and its processes, often translated through a series of abstractions and artistic expressions, and limited largely by cultural norms. Metaphoric device and a concern for natural process are central to the creation of work that eschews literal imitation of nature, but rather strives for understanding and emulation.

In *Theory in Landscape Architecture,* Simon Swaffield categorizes me as one who argues that meaningful landscape design should express a distillation of the essential qualities of human experience paired with a consideration of nature. He is silent about, or chooses to ignore, however, something that I tried to make clear—and that Marc Treib noted in his riposte, "Must Landscapes Mean?"—namely, that there are several ways by which landscapes come to possess meaning.[5] Some of these have little if anything to do with nature or the intent of a designer, for example, the landscapes that comprise the site of the nineteenth-century battlefield at Gettysburg, Pennsylvania, or of the Sioux victory over the US Cavalry at Little Big Horn in Wyoming. Their current cultural meaning derives solely from historic events, not the terrain itself or any designer's intent.

The bulk of my essay was devoted to considering some of those things that designers can do and what sort of devices can lead others—the public, visitors, whatever we call the users and perceivers of landscapes—to considerations, ideas, and thoughts about things not necessarily present on the site, whether they be about nature, the region, temporality, history, the human condition, or the medium of landscape. While I didn't make much of it at the time, it should be acknowledged that I was aware that designers can't make people think or feel anything. In the passage discussing rhetoric I tried to point out that one can proffer material from which others can then form impressions and thoughts of their own. As in any art, the skill with which one sets out the material—the selection and arrangement of the devices used to encourage others to think of particular (or general) things, to have both sensory experiences and discoveries of particular references, and the ability of an audience to be interested, to perceive and utilize such material—varies greatly with individuals and moments in time. Treib has questioned the efficacy or even the appropriateness of such endeavors, noting, as others have, that our population today is so diverse, ethnically, culturally, and spiritually, that it may simply be futile to attempt to construct a landscape that can be "read" coherently for any meaning that its author(s) may wish to embody.

A few years later I published a long-delayed study on aspects of the English landscape. One particular portion discussed at length eighteenth-century landscape gardens, and included an extended essay on the development of Stourhead, one of the greatest achievements of the period, or for that matter of all European gardens in the humanist tradition.[6] The narrative, my reading of the site, was based on extensive personal experience, as well as a survey of scholarship through the early 1980s. Since then various scholars have suggested other interpretations regarding some or all of the features I discussed.[7] None, however, has gone so far as to say that the men who created Stourhead were just messing about and that there wasn't intention in their work. Nor have any implied that there is no meaning to be found in the various pavilions, statues, inscriptions, the circuit of walks, views, and visual compositions. While I am convinced that this is one of the most literary or poetic of the gardens constructed in the English countryside of all times, I no longer believe (as I seem to have earlier) that it has a linear narrative such as one might find in traditional literature. I think it is laden with meaning, some accessible only to those who made it, some easily available to their contemporaries, and some for those of us familiar with their time and art. For many today, however, it almost certainly evokes things unintended by its authors regarding recreation, gardening, and class structures in the eighteenth century and today. For many I'm sure it is simply a huge and beautiful visual and sensory extravaganza.

Jane Gillette's critique of my essay on Stourhead (and her assertion, if I understand it) that landscapes can't really contain meaning at all, but that only written works, i.e., works composed of words, can do so, strikes me as simply untrue.[8] Gillette used the word *gardens,* not *landscape,* but it's the same quarrel for me. It is true that landscapes mean in a different way from literature. I made a particular point in the *Landscape Journal* article about this, quoting Nelson Goodman—a colleague of mine at the time in the philosophy department at Harvard—with whom several of us frequently met over lunch to discuss this very problem. As he put it, "Architecture and non-objective painting and most of music have no subject. Their style cannot be a matter of how they say something, for they do not literally *say* anything; they do other things, they mean in other ways."[9] I was troubled then (and still am today) by linguistic analogies that several members of Harvard's Graduate School of Design and other architecture and landscape faculties used repeatedly. I disagreed with Goodman that landscape in the hands of designers can't have a "subject," even while agreeing that it wasn't the same as in language. Despite my own struggles to find a way to discuss the strategies and devices employed in landscape design that could engender meaning, I knew then (and now), and wrote matter-of-factly, "landscapes are not verbal constructions. [But] they can express certain things, can possess symbols, and refer to ideas, events, and objects extrinsic to their own elements and locus, and in certain circumstances can be didactic and/or highly poetic. How they do it is not well understood. That they do it is."[10]

It seems to me that there are many forms of knowing and under-standing a variety of phenomena that are not linguistically based. A good example is music, that most abstract art. Despite volumes written on the subject, it (mostly) relates to itself and our knowledge of it is based on neither verbal nor linguistic data or processes. My favorite example is a story told of Beethoven: on coming to the end of a perfor-mance of a new piano sonata in a patron's drawing room, he was con-fronted by one of the guests who gushed how wonderful it was. But then she asked, "Please, could you tell me what it meant?" Silently returning to the keyboard he proceeded to play it through again. Upon completing the work he turned to her and said, "That, Madame, is what it means."

Another motive for writing "Form, Meaning, and Expression" was that I became aware of an enormous prejudice on the part of Har-vard's central administration and numerous members of other schools toward the faculty and students in visual arts and the Graduate School of Design, largely because the basis of our work and its measures were neither linguistically nor mathematically determined. Some of the most brilliant designers in the nation (or world) came to teach and lecture at the school (as they also do at the University of Pennsylvania, where I have taught for many years since), and their work has been considered extraordinarily beautiful, important as art, and a measure of the era's creativity—the stuff that embodies the aspirations and production of entire generations. Even so, we were not treated as intellectually equal to members of the humanities faculty, many of whom wrote articles for each other and small academic journals that in many cases are neither valued nor remembered today—and certainly can't be considered as critical elements of a lasting and meaningful cultural legacy.

I was convinced that designers knew things but that we knew them "in other ways" from our colleagues, as Goodman had remarked. Designers and artists know an awful lot—and not just skills or perfor-mance craft—but their knowledge all too often slips between words and is not easily discussed. Three of these topics in landscape of which we have knowledge, but cannot always articulate, are form, meaning, and expression. Despite their great interest to me I must set aside the discussion of form and expression for now, because they are huge topics, enormously important, and like meaning require extended discourse to treat them reasonably.

Just as there are levels of meaning and discourse in language, rang-ing from laundry lists to business letters, from narrative fiction to lyric poetry, so too are there levels of meaning in landscape. They range from the mundane to the profound, whether they are attractive, disheveled, beautiful or not, small or large. One must acknowledge that much of the built world is composed of banal, background places that are at most utilitarian or instrumental. This is probably a very good thing. At best they are merely a setting for something, whether for parking automobiles or marking a location for a building and its address. They are not called to do or mean anything more than this. The suburbs comprise a landscape largely made of such stuff. There are also land-scapes, like the Pennsylvania Turnpike, that are primarily infrastruc-ture or systems with purpose and character that do not denote much beyond their own intentions. They can be handsome and offer visual experiences that are powerful and rich, such as those offered by the Blue Ridge Parkway in Virginia and North Carolina. Along the way there can be places with particular references and meanings derived from cultural objects, events, or particular visions presented (the battle road between Lexington and Concord, for example). But it is fair to say that most parkways and their environs do not mean much more than an attractive way to drive through a portion of mountains or countryside, allowing driver and passengers a continual visual experience of variety and beauty. And then there are landscapes we purposefully make to remind us of particular things.

Unfortunately, my earlier writing may have muddied the waters a bit on this subject. By 1980, when I began trying to write on this topic, nearly all of the literature on landscape history had been made by a generation of scholars trained as art historians in an era heavily influenced by the War-burg and Courtauld Institutes and several of its key individuals interested in Renaissance iconography. This was the lens I began with. Architec-tural history and criticism at the time—the late 1970s and early 1980s—were emerging from a period of influence by prominent neo-Marxists or sociologists, especially French structuralists and the Annales group of historians, social critics, and philosophers. Deconstruction and post-struc-turalist ideas were flooding into American academia in literature and the humanities. It was difficult to find a way to discuss meaning in landscape that didn't fall into one of these thickets—what else to call them, pools of thought, swamps? It would be a few years before John Dixon Hunt would consider the realm of user/visitor/public perception as a way to construe sense and meaning, multiple and contradictory as that may be. His writing, especially as recently summarized in *The Afterlife of Gardens,* is very much in line with the post-structural, postmodern dethroning of authorial mastery and control, wherein the critic, reader, or others take control of meaning. There were also other sorts of attacks on artists and designers: "What do these idiot-savant authors and artists, Melville, Hawthorne, Wright, Olmsted, and the like, know?" It was for the critics to tell us, to become the new uber-artists, using works of art and design as grist for their creations. At its best this stance leads to a diverse set of readings with widely ranging interpretations, often rich in their interplay. At worst it has become a thick lens through which it is often difficult to actually see or experience the work itself.

As I see it now, much of the latter twentieth-century work that interests me does not lend itself well to an analysis based on iconographic models. At the same time, the close reading one enjoys with poetry can only be applied to landscape with great care and subtle examination of the myriad elements and their relationships. Landscapes are made of many diverse phenomena—visual, aural, tactile, olfactory—that may trigger the recall of things from our own personal environmental history, which in turn combine with a world of information from our education and experience. For this reason there is no question in my mind that the art of landscape design—when it is an art—is possibly the most complex and sophisticated art we possess. That said, despite some of the remarkable minds that have considered the topic, our ability to adequately analyze and discuss the designed landscape and its meanings seems to be among our least successful endeavors. It is easy to attack most of the discussions regarding meaning in landscape: for no matter how right they may be, at heart they are fragile constructions—unlike their subject.

IN CLOSING

Some landscapes demand to be extraordinary, if for no other reason than to sustain the pressure of expectation that they be emotionally moving, disturbing, and assertive. One such project is the Memorial to the Murdered Jews of Europe in Berlin, engaging as it does background and foreground: ordinary and non-striving versus assertive, attention-getting elements. What, you may ask, does this landscape or its myriad parts mean? People come away with a variety of feelings, impressions, and interpretations, especially regarding the thousands of concrete objects that make up the "field"—in all of their cold weight—rather the opposite of our usual association with the word "field." While the elements of the memorial—erected on the very spot where the fatal apparatus of the Nazi regime was located—are stated and constant, each visitor will perceive and independently construct his or her own views, ideas, and attitudes to the place and interpret them accordingly. And while it is common knowledge that the memorial's underlying subject is death on an unprecedented and barely conceivable scale—a reminder for both those who lived through the period of atrocities and those who have entered the world thereafter—it leaves those constructions partly, maybe largely, up to the visitor. Nowhere are there inscriptions, legends, mottoes, or figurative representations of any kind. In that way it differs strikingly from the work of Ian Hamilton Finlay at Little Sparta in Scotland or Lawrence Halprin's Roosevelt Memorial in Washington, DC. It is a landscape of concrete, granite, topography, and a few plants. The memorial is simply a landscape. The landscape is a memorial. It means a lot to me. What it means to other people I cannot say, but it must, of necessity, mean something.

meaningless *adj.* 1. Without meaning, significance, or value; purposeless; insignificant: *a meaningless reply; a meaningless existence.*[11]

Place Igor Stravinsky with its fountain and cafés, Paris, sketchbook notes, 1997

CIVIC REALISM AND LANDSCAPE

(2014)

For several decades my office and our practice have considered the relationship between the medium of landscape architecture and the making of civic places. A recurring concern has been that of purpose and attitudes toward real life, civil expression, and meaning.

The central purpose of landscape architecture is the planning and design of land and its features, including the positioning and relationships of diverse elements: earth, water, vegetation, roads, pavement, and structures, including buildings, for private and public purpose. Familiar topics include parks, squares, piazzas, campuses, systems of public space, community infrastructure, and reservations for the conservation of natural area and resources. In doing this work it is common to consider aspects of natural systems and physical character—the soils, geology, hydrology, climate, topography, and ecology, as well as the cultural artifacts and historical legacy of a given location—those things that define the "genius loci," to use a familiar phrase. In the course of developing plans and proposals for the development, redevelopment, or transformation of sites from one situation to another and considering the nature of the proposed result in addition to issues of ecological health and aesthetic merit—broad topics dealt with extensively in most

Originally delivered at the University of Virginia on the occasion of receiving the 2013 Thomas Jefferson Medal in Architecture. Revised for the Kenneth Helphand Lecture at the University of Oregon, April 2014.

academic institutions that teach landscape architecture—the design of public space raises ethical issues regarding social purpose, use, and behavior that are often inadequately addressed or understood in the discourse of either professional schools or practice.

Civic space has been central to the evolution of urban communities. Like them, it has taken different forms and has expressed and accommodated different needs and functions through time. While the vast majority of public space in nearly all communities is devoted to movement, circulation, and access, other spaces devoted to public encounter, gathering, recreation, and leisure remain important and among the most cherished and contested. We no longer have cattle markets and public executions in the heart of our cities, but we still use these spaces for civic events and public rituals, for sport, play, socialization, relaxation, celebration, and protest. The majority of parks, squares, boulevards, and civic spaces that we enjoy as a legacy of nineteenth-century planning and design movements in New York, London, Paris, Berlin, Chicago, or Philadelphia, as seen from the beginning to the end of that era, are in large part a direct result of social and economic changes that gave rise to a vast middle class for whom they were intended. With this development also came a democratization of art and literature that extended well into the twentieth century—developments that I wish to consider against a background of thought and behavior that accompanied these changes.

The question "What is real?" has preoccupied people who care to stop and consider it for centuries. Any number of academics, critics, and philosophers today would answer, "That depends on the cultural and relativistic orientation of one's conceptual apparatus."[1] Isaiah Berlin has remarked that "'realism' normally means the correct perception of the characteristics of events or facts or persons without the distortions produced by feelings like hope or fear or love or hate, or by a disposition to idealize or depreciate or anything else that interferes with accurate observation (or action founded on it) as a result of emotional pressure of some kind."[2]

Realism in the arts as an idea or problem appears in the mid-nineteenth century as a contrast and antagonist of romanticism and various forms of historical, eclectic, revival styles of painting and writing of the previous century. The movement was centered in France between 1840 and 1880, and its aim, according to the art historian Linda Nochlin, was "truthful, objective and impartial representation of the real world based on meticulous observation of contemporary life."[3] It is useful also to remember that this took place in the aftermath of a number of trans-formative revolutions and events, beginning with two in England in the seventeenth century (one that was bloody and one bloodless), and two more, one in America and another in France at the end of the eighteenth century, both violent and both setting in motion events, similar yet dif-ferent, that appear to still be playing out as social experiments—one can't help think of Chou En-lai's reply when asked about his thoughts regarding the French Revolution: that he didn't know, as it was still too early to tell. These social and political events focused on governance, individual liberty, and the universal rights of man took place within the context of the gathering Industrial Revolution, the redistribution of pop-ulation in Western countries from agricultural settings to urban ones, the dramatic growth of cities across Europe and America, expanding economies, worldwide colonial exploitation of resources and people, and the emergence of vast capitalist consumer product industries. A favorite painting of mine by Édouard Manet presents the mingling of classes in the Tuileries, depicting a mixed crowd of the haut monde and petite bourgeoisie, those in governance together with bohemian and artistic figures, grandmothers, artists, composers, and authors—a new dynamic social mix in a public park fashioned from a former private royal pleasure garden.

Realism in art and design emerged in this era as a deep interest in trying to see and understand what the world had become, quickly becoming ideological and controversial, initiating the situation of a self-proclaimed avant-garde. The collective and individual reactions of Géricault, Courbet, Daumier, and Millet, the writing of Zola (there are Manet paintings of his friend Zola and one of a woman in her boudoir titled *Nana*) along with the writing of Balzac, Flaubert, Baudelaire, and the Goncourt brothers, and the painting of Manet, Pissarro, Degas, Monet, Seurat, and Renoir, seem to us today the celebration of both the haut monde and the bourgeoisie: the shoppers, gossips, and flan-eurs, café society and workers—the entire world of souls who filled the new *grands magasins* that we call department stores, the arcades, boulevards, cafés, bars, and parks. This consortium of artists concerned themselves equally with the physical and social world of their day. The literature and painting of the time, especially that labeled "Impressionism," was a reaction against sentimentality, fantasy, and romanticism and attempted to directly and accurately present life and whatever subject matter came to the artist's attention—something also referred to by some as the "truth."

Among the last paintings of Manet are a group of close, very close, bold, loose, and powerful observations of flowers brought to him by his friends as he was dying: a portrayal of a palpable, immediate, energetic, and beautiful but transitory world. One of the things that his generation witnessed and engaged, which as often as not was both setting and subject, was the new public and civic realm produced by the bureaucracy of the prefect of the Seine, Baron Haussmann, and the engineer and landscape designer Adolphe Alphand, a remarkable series of grand projects of boulevards and parks.

The transformation of the urban structure and former royal enclaves of the city, along with the parks and squares that this bureaucracy created from scratch between 1840 and 1860, produced the Paris painted by Monet that we still know today. This prominent series of public works recently served as a model for the *Grands Projets* of the latter part of the twentieth century undertaken by Georges Pompidou, Valéry Giscard d'Estaing, François Mitterrand, and Jacques Chirac. An obvious motive for the creation of Parc de la Villette, Parc Citroën, Parc de Bercy, the Jardin Atlantique, Parc Diderot, and others was simply to enhance the city of Paris for the benefit of its citizens and the nation. Another, however, was that such parks were a device to instruct the large influx of immigrants from Africa, the Middle East, and a host of former colonies how to socialize and behave in public, how to be French citizens.

The period of the modernization of Paris during the reign of Napoleon III was also the era of Frederick Law Olmsted and his remarkable and innovative work. Following upon the thought of Emerson, Thoreau, and others, and as a contemporary of Marx, Engels, Lincoln, and Herzen, Olmsted proposed an urban agenda of reconstruction and infrastructure bringing aspects of the natural and rural world into the heart of large cities in an attempt to contribute to the betterment and health of the urban poor as well as the middle class that he represented and from which he'd come. At times in recent decades his work has been characterized by some of my former students and peers as romantic and out of date, pigeonholing and even dismissing his great works as "picturesque" and old-fashioned. This is debatable. Despite the fact that Olmsted was framing his views and work in the Victorian era, like the production of Manet and Alphand, there are reasons to take it as profound and prescient, regardless of how it may have aged or looks to young Turks today who have been raised on the internet and dreamy digital imagery.

From about 1870 to 1920, critical dispute in literature focused on the naturalism of Zola. Proust and others reacted strongly against what they perceived to be the overdetermination of works of art by their perceived content alone and what Peter Rowe calls "an almost total passivity before raw phenomena."[4] Painting, especially Impressionism, pursued light, color, and issues of the relationship between perception and representation, which eventually led without planning or intent to the radical departures of cubism, abstraction, and the abandonment of or eventually any interest in representation. In America, the so-called Ashcan School of John Sloane, Robert Henri, William Glackens, and others carried the earlier French agenda forward with a heavy dose of social observation and critique. As the Great Depression deepened, artists such as Edward Hopper and Walker Evans shifted the emphasis of realism away from the collective toward the individual and solitude, as did writers as different in style as James Joyce, T. S. Eliot, and Robert Frost had already begun to do. Debates about realism continued into the 1930s but were hijacked and debased by political agendas in America, Europe, and most dramatically Russia, where a form of radical propaganda virtually drove it from the stage of the most innovative and progressive design productions, at least in the realm of civic space, even while social critics such as Georg Lukács, Bertolt Brecht, Theodor Adorno, and Walter Benjamin astutely addressed the relationship between forms of production and the results, sociologically and politically if not often in a satisfactory manner aesthetically.

The world of what is called fine art wandered off and over the next fifty years went through a series of self-proclaimed avant-gardes, radical shifts of concept, production, and fashion that, regardless of the brilliance and merit of the work, had little effective engagement with the larger issues of the urban realm, the quality of life in cities, or the perplexities of design, whether it be of parks and landscape, emerging ecological crises, or architecture. This in part is due to an obsession with novelty and a fixation on what was only one aspect of early modernism—a desire for transgression, to shock and upset the established order, not necessarily a sound basis for the design of public space, especially if a major purpose is to engender community and health.

I'll now try to explain my interest in the fraught topic of realism. In 1967, I had become disenchanted with the design and creation of buildings, no matter how interesting, which I had been doing for a number of years in several of the leading offices on both the West and East Coasts. It was a time of questioning for every thoughtful person in my generation, whether about society and its behavior, or the world. It was a period that encompassed the civil rights movement, the war in Vietnam, wars in the Middle East, the Russian invasion of Central Europe, the Cuban missile crisis, and generally in both Europe and America a society at war with itself between generations.

I left architectural practice in Manhattan and retreated first to a cabin at the end of Long Island and then two years later to one on an island in Puget Sound in an effort to refocus on the world and life. I had studied with the poet Theodore Roethke for several years during and after architecture school and was deeply impressed by what we read, which included such hortatory remarks as Ezra Pound's one-line manifesto of modernism, "Make It New!" Yes, of course, I thought, but what *it* was we had to figure out. Another such line that bore deep was Wallace Stevens's "Not ideas about the thing but the thing itself." What we found in studies with Roethke in the work of William Carlos Williams, Emily Dickinson, Walt Whitman, and others pointed to a need for perception and confrontation with the physical world and its splendor in its ordinariness and minutiae—as had been the case with Emerson and Thoreau, whose work was a beacon for Olmsted and his circle.

Each in their way demanded that as individuals (or as a society) we must start afresh from a confrontation with ordinary things and the fundamentals of human existence and community. For several years I drew a lot and everywhere, in an attempt to take up the pleasures and burdens of daily life and nature. I "went into the woods" as Thoreau said. And yet, like him, I came out again to live and study life in the Skid Road neighborhood of Seattle and to reenter architecture briefly for three more years as my friends, teachers, and I battled City Hall and the business community to save the city's Pike Place Public Market.

Next I managed to leave America for several years to live, work, and study, to read, write, and think in Europe, mostly in Italy and England with doses of France and Germany. What I saw and absorbed confirmed my instincts to develop a focus on the landscape of cities and their civic realm—their parks, gardens, squares, piazzas, streets, and boulevards—the accumulated framework and infrastructure of the public spaces of cities grand and small, which provide the setting for social interaction that was so fundamental to the health and welfare of their citizens—places that played an important role in their daily life as well as in the spirit, understanding, and imagination of workers, poets, artists, business leaders, and politicians. I was fascinated by the evolution, form, elements, and management of the civic spaces that I admired and looked long and hard at them. I returned to America to teach in a department of landscape architecture that even then was internationally distinguished for its pioneering work in ecological planning and design, and almost immediately I became involved in an ambitious transportation and civic design study for Washington, DC, funded by the National Endowment for the Arts.

Among the many proposals we made as part of that work was one for a light rail system utilizing portions of the L'Enfant plan's street pattern, with one portion running along K Street. (Now, forty years later, this portion is apparently finally proceeding.) I was interested to see which of the things I'd absorbed of European public life could be applied here. I also had come to the conclusion that unless we could make our cities rich and satisfying places to live, and help Americans see a reason to live more densely, we'd never be able to stop the disastrous sprawl of suburban development, we'd never be able to save the rural and agricultural lands near cities that are so important, nor even the more distant forests and wilderness.

As I began teaching, I recalled a remarkable essay I'd read when a student myself in architecture school in 1959 that J. B. Jackson had written and published in his little, yet prescient, magazine *Landscape,* titled "The Imitation of Nature." In it he discusses the impossibility of doing so. Jackson wrote, "As a man-made environment every city has three functions to fulfill: it must be a just and efficient social institution; it must be a biologically wholesome habitat; and it must be a continuously satisfying aesthetic-sensory experience."[5]

Almost immediately upon opening an office of my own with Bob Hanna in 1976, we plunged into several significant projects in a brief five-year span of intense activity, risk, experiment, and optimism—some might also say with as much naiveté as ambition. These included the Sixteenth Street Transitway Mall in Denver, the master plan for Battery Park City in New York City, and the Fifth Avenue Terrace of the New York Public Library, which was soon followed by the adjoining Bryant Park. Building a young office staff with all of us learning on the job, we also began to gain an understanding of the difficulties of producing significant and workable public space in the latter part of the twentieth century in the United States. Within the next several years, while these first projects were under construction, we also began work on entire districts and significant public spaces in Europe and America, necessitating further consideration regarding the intersection of purpose, character, elements, and arrangement within particular environments and cultures to shape the public realm: the Playa Vista development in Los Angeles, and Canary Wharf, Bishopsgate, Ludgate, and King's Cross redevelopment projects in London.

Henri Lefebvre, a French social scientist, has written, "Each society offers up its own particular space."[6] In ancient Greece there was the *polis,* consisting of the agora and various public stoas, streets, and ways. After the developments in nineteenth-century Paris and New York referred to above, major Western cities incorporated what Lefebvre refers to as "bourgeoisie space," with their emphasis on places of exchange and commerce. As many understand, much of what we think of as public places today in this country are really not civic spaces at all. Much of our environment is really an expression of economic determinism, subject to privilege, exclusion, surveillance, and commercial management. As Rowe observes, Lefebvre posits that

> genuine social space is made up of an ensemble of vital characteristics. First, it is a matter of accommodating social practices, including necessary performance criteria and standards of competence—to be able to promenade down a street, for instance,

without having to concentrate unduly, or avoid bumping into other people, or falling into open basement areas. Second, it is a matter of having a sufficient "representativeness" to the space in question by way of signs and other codes, so that it is legible, imaginable, and so on. In short, not to mistake a church for a dry-cleaners, for example. And third, social practices require representational spaces embodying complex symbolism about, for example, identity, ownership, or civic pride. In civic realist terms, . . . this means creatively making environments for those practices involving the state and civil society in everyday life, which are either widely regarded or warrant distinction.[7]

Another key criterion for social space that emerges is the tolerance for a real variety of social practices within limits that are well defined by custom and the physical attributes of a place itself. Over the years, as I worked on these urban projects and thought about those that I felt were exemplary and began to watch how the places we'd been making were working, I also realized that Olmsted had got something rather profoundly right, namely our need for contact with natural phenomena. Considering the increasing urbanization of world culture, questions of human and social well-being, and our relationship to nature and its attributes as a matter of health, personal self-understanding, physical development, and social justice are topics facing all those who plan and design public space in urban situations. The needs of children and the elderly, for example—not a central audience for civic design in the past, largely because their needs were accommodated through a looseness in the settlement and urban fabric as well as family and social structures unlike most today—are rarely addressed as influential in the design of cities or public space. As the middle class struggles in America and elsewhere today just to maintain the situation it enjoyed in the past century, and other cultures attempt to achieve or deny a successful and open middle class and its amenities, questions of resource allocation and content, design character and elements pose questions for those involved in planning and design.

The work of my office has from the start taken a clear position on these issues through what I have referred to as a conscious concern for the "perfection of the ordinary." This stems from an interest and conviction that commonplace and everyday environments—provided they are of sufficient quality—can bring people into contact with the essence of things and thereby provide them with an excitement or deep comfort about the world they inhabit. Moreover, if one's daily routine and spatial experiences can be rendered well in ordinary terms, both the meaningfulness and congeniality of public life will be greatly enhanced. Instead of being banal or mundane, brutal and disorienting, carefully orchestrated ordinary spatial and sensory experiences can bring us close to the world and in a natural relationship to it.

At about the same time my partners and I were developing much of our early work in the office in Philadelphia, I moved my teaching activity to Harvard. Across the street in Emerson Hall, home of the philosophy department, Hilary Putnam, Stanley Cavell, and Nelson Goodman were debating and working their way through what has come to be referred to as "ordinary language" problems, in part having to do with nagging doubts about our relationship to the existence of the world, or at least our ability to deal with persistent problems of meaning. I found their work inspiring in part because of their interest in our capacity to have meaningful, useful exchanges and shared lives through the employment of "ordinary" language.[8] My interest in the "ordinary" was a decidedly quotidian one. I felt that pursuing it in our work provided a useful basis for deciding things that my colleagues felt to be truly "un-decidable aspects of expressive meaning."[9]

There is a lot of talk about sustainability these days, a topic that landscape architects have been concerned with for centuries. A central premise of sustainability is (or should be) that of sustaining health, both mental and physical (as if they could be separated!). Many since classical antiquity (philosophers, artists, social critics, architects, poets) have posited that urban areas and cities are harsh and unhealthy environments and that natural and rural ones are healthier, even morally superior. They discount, however, that there are serious problems and issues in rural environments as well. One can behave ethically or unethically, morally or immorally, in any environment, especially today. I can personally attest to the fact that rural poverty can at times be even more bestial and hopeless than that of urban areas, certainly for children, who often have more options and opportunities in cities than their country cousins. Nevertheless, this recurring feeling about cities is grounded in something that has a factual basis. Thoreau, Emerson, and Olmsted all felt the profound attraction of nature and wrote extensively and passionately about the subject, even while attracted to and working within the context of community and rapidly expanding cities.

A few years ago Richard Louv gathered together a worrying and well-considered amount of information from scientific research, educational studies and reports, clinical data, and the writing of thoughtful journalists and governmental agencies in a remarkable book titled *Last Child in the Woods*, in which he makes a case for what he described as "nature-deficit disorder."[10] He presents the case that contact with nature is essential for the healthy physical and emotional development of children. He doesn't propose it as a cure-all for the wave of obesity, attention-deficit disorders, depression, anxiety, and other ills afflicting more and more people, especially the young in developed societies, but the many studies and researchers he surveys make a compelling case for the role that exposure to and familiarity with nature and natural phenomena play in the care and feeding of our nervous system, mental development, and acuity.

More recently, researchers at Heriot-Watt University and the University of Edinburgh, both in Scotland, have conducted a series of studies to test the ancient assumption that the combination of contact with nature, fresh air, and moderate exercise as a break from urban routine is fundamentally good for people. Many of us have had the ad-hoc and personal feeling of well-being or an improved mood after a breath of fresh air and a stroll through a park on a lunch break or weekend, but these academics decided to see what basis, if any, there might be for such a conclusion physiologically. As reported in the *British Journal of Sports Medicine*, they attached portable EEG (electroencephalograph) machines to a number of healthy young adults and sent them out on a predetermined walk through three different urban scenes for a mile and a half. It included a historic shopping district with handsome architecture, numerous pedestrians, and light traffic, then a park-like setting, and finally a busy commercial district with contemporary concrete-and-glass architecture and heavy traffic. The result was what one might expect. The recorded brain waves showed mental activity in areas associated with frustration and coping with difficulty while in the busy commercial area and a calmer state as the subjects moved through green spaces. Furthermore, rather than merely exhibiting fewer signs of stress, the recorded data even showed patterns similar to those of subjects involved in meditation or quiet concentration. As one researcher remarked about the mental activity observed in the more natural setting, "It's called involuntary attention in psychology; it holds our attention while at the same time allowing scope for reflection."[11] In other words, a brief stroll through a park area is more than a mere palliative against urban stress; it is also a situation that allows for and encourages mental acuity and activity of a productive or creative kind.

On the roof of a conference center in Salt Lake City that I designed with the architect Bob Frasca, from Portland, Oregon, is a subalpine meadow. It is a version of what Alexander Pope referred to as "calling in the country." As suggested earlier, designers, poets, and potentates before Olmsted on numerous occasions proposed the importation of natural landscapes into cities, literally *rus in urbe*, creating landscapes that attempted to reproduce aspects of natural scenery in parks, gardens, and estates. Many of these were developed in conjunction with natural features such as streams, rivers, escarpments, and sites that posed difficulty or hazard for development and opportunity for gardens, villas, parks, and recreation. As a result, many historic urban areas have a legacy of great parks that are well loved and heavily used. Unfortunately, as most cities around the world and their economic problems have grown in recent decades, many societies have been unable or unwilling to continue such practices at a scale commensurate with the needs of their population for such beneficial domains, or at least not at the scale of the need. But even on a smaller scale there are a lot of things one can do.

One example of this is our project for Columbus Circle in midtown Manhattan. Many civic spaces from the past that I've studied and grown fond of—whether in Europe, America, or Asia—possess a spirit of generosity, a largesse or surplus of some kind, whether it be of space, materials, scale, furnishings, or delight in some form. Columbus Circle was a space that had been through many iterations before its devolution in the 1980s into a bewildering and dysfunctional intersection.

In 1988 Bob Hanna and I were asked by the Central Park Conservancy to see if we could fix it, but were dismissed by Henry Stern, the city's parks commissioner at the time, when we tried to straighten out the awkward entry to Central Park created by Robert Moses that was a complete mess, including the removal of a number of weed trees that had obscured the original spatial composition of the Olmsted and Vaux design. Other professionals later executed some aspects of our proposal for the park side of the circle after Stern left office. We returned to work on it for a second time in 1997 as part of an ideas competition sponsored by the Municipal Art Society, which ended without any result.

On that occasion I was interested in the potential of revealing the layers of subway concourses beneath it, and the possibility of connecting the spaces visually with skylights, fountains, and seating that would create a public theater of sorts around the monument to the eponymous ancient mariner. When it finally and oddly became a viable project in the late autumn after the terrorist attack of 9/11, in the waning days of the Giuliani administration, the MTA forbade us from opening up their concourses with a skylight, and the Streets Department prevented us from unifying the entire circus—center island, roadways, and surrounding walks—with unit pavers of any sort, let alone in stone as I thought would be a good thing to do.

Nevertheless, I was determined to create more than a mere refuge from traffic, and pushed for an open, attractive place into which one could step out of the city for a moment even while still in it, to create a place where one could look around, relax, meet friends, merely just be, or take a shortcut across the intersection. All of this we have done through the employment of several devices. I posited that because it was called a "circle," it should return to being one. First, the traffic was reorganized by Philip Habib, a brilliant transportation planner and civil engineer, with three new carefully located signals and pedestrian crossings. Next we manipulated the topography, creating a planted berm around the outside of an island with stepped fountains on the inside and broad walkways sliced through. We then inverted what had existed before. Formerly the monument to Columbus had stood in a basin, a miserable puddle, which even with its peculiarly small size kept people away from the monument. The entire ensemble had been wide open to the streets and the traffic that swarmed about.

Instead we removed the midget moat and railing around Columbus, created a true island surrounded by water in large and generous fountains backed by mounds, which in combination mask the noise of traffic and the city, and added a ring of native American trees (yellow buckeyes,

Aesculus flava), an ensemble of elements providing movement, light, color, and cooling on hot summer days. I liked that it was an island; after all, Columbus discovered a group of islands, not a continent.

Conventional wisdom holds that seating, especially park benches, should always have backs to lean against comfortably. Here I concluded, however, that there was no correct direction to face—some would want to look at the fountains and some at the statue or across the circle— and that the vertical presence of bench backs would chop up the rela- tively small space and cut off the fountains from the center and across the space visually. So we made enormous long curving benches with the cross-section of a wide wooden pillow. As a result, people come at all hours of the day and night, in groups, couples, and singly, to sit or stretch out in all directions on these benches, as well as on the rescued steps of the base of the historic monument in the middle.

It has become truly a new place to be in the city that never existed before, and it is in the middle of a five-way intersection. There is a remarkable sense of amplitude and civic welcome within this relatively small space. Additionally, people also now use it as a convenient and pleasant way to traverse the intersection, something unheard of before.

Imagine my pleasure when, less than a year after it was completed, the *New Yorker* magazine used a drawing of it as seen from the win- dows of the Jazz at Lincoln Center facility in the adjacent Time Warner building as a graphic image of the city for one of their festivals—it had already become a recognizable and memorable place that was part of their self-image. It had taken a place on the mental map of New Yorkers as an iconic spot, and a pleasurable one at that.

The principle of making places particular and not generic is as important as making them well. On one of my first projects, Denver's Sixteenth Street Transitway Mall, back in 1977, I was asked during a public meeting by the head of the metro area's Regional Transporta- tion District why I was proposing to pave twelve blocks of a street with polychrome granite (and trees). I responded that it was a better deal than building such an important street at the heart of the city of out of concrete or asphalt. I suggested that it was the single most important public space in the heart of the polis and that they couldn't afford to build it cheaply or badly. In my view it was a place where the citizens could come and be together, to see and interact with each other, and as the commercial core of the metropolitan region it needed to be special. I pointed out the relatively short and shorter life of concrete and asphalt roadways in the Denver region due to the remarkable freeze/thaw cycles of their climate, and that stone, especially granite, a material produced under intense heat and pressure, was one of the most durable materials on the planet—that we didn't know how long it would last before needing to be replaced, since most of the ancient Appian Way was still in place except for a portion that had been stolen by the Mafia for resale as a durable building material. How could Denver not afford to build seriously in their most public space?

The scheme our office developed in collaboration with Henry Cobb, I. M. Pei's partner, was conceptually very simple. It consisted of a pavement conceived as a carpet runner, albeit twelve blocks long, with two rows of trees and lights that were more like floor lamps than street lights, which shone down on the pavement and up into the trees. The carpet pattern was largely inspired by several nineteenth-century Navajo trading blankets, although I will admit I had noticed some rattlesnake-skin belts in a tourist shop on the street when I was doing my initial site reconnaissance. Also, the ghost or memory of the pavement in the Pantheon in Rome hovered somewhere in the back of my mind.

There were small fountains at the beginning and end of the central portion for punctuation and a handful of benches. I proposed movable chairs as I was familiar with in Europe and would propose for Bryant Park a few years later. I didn't want to do much else, so as to allow the community to figure out how much else they wanted and how best to use it their way.

Our details weren't perfect—and as with many young design professionals when their office is starting out, we were learning on the job. Our work has always been an experiment. Over the years there have been some necessary repairs and maintenance; however, the net effect has been overwhelmingly positive. Recent efforts by Downtown Denver Inc., a business organization, and the Regional Transportation District to make changes ran into strong opposition from the citizenry, who have declared it a well-loved historic landmark. When I informed a public meeting on the topic that I was the original designer and that several improvements would be appropriate, I was told to forget it. The Mall was theirs and they didn't want anyone messing with it!

This public scheme has helped to generate hundreds of millions of dollars in investment and construction and is the most popular and visited site in the city. Our notion that a well-built, handsome street of granite with trees, something similar to Barcelona's Las Ramblas or a stretched piazza, might work as a sociable space even in contemporary America proved successful. So much so that it was subsequently expanded further to extend the urban regeneration. The degree to which for a time it became attractive to homeless people and young teens with nowhere else in particular to go didn't mean there was something wrong with our design, only with its surroundings and management, along with larger problems in the general society regarding inequity, poverty, and drugs. I'm happy to say that today it is managed well once more, and ordinary middle-class office workers, shoppers, and visitors as well as disadvantaged individuals are all happily accommodated. It is a truly civic space: open, communal, democratic, generous, and life-affirming.

We began that project in 1977—thirty-seven years ago. Twenty-four years later, in 2001, I joined a group of local professionals in the city of Portland, Oregon, to study an urban situation they'd puzzled about for several generations: what to do with an area facing redevelopment that was located between two distinctly different but important and well-loved sequences of parks. A design charette sponsored by the City Planning Department and the American Institute of Architects had concluded that what was at the time an open city block used for surface parking should become a park. It belonged to an adjacent property owner, who agreed to let the city build a park, which would thereby enhance his property, if he could build a below-grade multistory parking garage. This was approved and went into construction before design for the park—not the best order to do things, but one we often encounter.

When interviewed for the project, I proposed to my colleagues (landscape architect Carol Mayer-Reed and the architecture firm ZGF) that we create a small urban piazza, partly in contrast to all the other public spaces in the city and region and partly because it seemed to offer something that I believed would be popular and well used in that particular location, climate, and city. This led to discussions about what should constitute a park today. Despite my thoughts about the need for access to nature in cities, I was not particularly interested since too much of the debate centered around lawn, naturalism, and the appropriateness of a café. The city and region are as verdant as anywhere in North America, literally dripping with vegetation, so I felt that something else could be welcome. I am neither a formula nor a rules guy in terms of public space. I simply felt that it would be nice to create a lovely place that looked good even when damp on a gray drizzly day and where one could sit under shelter and socialize, read a paper, have a coffee or snack, meet a friend, watch people, and relax. I was interested in comfort and in making it welcoming. This meant that it needed to be open and have a variety of comfortable, attractive, and generous seating. I also knew that there are few truly special public squares and parks I really like that don't have water and trees. So, Simon and Helen Director Park ended up with just that mix of things.

I began some sketches. In this return to the Pacific Northwest, my interest in its damp atmosphere and fascination for constructed lithic (stone) surfaces to some extent drove the scheme. Why, I wondered, didn't people in the rainy Northwest cover public squares with glass, like the great train sheds and arcades of nineteenth-century Europe? I'd spent many hours outdoors in winter on a porch when I lived on Bainbridge Island in Puget Sound. One could read, write, draw, paint, eat, and be with friends out of doors most of the year if under cover.

Also, as every landscape architect knows, water runs downhill. The site was a small one, measuring only 30 by 60 meters, and sloped considerably from south to north. In response, I proposed a couple of level terraces with a high canopy of glass, a small café, and loose tables and chairs, with a fountain at the low end of the site to catch, gather, and hold water when it rains or that is sprayed up out of the pavement a bit further uphill when it was sunny and dry.

There are also benches, and various furnishings such as movable chairs and tables, as well as a giant chessboard in the pavement under a small grove of trees. Like many of our projects, the whole thing is built over structure—here, five levels of a subterranean parking garage—which necessitated sizable vent and stair structures amounting to small pavilions as well. Despite concern expressed by some that it needed to be softer, with more planting, I argued that Portland was awash in vegetation, that its citizens lived in the most verdant region of the United States, and that this wasn't what they needed more of in this particular space. I also argued for a café with public toilets, convinced that it was

wrongheaded to build public places without such fundamental amenities, and that one could not depend on neighboring businesses that are
subject to the vagaries of economic cycles and would likely not want
noncustomers using their facilities, especially individuals fallen on hard
times or mothers who just wanted to change their infants' diapers.

Making a case for a fountain of some sort, I suggested that it needed
to be rather modest, possibly even silly, not grand. This was because
just across town is located one of the great works of twentieth-century
landscape design, the Ira Keller Fountain (formerly known as the Auditorium Forecourt Fountain) by Lawrence Halprin, which possesses tons
of water in cascades and can only be described as majestic. Larry was
one of my heroes, and that particular work along with its earlier com-
panions, Pettygrove Park and Lovejoy Plaza and Fountain, were enormously inspirational to me when I was entering the field. I recall saying
in one of the presentations for this new park that with Beethoven down
the street one didn't do Beethoven, but something else, something with
a lighter touch. I thought of this space as analogous to a small salon
in the palace of the city, one for chamber music and intimate gatherings, not grand balls and orchestra concerts. My associate at the time,
Tiffany Beamer, who has since become a partner in the Los Angeles
office, made a delightful small study model for us to play with and to
use in talks with our fountain consultant, the CMS Collaborative from
California, who had done the hydraulics for Halprin two decades earlier
across town.

As with several other projects of mine, the plaza surface was conceived as a fabric of stone. While it began with the memory of woven
baskets, in this case several by Native tribes who once lived in the
Columbia River basin, it is monochromatic. Here I wanted the pavement to be quiet, calm, and elegant, with its visual interest and richness
coming from texture and pattern. I began exploring various herringbone
patterns and block sizes, shapes, and textures. The lovely blond granite
we found, reminiscent of the pale grasses, straw, and roots of the Native
American baskets, is cut into long, thin blocks. Most are bush ham-
mered, which gives a uniformly textured finish, but a series of lines runs
diagonally through the pattern, made from blocks that are "reeded,"
that is, tooled with a corrugation. Water, light, and dirt enhance these
textures whether dry or wet. On some days and from some directions it

is sharp and noticeable, and on others and under different conditions it is more subtle and barely noticeable to some.

Stair treads from the terraces that feather into the slope are handsomely tooled and modular with the pavers. As often happens on our projects, the workmen building it became intrigued, realizing it was special, and got into what they were making, producing a beautiful product.

Another aspect of this new urban *place* is that we persuaded the city government to extend the biscuit-colored stone pavement across two vehicular streets and sidewalks from building face to building face from east to west, creating a continuous carpet. Vehicles entering the space driving north or south, therefore, move into and through the square, sharing the same paving as pedestrians. This stone and its texture cause drivers to move more slowly than on other blocks. It makes it safer and makes a statement of civic purpose—it is a place for people, comfort, and enjoyment, not automobiles and traffic.

Such things matter.

For a number of years our office has conducted an ongoing set of experiments in public seating, the most famous being the introduction of moveable chairs in Bryant Park in Manhattan. This is an old-hat thing in Europe but was a real stretch for New Yorkers thirty years ago. In several projects I have explored what was deemed another counterintuitive notion, the backless benches mentioned earlier. Most people, myself included, believe that public seating should have backs, for obvious reasons of comfort and a sense of support and security. There are, however, numerous instances when backs on benches are undesirable due to contextual issues of sightlines and views and a need to allow people to face in more than a prescribed way, as I noted above regarding Columbus Circle. How then to make such benches attractive?

The first time I experimented with backless benches was at Robert Wagner Jr. Park in Battery Park City, also in Manhattan. I decided to try to make them overly generous, to make them unusually broad and very long, theorizing that it would be an attractive thing in itself. This would also allow people to sit in opposing directions without impinging on each other—they would not have to touch or accidentally bang into strangers—while it would allow people to sit, sprawl, or lie about as they chose. We gave this bench the profile of a great cushion, while it also vaguely recalled a boat deck, docks, piers, and other wooden structures. Later evolutions of this idea, at the Washington Monument and Columbus Circle, convinced me that there were times and places for this device as well as for the ubiquitous loose tables and chairs and continuous wall-mounted benches that we also have employed.

We ended up using all of these seating approaches at Director Park, which is not a trivial aspect of the sociology of the place. People are free to select and associate with others or maintain their independence in a remarkable variety of ways. This allows for a truly open and civic space that is used by all manner of individuals: old people, young people, office workers, shoppers, the homeless, mothers with prams and infants, teenagers, opera goers, movie goers, people of all classes and incomes can be seen in Portland's Director Park at various times throughout the seasons.

The frequent light rain of the region falling on the tall civic-scaled canopy is led to a series of planted filtering troughs that form the support for a bench at the terrace while resolving the difference between the sloping street and the level terrace. Water that falls on the stone streets and much of the square is led to planters along the two streets for filtering before being passed on to storm drains—where eventually, according to earlier planning, it will arrive at O'Bryant Square, two blocks away downhill, which is intended to be designed to cleanse and detain in a contemporary water garden. Water that runs into the fountain, whether rain or recycled, is caught, filtered, treated, and recycled. The small café structure has a green roof.

When Director Park was completed, journalists and landscape architect design award jurors who looked at the park were mildly friendly but have referred to it as stark, and appeared to be puzzled that it seems to work and be heavily used by people—in short, that it was OK—partly, I suspect, because it was unfortunately called a "park" and didn't possess any lawn or bounteous planting. They didn't seem to notice that it's bounded by trees, which, if my colleagues and I have gotten our homework right, will continue to grow for many years until they are quite large and have a significant presence in this small place. Time is an aspect of our medium that most people can't see or feel. The bosque at the small space with the chessboard is composed of yellowwoods (*Cladastris kentukea*), a lovely tree from the Appalachians discovered by John Bartram that will surprise people with long pendulous racemes of white blossoms hanging down in spring—more or less heavily every other year. While all the parts are perfectly ordinary, the ensemble is not.

Simon and Helen Director Park seems enormously popular. Despite its small size and lack of lawn, it attracts a wide diversity of people of all ages and economic strata throughout the day and into the night. In 2012, the city's park department took counts of users every day through the summer. Between the hours of noon and 7 p.m. there were typically more than a hundred people per hour using this small space. In August, an average of over two thousand people were counted in the park between 10 a.m. and 10 p.m. Old people, mothers with prams and children, office workers, shoppers, all find their way to it and hang out. While one must be wary of such quantitative methods in judging quality—the high body counts during the Vietnam War are one of the most dramatic proofs that quantitative measurement does not necessarily equate with qualitative or other success at all—even so, the people in Portland have embraced this new portion of their public realm with enthusiasm. Despite the "useful" nature of our work, I continue to believe that what we do remains very much an art, not a science, and that contrary to popular belief, it is easier to teach science and technocracy than art and humanism. Every place is different, and to try to fit the design of good civic space into some procrustean bed of urban design rules and formulae is both fruitless and wrong.

Earlier I linked the emergence of realism with the emergence of the middle class in modern society as well as a dramatic increase in the creation of civic space for public health and recreation. The economic and political developments that accompanied this have delivered remarkable benefits and great disappointments in the successes and failures of democratic governments and materialist (capitalist) consumer society. The worries of Alexis de Tocqueville, Thoreau, and Emerson about the competition for control between the individual and the group, the threats to minorities and tyranny of the majority, have played out against a background struggle for self-realization and freedom. The work of our office takes a firm stand on both—that public spaces must be open, accessible, generous, and welcoming to individuals of all sorts, and designed so as to discourage domination by any, all the while encouraging respectful and sociable behavior. This has been one of the great lessons of the rise of the middle class in Europe and America, something envied around the world.

These attitudes, approaches, instincts, and feelings, when employed with care and informed with appropriate knowledge and concern for beauty and the human spirit as well as affection for life and society, can make the chances of success high. Much of what one does while in the act of working seems to flow from instinct and to be dependent on the myriad things one has seen and done, learned and filed away somewhere, often deep down.

All of this leads to a recurring paradox within modernity: we have a deep yearning—and apparent need—for new, fresh, and innovative paradigms that can cope with the scale and character of our contemporary urban landscape, while at the same time we have a continuing need for older, timeless relationships and essences, for ancient tropes regarding humans and nature. One of the hallmarks of nearly all avant-garde movements and youth is a desire to challenge authority and the way things are or have been. Transgression, as an opening career move, is a default position for those who wish to make their mark in the arts and design. Yet a disruptive public realm is not particularly useful or of benefit to society. In recent times many prominent designs, especially in architecture, that have been widely publicized in current journals show little concern for the success of cities and society or even the many aspects of the current understanding of "sustainability."

Do not mistake this as a conservative argument in disguise, or a rear-guard attack on contemporary design. It would be more proper to call me a "good old-fashioned modernist" of the sort that pursued an overt progressive political agenda. I have purposefully distanced myself from postmodernism, New Urbanism, Landscape Urbanism, and the more extreme self-proclaimed ecologically determinist camps. Peter Rowe has written that underneath our work at Bryant Park and Battery Park City there was a use of classic typologies and a slippery use of precedents that directed people toward familiarity, use, and behavior which was as ethically based as it was aesthetic.[12] I'm sure this is as true today as it was in this early work. I also know, as hinted earlier, that well-designed cities cannot imitate all or very much of nature, but they can incorporate aspects of it that we find stimulating and essential—

those aspects that set in play the beautiful shapes and forms, elegant and simple, elaborate and complex, changeable and recurrent, stable and moving, with passages of shade, pools of light, the play of vegetation, changes of surface and level, varying views and perspectives—"the splash of water in fountains, echoes and music; . . . the harmony of colors and the unpolluted sun" that J. B. Jackson evoked.[13] These are all very ordinary things, but to make them available for citizens in their daily routine at the heart of our cities is to serve up a dose of reality and its life-affirming nature.

To conclude: my interest in the "ordinary" or "common" is not to be confused with an anti-intellectual stance or the attacks on elites or sophistication such as one encounters all too often in the popular press or the unfortunate political posturing of numerous individuals and organizations in America today. Philosophers such as Heidegger, Wittgenstein, and Stanley Cavell instead relate an interest in ordinariness to attitudes one finds in a number of ancient poets and thinkers in Asia, and particularly to an attitude expressed by Emerson and Thoreau as well. This is an eschewing of derivative secondhand stimulus and a desire to partake of existence and life directly, firsthand. As Cavell puts it, "an intimacy with existence" and a "natural relation to existence is what Thoreau means by our being *next* to the laws of nature, by our *neighboring* the world, by our being *beside* ourselves. Emerson's idea of the *near* is one of the inflections he gives the common, the low." He goes on to say that the "recurrent appeal to ordinary language in the history of philosophy [from the time of Socrates through the Enlightenment and modernity] is a sign that there is some inner wish of philosophy to escape as well as to recover the natural."[14]

Emerson's "embracing the common" is not a repudiation of culture and science, of the advancement of art and intellect. He does, however, specifically state his preference "not for the great, the remote, the romantic," but for what has been described as a "continued search for a new intimacy in the self's relation to its world."[15] His stated goal in "The American Scholar" is to call upon his fellow citizens to turn away from imitations and foreign styles and derivative thought, and to discover or rediscover the world within themselves and the world around them. This was not a jingoistic, nationalistic, or ethnocentric call to arms, but rather a directive that asked, as Thoreau does in *Walden,* for us to create a life, art, and a nation that is fresh, authentic, and whole—in a word, as natural as nature when we draw near to it and take it in, with both understanding and passion.

My invocation of the middle class, or of children, as the consciously intended recipients of my efforts in the design of civic space and landscape, is not to miss the irony of their usual and general obliviousness to their situation or the topics of my concerns. The suspicion, anger, and attacks on the middle class (vilified as the bourgeoisie, whether petite or haute bourgeoisie) on the part of numerous intellectuals and artists throughout the last two centuries that continue today might appear to be directed toward generations of those who have labored through misery, hard work, tedium, and deadening decades in industry, commerce, and homes, who have suffered and struggled to make a decent life for themselves and their families. But in fact it has really been intended toward the hypocrisy, petty concerns and ambitions, self-deception, waste, pretension, and thoughtless expense, competition, and escapism, along with the lies and manipulation of leaders and politicians who have used and abused them on every continent. The critiques of both capitalism and collectivism are many and often correct and well founded.

As a landscape architect and artist it is my firm belief, however, that it is neither romanticism nor pandering to attempt to create rewarding public environments that are accessible to all—rich, poor, young, old, able, disadvantaged—especially for the many who work and strive and are buffeted by the forces of society and life, a populace sorely manipulated by commerce and politics. It is not a sop or mere palliative to attempt to create places that allow them to come in touch with natural phenomena directly, with themselves and their senses and sensibilities, along with their fellow citizens and the larger community.

For me, this seems a direct response to the problem of realism, and to both Ezra Pound's directive to "make it new" and Emerson and Thoreau's challenge that we "draw near" to the world, to nature, and to ourselves while in the heart of our cities.

GLOBAL, REGIONAL, LOCAL

(2015)

What is one to think today of traditional concepts related to regional issues of heritage and of the local, or the hoary topic of *sense of place,* in what is frequently referred to as the age of globalism? I propose to survey such concerns as expressed in the work of the OLIN firm over forty years of practice, particularly in relation to the twin poles of culture and nature, in an attempt to address a contemporary civic realm and the making of robust and meaningful places.

Twenty-some years ago I delivered a paper at Dumbarton Oaks on regionalism in American landscape design and in the work of our office.[1] I thought I had dealt with the topic adequately from my perspective and turned to the consideration of other things in addition to practice and teaching, particularly how to produce landscape meaning and value in a manner other than through iconography, inscription, or overt symbols, namely through artistic deployment of the medium itself. The topic and problems raised, however, haven't gone away. Respected colleagues and friends have taken me to task regarding some of my statements in this effort, while issues of authenticity and meaning, along with slippery aspects regarding the nature of identity and place, keep surfacing thanks to globalism and the evolving nature of practice and urbanism.

Not infrequently people ask me, "How is it you can work in such

Delivered as the Ian McHarg Memorial Lecture, University of Pennsylvania, School of Design, Spring 2015.

different locations or regions or countries?" It is, I suppose, a reasonable question and expresses genuine curiosity. The implication is that they are suspicious of a landscape architect who attempts to work somewhere other than where he or she lives—and particularly if one's inquisitor is in America somewhere, the implication is "How can you adequately know about our plants, soils, and climate?" Or if one is talking with someone in Europe, Asia, or somewhere other than the United States, "How can you possibly understand us and our way of being, habits, values, and heritage?" Underlying these questions and assumptions are two others. First, that landscape architecture is mostly about plants, and therefore, if you live in one place you must know it and its flora and ecology well, but everywhere else is so different and special that it would be unlikely for you to know their environment adequately. This is probably true for many individuals and laymen, even some professionals, but certainly not for others.

Admittedly, despite what appear to be similarities, the ecology, climate, and topography of the high Sierras is considerably different from that of mountainous islands in the Atlantic off the coast of Maine. It is certainly true that for centuries many people went about the world doing inappropriate things environmentally, such as introducing, all over Phoenix and Southern California, many square miles of cool-weather grasses of European origin that have had to be artificially irrigated ever since. But this line of thought is flawed in that landscape architecture entails much more than planting, despite the fact that plants, horticulture, and ecology are fundamental aspects of our medium in the way that bricks and structural engineering are part of architecture, which also happen to be part of landscape architecture's vocabulary as well.

A second assumption, that the cultural history of a particular place makes for differences that cannot be understood or adequately addressed by an outsider or foreign professional, today is equally flawed, although it too derives from clichés that are based on centuries of misunderstanding and poor performance on the part of many travelers, governments, missionaries, traders, and design professionals. Inappropriate agriculture has led to starvation and disastrous plant invasions; inappropriate planning and buildings have led to dysfunctional cities and social misery, even chaos—from the tropics to the arctic. Many centuries of cultural evolution and artistic invention in different parts of the globe are an essential part of what makes humans so special. In the past this has been part of what kept us separate. But the legacy of sixteenth-century gardens created on opposite sides of the globe in China and Italy belongs to all of us today as an inspiration of what the imagination is capable of.

So—let's take stock of the situation and possibilities. First, what is commonly meant by the term "regionalism" ecologically, culturally, and in design? In my Dumbarton Oaks paper I wrote, "Generally, *region* is a term used to connote a geographic area of considerable extent, indefinite in size and shape, that despite considerable diversity within its parts exhibits some overall commonality or possesses a set of shared properties that render it distinct from other areas and their general properties, which are in some way(s) different."[2] Regions can be described in terms of geology, such as the Triassic Basin of the mid-Atlantic coastal region, or in terms of biomes at several scales, such as the oak-deer-maple or temperate deciduous forest region, the maple-beech-hemlock or eastern and northern and upland regions, and so on.

Mountain ranges in regions thousands of miles apart may look similar, but we know that they aren't really. As often as not, each region grades into another and is a constellation of various factors having to do with dynamic communities within a physiographic setting. Social scientists, particularly anthropologists and ethnographers engaged in the study of human settlements and communities, have likewise described cultural regions around the world. And here other differences emerge. As I noted in my earlier paper, Henry Glassie has observed that variations in folk culture are spatial (that is, regional), while those in popular and academic culture are temporal (that is, they tend to fall into periods). In Glassie's view, works of art and other products of the dominant culture exist not in regions but in a placeless continuum.[3] This fits well with the way we generally use the terms *regional* and *regionalism:* to distinguish a broad range of work that is not seen as part of mainstream or contemporary culture; in broader movements it often reflects a group's intent to express its identity, particularly in resistance to the cultural hegemony of distant centers of power and influence. Geographic isolation or separation also contributes to regional identity. Glassie suggests that folk culture is backward-looking and resists change; thus there is a conflict between regionalist movements and dominant trends such as international modernism.[4]

I also observed that *versions,* or "regional" variations, are a key concept, as with regional schools of painting and writing as compared to the more dominant or "standard" models. For example, in my own life there have been different groups of painters in the Pacific Northwest, the Bay Area, and New York City that were considered local or regional "schools," each with its prominent figures and what were generally regarded as shared stylistic characteristics, but all very much twentieth-century modernists, whether their work was deemed abstract or more narrative and representational in expression. The work of Frank Lloyd Wright and his colleagues in the Midwest in the early decades of the twentieth century produced one of the most distinctive "regional" styles in American architectural history, the prairie school, which began as a local interpretation of the more general Arts and Crafts movement in late Victorian domestic design that was prevalent on both sides of the Atlantic.

A key strategy employed in the first half of the twentieth century to "ground" a building regionally often entailed the transformation of a somewhat generic building program into something recognized as reflecting aspects of a local nature. Remarkable examples of this can be found in the American West, where architects like John Gaw Meem, Gilbert Stanley Underwood, and others were able to shape contemporary typologies—movie theaters, vacation hotels, post offices, museums, railroad stations, and other structures—into evocative works that employed historic motifs, ranging from Spanish Mission forms and details along with American Indian symbols to frontier imagery utilizing local materials along with Art Deco and Beaux-Arts compositional devices. This effort produced a number of romantic yet highly functional and pleasing buildings that continue to work well today while giving identity to their immediate setting. Residences by Greene & Greene and Irving Gill in California, the KiMo Theatre in Albuquerque, National Park lodges at Zion and the Grand Canyon, as well as the Awahnee Hotel in Yosemite and the central post office in Los Angeles, the last two by Underwood, and the Santa Fe art museum, are all now treasured period pieces. At the time they were constructed they were seen as up-to-the-minute, "contemporary," and thought of as both modern and regional in style. They may seem charming, but one can't help asking what we can learn from them—of what use are they to us today?

Two decades ago the answer for me seemed to be offered by Kenneth Frampton's essay "Towards a Critical Regionalism," and I thoroughly accepted it as a good description of my own office's work and ambition at home and abroad. He stated clearly that "the fundamental strategy of Critical Regionalism is to mediate the impact of universal civilization with elements derived *indirectly* from the peculiarities of a particular place. . . . Critical Regionalism depends upon maintaining a high level of self-consciousness. It may find its governing inspiration in such things as the range and quality of the local light, or in a *tectonic* derived from a peculiar structural mode, or in the topography of a given site."[5]

Nothing in recent memory fits this description better than some of the masterpieces of Frank Lloyd Wright. Few buildings of the twentieth century are better wedded to their location than his two homes, Taliesin in Spring Green near Madison, Wisconsin, and Taliesin West in Scottsdale, Arizona, or the Kaufmann home (Fallingwater) in Mill Run, Pennsylvania. In each case they employ local building materials in combination with advanced structural materials and ideas. In each case they transform an ordinary piece of a region into an intense landscape and a unique place to experience the physical properties of the region— its light, its topography, vegetation, seasons, and climate.

As with Wright's example, Frampton was not arguing for a dependence on indigenous or primitive architecture as a crutch, and he noted that "Critical Regionalism cannot be based on the autochthonous forms of a specific region alone." He went on to say, "The case can be made that Critical Regionalism as a cultural strategy is as much a bearer of *world culture* as it is a vehicle of *universal civilization*. . . . [It] is contingent upon a process of double mediation. In the first place, it has to 'deconstruct' the overall spectrum of world culture which it inherently inherits; in the second place, it has to achieve, through synthetic contradiction, a manifest critique of universal civilization."[6]

Around the time that he wrote this, a number of people were puzzling over the issue of global architecture versus place identity, often in terms of a discussion around regionalism. Alexander Tzonis and Liane Lefaivre optimistically wrote that regionalism had suffered an ambiguity since the late nineteenth century and that in general, regionalism "upholds the individual and local architectonic features against more universal and abstract ones. On the one hand, it has been associated with movements of reform and liberation; . . . on the other, it has proved a powerful tool of repression and chauvinism."[7]

Tzonis and Lefaivre continued to publish their analyses of critical regionalism in a series of studies throughout the 1990s and early 2000s.[8] Like Frampton, they used work by Alvar Aalto, Richard Neutra, Oscar Niemeyer, and a number of more recent designers to argue that there was no problem being thoroughly modern or contemporary while at the same time being deeply responsive to place and cultural situation. The work of Aalto, Neutra, Niemeyer, and later architects such as Balkrishna Doshi, Charles Correa, Álvaro Siza, Rafael Moneo, Peter Zumthor, Tadao Ando, and Glenn Murcutt is satisfying aesthetically and is adjusted to its location and climate, society, and use. It is handsomely made and invariably highly valued. While nearly all of these architects produced superb private dwellings, nearly all also created successful major cultural, commercial, and industrial projects as well: a roster of work that passes muster as high-style, mainstream design, while it can also be considered "critical regionalism."

For those who think this is something for the rear guard, let me cite a brilliant example: a project by Frank Gehry in Prague known as Fred and Ginger, or the Dancing House (the Nationale-Nederlanden building)—as magnificent a work of design as it is whimsical. Gehry dexterously fits this building into its context in a number of ways, first in the palette, materials, and colors—creamy stucco, stone, and metalwork—all derived from the precedent of historic buildings of the old city. Next, he plays with moldings and frames, picking out elements in a way that recalls those of the neighbors, drawing a set of rococo lines across the facade while mixing prefabricated industrial components with the traditional plaster and stucco. From the river, in an allusion to the famous dancing film-star couple Fred Astaire and Ginger Rogers, two contrasting small towers, one with a little dome, act as a hinge that marks the end of the block, much as any number of such corner turrets and bays do throughout the old city. A tongue-in-cheek reference to the dome of the Secession Hall in Vienna by Joseph Maria Olbrich shows how closely Gehry has studied the work of his elders, while the nipped-in waist of Ginger, as he jokingly points out, was a nod to Václev Havel and others living up the block—deferring to and enabling their view down the street past his building toward the river. This is a building that is deeply contextual, highly personal, and of its moment. It is a testament to the possibility of critical regionalism in architectural design today.

What then of landscape architecture? As I noted in my Dumbarton Oaks paper, to a degree it is the same thing as in architecture, but as with other aspects of the two fields, the means are somewhat different, and the results often completely different, partly because the medium of landscape leads to different concerns, and partly due to a different perspective regarding place that is not tied to making objects, especially in an era when buildings are often conceived as "products" like other commercial items or gadgets. The physiographic factors of location are the main implication of difference; secondarily, but ultimately as important or more so, are considerations of cultural attitudes, ideas, and conditions.

Harwell Hamilton Harris, a protégé of Frank Lloyd Wright, once wrote: "Opposed to the Regionalism of Restriction is another type of regionalism, the Regionalism of Liberation. This is the manifestation of a region that is especially in tune with the thought of the time. We call such a manifestation 'regional' only because it has not yet emerged elsewhere. . . . A region may develop ideas. A region may accept ideas. Imagination and intelligence are necessary for both."[9] To see the truth of Harris's remarks one need only think of the indoor/outdoor living of postwar California and the development of a local idiom of domestic landscape design that evolved into a modernist style that fused the formal language of School of Paris painting and present-day construction methods with contemporary experiments under way in Latin and South America. It proved a revolution in American landscape design that then spread out into the world and was absorbed into the mainstream, possibly the first "international" design upheaval in style and taste in landscape design since eighteenth-century England.

The work of my office from the very beginning has certainly explored some of the possibilities suggested in the literature of critical regionalism: the employment of a somewhat dialectical relationship between nature—through the incorporation and reference of local vegetation, geologic and natural materials, forms, and processes, and more contingent properties such as climate and light—on the one hand, and more abstract formal and artistic traditions, cultural products, and human needs and behavior on the other hand.

Any journeyman landscape architect just off the boat can usually figure out which plants and materials bespeak a region and should be able to use them effectively. In New England I purposefully settled projects into place with stone walls and maples, but also by using water, in one case as a portion of the mechanical system of the building. Working with mechanical engineers, we took water from the ground, pumped it through the building, returned it to ponds reminiscent of the industrial mill ponds of previous eras, and thence through the stone walls back into gravel beds and the alluvium of the site and the aquifer. This worked technically because of the unique alluvial properties of glacial deposition in the region, which we were familiar with.

On other projects in New England we have used the conifers and native evergreen ground covers that grow on the granite ledges of the coastline, along with erratic boulders left by the retreat of the Wisconsin glacier and stone in various forms, shapes, and situations. One needn't know or quote Robert Frost to take in the local reference and utility of such touches. That one can use such satisfying material for practical purposes as well as to make reference to geologic history and the struggle of early settlers—including their eventual decision to give up and go somewhere else where the soil is deeper, richer, and has few or no stones—is deeply rewarding.

In projects in other regions, a comparable approach to local materials, plants, and stone invariably leads to specificity of place, a wealth of associations, and pleasure. In Rome, working with pines and Mediterranean shrubs and herbaceous plants seemed obvious, but also the use of local tufa from the soft brown volcanic beds found throughout much of the Lazio region, along with the soft Travertine marble and black basalt that characterize so much building there. This was not difficult to understand or do. So too, it was appropriate to acknowledge that there is a history and familiarity of working with water flowing down from the Apennines. What one makes with such regional material, however, is a matter of design and artistic choice. It can be ghastly, ordinary and workmanlike, or something special. With some effort one can produce design that exhibits the sort of critical and thoughtful understanding and achievement associated with the architecture just discussed.

Rarely, I might add: due to its non-objectified nature and because it is spatial, often with considerable extension as a field of inhabitation, it is not as obvious with landscape design or as noticeable as in an isolated building. Thus it is often only in a handful of furnishings or details that one becomes aware of this situation. Normative qualities often pervade landscape design that is well situated in its context or region.

There are or have been, as well, two other related concepts that hang about discussions of regional and local character versus universal, international, or global influence and design. These are the phenomena that are referred to by such words as "place" and "authentic," both of which are frequently employed in design conversation and criticism.

The phrases "genius of the place" and "sense of place" have hovered about discussions of landscape design ever since the former appeared in Alexander Pope's "Epistle to Lord Burlington" of 1731, wherein among other things he wrote, "let Nature never be forgot" and "Consult the Genius of the Place in all; That tells the Waters or to rise, or fall." Borrowing an invocation to the "genius loci" from Virgil's *Aeneid,* Pope and Horace Walpole later referred to a conceptual approach and content in landscape design that today we identify as the English Landscape Garden.

It was a remarkable mixture of classical Roman attitudes, seventeenth-century Italian villas, pastoral visions, and contemporary British agriculture and political activism. The fact that the English climate, topography, and vegetation prevented the adaptation of Italian motifs and design elements from looking Mediterranean, but instead altogether different, underlies the seeming "invention" of this so-called style of design, namely the English park or *jardin anglais.* It is also true that in its overt rejection of baroque details and expression that had been a favored design idiom of the rich, powerful, and famous patrons and builders of the late seventeenth century (the work of John Vanbrugh, Christopher Wren, and Henry Wise especially), the designs of Lord Burlington, William Kent, and Lancelot Brown smudged over and veiled the remaining underlying baroque compositional strategies of this new work, whether knowingly or not.

The point here is that this work was a combination of importation and invention and was in no particular way derived from local forms, traditions, native vegetation, or physiographic underpinnings. It was a fabrication and imposed. These parks and gardens were works of art that were clear, identifiable, and unique. They came, however, in a short period of time to be thought of as characteristic and indigenous, even "natural." Despite what people have thought or written (including myself) about Henry Hoare's Elysium at Stourhead, possibly the high-water mark of this movement, it, like other English gardens, bears little resemblance to anything that had existed in the chalk downs of southern Wiltshire's agricultural landscape prior to its fabrication. All of which brings up a little understood feature about many of the most familiar cultural landscapes that are particularly considered to be unique in terms of defining a "sense of place." They frequently have little to do with the historic site, or preservation.

While in the midst of producing some of my own projects that are most consciously concerned with locality and identity, I attended a talk on "Place Identity" at the University of Pennsylvania given by Karsten Harries, a philosophy professor at Yale with an interest in art and architecture as well as phenomenology and Heidegger. Among the notes in my sketchbook from that evening are that his first thoughts were not surprising, and sounded like the sort of advice one would give a student or young employee: "Anyone who wants to use or become involved in the determination of a place must have an understanding of its nature, just as a craftsman must understand the properties of his materials— leather, stone, etc. Understanding alone does not ensure respect. A sense of place requires or implies constraints, or at least respect does."[10] Grounding a place in the spirit of a local ecology or nature is something that my office has done on numerous occasions, and I will say candidly that it is not that hard to conceive, although at times requiring considerable effort and technique.

In Salt Lake City we created a four-acre meadow on the roof of a conference center for the Church of Latter-day Saints. Thinking of the region and the alpine meadows of the nearby Wasatch Range and the vegetation of its canyons, we conceived a project that spoke directly to the value placed on the natural features of the region by the citizens of Salt Lake. It entailed contract-growing tens of thousands of native grasses, forbs, and herbs, along with a commitment to the structural support and soils necessary for their success. The roof meadow was planted by members of the community under the direction of my partner Susan Weiler. It now amounts to a significant wildlife habitat and exists in concert with a giant building that seats more than twenty thousand people. It participates in ameliorating the heat-sink tendencies of the city, assists in stormwater management, and provides habitat for numerous small animals, birds, and raptors, while giving pleasure to the populace.[11]

At times such endeavors to recall or invoke a regional ethos are rather abstract, as with the grasses in raised plinths I employed at the Wexner Center for the Visual Arts at Ohio State University, or are more literally representational or referential, as will be the hills, grasses, wildflowers, and live oaks currently being grown for a large corporate project currently under construction in California, or the recollection and reestablishment of fragments of a relict native forest at another project at the University of Washington in Seattle. In a way these are easy to conceive, but difficult to achieve technically and artistically so that they do not become fake imitations of scraps of wild nature. When the scale allows, and the artifice is adequate, however, they are deeply satisfying.

As recorded in my notes on his lecture at Penn, Harries went on to say something else that was certainly unexpected and possibly even more interesting:

> Respect can become an obstacle to action; so can analogies—however, the words Boston or Philadelphia invoke a sense of personality.
>
> The creation of Baroque Rome speaks to the ability and decision to destroy or change Renaissance Rome. . . . Sites don't want to be anything. We want them to be something. . . . [One needs to ask] how are human beings best served by what we do or fail to do. . . . The establishment of a strong place identity may be prevented or compromised by a desire for preservation or timidity to change or destroy things.

Certainly the number of historic towns and villages to which we allocate strong place identity as a result of preservation undergirds the tourist industry of many countries, with examples ranging widely from Montepulciano and Arezzo in Italy to Suzhou in China and Kyoto in Japan. Conversely, one can demonstrate that strong place identity can

Royal Tombs, Marrakech, Morocco, 2018

be generated through an imaginative act of creation as well as through the conservation of historic fabric. Implanting something totally new and in vivid contrast to heritage and setting can establish unique and iconic status for a location, as can be seen with two examples from Paris, the Eiffel Tower and the Pompidou Center.

Both caused outrage when built and today are vital icons and fixtures in the city, heavily visited by locals and tourists and memorialized by artists and merchants alike. New, brashly contrasting elements are not assured of acceptance and success, however, as the unfortunate Tour Montparnasse, also in Paris, equally demonstrates. Poorly conceived and executed, it caused a backlash against contemporary architecture sufficient to have all tall buildings banned for decades in the city center. What was different was surely not a simple matter of scale, modernity, or color, for the Eiffel Tower, the product of boosterism accompanying a temporary mercantile exposition, was and still is obviously and dramatically not in scale or harmony with its surroundings. Likewise, the Pompidou Center rises in structural exuberance and lively colors amid the uniform gray-and-white monotony of its Haussmannian surroundings. (In some ways this work of Renzo Piano and Sir Richard Rogers was originally a companion to a now absent neighbor, the majestic iron and glass structures of Les Halles by Victor Baltard.) No one can deny that these two concoctions, these total inventions, have engendered a strong sense of unique "place," or that it is the survival of their context that contributes greatly to this.

The Tour Montparnasse failed on several accounts: it did not make or shape a space but merely occupied space; it is lacking in grace, form, or delight. It is merely a lump that has been sadly raised into the sky to no purpose beyond financial gain. It is a story repeated daily in America, Europe, Asia, and the Middle East, where vast accretions of placeless structures occupy space rather than shaping it, each one saying "Look at me," with no resulting dialogue with neighboring structures or the community.

While monuments and iconic structures have contributed to the establishment of "place" historically—whether Rouen Cathedral, the Colosseum, or the Eiffel Tower—the proliferation of objects, especially mere office or condominium residential buildings attempting to be monuments, aspiring to be unique while merely achieving a sameness and banality such as we experience today, produces the opposite effect, that of placelessness and ennui. In landscape design, we see this same paradox—the creation of a unique sense of place, of specific locality, through the introduction of something other—in the long sequence of famous gardens, villas, parks, squares, and memorials such as the Memorial to the Murdered Jews of Europe in Berlin, which we designed with Peter Eisenman. They are inventions, not something quarried from the site. They are constructions. Even though many are remarkably fitted to their location, they were not inevitable, nor the result of some scientific or mechanical process of distillation. They often derive as much of their poetry from memory, wit, literature, historic homage, and reference as from any indigenous properties of topography and ecology.

Consider other examples from our work. When we began design for a bus transitway through the center of the downtown commercial district of Denver, it was conceived as the central link of what was initially intended to become a twenty-five-mile-long transportation project proposed by Wallace McHarg Roberts & Todd for the metro area's Regional Transportation District. The Federal Transportation Agency of the Nixon era, dominated as it was by General Motors and the automotive industry, succeeded in preventing a rail system from being built at that time. We worked on the resulting project of reduced scope with I. M. Pei's New York office, which was hoping to land significant mixed-use design projects at the two ends of Sixteenth Street—and that didn't happen either. But our part, the mall in between, did. There was no precedent in Denver, or for that matter in the United States at that time, for what we proposed: a twelve-block-long carpet of polychrome granite paving with trees and lights, largely in a format suggested by Barcelona's Las Ramblas. This project, which I've described in detail elsewhere, was a complete invention, not derived particularly from its surroundings, client requests, or any citizen workshop, and it was a tremendous success.[12]

On a number of occasions, we have had such an experience: that of inventing something to serve a client and solve particular problems while inventing its parts in what can only be considered an artistic venture. These are deeply dependent on craft and technique suitable to their achievement, of course, but often there is no particular or overt narrative toward achieving meaning, no traditional iconography, no inscriptions. There are suggestive forms and elements, some of which may mean one thing to one person and something altogether different to someone else. As John Dixon Hunt points out succinctly in his 2014 book *Historical Ground,* the narratives a designer tells himself may or may not be perceived by viewers and visitors, but more often than not they will not.[13] Nevertheless, any number of our projects are as dependent on social or artistic gestures and references as on natural or biophysical referents.

In Harries's brief talk I noted something else he said that I believe pertains to the topic of critical regionalism, landscape architecture, and focus on central places and communal space:

> Built environments are not organisms; some do resemble them, some do not. . . .
>
> Squares are paradigmatic places where individuals come together and develop or enjoy a sense of community. Many squares establish a sense of harmony, a sense of well-being and of being at home in the world, even though many were created by violent action. . . .
>
> It is the peripheries of our cities that most often invoke reverie and a sense of loss in our cities, where we most often sense a loss of place. Much of urban development today merely *uses* sites rather than appropriating and inhabiting them or coming to rest.

In this he was circling the issue of community and the expression of it through spatial means. The historic squares, spaces, parks of quality that we value are often in large part framed, shaped, and given aspects of their character by structures and elements of particular quality and conviviality—they are not just voids in an otherwise monotonous or oppressive fabric. Whether empty or full, treed or paved, there is amenity and coherence, some commonality and physical merit that often lend character, the sum of which we regard as particular.

The most successful squares and spaces we have produced invariably have a heart, or some sense of spatial interior and perimeter boundary, with an inside and outside to them, regardless of size—from tiny single spaces such as Director Park in Portland, to bigger ones such as Bryant Park in Manhattan, or larger, more complex ones such as

Hermann Park in Houston. Each of these places is also developed in one or more ways that establish a human scale and allow people to feel at home. While inhuman scales move us, and not always in negative ways—consider the pyramids and Great Sphinx, or certain monuments and natural formations—even so, we frequently need to add elements of middling size, such as trees or sheltering structures, as an intermediary in scale between gigantic buildings and ourselves. Another point is that especially when making something up out of whole cloth, consideration of how a particular spatial order and the choice of elements is related to a larger context, particularly regional patterns and situations, matters. There is also usually an expected behavior and set of activities that an environment signals vis-à-vis movement, places to rest, decorum, and use, while allowing a certain freedom of choice to allow for random and casual encounters and experiences.

A fundamental proposition if one wishes to be self-critical regarding regional or local issues is to understand that there is no such thing as a blank slate. Every site is somewhere and has a history. In addition to climate, there are memories and ambitions. Even when working on roof decks, one is always somewhere, whether the eleventh floor of a garage, at the sky lobby of an office tower, or over a subterranean parking garage. While planning and designing Canary Wharf we were savagely attacked by the British press for bringing Manhattan to London, for being ugly, gross, commercial Americans. The project was intended to provide sufficient built space at a scale that would have destroyed the historic financial center of the city and the area around Bank Corner, Lloyd's, Leadenhall Market, and St. Paul's. In fact, it saved and secured the financial future of London as the heart of the European trading and financial exchange market for eight of the twenty-four hours of the trading day that followed the "Big Bang" in global financial markets that occurred in the early 1990s, when money, stocks, and trading went global round the clock. (The other sixteen hours ended up being divided between eight in New York for the Americas and eight in Shanghai and Tokyo for Asia.) Criticism centered on the scale of the buildings and our plan, which was perceived as too "formal"—there were straight streets, squares, and trees in rows, among other features. I pointed out that it was very much in the tradition of British commerce, urban design, and building.

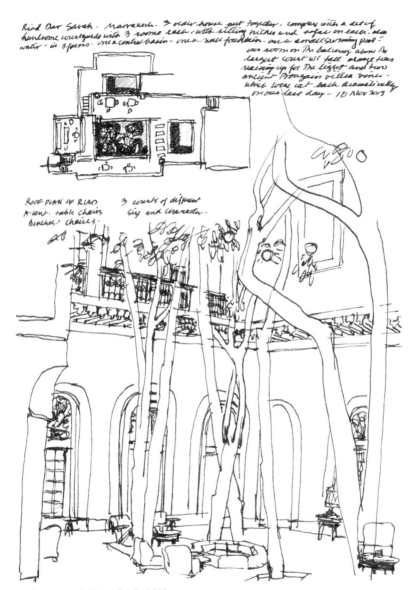

Riad courtyard, Marrakech, 2019

Apart from the fact that our site was a rectangular dock, and setting aside the superb Baroque work of Wren, Hawksmoor, and Vanbrugh, their sense of geometry and trees in rows, I pointed to the Bedford estate and other commercial developments in Westminster, Kensington, and Knightsbridge, noting how squares and blocks had been developed as real estate ventures, and that God *was* in the details and particularly the proportions. I pointed to the Adelphi by the Adams brothers, a multilayered effort with service vehicles and such on one level and large, high-style commercial buildings above. I argued that these critics hardly knew their own history. As it has turned out, the project was not only highly successful—like the Adelphi and the Bedford estate—but also is quite comfortable physically on the ground level. Services and trucks are below grade, and the squares and esplanades above are sunny and heavily used daily and for special events. Development, housing, transport, and more commercial building have followed, but little of it (except the Olympics site) has been composed as an ensemble the way that Thomas Cubitt, John Nash, and Decimus Burton did in their work at Regents Park and the Mall, or that we attempted.

The effort to produce places of character, which might develop a life that remains particular and special, is challenged today by the homogenizing forces of global commerce. There is, as far as I can see, nothing that cannot at some point be, or has not been, coopted by commerce. This involves another concept, that of "authenticity," which comes up at times when we talk of "sense of place," regardless whether new or old. The idea—or phenomenon, maybe—of "authenticity" conjures something that is *genuine,* or has integrity and an inherent nature that is truly and exclusively of one place or author, and not of another. We smile when we eat a particular dish or hear a particular piece of music and say, "That is really authentic"; or when having an experience in some particular place—a local festival or a trip through a natural area of distinction—we might say to ourselves or others, "This is the real thing."

We mean, of course, that it isn't adulterated, a simulation or fake, and that the ingredients and performance are truly of one particular and memorable place, artist, or community and not some other. I can recall that after tasting the wares of a particular vendor at a weekend market in Palo Alto, California, I remarked that his porchetta was

"authentic" and reminded me of some I'd particularly enjoyed one after-
noon in Bagnaia, the small town north of Rome where the Villa Lante
is located. In this particular case it was the performance and taste that
were authentic, not the place, for Palo Alto is a far cry from the village
of Bagnaia. Places, unlike food, have characteristics that are not portable, replicable, or transferable.

Global commerce today is rapacious in its continual search for items
and stratagems to perpetuate and expand consumer markets and sales.
At times it seems that there is very little that cannot be coopted, appropriated, or debased for commercial gain. If you can't travel to particular
places, an effort to fabricate artificial attributes of them and bring them
to you has become the approach of many entrepreneurs. Whether one
considers the clever, crowd-pleasing pastiches of the Disney enterprise,
the pathetic and vulgar concoctions of Las Vegas, or various themed
entertainment parks in America, Europe, and Asia that trade on cliché
and familiar imagery, these "places" inevitably are separate and not of the
locale where they are situated, nor are they what they pretend to be. From
Hadrian to Marie Antoinette to Walt Disney and Steve Wynn, through
the centuries people have devoted time and energy to the fabrication of
fantasies and amusements based on something else, something real and
specific that possesses a character perceived as attractive. At times we
are amused, even charmed, and at other times repulsed or condemning.
Las Vegas may have amused Bob Venturi, Denise Scott Brown, and Steve
Izenour, but it doesn't really amuse me. A few weeks ago, I ran into the
following in the business section of the *New York Times:*

> The French researchers Delphine Dion and Stéphane Borraz
> have reported in the *Journal of Retailing and Consumer Services*
> that luxury brand managers use myths and rituals to cast his-
> torical shops as sacred, which then lends authenticity to the
> merchandise and the brand. Talking to the researchers about
> Christian Dior's first outlet on the Avenue Montaigne in Paris,
> one manager said, "It's a mythical place." He added, "These stores
> keep the traces of something that has gone."[14]

Marketing language from companies today often plays up a sense of tradition and locale, whether it's the famous Marlboro Men appropriating

the American West and advertisements depicting cowboys and Monument Valley—which happens to be an iconic portion of the Navajo Nation reservation, widely known around the world thanks to movies made there by John Ford—or recent advertising campaigns with Ralph Lauren's British expats on safari in the bush of East Africa. The *New York Times* article quoted just above cites advertisements from the Hershey candy company in Pennsylvania and Fuller's Brewery in London, both proclaiming their nineteenth-century origins. The reporter also recounts that the Brooklyn-based online retailer Zady sought out J. G. Littlewood & Son, a long-established fiber dye house in Philadelphia, to produce materials for Zady's new clothing line, in part for Littlewood's historic craft and apparatus—its nineteenth-century brick plant and giant dye kettles, dryers, and bale pressers—and in part as an element in a process the more recent Brooklyn firm could assert is traditional craft with a venerable American pedigree. Such developments are undoubtedly a response to consumer antipathy toward (or even a backlash against) less expensive global products from Asia that now fill not only chain stores but also high-end shops in cities throughout the industrial world—ubiquitous bargains, mass produced, some of them as well made as a flood of others are shoddy, and all of them part of today's global consumer market economy.[15]

Landscape architecture today is global as well, and has been for decades, in terms of ideas, materials, and manufactured products. Stone that we use on projects in Washington, DC, and Philadelphia comes from Quebec; stone used in Portland or Seattle comes from China; in the San Francisco Bay area it is from China and Italy. Trees we recently planted in France and Switzerland were purchased from Bruns's and Lappen's nurseries in Belgium. Colleagues of mine are using black locust wood (an American tree) from plantations in Central Europe for decking in New York and Boston, and we are all dependent on tropical hardwoods from Malaysia and South America for exterior furniture, whether custom designed or off-the-shelf.

Lighting firms in Spain and Germany supply our favorite fixtures, regardless of where we are working. Stone quarried in Portugal or Africa is shipped to Italy for fabrication for use in any of a dozen countries on both sides of the Atlantic. In order to evoke the red sandstone that gave a regional flavor to architecture in Ohio in the nineteenth century, we had to choose stone from India, Germany, or the Peaks district in England because no quarry in the region could supply it. We settled on India for cost reasons. One client of ours still uses American glass in their industrial products but had competing offers from China and Germany for the glass of their new headquarters building in California, settling at last on the German product.

My office ended up using a paving brick from England on a project in Los Angeles because American manufacturers couldn't meet our dimensional specifications at the time. Whether we like it or not, it is, therefore, a global world today, even in the making of landscapes, no matter how hard we try to use local materials in an attempt to ground projects in their time and place. An awareness of such logistics is not new, of course. Well-known designers of the seventeenth, eighteenth, and nineteenth centuries were masters in such matters, finding, growing, and shipping, often great distances, vast quantities of plants and building supplies as they transformed enormous tracts into the parks and estates we admire to this day and think so suited to their place.

A common yearning for something that is special and not generic is in part a reaction to the leveling and homogenizing nature of so much in our lives, particularly in urban architecture around the world. While private and domestic structures, as well as numerous moderate-sized buildings, frequently manage to retain a particularity tied to regional, historical, or local character, larger institutional and commercial structures have attained a near-universal look and feel. This is in large part a simple matter of economics and the interconnected nature of society and the business world internationally (along with the worlds of fine art, engineering, finances, and design). Looking at cities around the world, one begins to see a new universal (or global) vernacular of tall buildings. While a discerning visitor may detect something of a regional flavor, as each community turns yet another product to its own particular use and habits, the sameness is striking.

If shown a group of images of the current skyline of a number of cities, some individuals might know which is Shanghai, which Hong Kong, London, or Houston, and which is Beijing. The numbing crunch of drab buildings in the latter city, at a new scale in the miles and miles of serviceable but nearly identical structures, forms what amounts to a new gargantuan *hutong* with little community social space or any amenities. The natural world is held at bay or simply flattened out and eliminated. In London this remarkable new vernacular in contemporary tall buildings has taken on a local character of expensive, bespoke (one-off, tailor-made) objects, familiar in their overall diagram, but with an elegance once expressed in Spitfires, Aston Martins, handmade shoes, the Mayfair clubs and country-house gardens we associate with English furniture and style. Even so, there is a growing sameness in London as elsewhere from the increasing quantum.

Dubai presents an ongoing monstrous demonstration of the inability of a group of such self-centered towers to shape and create community, surpassing Dallas or Shanghai. There is a "lost in space" placelessness, along with an unfettered display of somewhat woozy, adolescent male obsession hardly worth describing. Around the world there has been an enormous amount of building and construction, even instances of real "architecture," but it has rarely succeeded in making places in any of the ways regarding regionalism or local genius that I have been discussing.

Among the replication and mass production of tall buildings, few have developed the character and "sense of place" that the ensemble of structures of Rockefeller Center engendered in 1930. This is largely because there has been so little attempt recently to use these redundant buildings to shape human space at the ground level to achieve any social use beyond that of circulation, mostly for automobiles. The few efforts, such as Canary Wharf, stand out in contrast to the jumble at Potsdamer Platz in Berlin or other attempts at ensemble development, such as the claustrophobic and hideous scrum of towers at Hudson Yards in New York or the new commercial cores of Beijing and Shanghai.

A common factor behind the general global sameness, regardless of place, has been technology that allows for climate modification through the application of vast quantities of energy and expensive mechanical systems. The costs of this are enormous, and the effect on the biosphere from the production of the energy needed has been all-consuming and damaging. How long it can continue is anyone's guess, but the results are more and more clear. If at the upper level of global economics there is a universalizing of development, so too at the lowest levels of society and poverty there has emerged a ubiquitous and similar set of urban habitats, and whether one calls them barrios, favelas, slums, informal settlements, or shantytowns, hundreds of millions of people are living in and moving into similar harsh, unhealthy, and inhuman environments today. This is another side of globalism, and the merging of human habitat into a continuum regardless of continent and place. Critical resources such as food, water, health services, and access to viable employment and income are equally more and more difficult for large populations in what once were truly different settings.

Traditional nation-states and borders are under assault today, as any glance through current news will reveal, whether the topic is communication and connectivity via the internet or cellphones, cyber hacking and terrorism, global warming or global trade, immigration, refugees, epidemics, sports, entertainment, or art and design. If one were to see these phenomena together and from an ecological point of view, especially recent climate and species data, one might begin to think finally that the whole planet is really one large and interconnected habitat. The nations, their boundaries, and a lot of our cherished notions and heritage might have to give way to a new attitude, one that finally and truthfully is "Think globally and act locally."

If there are to be any meaningful "regional" differences in the emerging habitat of humanity, it seems that they will not be so much in our daily goods and technical apparatus—in our clothes, workplaces, machines, transport, or architecture—as these have become universally marketed products. Rather they will be in the ground layer, the famous "space between buildings" and around, under and on top of our architecture: the surface of the earth and our settlements, its elements and products, the soil, its plants, water, geological and climatological processes, and in the spaces we invent with them in our environs. These make up the context of our rather ubiquitous architecture and the spaces we share in dense cities that comprise the public and private realms. One must accept that biological and ecological principles will continue to determine and limit what is possible. Equatorial lands and those of the north temperate zone will continue to persist in their differences. Cold and hot deserts will support plants and animals that have evolved to thrive in each. As the global climate changes and shifts around, these creatures will be pushed about, for many fatally. Nevertheless, regional differences will persist. So, I hope, will differences in food and cuisine to a degree, along with sensitive and imaginative ideas and attitudes toward design, albeit largely as a function of aesthetic preference derived principally from cultural attitudes, memory, and imagination.

Nearly all of the examples I have discussed have been sites and projects—places limited in the extent of the scene designed. Landscape architects around the world today are frequently engaged in large district and regional plans that are ambitious in their scale and scope. Many are largely infrastructure or framework plans for urban development that propose to shape the nature of extensive, even vast territories of cities and their attendant supporting topography and natural systems, as well as historic and contemporary built fabric. Our students are ambitiously proposing to reset the balance between amenity and service, priorities between resources and established habits, often based on a revised aesthetic and values regarding natural phenomena. It is exciting and brave. But if any of these plans and ambitions are to be realized, it will be through the implementation of projects, through the making of things physically. These plans will ultimately be executed and judged through project designs. The designs will be subject to evaluation and criticism regarding their success as supportive and meaningful habitats for society—for men, women, and children to live and work in. Once safety and services have been achieved, the worth of all this effort will be measured by the quality and spirit, the information and opportunities, and frankly the ideas and pleasure these environments afford. J. B. Jackson's thesis that all cities must function justly and efficiently, be ecologically sound, and provide "a continuously satisfying aesthetic-sensory experience" is as apt today as when he wrote it nearly sixty years ago.[16]

Something R. Buckminster Fuller once said in a lecture I heard at Columbia University in the 1960s has also stuck in my mind ever since: "The opposite of *natural* is *impossible*." Well, nature is with us and we are part of nature. A lot of what we do is terrible, but a fair amount is rather remarkable, even wonderful. We mustn't confuse many unfortunate things that we despise or regret in the work of others with what is "natural" or "unnatural." Most often they are merely human and regrettable, unjust, wasteful, destructive, or offensive to our way of thinking and feeling. As a designer, I will continue to be optimistic and agree with Lewis Mumford, who maintained through his criticism that trend is not destiny. Francis Fukuyama was dead wrong when he posited that "history is over." The digital age has made us all members of a global community that has not comprehended the full meaning of this fact. While regional differences may now be limited and largely a function of natural processes and phenomena and less and less that of cultural products, I have no doubt that there will be a continuing concern for the assertion of local character, for what has been referred to as "place," and that it will be, as it always has been, a function of invention and interaction with nature, the nature of the world and ourselves, and of heritage—in short, of life.

It seems to me that as planners and designers, what all the mumbo-jumbo about globalism, regionalism, and sense of place comes down to for us is that the situation of humanity and events today means that we must understand globally, plan regionally, and design locally, for that is where we actually build and live. In short, we must be able to *preserve* and *contest* and be able to keep two scales of life and reference, the *grand* and the *human*.

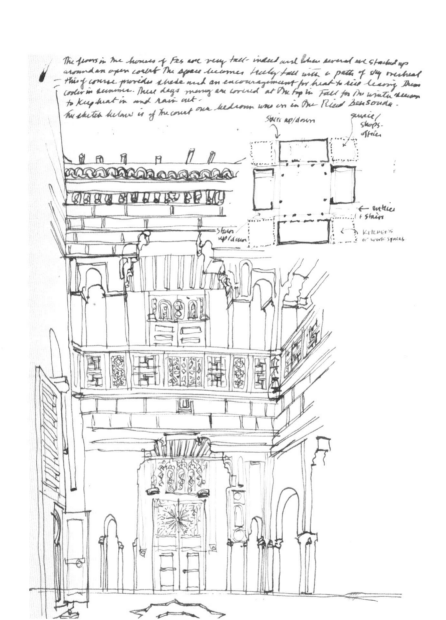

The floors in the houses of Fes are very tall - indeed and when several are stacked up
around an open court. The space becomes truly tall with a patch of sky overhead -
this of course provides shade and an encouragement for heat to rise leaving them
cooler in summer. These days many are covered at the top in Fall for the winter season
to keep heat in and rain out.
The sketch below is of the court over bedroom was in in the Riad Bensouda.

stairs up/down

service/
shops/
offices

← entries
+ stairs

stairs
up/down

← kitchens
or work spaces

Riad courtyard, Fez, Morocco, 2019

WATER, URBAN NATURE, AND THE ART
OF LANDSCAPE DESIGN

(2016)

There is an ancient character in both Chinese and Japanese that means water—*sui* in Mandarin and *mizu* in Japanese. It is used in combination with hundreds of other characters to form myriad words and thoughts. Made with four strokes basic to calligraphy, this character for water is familiar to all those learning and practicing calligraphy in these two ancient cultures. Equally venerable are great works of art from both cultures depicting water and its many forms: in poetry, paintings, drawings, and gardens; as streams, canals, basins, ponds, and lakes. As elsewhere in the world, water was understood to be fundamental and dynamic, essential and life giving. At the same time, it was treated with great respect and the knowledge that it could also be tempestuous and violent.

In 1993, Frederick R. Steiner and George F. Thompson summoned a group of landscape architects and planners to a conference at Arizona State University titled "Landscape Architecture: Ecology and Design and Planning." At that time, I gave my views on what I understood about nature, art, and landscape architecture and presented a number of projects from our office that illustrated the degree to which we were able to act on such ideas in practice.[1] Feeling generally the same today, I will try not to repeat myself. One element briefly touched upon in that

From *Nature and Cities: The Ecological Imperative in Urban Design and Planning,* ed. Frederick R. Steiner, George F. Thompson, and Armando Carbonell (Cambridge, MA: The Lincoln Institute of Land Policy, 2016), 16.1–16.47.

essay, however, has become a topic that every practitioner and student of landscape architecture has come to dwell on considerably since then: water. At times one grows weary of the topic, wanting the conversation to move on. but among the many factors that contribute to the miracle of life on Earth and its remarkable history and diversity, none is more important than water.

Seen from space, Earth is truly the "blue" planet, one predominantly covered with water in a form we refer to as oceans, from which all plant and animal life emerged—and on which all life still depends for survival in a variety of ways. On land, the home of humans, fresh water has enabled the evolution of agriculture and society and is every bit as essential today as it has been at any moment in history. As much as 60 percent of our very bodies, organs, and selves, as most school children learn, is composed of water—H_2O, hydrogen and oxygen—thus accounting for the serious consequences of dehydration in humans. Only 40 percent is minerals, chemicals, and other solid stuff.

Nature and Water

Water is a peculiar and changeable substance that can be a liquid, solid, or gas. Above the molecular level, it has a weak structure and takes the form of its surroundings or containers—whether a valley, basin, channel, cup, bowl, or glass. Lacking the ability to stack or stand up in a pile, it flops and falls, and, as we usually say, "runs" all over the place. This seeming formlessness causes it to be almost never at rest. As a result, water has repeatedly shaped, carved, and molded Earth and its lands, above and below the oceans, as streams, rivers, lakes, bays, or oceans, and as ice in floes or massive rivers called glaciers, with relentless and perpetual dripping, lapping, running, rushing, pounding, rubbing, scouring, and scraping. It soothes us with its cool showers when we are hot and freezes us in the winter. It lulls us to sleep and crushes or drowns us when it arrives in typhoons and hurricanes. Water sustains plants, animals, and humanity. It is our friend and necessity. It is also our adversary and threat.

Historic Perspectives

Beyond hydrating our animal bodies for health, water has been essential to human society for agriculture since the dawn of civilization. Our need and use for it has grown dramatically as the population has spread, increased, and developed myriad industries, many of which use it heavily. For thousands of years, we have developed techniques to harvest, store, and transport water through all manner of ingenious devices and structures, from great distances to areas and regions where we desire to use it. Examples of cisterns and basins that collect rainfall and the aqueducts and canals that transport it range from the ancient Middle East, Egypt, Greece, and Rome to those of the ancestral Puebloans and their modern descendants on the Colorado Plateau and the desert of southwest North America. On all continents, wells, tunnels, aqueducts, pipes, drains, and a wide variety of mechanical devices have lifted and moved water from below ground, from rivers and lakes, and from distant watersheds for centuries.

Agriculture may be the most critical industry and largest user of clean, fresh water, but many other industries have emerged that require enormous amounts of it for their processes. And as everyone knows from their own domestic routine, billions of people in cities and other areas around the world use water to drink, bathe, cook, and clean each day. In the course of all this use, most of the water becomes dirty, contaminated, or, worse, is lost and unavailable to be treated, cleaned, or reused. It was not a problem when there was only a handful of us. But today it is a crisis of great seriousness in much of the world, where many millions of people do not have access to clean water, where its overconsumption has led to depleted aquifers and desertification, or where climate change is engendering droughts in some regions and cyclonic storms, floods, and sea rise in others. I will return to this situation later.

To make matters worse, cities in particular consume enormous quantities for daily domestic use. Some of the fastest-growing urban areas in arid regions are plunged into long-term droughts, while other cities are expanding constantly into, or adjacent to, estuaries. In nature, such estuaries have functioned since time immemorial both as natural filters for cleansing water and as the breeding ground for vast amounts of plants and animals that serve as major players in global ecology. Unfortunately, as cities around the globe have grown (in many cases exponentially in recent decades), they have done so by filling and destroying staggering amounts of wetlands. Such a situation suggests that landscape professionals must think globally and plan regionally, but normally practitioners can only act locally on a project-by-project basis, as I hope to demonstrate at a variety of scales and purposes.

WATER AND LANDSCAPE ARCHITECTURAL
PRACTICE IN RECENT DECADES

The first two projects ever undertaken by our office, in 1976 and 1977, had water elements. One was on a suburban (at the time, rural) site near Princeton, New Jersey, for Johnson & Johnson's baby products division; the other, for Johnson & Johnson's international headquarters, was in a city—downtown New Brunswick, New Jersey—but seemed somewhat suburban. For the first, I proposed a lake that would be a visual amenity and also function as a pioneering stormwater detention facility to satisfy the recently enacted Clean Water Act of 1972 and some of the earliest state regulations on the issue. For the other, we proposed a small fountain set within a grove of trees in a garden atop a roof over a loading dock, storage, and food-service kitchen. The good news was that both worked fine hydraulically and functioned well as amenities for the employees and various birds and animals. The bad news was that a flock of geese suddenly appeared and in one day ate nearly all of the emergent lakeshore aquatic plants I had talked the owners into letting me purchase and experiment with. Eventually we managed to establish them. Since that summer many years ago, both the profession and I have learned a lot about water, vegetation, habitat, and their implementation. These two projects also represented the twin poles of water design: efficacy and environmental mechanics, on the one hand, and art and *poesis,* on the other. Both have seemed of equal importance to me and to our firm ever since.

At that same time—and for two years previously—down the hall from my office at the University of Pennsylvania, Joachim Tourbier, Richard Westmacott, and several other young landscape architects were working under the encouragement of Ian L. McHarg, our chairman and the recent author of *Design with Nature* (1969), and in collaboration with Ruth Patrick, a distinguished limnologist at the Franklin Institute.[2] Their project was to develop ideas and techniques of bioengineering for stormwater management, not only as methods of detention and retention to alleviate flooding caused by urbanization, but also as experiments in what we now call phytoremediation: the cleansing of water with plants through the removal and absorption of deleterious materials (chemicals and minerals), leaving it fit and safe for wildlife and human use. Since then, many individuals and institutions around the world have continued this work. Happily, what used to be seen as award-winning and cutting-edge experiments have become the state of the art—the normal sort of thing that responsible professionals are expected to know about and do.

Also, in the decades since the Environmental Protection Agency (EPA) and various US states promulgated numerous regulations regarding clean water in lakes, streams, and rivers, as well as treatment standards for detention, retention, and methods of handling the volumes of water involved, landscape architects and civil engineers have developed a vocabulary of design strategies and methods in response—at times taking turns leading and then following each other and the regulators. Twenty years ago, we could find client support only in Europe for fundamental techniques such as pervious paving, infiltration beds in parking lots, and vegetated swales, which we employed in the Siedlung Goldstein social housing project in Frankfurt, Germany. Today, these methods are well known and widespread, although still not in common practice in the United States. The concept of planting wetland species in swales and detention basins, as a number of us began doing during the 1980s, was appealing, for it allowed the introduction of corridors and strips of habitat for birds and small animals into projects under the mandate of flood prevention and compliance with clean-water legislation and initiatives.

As it became standard practice to capture stormwater in order to prevent flooding caused by its rapid discharge from the increasing acreage of urban development, detention basins have become more and more common as a means of temporarily storing the volumes generated. Throughout North America today, especially in suburban, residential, commercial, and industrial areas, one sees an endless supply of awkwardly shaped, barren, or riprap-lined holes designed by civil engineers. Flying over suburbs, one sees an array of these barren craters dotting the scene.

Landscape architects have come to realize that such facilities offer an opportunity to do more if they are planted with mixtures of native and water-tolerant plants—not just to make them visually more attractive, but to make them valuable as habitat, especially if linked coherently to riparian corridors where the water almost inevitably wants to go. Rain basins, as many have come to be called, can reintroduce a diversity of plants and animals, whether for amphibians and small mammals or migratory insects such as butterflies or songbirds, many of which suffer from the loss of habitat along their seasonal routes, especially in coastal and river corridors where a majority of development has been taking place, or for threatened resident populations of mammals, reptiles, amphibians, and birds. The resulting mixture of water and wetland plants that is the most appropriate for stormwater facilities is often the most common to the natural areas being filled and plowed under. Because of the increasing interest and demand for such qualities on the part of many community boards and county officials, one side effect has been that engineering firms are now specifying such planting and have even mastered the concept of groundwater recharge. I have heard landscape architects bemoan that engineers today are doing something they pioneered, seeing it as a loss of work and fees. It is, however, a successful case of educating others to do basic tasks—environmental housekeeping and maintenance—that frees us to work on other important and rewarding projects and goals. This should be the basic state of the art, rather like knowing how to lay out a safe and handsome road.

More important and at another scale, by 1990 many landscape architects began to advocate the creation or re-creation of wetlands within or adjacent to urban development. For a large, nine-hundred-acre urban development on the former Howard Hughes industrial site near the Los Angeles Airport begun in the mid-1970s, I advocated the re-creation of a long-vanished creek and reestablishment of a freshwater and saltwater marsh—in part to create a stormwater device at the scale of the problem, but also to preserve open space, create habitat for native and migratory birds, and ensure clean and safe effluent for Santa Monica Bay, a major recreational resource for the region.

Where and how one locates such features matters. Originally, I positioned the stream corridor as a spine within the proposed urban development so it could function as an amenity in a linear park for future residents. Later, we shifted it to be adjacent to the Westchester bluffs, an escarpment we were trying to revegetate and preserve. This was with the encouragement of restoration ecologists and engineers with whom we were collaborating. We all came to realize that it would be more useful and successful ecologically if the corridor were located at the edge of the housing and not within, thereby allowing birds and animals to move back and forth between hill and stream without confronting human activity. Another benefit was that we could design it to have more capacity for floodwater surges than would have been comfortable in a more refined and constrained urban park.

This award-winning stream and marsh project, which began as a stormwater measure, is seen today as a nature preserve and bird refuge. It was so successful that, since our early proposals, it has been expanded from about fifty acres on one side of Ballona Creek to more than two hundred acres occupying land on both sides. In one case after another, in our work and that of others, I have noticed a frequent leveraging of water management features for significant social or ecological benefit.

One lesson along the way has been that one should not think it necessary to do everything oneself. A number of years later, I was on a committee assisting the National Park Service to develop mechanisms and programming for the Golden Gate National Recreation Area in San Francisco and adjoining Marin County. Most of those involved were preoccupied with legislation, finance, architectural historic preservation, resource and facility management, and a wealth of issues involved in creating and managing such an ambitious new federal entity. Gyo Obata (the O of the architectural firm HOK), Maya Lin, and I, the only designers in the group, quietly pondered the physical attributes and design potential for the historic Presidio site that we envisioned could be undertaken. A doodle in my sketchbook records part of the conversation wherein we concluded that it would be beneficial to remove the relict airstrip of Crissy Field, regardless of its historic interest as a wartime airfield, and that we should propose re-creating a tidal marsh and natural shoreline (restoration was literally impossible, since there was nothing to restore). This simple but important thought rather quickly became embedded in the plan for the park, and several years later a version was executed by the San Francisco office of George Hargreaves. It has proved enormously popular and is a highly successful example

Fresh Pond, Amagansett, New York, 1968

of getting the big picture right—for the birds, fish, mollusks, and the people, the city, and San Francisco Bay.

The concept of a "blue roof"—using the roof of a building as a detention basin for the rainwater that falls on it, as opposed to a "green roof"—emerged in northern Europe during the 1960s. Since roofs are supposed to be designed not to leak, why not detail them as a detention basin to catch and hold water falling on them, allowing for a measured slow release of a predetermined quantity in the same manner as a detention basin on the ground? In terms of weight and supporting structure, this seemed preferable to green roofs and their supporting soil and drainage apparatus, simply because water, at 62.5 pounds per cubic foot, is lighter by itself than wet soil, which is basically a bucket of water with rocks in it, at about 100 pounds per cubic foot. Architects and clients have been stubbornly resistant to this idea, as much from habit and superstition as anything else.

Strangely enough, architects and clients alike have embraced the green roof as a common tool in the repertoire of devices and strategies for working with water in developed areas. This is truly an old idea. My grandfather was born in a sod hut in the Dakota Territory during the nineteenth century, and, as a child in Alaska, I was quite familiar with the merits and hazards of sod roofs. During the early 1970s, when I began paying attention to such things, the use of intensive or extensive green roofs had become common throughout northern Europe. By the 1980s, they were required by law in many cities there. Today, most architects worth their salt know how to do minimal green roofs, and many landscape architects have helped them with more ambitious projects. Independent study at the American Academy in Rome, prior to my having an office, also pointed me to the frequent creation of impressive gardens and parks atop masonry structures intrinsic to the palaces and villas of the first and second centuries CE in Tivoli, Terracina, Rome, the Alban Hills, Capri, and elsewhere. One result of experiencing these sophisticated mergers of architecture and landscape is that, since the earliest days of our office, my partners and I have unabashedly treated buildings as part of the landscape. On numerous occasions, we have literally used structures designed by our friends and colleagues for diverse purposes as sites for landscape invention and construction.[3] One of the best-known benefits of such a landscape over a structure is the use, cleansing, and delayed release of rainfall. Green roofs also prolong the life of waterproofing, protecting it from harmful ultraviolet light while significantly helping to stabilize temperatures within a structure, lowering the heat island effect as well. And, once again, the rooftop environment offers food and habitat for birds and useful insects.

Two quite different urban projects from our office bracket the range or twin poles of such endeavors. One utilizes several small features, and the other employs a dramatically large one—rather like the juxtaposition of two sorts of knowledge that Isaiah Berlin playfully pointed to in his classic essay *The Hedgehog and the Fox*.[4] The first is Director Park, which is more of a small urban piazza (only 100 by 200 feet in plan area) that our firm recently completed in Portland, Oregon, atop a five-story subterranean parking garage. It is entirely paved; even so, it catches, cleans, and then either uses, reuses, or releases as clean effluent virtually all the water that falls on the site and adjacent streets. Because the Pacific Northwest's climate is generally quite mild but also seasonally moist, misty, and rainy, I proposed covering part of the park with a high glass canopy so that people could sit outdoors at all times. Rain that falls onto his canopy is directed to a long planter, something like a civic-scale window box, which doubles as a back for benches and mediates between a sloping street and two level terraces with tables, chairs, and benches for seating, dining, and relaxing under the canopy. The planter is designed as a mini-detention basin with freeboard sufficient to accommodate storms, and, of course, it uses, filters, and, for the time being, slowly releases clean, unused water to the storm system. Rain falling elsewhere is directed either to vegetated basins on the streets or to a fountain designed with a surcharge tank and filters for the reuse or release of water directed to it.

This square (or park, or piazza—the name confusion indicates the evolution of public spaces and their use in contemporary cities) is the uppermost of three small public spaces that are linked by two small lightly trafficked streets, Park and Ninth Avenues. Lying between what are known in Portland as the North Park Blocks and the South Park Blocks, all three parks—Director, O'Bryant, and Burnside—were planned in an earlier effort by the city. The design team (which included landscape architects Carol Mayer-Reed and Brian McCarter of ZGF, as well as those from OLIN) had proposed that they be linked for the treatment of stormwater; excess water from Director and Burn-side Parks was to be directed to O'Bryant Square to create a public water garden, where it could be kept and used with virtually none of the water going to the storm-sewer system, except in truly extreme conditions. A small café designed by ZGF Architects was covered with a green roof that has a bit more exuberance than the thin mats of sedums and succulents so common in the industry today.[5]

Director Park is modest, less unexpected, more ordinary, and far less ambitious than the second project, which Berlin might have termed the "one big thing." It is an extreme form of green roof for a very large conference center for the Church of Latter-day Saints, the religious faith generally known as Mormonism. It seats 21,000 people who come twice a year from around the world for conferences at their mother church. This ambitious structure occupies virtually a full city block, which in Salt Lake City is enormous to start with: ten acres. After visiting the site and thinking about the project, I proposed to the architect, Robert Frasca of ZGF in Portland, that it be conceived in terms of a landscape and not as a conventional freestanding building. "Think of it," I suggested, "rather like one of the mesas in southern Utah in the Four Corners region where the ancient Puebloans built communities such as Mesa Verde in large caves and under overhanging ledges along arroyos that were often forested." Bob said, in effect, "You mean put a park on top?" I replied, "Yes, I guess so"—and we did. We managed to plant quantities of native trees against the inevitable blank sides of this giant auditorium, not unlike the canyons nearby at the edge of the city. On the roof above, we created an open, alpine meadow, the whole inspired by and referring to the natural setting of the nearby Wasatch Range.

Inside the building is a spectacular hall seating more people than attend Utah Jazz basketball games a few blocks away. The team's arena has a traditional built-up roof that dumps its acres of runoff rapidly into the storm sewers. The majority of our roof over the conference center became a four-acre subalpine meadow composed of plants indigenous to the region, thousands of which were grown for us by contract with a number of regional nurseries. We added groves of conifers and places to sit and stroll about to view their historic temple and tabernacle, the city, the Wasatch Range of the Rocky Mountains, and Great Salt Lake.

Placing a source-fountain at the highest portion of the roof, we developed abstract runnels that lead water to the edge, where it then cascades down to the street level. On North Temple Street, we convinced the church and city to allow us to daylight a controlled amount of flow from City Creek, a historic stream that partially accounts for the location of the city, street, and Mormon temple. Like so many urban watercourses, it had been placed in a giant drainpipe alongside the site in the nineteenth century because of its habit of flooding in early summer as snows in the mountains above rapidly melted. This project deals directly with storms, seasonal rain, and snow in a dense urban area, establishing a great sponge across a vast expanse of what conventionally would have been an extensive, impervious surface. At the same time, it reveals and exploits the natural tendencies of the region, making reference to its hydrologic cycle while utilizing water that, although hidden, is already there, either in a somewhat seasonal, historic stream or with recycled rainwater.

Putting water to beneficial work has been a hallmark of civilization. Thirty years ago, I proposed creating several ponds on an early project outside Boston on Route 128 for Codex, the corporation that developed modern modems. Working with superb civil engineers from the firm of Flack & Kurtz, I suggested that we use the ponds as basins, with enough freeboard to accommodate stormwater that might also be used to assist with cooling. Like most high-tech companies, especially those with massive assemblies of mainframe computers, Codex had an issue with heat reduction. Our engineers suggested we use wells to pull water from a rather extensive aquifer under the site, run it through the building for coolant, and dump it into the ponds. I, in turn, designed stone retaining walls that would allow water to move from the ponds back into gravel beds that would allow it to sink back into the aquifer. This trick only works in certain geological situations—in this case, extensive and porous glacial alluvium. Since then it has become common to do a similar thing with injection wells. The nice thing about this return was its reliance on gravity to do much of the work; it was also visible. In addition to other awards, we received the President's Award of the American Society of Landscape Architects for the project. Aside from pride, the reason to mention it is to encourage colleagues in the field to push clients and allied professionals toward nonstandard experimental work, especially with the wonderful element of water.

This idea of catching water and putting it to work is common in our recent experience, but for generations water was seen as a nuisance that people simply tried to get rid of. While working on a campus development plan for the Massachusetts Institute of Technology, I realized that the site and most of the campus were built largely on landfill in the Charles River's estuary and that a significant amount of surface runoff from Cambridge farther inland was trying to get to this river through the campus—which, when combined with precipitation that fell on the MIT's buildings and pavements, constituted a considerable problem. In response, I suggested not only that we think of building roofs as landscape spaces that could absorb and use water, but also that we catch everything possible in the vicinity and create a storage area for its reuse. Working with Stephen Benz, a superb engineer and hydrologist who has since left Boston and joined our office as a partner leading Green Infrastructure efforts, we developed a large, below-grade cistern, which we covered with a planted basin and boulders left in the region by the retreat of the Wisconsin Glacier at the end of the Pleistocene era. Water captured on the site and adjacent buildings is directed to this cistern, and from there it is pumped up into the new Stata Center for Computer, Information, and Intelligence Sciences designed by Frank Gehry, where it is used for toilets. At any given time there is always at least a week's worth of flushes available, saving MIT a considerable sum on its water bill. The pumps are powered by solar panels on the roof of the building. It is a functional and attractive landscape that challenges the habitual Ivy League lawns of the region and culture while referring to the nature of the larger environment. As bold as some aspects of it appear, the actual movement of the water was subtle and unobtrusive.

I was criticized by some of my peers for not making this process more visible and thereby instructive. Therefore, on two subsequent projects at Yale University I asked, Why not make the banal capture of stormwater, its use, and its reuse a more visible amenity? Preparing a development plan for more facilities in a district known as Science Hill, which Yale's board of trustees, administration, faculty, and students wanted to integrate more fully into the rest of the university, we studied the topography, watersheds, and potential for building sites while developing strategies for service, circulation, social space, and water management. The first project implemented was Kroon Hall, a new building for the School of Forestry and Environmental Studies, designed by the London-based architect Michael Hopkins. Working again with Steve Benz and his former firm, Nitsch Engineering in Boston, we collected stormwater from the building and site, stored it in a cistern, and then directed it through a basin filled with water plants that help to clean and filter it before it is used in the building again for toilets and other non-potable uses.

I have, for some time, thought that it is foolish to imitate or attempt to copy the appearance of nature. As one ecologist told me, "Nature does not care how it looks—it cares how it works" (which is generally true, except for some aspects such as sexuality). This is not to say that while finding ways to use or replicate natural processes, we cannot and should not be conscious of aesthetics and the gorgeous combinations of color and visual form that one finds in nature. Professionally, we must do so if we want to attract people to our work and get them interested in, and to value and care for, the landscape and the environment as much as or more than they do their clothing, furnishings, cars, and homes.

We live in a culture of metrics, assessment, and accountability, and it is always helpful to point out that good environmental design is good for business. Furthermore, a significant part of sustainability, as my partners and I see it, has to do with social value and involvement. Thus, knowing that we were not really creating a natural marsh in the middle of Yale's campus on top of a service dock, we selected plants that not only could do the work needed, but also had a strong cultural legacy that would make clear that this was a water "garden," albeit a working one. The students liked it so much that they added fish, leading to the decision to keep it active year-round, which, in turn, has contributed to another happy aspect of this case: reducing the purchase of water by half a million gallons per year.[6]

Our next effort at Yale was to restore and transform the landscape of two residential colleges—Stiles and Morse—both built in 1961 and originally designed by the architect Eero Saarinen and landscape architect Daniel Kiley. Working with former students of ours from the University of Pennsylvania, the environmentally sensitive Philadelphia architects Kieran Timberlake, we developed a system of green roofs and storage tanks, again circulating the water in two ways: one for use as non-potable water for toilets and the other for fountains that we used to transform and enliven a particularly awkward aspect of Saarinen's original scheme. For whatever reasons, the two colleges had ended up with dining halls that, despite their generous proportions and ceiling heights, were nearly a floor below the grade of their adjacent courtyards. In an effort to make sense out of what was and normally is a dysfunctional situation—courtyards draining toward buildings, as these did—I proposed that we create outdoor decks adjacent to the dining rooms on the courts and suspend them over a new, even lower portion designed to contain receiving basins. We were then able to create shallow cascades or rapids with recycled stormwater, once more utilizing solar power. It has been a smash hit with the two colleges' residents while helping, as in a number of our projects, to win design awards and high environmental ratings. This, in turn, has helped Yale feel good about all the fuss and effort we endured to accomplish this work.

In addition to site-scale projects such as these, our office, like many in the field today, has been involved in larger water-related projects of vital interest to broader communities, particularly urban waterfronts, whether on rivers or harbors. For more than thirty years—from London's Canary Wharf and Long Beach, California, to southwestern Manhattan's Battery Park City, to Philadelphia and Alexandria, Virginia—we at OLIN have worked to reclaim access to water for residents of cities that have been cut off for a century or more by the industries, railroads, and highways that once fed their growth and success before decline set in. Today, reclaiming and redeveloping these areas at the heart of many cities is directly related to economic opportunity and ongoing urban evolution.

A generic project currently common across the United States is the removal of dams that may have once made sense for industry and employment but are now dysfunctional, having silted up, devastated fish stocks, and, in numerous cases, exacerbated flooding. For the past half-dozen years my partners have been working with the city of Stamford, Connecticut, and the US Army Corps of Engineers to restore Mill River as it passes through the city and enters Stamford's harbor and Long Island Sound. During the late summer of 2013, families and children began to engage the river in ways that had been impossible for more than a century, beginning to appreciate and use the first two phases of a new linear urban park and river restoration project that will continue for at least another half-dozen years.

The restoration of rural and wilderness water systems is equally worthy of the landscape architect's attention, and our firm has had the great pleasure of working on such projects. Even as our designs seem relatively straightforward compared to the difficulties of doing such work in dense, urban areas, it is a necessary effort that must be made, in part for fundamental aspects of civic health and in part because of the emotional strength and commitment it generates on the part of the populace and the catalytic effect it commonly bestows on adjacent territory. Frederick Law Olmsted and his sons' successor firm are renowned for their utilization of watercourses and drainage ways as devices to give structure, form, and direction to a community's layout and circulation, as well as to provide specific local character, amenity, and recreation for new and expanding urban situations. Frequently, however, one must work hard to find, pry apart, and reveal watercourses that are lost, hidden, degraded, or rendered dangerous, and then work to reclaim and provide access to them, restructuring and improving what can, at times, amount to a major portion of a community, one that has lost not only charm but its basic health and identity.

This was very much the case in our work on the master plan for Mission Bay, a large urban redevelopment on a former landfill and industrial area at the mouth of Mission Creek in San Francisco, where we insisted on placing the entire shoreline into public access. It turns out that linking the waterfront's parks and open spaces to the site has helped spur remarkable real estate development, despite difficult financial cycles. This has included the creation of a new campus for the University of California–San Francisco's extraordinary biomedical research endeavors, a large residential community, new commercial office and research facilities, and enough residential structures to make this a legitimate new neighborhood or district. In an area adjacent to San Francisco Bay that had been removed from the public for nearly a hundred years, the newly constructed beaches, habitat, public esplanades, and recreational facilities have a direct appeal to those who have arrived to live, work, and play here, as well as for others in the adjacent South of Market high-tech neighborhood and nearby downtown core.[7]

More recently, my partners and office have worked together with a team of architects, planners, engineers, and economists to complete a plan for seven miles of the central Delaware River waterfront in Philadelphia, which has subsequently been adopted by the city and by regional planning agencies. One driving purpose of the plan has been to reconnect the city to the water for the sake of economic development and an improved quality of life, health, civic sociability, and recreation for the general population. This transformation will take a generation to accomplish. It is important to know that key elements are not only the parks and created areas of wetland habitat near, on, and in the river, but also a series of lateral greenway connections that reach back into the city and its many neighborhoods. While some of these follow and rehabilitate historic drainage ways, others are pure inventions devised in the absence of such embedded natural features and yet necessary if one is to make a plan that equitably provides broader access to more of the city's residents.

As is happening in numerous places around the world, the Delaware River is currently in the long, slow process of becoming cleaner as a result of decades of struggle between the EPA, a number of industries and communities, and the often-problematic governments of Pennsylvania and New Jersey. The degree to which this plan for the waterfront succeeds and engenders a vibrant community adjacent to water—one that is healthy and attractive—will depend, ultimately, on political will and economic cycles. But once enough of the project is implemented, it will undoubtedly attract visitors and tourists as well as residents, further adding benefit to such an effort. Perhaps few in the community will focus on it, but the water is the magnet, and without the river there would be no city, no address, no desire, no project, and very likely not much of a future.

TODAY'S CONCERNS: LANDSCAPE PRACTICE AND CLIMATE CHANGE

As international conferences are held and the worst of our politicians go into hysterics demonizing scientific and academic messengers about our Earth, the news is clear: as a result of deeply entrenched and financially rewarding habits of industry and our cultural way of life, *the climate of much of the globe is changing.* This of course is something many of us began to suspect even decades ago, as the facts came in and scientific studies were published. We also know that this change is not happening slowly but somewhat rapidly.[8] The resulting situation is very serious and probably disastrous for much of human society—both rich and poor—on all continents, and it poses myriad planning and design challenges. While the US federal government, for the time being, may be tragically hamstrung on this matter because the leaders of one political party are far more interested in regulating my sex life than in caring for the environment and the fate of our cities and populace, those with serious responsibility at the Pentagon and in a handful of agencies, along with a number of states and many colleagues in academia and practice, are acting on the problem in areas where they can initiate a response and have some effect.

Our practice and the department of Landscape Architecture in the School of Design at the University of Pennsylvania have stopped talking about "global warming" and embraced the more encompassing, accurate, and useful phrase "climate change." Why? Because so many things are happening climatically in addition to the warming of particular places and regions. Some regions will be deluged with snow and rain or a rise in sea level or both, submerging significant inhabited and developed areas. Other regions are in a process of rapid desertification, with droughts and depletion of aquifers that will have equally devastating effects.[9]

Consider two incontrovertible facts: first, a vast proportion of humanity currently lives within one hundred feet of sea level. During the last Ice Age, when the Wisconsin Glacier covered most of what comprises Canada and the eastern half of the United States, there was an open ocean free of ice at the North Pole. Water formerly locked up within the polar ice cap had gone into circulation and rained down in the North Temperate Zone as snow and ice. Second, today the circumpolar north is heating up faster than anywhere else on the planet, and the ice cap is retreating rapidly, so much so that ocean navigation between the Atlantic and Pacific is about to begin for the first time in human history. Permafrost is melting at such a rate across the Arctic that 10 percent of all the stored organic matter on Earth will be released into the atmosphere in the next sixty to eighty years; a large portion will be in the form of methane, thereby exacerbating the problem of our changing atmosphere. No one is expecting to see glaciers growing any time soon, partly because they are melting everywhere—in Antarctica, the Himalayas, the Alps, the Sierra Nevada and Rocky Mountains, the Cordillera and the Andes of South America—but the water has to go somewhere into the new global water cycle. Most predictions are for significant rises in sea levels and for more frequent and more violent storms.[10]

As long as we have been in practice, my partners and I have habitually sought to see whatever possible social and environmental improvements might be leveraged by projects we have been asked by clients to work on, regardless of their nature. A well-publicized recent example was our endeavor to turn antiterrorist projects into civic improvements. In our schemes for the Washington Monument and new US embassy in London, we conceived of defensive barriers as devices that served other purposes as well. A crash wall was transformed into a generous seat wall holding a meadow, and a moat turned reflecting pond offered habitat and functioned as an element of the building's rain-harvesting and cooling system. Another such effort currently involves problems associated with climate change affecting native plant communities on California's coast. While engaged on the design for a large corporate facility there, we are working with plant biologists, horticulturalists, nurserymen, and local experts to experiment with alternative Mediterranean and arid-zone plants from elsewhere (particularly the high-desert and Intermountain West), which should survive changes under way throughout the coastal region that will likely destroy a number of key native species. Increase in interest on the part of many institutions, industries, and governments in water-related projects likewise suggests potential challenges and opportunities regarding social import, equity, and physical design that go beyond the mere management of water to issues of allocation and social justice.

Three current projects in our office respond, in varying ways, to this changing perception and need. One is in Philadelphia; the second is in Cleveland. The third began encompassing a large portion of the New Jersey coastline and western Long Island in New York, but has come to focus on a vital portion of New York City.

Philadelphia

The Philadelphia project, one of many such initiatives under way in the United States, was a national design competition cosponsored by the

EPA and the city's water department and managed by the Community Design Collaborative of Philadelphia. Titled "Soak It Up," its mission was to seek alternative and innovative solutions to prototypical problems associated with stormwater. Firms could compete on whichever of three large, specific areas of the city they chose. Each one involved how to catch, clean, use, and/or release stormwater in a beneficial manner that would show how a "green" infrastructure can transform a city such as Philadelphia. The first involved industrial land, the second was a somewhat suburban commercial area, and the third was an aging, dense residential area in South Philadelphia. We chose not to work on the first, because stormwater has been addressed adequately by existing programs and strategies that include runoff fees, incentives, green roofs, and cisterns, and it generally possessed considerable open land with which to work. Likewise, we chose not to work on the second, because most suburban areas are relatively known, understood, and have substantial slack in their development pattern that has been amply shown to accommodate runoff through a variety of by-now conventional measures. The third area—the aging, dense residential neighborhood— seemed by far the most difficult, and it represented a problem typical to a great number of cities in North America and the world.

At the time, it appeared nearly impossible for Philadelphia's city government to meet the objectives set forth by the EPA without demolishing substantial portions of the community. With a near-continuous pattern of multistory, masonry row houses similar to large areas of Baltimore, Boston, Washington, DC, Wilmington, and other older industrial centers, there was almost no open land to speak of. It presents a continuous matrix of impervious surfaces composed of streets, pavement, and aging buildings. Unlike in Detroit or even portions of North Philadelphia, there were few or no missing teeth—gaps where buildings had been abandoned or torn down. It was also full of people and businesses. It was soon obvious that no single strategy or device could generate the numbers or volume needed to deal with the problem, which was unlike the other two urban typologies in the competition.

My partners and our ambitious young staff produced a winning scheme that employed a phased combination of many parts at several scales, which would work together to accommodate the region's troublesome and increasing precipitation. The multilayered and patchwork approach we developed included work at the individual building and block level with roofs, sidewalks, streets, and alleys; above and below ground; the creation of new pocket parks, larger neighborhood parks and recreational spaces, and gardens; and the appropriation of land adjacent and beneath local arterials and elevated highways. If implemented, the results would easily justify the costs. As a result, the city and its water department, one of the sponsors of the project, are now working on a number of the proposed strategies.

Cleveland

A second ongoing project is in Cleveland, Ohio. Because this city is immediately adjacent to one of the Great Lakes, it has severe pollution cleanup issues and (like every metropolis in the nation) is under an EPA mandate to separate stormwater from its sanitary sewers. To stop the dumping of raw sewage into the lake with every major and many minor storm event, it has been directed to commence capturing and treating 98 percent of its rainfall and will only be allowed credit for 2 percent treatment through ground absorption and vegetative remediation. (By comparison, Philadelphia—which is adjacent to two major rivers, the Schuylkill and Delaware, but with a different geology and topography—is allowed 15 percent absorption into the ground and vegetative areas while treating and discharging the rest.) Given both the severity and the difficulty of the problem, Cleveland's water and sewer authorities have been forced to begin a massive infrastructure project that proposes to create a series of 24-foot-diameter tunnels, in some cases running for miles through the city to several large treatment centers near Lake Erie.

This giant public works project was expected to be costly and enormously disruptive to the urban fabric and numerous communities. In 2013 we were approached by Land Studio, a not-for-profit organization that helps the Cleveland Foundation implement physical projects, to do a feasibility study for landscape opportunities that might come from working with this project. Our office has completed a preliminary design for the first phase of the Doan Brook portion, referred to as "Green over Gray." We proposed shifting several roads as they pass through the area, which includes Euclid Circle, the Cleveland Clinic, and Case Western Reserve University, to take advantage of the massive excavation and replacement of cover over the stormwater tunnel to create a new linear park connecting them to the Olmsted Brothers' Rockefeller Park (built between 1896 and 1900) and the outfall area farther north. More than merely putting the existing hodgepodge back atop a giant cut-and-cover civil engineering project, this proposal allows the adjacent campus and community to open out and use a new green corridor where once was a highway-infested ravine and ravaged stream.

At the location where this new buried version of Doan Brook will reach its outfall after treatment, we have suggested transforming what was once a heavily polluted alluvial fan and landfill known locally as "Dike 14" into a nature preserve and park along Lake Erie. A portion of the clean water will be released and used on the surface to re-create the former stream and provide a constant flow through a riparian habitat. The scale of the proposed preserve is revealed by the presence of several lake freighters buried within the site like large toys in a sandbox. To succeed, all such projects that attempt to deal with urban water issues at the scale of the problems created in recent centuries must engage successfully and equally with the community, industry, and government. And they can only be achieved through incremental steps. Those involved in this work see it as a twenty-five-year plan that will inevitably evolve as it is implemented, very likely with unforeseen and differing plans, situations, and opportunities emerging in the future for this segment and other subsequent portions.

The New Jersey and New York Coast

The third of our current water-related projects, at yet an even larger scale, is one of many responses to Hurricane Sandy, a Category 3 storm that struck the East Coast in October 2012. Our firm is the prime consultant for one of ten separate design and planning teams engaged by the US Department of Housing and Urban Development in a multistage attempt to help figure out how to fulfill its mandate to spend many billions of dollars appropriated for recovery in coastal communities, from Maryland to New England; that is, how best to rethink and rebuild in the wake of increasingly costly hurricanes, storms, and floods so as to engender *resilience* within the affected communities. The current cost estimate for all of the related projects is $50 trillion, but that number is certain to grow in the future. The particular region of our portion of the study, undertaken in conjunction with Penn Praxis, the research and public service arm of the School of Design at the University of Pennsylvania, is the entire coastal zone of New Jersey and a portion of western Long Island Sound, including parts of New York City that were heavily affected by Sandy.

Although this portion of the US coastline has weathered a long history of such storms and figured prominently as a cautionary and prophetic case study in McHarg's *Design with Nature,* the puzzling and stubborn insistence on merely rebuilding time after time and the continually escalating costs—especially those of insurance rates and construction—are finally not being accepted by many. While some, whether affluent or not, are simply trying to put their beach houses back in place or on higher, sturdier stilts, others are asking, What would real resilience for a community look like? What are better outcomes? What can planning and design suggest that is different from local tradition and business as usual?

In addition to searching for particular local solutions, HUD is hoping to use the findings of our work and those of the other teams as a model for resilience and emerging responses in other regions of the nation and possibly even other types of disaster, such as fires in the West. Despite the fact that the towns in New Jersey are site-specific places and ultimately unique, tempering the degree of universality of solutions, we have also come to realize that models in the abstract are often useless for most real places and communities. The hope, therefore, is that a menu of strategies and alternative responses to a variety of topics and situations will emerge, and that more than a few may be useful at other locations.

We purposefully use the term *resilience* and not *sustainability.* The word "sustainability" has become so overused (like "ecology" or "nature") that it has lost much of the particular meaning first suggested in 1987, when the United Nations Commission on the Environment and Development produced what has come to be known as the Brundtland Report. It advanced a concept of sustainable development in opposition to one based on economic growth. It specifically defined sustainable development as that which "meets the needs of the present without compromising the ability of future generations to meet their own needs."[11] What the HUD project design teams are dealing with for the coastal zone is to devise alternative strategies that will engender continuity of communities subject to repeated major storms. It has little to do with growth per se, but more to do with survival and health for what currently exists. Even so, some form of change and growth is an almost inevitable aspect of the communities in our study area. Whatever strategies emerge can and should be incorporated into any new development within the coastal zone, and some or all can also be seen as sustainable practices.

The first step in the process has been to attempt an analysis of the scope and nature of the problem. Our findings have been revealing. The coastal zone of the United States is six times denser than the rest of the nation. Sixty-five percent of the country's GDP (gross domestic product) is produced in the coastal zone, and 40 percent of the income in these regions is derived from tourism. People enjoy the seashore and living near the water, except when it is raging and flooded. Disasters such as those caused by increasingly severe storms, therefore, have a significant impact on the health, welfare, and economies of a significant portion of the nation, just as further privatization and removal of additional portions of the coastal zone from public access have a negative impact on tourists and residents alike, except for a minute portion of the population. Acknowledging this, we concluded that whatever we proposed should not separate people from their land and heritage. We could not seriously propose to have all or even a substantial number of America's coastal communities—Boston, New York, Newark, Cape May, Hampton Roads, Charleston, or Vero Beach, for example—pick up and move inland or to higher ground, as have at least one Inuit village on the Bering Sea and several towns on islands in the Pacific. The sheer cost, however one calculates it, would be unaffordable and unworkable in terms of the number of people dependent on the coastal resource, with livelihoods in the cranberry, fishing, and marine industries or in tourism, services, military, and recreation.

To understand the communities under study, we began to focus on issues of income, poverty, and topography. As economic advisors, the firm of HR&A helped us study how changes in public policy affect diverse costs such as insurance, construction, mobility, and public services, and led us to develop alternative scenarios. One is that enclaves of the wealthy will not be significantly affected, for they have the money and ability to do as much or as little as they desire, and they can rebuild as often and however they choose. A second scenario is that communities with many middle-class residents, who can't afford new insurance rates or can't rebuild or modify their homes sufficiently to adapt to change and emerging conditions, would be able to leave and move elsewhere. This would leave only the poor in place, unable to pay new insurance rates, meet the costs of rebuilding, or go elsewhere for alternative employment and homes. Such communities would then have a reduced tax base and be unable to pay for public services needed. It would be a wicked, downward spiral. Thus, without some sort of new strategy for resilience in the face of climate change, some communities would see what might be described as a Hamptons effect, and others would resemble Detroit—that is, a few coastal communities would become more and more exclusive while numerous others collapsed.

With this potential crisis in mind, we mapped several factors. Areas that will be flooded repeatedly were easy to define with GIS (Geographic Information System) survey data or old topographic maps that have existed for decades. We then overlaid areas with high rates of poverty and subtracted them from the inhabited zones to locate areas where the tax base would remain. While there is almost continuous development throughout the coastal zone, we focused our attention on communities with this particular combination of issues and followed up with field visits, spending time correlating the data with the situation on the ground. What we found in speaking with knowledgeable people in the area, such as the mayor of Hoboken, Dawn Zimmer, is that current government funding for disaster relief and preparedness is predicated on piecemeal, standalone projects, essentially an isolated property basis. She pointed out that funds currently can't be aggregated or allocated for broader, systemic solutions to flooding. Funding today is also means-based, not performance-based. Currently, one can receive funding to build a dike around a single property or building, but not for one that is a quarter-mile away in another place or a property on a bay that would prevent flooding on a larger number of properties, including the qualifying fundable one.

There is, therefore, a clear need to restructure the process from the current dysfunctional system of awarding grants for individual property, and to study the nature of different kinds of problems created by storms. First, one cannot elevate all the existing cities, streets, buildings, and harbors ten or more feet from their current situation. New York City, Newark, Hoboken, New Brunswick, and Atlantic City are not a bunch of wooden beach cottages that can be lifted onto stilts like Neolithic lake dwellers. Nor can any reasonable person expect everyone along America's coasts to abandon their homes, communities, and vocations. We need solutions for the new sea level and so-called hundred-year floods (which, of course, every student and citizen knows have and will continue to occur more frequently than that; in our study region alone there have been several during the past decade).

Our team has been inventorying a menu of design strategies and responses, settling on a number of alternative solutions, each appropriate to particular situations. One is the construction of offshore reefs and barrier islands, which can greatly attenuate storm surges and prevent their crushing impact on exposed shoreline and development. Another is to rebuild or create the equivalent of a sizable primary dune (which is what dikes and levees really are) that can prevent or mitigate flooding of the area behind them. Another alternative in urbanized areas is to create a new set of linear structures—multistory buildings for different purposes, whose lower portions would largely be "sacrificed" in order to serve as a dike or levee. Such a strategy would be highly effective in areas such as the Hoboken Terminal and Hoboken University Medical Center, both of which are currently in the floodplain and suffered severe damage from Sandy. The food-distribution system for the greater part of New York City, located at Hunts Point in the Bronx, at the confluence of Long Island Sound and the East and Harlem rivers, could profit from such a strategy as well. The right sort of storm could virtually knock it out, leaving several million people in considerable danger of starvation, making the project especially urgent.

To a degree, most environmental problems are cultural problems. Hurricanes Sandy and Katrina were not so much "natural" disasters as they were "human" disasters, because of historically poor land-use decisions. Nature was merely releasing energy that was in circulation, had built up, and then was dissipated through these storms across their respective regions. Such phenomena will continue with increasing frequency as a result of the global changes in climate currently under way. Therefore, we need a cultural shift and new alternatives: to change codes and regulations, prohibiting further construction of single-family houses in particular areas, such as barrier islands; to mandate mobile dwellings that can be shifted out of harm's way and returned later after a storm event has passed; and to create maritime forest reserves that offer habitat and amenity around bays in areas that currently do not receive ocean storm surges but have flooded in nearly every recent storm, due to water from heavy rains inland moving down streams, rivers, floodways, and ravines on the way to the sea and piling up in coastal communities and harbors. This manner of flooding can and should be readily addressed upstream at the source, as discussed earlier, through traditional means such as using parks for storage and sponges, as shown in our earlier projects and those of our peers.

Finally, we propose the creation of a series of "resiliency centers": places where communities learn about the issues and alternative strategies, share and find information about climate change and the diverse proposals and means to accommodate climate and weather events, to provide refuge in emergencies and assist in developing resilient communities. Also, new industries can emerge from efforts to produce such resilient communities—including new firms, businesses, products, manufacturing and construction methods, tools, and materials—developing products and processes not yet imagined or available that will prove useful in such circumstances.

RUS IN URBE: COVETING WILDERNESS— A NEO-FAUSTIAN DREAM?

Throughout society and even within the academy, there is the notion— or implied thesis—that nature and the city are not only different, but historically in opposition to each other. Thus there is often a motive to develop and present proposals that bring nature and the city together— surely to improve cities and their citizens but not necessarily to improve on their perceptions of nature. This is an interesting double proposal, which may or may not work.

In our experience at OLIN, it has been relatively easy to conceive, explain, and gain support for what is called "natural restoration" in non-urban and rural settings, whether in Europe or North America. Despite technically complex issues regarding hydrology, topography, soil, and plants, such projects are generally not that difficult to implement. To do such work in a city is another matter. The idea of nature or of "natural restoration" in an urban setting raises a number of important questions: What do we mean by the phrase *nature in the city*? Or, for that matter, what do we mean by *nature,* and what sort or aspects of nature? How wild? To what extent and scale? Depending on the answer to those questions, how do we feel about wilderness and wildness, and what they mean? Which aspects, processes, and creatures of nature do we truly need and desire to bring into cities, and how can we do so effectively? How far are we prepared to go as a consequence?

For most people, nature implies the existence of phenomena, creatures, objects, processes, or events that are not of human creation or control. Many people (even a lot of designers and planners) think that nature is somehow not part of a city, that cities are in some way different entities, and that one can bring nature into a city and park it there like a car in a garage, or install it in a piazza like art, or insert it into and through a neighborhood like a street, greenway, or even a stream. But cities are already within and a part of nature, and so are we, all the time, all day, every day. We are not separate, and thinking that we are has resulted in many of the problems so frequently associated with the general notion of "environmental crises." What many people mean by phrases such as "introducing nature into cities" is that they are referring to particular aspects of natural processes and ecological associations, even biomes or, more likely, portions of them: mainly forests and hydrologic regimes such as rivers, streams, ponds, lakes, bays, marshes, and meadows. Often, it seems there is a literal (if unstated) notion that one can have fragments and working portions of wildness not only immediately adjacent to developed parcels of land, but also threaded and woven right into, across, and through the heart of the polis, through the residential, commercial, and industrial districts of a city.

To a degree, this is a highly desirable dream. As one who grew up within a true wilderness in a small Alaskan town, where there was forest with moose and bears at the end of neighborhood streets, and one could occasionally hear wolves at night while falling asleep, I can attest that it was a marvelous place to be a child, with the best possible playground always close at hand. It is what life on the frontier was during several centuries of North American history. It does pose issues, however, that are not much discussed, at least not in the articles I have seen about the prospects and advantages of "re-wilding," whether in the Netherlands, New Orleans, New England, or Montana. The complications or difficulties most likely to arise by reintroducing a wilder form of nature into cities are matters neither of feasibility nor of cost, political will, or even resistance to change in the current physical accumulation of infrastructure and building stock but of tolerance. What sort of "wild" nature are people capable of accepting or willing to coexist with in areas of density? This returns us to a fundamental aspect of nature found in the wild, namely its stochastic nature: random or accidental events that can and often do lead to a cascade of other events that are not only dynamic, but are dramatically transformative, including landslides, forest fires, floods, droughts, disease, and population explosions (or crashes) of plants, animals, insects. Climate, for example, is a statistical abstraction, whereas weather is a series of unique events in real time that can fluctuate wildly within statistical probabilities and the history of a given place. Currently, both are changing in dramatic ways. For example, decades of drought in the American West are leading toward a new norm that will likely include the disappearance of all but a few glaciers in the mountains and the end of snow as we have known it by 2050, with the subsequent nationwide collapse of the winter resort industry, the disappearance of many subalpine native forests and concomitant plant and animal communities, and the occurrence of frequent and widespread fires.[12]

In addition to personal anecdotal experience, one frequently reads about current or growing problems of urban life coming into confrontation with nature and its processes and the steps taken to deal with it. Communities need to face and resolve the regular occurrence of incidents with bears, coyotes, and even mountain lions in suburban areas of the West; or of deer, coyotes, foxes, raccoons, and opossums in the heart of cities in the Midwest and Appalachian East (usually leading to the death of the animals involved); or of wildfires in new and older communities; or of the flooding discussed earlier. In all likelihood, this will lead to the "management" of any new natural areas introduced into cities, to prevent such confrontation or "accidents."

One such example occurred with our project for the Ballona Wetlands, a refuge in the Los Angeles basin. Many birds in this particular

habitat favored nesting on the ground in dunes and grasses, and a population explosion of foxes occurred that threatened to wipe them out.
This led to live-trapping all the foxes and transporting them for release
east of the city in the San Gabriel Mountains. Bear-proofing all the
trash cans in the many increasing suburbs near forested areas usually
proves inadequate for government officials and citizens worried about
the safety of their children. The probable result will be to make supposed "natural" or "wild" areas in cities no different from the parks we
have had for centuries, only dissimilar in their appearance. Rather than
exhibiting a "pastoral" imagery, they will be "naturalistic" in appearance, but only partially so in process and reality. What many people
really want and expect is a nature with its problematic and unpredictable aspects removed—no mosquitoes, ticks, or mice, which are vectors
for serious diseases in humans; no snakes, snapping turtles, or bats,
regardless of how helpful they may actually be. This process of selec-
tivity has been under way for centuries and has accelerated drastically
during the past century with the extinction of vast numbers of plants
and animals.[13] Even as there is talk of reintroducing nature into cities,
I try to imagine what is meant beyond plants, meadows, forests, and
watercourses in a representative but somewhat abstract and de-natured
way, or a concoction that is basically a sanitized imitation of nature.

Worse than my fear of a misbegotten "imitation" of nature is a fear
of ecosystem designers who believe they can, in a godlike way, fully
create large-scale natural areas within cities and that they have the
knowledge, wisdom, judgment, or authority to do so. This is a Faustian
scenario. How are we to ensure that the profession does not fall into
the hubris and situation of engineering, especially civil and mechanical engineering, with all of their environmental mistakes in the recent
past that are explained away or excused by saying, "If only they had
better data, more information, more money, more scope, or improved
technology, then all would have worked out better"—the hydro projects,
the flood-control projects, the uniform highway designs, the chemical
treatment systems and precautions, the irrigation projects. Too often,
the disasters and ruined landscapes and lives resulted from single-fac-
tor goals and solutions. But simply doubling down and having more and
better data and larger applications will not make mechanistic solutions
work, even imperfectly. This was not the underlying problem that led to

bad housing, disastrous transportation systems, flooded regions, toxic waste, and climate change. As with Faust, the values and limited purpose and motives were at fault, not technique. The ideal of a perfect design and planning process, with infinite inputs, is a phantom. So as we embark on the worthy goal of reintroducing more thoroughgoing aspects of nature into our cities, we need to check carefully to ascertain our understanding of the proposed situation as well as our beliefs and motives.

Ever since I began practicing landscape architecture more than forty years ago, I have been an advocate for versions of rus in urbe (meaning, literally, nature or the country in the town or city). Rarely have my proposals been for full-blown wild territories; rather, they have incorporated select aspects, fragments, processes, and systems at a smaller scale. To greater or lesser degree, our designs have been works of art or representations, often in conjunction with particular functional services. For me, several of the issues discussed above raise problems as old as Western civilization. These pertain to different meanings of the concepts *natural* and *artificial,* as well as *imitation* and *art.* During the fourth century BCE in Athens, the Doric style was considered more "natural" than the Corinthian, which was seen not only as more elaborate and ornamental, with its carved acanthus leaves and occasional added florets and palm fronds, but also as more decadent. Part of the argument was that the columns, capitols, triglyphs, and metopes of Doric architecture were more elementary in their simple forms as expressive structures, more direct in the use of materials, and closer to their predecessors, which had been made of timber. The representational quality and, one might say, the virtuosity of Hellenistic carving in the Corinthian style was seen as more artificial, as it imitated plants in stone. The simpler, more abstract work (Doric) was considered to be more virtuous or truthful than the more representational work that copied the appearance of natural forms.

While it was already a cliché that art, in one way or another, was derived from or representational of nature and, therefore, was valued or derided because it was seen to imitate nature (see Plato and Socrates), there were other concepts of imitation. One was "naturalistic imitation." If well done, it would give the illusion that the object itself was imitated. A contrasting view was that a "good imitation" would convey the essential information about the object without emphasizing all the accidental detail. This version allowed distortion, editing, and exaggeration of particular aspects that gave the character of something and not necessarily the appearance or facsimile.[14] Thus, for the ancient Greeks, the more abstract work was seen as "natural," and the more imitative work was seen as more "artificial." That framework has been with us ever since, at least in Western civilization.

The profession of landscape architecture, from time to time, exhibits a surfeit of mimesis, of efforts to artificially produce environs that attempt to imitate, mimic (a word and concept I hate), re-create, or even newly create natural and largely wild landscapes. As acknowledged, my office and I have indulged in aspects of this at times, and so have a number of my peers and predecessors, with greater or lesser success. In part, the medium invites such attitudes, for our culture is beguiled by imitative work in all the arts, by simulacra and fakes, by images, copies, and reproductions, and, most recently, in all manner of digital productions. Interestingly enough, however, landscape design has, like music, for centuries offered the opportunity to produce remarkable compositions and works of art that are derived solely from formal exploration of the medium. Some landscape architects most revered for their art and accomplishment in the distant and recent past—Giacomo Barozzi da Vignola, André Le Nôtre, Lancelot "Capability" Brown, Roberto Burle Marx, Daniel Urban Kiley, and Lawrence Halprin—avoided naturalistic work. Yet each produced work that reveled in aspects of nature: water, stone, and plants; abstractions of natural processes and forms that dramatically exploited a number of its attributes—generosity of scale, redundancy, amplitude, color, pattern, texture, movement, sound, modulation of topography, and light. And, in case after case, they encouraged movement (choreography) through a sequence of rich and varied spaces and stimulating sights, engendering sheer joy for many, and in a manner we associate with *being* in nature.

Some of my colleagues disdain such work as old hat, non-ecological, and representative of societies, political systems, and environmental attitudes no longer seen as valid. This is in step with what has been a central tenet of art and design criticism for some time: that architecture and landscape design can and should be judged socially and ethically, that work in the public realm is inevitably political, that the true measure of the worth and meaning of a project is determined by who suffers, who gains, and who pays for these benefits, in both the short term and long run. There is considerable reason to support such a position.

Unlike the humanities—the academic disciplines that study the arts and the human situation, often without prescriptions for change or improvement or the production of any "practical" action or product—landscape architecture as a profession is, like medicine, law, engineering, and architecture, an instrumental field. It is a commonplace, remarked upon from time to time, that professions have the job of developing such things as laws, medicines, bridges, hydraulic schemes, and bombs. This can generate a certain melancholy on the part of those in our profession who are reflective, which, while probably not as great as that of Robert Oppenheimer and the others who created the atom bomb, does compel scrutiny over the ideology and motives or veiled moral judgments of every reformer and "good soldier," of all those who propose to wield instrumentality over the human environment. Shifting the mood, however, to considerations of art, one is reminded that Marshall McLuhan termed one of the basic strategies of modern (twentieth-century) art to be a "juxtaposition without copula"—placing disparate things in the same composition without an attempt to relate or explain them, such as Giorgio de Chirico's classical statue, railroad train, Renaissance arcade, and rubber glove.[15] Yet, for thoughtful viewers, the urge to find meaning, an intelligent link to the combination or success in its composition, is expected, desired, and possible. So, too, one might say that the juxtaposition of wild and chaotic nature with the works and context of human order makes possible the creation of art of high ambition.

SPIRIT AND POETICS: LIFE AND DESIGN BEYOND SURVIVAL, PRAGMATICS, AND INSTRUMENTATION

Paul Fréart de Chantelou, the chronicler of the artist and architect Gian Lorenzo Bernini's visit to France in 1665 at the request of King Louis XIV, tells of an incident when the two of them were traveling across Paris. Stopping their carriage on a bridge over the Seine, Bernini descended, walked to the rail, and stood staring at the river below "for a good quarter of an hour looking first from one side of the bridge and then the other. After a while he turned to [Chantelou] and said, 'It is a beautiful view; I am a great lover of water, it calms my spirits.'"[16]

I could say the same. Recently, in leafing through a number of sketch-books filled over time, I found that a surprising number of drawings were either exploratory depictions of some aspect of water or sketches done in its presence. I spent my childhood and young adult life in Alaska and the Pacific Northwest, two regions of extraordinary natural beauty and power that are blessed with ample water in all of its magical forms, at times seemingly too much. For some, the ocean surf is like mother's milk, but where I lived if you went into the water, you would probably die, whether from silt, the current, or the cold. I eventually learned to swim or at least to float when nearly thirty years old, while living on the eastern end of Long Island, where I discovered the pleasures of relatively warmer water and the buoyancy afforded by the ocean's salt. Earlier, though, like most humans, I delighted in playing in water as a child, squirting and splashing it about, building dams and ditches, and messing about with it, whether in puddles, ponds, or streams. I made rafts and waded in it on hikes and fishing trips. I grew up, moving from one coast to another, coming to enjoy beaches, waterfalls, and all man-ner of water—spending time in diverse natural settings, and drawing and painting it in a number of manifestations. Later, I observed many of the ways that water has been treated as a subject and element of landscape and urban design, from the artificial yet compelling bodies of water created in English landscape gardens to the exuberant fountains and waterworks of classical antiquity and the Renaissance to those in Mannerist and Baroque gardens, parks, and urban piazzas.

Although many of these landscape creations may be stimulating works of original art, they often have other desirable attributes. The lakes of Capability Brown, Humphry Repton, and others may have orig-inated as visual and scenographic artifice, but they are, in fact, com-posed of natural elements that, once in place, have developed a life in the world, inevitably becoming the habitat of numerous plants and animals. In a world of agriculture and human settlement, they became de facto sanctuaries for fish and birds, insects and amphibians, aquatic and riparian plants, as well as watering holes for numerous mammals, domestic and wild. There is a shift in their designs from the artificial to the natural, along with a deepening in artistic meaning. The fountains and basins of Italian cities, on the other hand, began as purely functional devices—namely, like the wells and basins in a monastery's cloisters, as devices to bring potable water to communities that had little or no access to it. These fixtures where urban citizens came to fill buckets and jars with fresh water to take back to their dwellings for drinking, cooking, cleaning, and bathing became foci for social contact and activity. As such, they also offered opportunities for those of wealth and power to demonstrate largesse, to exercise noblesse oblige and show off a bit by enhancing these fixtures and commissioning superb craftsmen and artists to design and produce impressive waterworks as vehicles for display, complete with sculpture and architecture. Like numerous arcades and bridges that have enhanced so many Mediterranean cities since antiquity, bits of urban infrastructure—things that began as a utility or even a necessity regarding climate and circulation—time after time were transformed into works of art that enhanced life for all who encountered them. Repeatedly, villas, parks, and urban scenes have afforded a surplus of delight; such production of beauty and wit, of pleasure and amenity, would appear to far outweigh utilitarian necessity by serving another deep purpose and need: elevating the human spirit and imagination.

Fountains and water play may well be a welcome yet unnecessary pleasure in a country estate or retreat, but they are far less gratuitous and much more purposeful, even necessary, in today's urban scene. Recent medical and psychological studies have concluded something that most landscape architects have known for generations and many laymen not only suspect but act upon regularly if they have sufficient means to do so: being in proximity to nature and experiencing its elements, even if only on a short walk, is good for us.[17] Hence the centuries-long tradition of having private estates, gardens, and country retreats, and of taking trips and vacations to wild and scenic spots. We are creatures of nature and need it for our physical and mental well-being. Fresh air and exercise are only part of what is required. Our brains, eyes, and spirit are stimulated and nourished by the sights and sounds of natural phenomena, by trees and flowering plants, water and topography, sunlight and shade, the movement and sound of water and wind, birds and animals, varying textures, infinite shades and colors, along with varied focal lengths that differ from those within our architecture—our habitual interior living and work spaces, with the fixed and often standardized dimensions of rooms, corridors, desks, and computer screens.

The pleasure that one obtains from time spent in the woods, mountains, or seashore and the conclusion that it is healthy and restorative are simple yet profound facts. But for many millions of people, whether rich, middle-class, or poor, such experiences are fewer and farther between these days. An increasingly greater population of the world is born, lives, works, plays, and dies in urban settings. It is thus incumbent on those involved in urban planning and design to find ways to introduce into the heart of our cities elements and attributes of nature that are restorative, that stimulate us, that engender health and well-being. In this, nothing is as potent or effective as plants and water, as study after study with hospital patients, the elderly, children, and office workers attest.[18] Simply being in the presence of water has a calming effect on everyone, whether Alzheimer patients or energetic businessmen, mothers and small children, teachers or laborers on a break.

While rarely articulating this perspective in so many words to my colleagues (or to myself), for many years I have quietly been concerned with introducing water and other aspects of nature into our projects, working with them in diverse ways and in any number of different sites, whether public or private, urban or rural. These have ranged from ponds and basins in parks, such as Hermann Park in Houston and Wagner Park in New York City, to a variety of fountains in plazas in London, Los Angeles, New York City, and Portland, Oregon, to fountains in gardens and grounds of institutions such as the National Gallery of Art in Washington, DC, the Cleveland Public Library, the Barnes Foundation in Philadelphia, the Getty Center in Los Angeles, and the American Academy in Rome.

In reflecting on the pleasure we may derive from nature and art, my thoughts return again to ancient Greece and the emerging relationship between *truth, beauty,* and *morality.* It is impractical to explore such enormous and difficult topics here, except to say that there are many occasions and aspects of nature that humans have seen and described as beautiful through the history of all societies. Enormous effort has

been devoted to describing and explaining this phenomenon. Philosophers, poets, artists, writers, and critics have said profound and contradictory things, especially regarding the relationship of perceived beauty
in nature to that resulting from artistic creation. At least as far back as
St. Augustine, people have debated the relationship between the beautiful and the useful. In 1965 the French philosopher Étienne Gilson
wrote, "There is no opposition between the beautiful and the useful,
for beauty may serve useful purposes (in a sense it always does), yet
beauty is not made in view of its possible utility—it is desirable for its
own sake."[19]

If one can say there is a common aspect to many of the things
deemed beautiful—whether it be a machine, poem, sunset, or an
unusual person, painting, or landscape design—it often can be seen
as an aspect of form. Nature and natural landscapes as commonly
perceived are "form full," which is part of their wonder and equally
overwhelming essence. "Form" here means more than mere shape or
visual attributes. Gilson writes, "We call beautiful . . . what causes
admiration and holds the eyes. It is of the essence of the beautiful in
art, even from the simple point of view of its nominal definition, that
it be given in a sensible perception whose apprehension is desirable
in itself and for itself."[20] It was this truth that another philosopher,
Hegel, wielded as a club in his insistence that, for him, human works
rank above those of nature aesthetically. He disapprovingly stated that
one's sensory power is "deeply rooted in the earthly."[21] This, of course,
is one of the fundamental aspects of our humanity and of our bond
with nature, and, therefore, it is a source of the deep pleasures we
derive from it in particular circumstances. I agree with Denis Donoghue when he says that "form entails the conversion of matter, so far
as is possible, to spirit."[22]

How this is done in nature is through the production of forms we find
rich and compelling and that, to a degree, are described by science as a
matter of chemistry, physics, thermodynamics, and the flow of energy
along with the various processes of evolution, tectonics, and randomness. In art, including that of landscape architecture, it is accomplished
through craft and artistry, making and shaping, experimenting and testing ideas about forms and materials to create something—a place—that
did not exist before, ideally with materials from the so-called natural

world. There are innumerable gardens, parks, and designed landscapes that have been deemed beautiful, but are they natural? As I've noted elsewhere, I firmly agree with R. Buckminster Fuller that "the opposite of natural is impossible." There are beautiful places and events that are not human, that have been deemed beautiful yet are oblivious to our feelings and thoughts; some of them are benign and some terrible. This, in combination with the many attitudes toward art, has led philosophers to feel a need to construct and describe a gradient of emotion-related perceptions that include terms (concepts) such as *sublime* and *pretty,* with that of *beauty* somewhere in between.

Creating something pretty, while pleasant and attractive, is more common, predictable, and relatively easy to achieve through design. Prettiness often underlies much that is attractive in bourgeois culture, and it is regularly employed in marketing everything from automobiles and clothing to movies and vacations. Prettiness is the quality often under attack and judged offensive when it is detected as the character and motive of landscape design, especially when it is seen to be employed as a palliative to mask the true nature of a place or of an endeavor, such as a commercial or political condition, that is exploitive or destructive in some form, whether social or environmental. Pretty—while charming in children and small gardens—has often and easily been manipulated by commerce and industry, giving rise to fairly universal attacks and rejections by many twentieth- and twenty-first-century artists, architects, and landscape architects.

Beauty, on the other hand, cannot be truly controlled or manipulated. It is a property that one might hope to coax into being, but it is extremely difficult to achieve by running straight after it. As recorded in a conversation with the poet Michael Palmer a few years ago, I remarked that I almost never mention beauty to a client, largely because it makes them nervous. Michael responded, "They might carry so many preconceptions about what 'the beautiful' is. It is an earned thing, not something that preexists at any point, and you don't want them conceptualizing that from constraining assumptions. . . . Beauty includes difficulty as well. . . . It's the unstated goal. . . . [If you aim for it] you end up with pretty instead of beautiful, without the depth because the primary consideration can't be in surface terms of beauty. Pretty is about surface."[23] That beauty has confused so many is understandable.

CONCLUSION, FOR NOW

My enthusiasm, on the one hand, and my unease, on the other, about the invocation or desire for a more representational and functional presence of nature in the city is, therefore, often tied to the differing perceptions not only about nature but also about its meaning and possibilities: how does nature—in these many guises—relate to the instrumental and artistic qualities of landscape design and landscape architecture? My answer is and has long been that what I and other landscape architects do, in addition to being responsible social professionals licensed by public authorities, is an art and not only an applied science. I hope I have shown, through a range of my projects, that even as much of our work is primarily instrumental toward particular social and environmental goals, we also strive to make our designs palatable and as handsome and beautiful and meaningful as possible. At certain scales, a design can reflect fairly dramatic presentations of aspects of natural processes and materials; at other times, it is quieter and less obtrusive. Design varies in its expression, but there are times when one has the opportunity or the urge to be more expressive and less concerned about the instrumentality of a place. Let me present one last example.

Several years after working on a design with an international team, we at OLIN have recently begun construction on a large corporate facility in Silicon Valley. For some who live in the heart of big cities with big skylines, such as Chicago, San Francisco, and New York City, the low-rise sprawling community of Cupertino may seem inadequately urban. Nevertheless, ever since World War II, a large percentage of the American population has lived by choice in such spread-out, automobile-dependent, low-density matrixes, not in densely packed Manhattan. Citizens in this broader American urbanism are as much in need of thoughtful, stimulating, and challenging environments as anyone else. As can be imagined from my previous remarks, my partners and I have devoted considerable effort to stormwater management and plant communities appropriate to a region, in part to ensure low usage of water. At the heart of the project, seemingly almost as an incidental anecdote, we have designed a pond that appears as an abstraction, not a reproduction or copy of nature. On the plan it is a smallish detail, but in the overall site it is a relatively large, circular basin, 180 feet across. It is designed to have gentle waves moving from its center outward to the circular margin, lapping the perimeter with constant, random ripples and gentle sound. Working with the California fountain-design firm CMS Collaborative, we built a full-size mockup of a sizable portion of this pond to work out its mechanics and limited elements to ensure that it would work as envisioned.

Looking at my initial design sketches and proposed materials, one of the clients realized that this feature incorporated aspects reminiscent to him of the shoreline of Lake Tahoe, where he had gone since he was a child. He immediately reacted with passion and enthusiasm, suggesting how powerful memories are in connecting sensations stimulated by natural processes and elements with place. And yet, he and I and everyone involved knew that the proposal was not a reproduction or copy of a natural wonder such as Lake Tahoe, where I have never been. If this pond is successful, it will be a work of art, landscape art, that embodies and brings into the heart of an urban campus particular aspects of nature that not only appeal to us today but also, over millennia, have proved vital to our well-being. These natural elements include the constant movement of water, the shifting and dancing of light and reflection, the sibilance of small waves moving across shallows of polychrome stones— truly fundamental attributes of nature. The simple, even calm resolution of shape or vessel in contrast with such a mercurial and animated presence is a cultural product.

In *Speaking of Beauty,* a book largely devoted to literature, especially poetry, Denis Donoghue writes, "When I look at a wave breaking along a beach, I see a force becoming its form."[24] This recognition of the production of form through movement and repetition in the natural world and its analog in works of art are noted astutely by T. S. Eliot in "Burnt Norton," the first of his "Four Quartets":

Words move, music moves
Only in time; but that which is only living
Can only die . . .
. . . Only by the form, the pattern,
Can words or music reach
The stillness, as a Chinese jar still
Moves perpetually in its stillness.[25]

These lines point out that, although life moves on relentlessly, some arts are evanescent and exist in time, while others present us with timelessness through their form. Among other things, Eliot seems to say that we are to avoid setting up an opposition between force and form, and that we can experience time in the manifestation of form and vice versa.

It is commonplace to note that everyone comes to see the world through their own experiences, as did my client who loves Lake Tahoe, and to filter the world through the particular constructs of language and imagery, dance and music. And yet—and yet—there is still that world out there, independent and uncaring of us, even as it is there to nurture. How do we present the natural and built environment not only for ourselves, but also for others? How do we embrace that larger world as a true companion? In a way, just as the fountains and water gardens within the arid lands of Islam have presented the precious, life-enhancing element of water through superb abstractions, so, too, on a project in the quasi-Mediterranean climate south of San Francisco did we employ native, drought-tolerant plantings with a strict water regime throughout the overall site, at a key central location within a shady grove of trees, to create a quiet yet gently active pool as both a social and spiritual center for a working community.

There are several manifestations of form in this perfectly round basin or pond: the container itself, the waves and their patterns of movement and shifting shapes, the stones, the reflections of trees and clouds and people, the seasonal trajectory of the sun above and the light in and on the pond, the seasonal rising mist, and on and on—creating an almost Olmstedian delight in the power of contemplation of the senses. One can easily say that the idea of form has become hopelessly "entangled in its relation to content," as Donoghue puts it. Nevertheless, in any thought of nature that becomes combined with that of design, *form* cannot be evaded, and here I quote again from Donoghue: "If we try to separate form from substance, we turn form into abstraction that . . . makes it an ally of reactionary art. . . . Form transfigures what otherwise merely exists. . . . It is not a creation from nothing, but a further creation from the otherwise created. Form is substance as imagined, not merely received; *transfigured, not mimed*."[26]

And in Charles Baudelaire's "Le Peintre de la vie moderne" (The

Painter of Modern Life), a landmark essay of modernity published in 1863, he asserts: "The beautiful is made of an eternal, invariable element, whose quantity is excessively difficult to determine, and of a relative, circumstantial element, which will be, . . . whether severally or all at once, the age, its fashions, its morals, its emotions. . . . I defy anyone to point to a single scrap of beauty which does not contain these two elements."[27] There we have it: the inevitable combination of the momentary and the eternal.

I am absolutely convinced that this pond will become a particularly treasured spot for people to gather, relax, and socialize. Although it is part of a place of private employment, for the twelve thousand or more employees who will work there every day (a population nearly as large as the town where I grew up), many of whom will often work late hours, the pond can become a kind of refuge.

I have said elsewhere that, because streets normally comprise the bulk of the public realm of most cities, they are too important to leave their design solely to traffic engineers. They serve too many important roles other than simply moving automobiles and trucks about. So, too, I can state with conviction that water is far too important to leave solely in the hands of engineers and utilitarian planners. That we must design and plan to accommodate water, its conservation and care, its stewardship and wise use, should go without saying. It must be fundamental to our art—rather like assuming that an architect and her engineers will produce a building that will not fall down. But one expects and should demand more, much more. When we as landscape architects think about nature in cities, we should expect more than instrumentation and utility. We must also address the spirit.[28]

Like Cato the Elder, who ended every speech in the Roman senate with the phrase "Death to Carthage," I am fond of sharing J. B. Jackson's ideas about the functions of a city in his essay "The Imitation of Nature." After asserting that it is impossible for us truly to *copy* nature for a number of reasons, even if it were a good idea, Jackson proceeds to discuss our need for nature and how we must strive to bring important functions and attributes of nature into the heart of our cities. He concludes by paraphrasing Vitruvius's hortatory triad, which has been translated as "firmness, commodity, and delight"; to Jackson this means that a city "must be a just and efficient social institution; it must be a biologically wholesome habitat; and it must be a continuously satisfying aesthetic-sensory experience." He goes on to observe, "Up to the present we have given all thought to the first of these. There are signs that the second will receive its due attention before long; for it is already outside the city gates. But the third will be realized only when we learn once again to see nature in its entirety; not as a remote object to be worshipped or ignored as it suits us, but as part of ourselves."[29]

My partners and I have tried to act on this invocation, in part by devoting most of our careers to landscape projects in urban contexts. If water is a key factor in the creation and ongoing sustenance of life and in nature itself, then it must follow that water and how we accommodate it will play a vital role in each of these powerful and all-embracing goals as we attempt to produce livable, sustainable, desirable, and rewarding cities. As the eighteenth-century landscape designer William Shenstone once wrote, "Water should ever appear."[30]

Stone pines adjacent to the Palatine, Rome, 2008

TREES AND THE GETTY

(2018)

. . . what the trees try

To tell us we are:
That their merely being there
Means something . . .

—John Ashbery, "Some Trees"[1]

"Landscape" is a word used to describe the combination of things that make up the human environment. It includes topography and buildings, vegetation and infrastructure, rivers and roads—not to mention all the objects and furnishings that go along with them. Landscape architects shape and give character to the landscape, endeavoring to bring not only order and beauty but also utility, safety, and health to what are often complex combinations of these elements: a garden next to a parking lot, say, or a museum above a highway. And one of the most powerful means they have of transforming and giving character to landscape is by planting, shaping, and removing trees.

Humans, having evolved surrounded by nature, are highly responsive to trees and their particular properties, which are often seen as having moderating influences on urban environments. Trees have form, color, texture, and movement. When fully grown, many reach four or

From *Site/Lines* 13.2 (Spring 2018): 7–13.

five stories in height. They can provide shade and protection from wind as well as habitat for birds, beneficial insects, and small mammals. And they are excellent for shaping the nature of spaces.

Sometimes landscape architects find themselves exerting a moderating influence also—functioning, as trees do, as intermediaries between contending forces (in this case, architects, engineers, builders, and clients), often in the midst of competing political and economic pressures. The story of the Getty Center's vexed beginnings, which unfolded in the Brentwood section of Los Angeles more than twenty years ago, includes a succession of such interventions—by both landscape architects and trees.

J. Paul Getty's first museum in Malibu had been created in 1954 to accommodate his substantial collection of ancient classical art in a wing of his house. In 1974 the museum opened a new building, with architecture based on the design of a villa in Herculaneum and a garden derived from archaeological knowledge of first-century precedents. The museum garden and its surrounding landscape—a buffer of trees, most of which were native to the region or from countries around the Mediterranean—had been designed by Emmet Wemple, a highly regarded Los Angeles landscape architect. After Getty's death in 1976, however, the board of the Getty Trust decided to consolidate the organization's disparate enterprises in one location: an integrated campus on a mountainous, seven-hundred-acre site above a freeway on the west side of Los Angeles.

When the architect Richard Meier won the commission in 1984, he turned to Daniel Kiley, who by then was one of the most respected landscape architects in the nation, to assist with the site design. The selection was no surprise; Kiley had been the go-to landscape architect for a number of modernist architects for decades, including Eero Saarinen, Gordon Bunshaft, Nathaniel Owings, and Edward Larrabee Barnes, as well as, more recently, Meier himself.

The board of trustees wanted to ensure that everyone directly involved shared its vision of the new center. Therefore, to kick off the project, Meier, members of the Getty's team, and several of the Getty's administrators journeyed to the Mediterranean to visit historic precedents of the highest aesthetic level, ranging from Italian hill towns and villas to ancient sites in Greece and Jerusalem. Upon their return,

Meier began developing plans for the immense task at hand. The new Getty was to include a museum with permanent and temporary galleries; conservation facilities; a library and archives; a study center for visiting scholars; foundation headquarters; offices for grant and program administration; an auditorium and theater suitable for conferences, lectures, and performances; shipping, receiving, and storage facilities; and a café and restaurant. At the same time, Kiley began to develop a strategy for the overall site.

The Getty and its lawyers, attempting to placate privileged and cantankerous neighbors who opposed the project, had already agreed to restrict architectural development to about a hundred acres of the property on a single hilltop. This both reinforced the acropolis or citadel nature of the building scheme and placed considerable restraints on the landscape design, since it guaranteed a vast peripheral buffer of steeply sloping hillsides and canyons. Kiley was already well known for his bold schemes deploying trees. On a number of occasions he had expressed a deep interest in the work of André Le Nôtre, especially his use of geometry and his fondness for trees in plantations, bosques, and allées. Still, everyone was surprised when he proposed to establish a grid of trees planted at fifteen-foot intervals over the entire terrain—a geometric forest over an arid and wildly uneven landscape. The tree he selected was a California native, the coast live oak (*Quercus agrifolia*).

Meier embraced the scheme, which entailed the purchase and planting of what eventually amounted to ten thousand trees. After a period of delays, construction began in 1989. The slopes had to be benched to provide a series of narrow terraces where the trees would be planted and irrigated, to prevent erosion of the steep terrain. Because Kiley lived in Vermont and had a small office, he and Richard Meier decided to engage Emmet Wemple's office to document and supervise the operation.

Several dozen old and large handsome live oaks—remnants of an ancient forest that had once covered the Santa Monica Mountains—were already scattered throughout the 110-acre parcel selected for the complex. In clearing the scrub and chaparral for construction, these oaks were carefully dug up and removed to a holding area north of the construction site, where they were recorded and numbered. Several years later they were replanted in the final scheme, often in distinctive locations within the larger hillside oak plantation. Additionally, a number of Lebanon and deodar cedars—majestic trees associated with historic landscapes in both the Mediterranean and Southern California—were distributed in clumps and drifts in several spots within the oak matrix; these evergreens provided a harmonious vertical counterpoint to the somewhat uniform height of the live oaks. By 1999, what had been an unstable mountainside of highly flammable chaparral had been transformed. In part due to topographic variance and the exigencies of terracing the natural terrain, there are numerous gaps in Kiley's tree grid, and a few oaks have died. Still, the general effect is of a continuous blanket of trees covering the mountain, with the buildings floating above.

In a number of ways Kiley's forest of live oaks was a truly brilliant design gesture with both historic and environmental logic on its side. Perhaps unbeknownst to recent denizens of Hollywood and Beverly Hills, this venerable indigenous tree had provided food for wildlife and the native inhabitants of the area for millennia, and had remained an icon of the place. Once found in vast forests all the way from southern to northern California, the coast live oak had largely been replaced by towns and cultivated land since the arrival of early Spanish expeditions.

Donald Culross Peattie, writing in his unsurpassed *Natural History of North American Trees,* notes that Padre Junípero Serra's first missions were associated with this tree. In fact, he planted a cross beneath one after anchoring in 1770 in Monterey Bay, and that oak became a venerated tree for the next century. It was also one of the first two plants collected and identified by the Malaspina scientific expedition of the Spanish government in 1791. Unlike the highly explosive and flammable coastal sage scrub and chaparral plant communities or the windbreaks of eucalyptus that replaced them, these oaks, once established in a solid stand, are difficult to set ablaze. Kiley's oak scheme was a brilliant strategy for protecting the Getty from the recurrent wildfires that plague the region today.

All of this was irrelevant, however, to some important members of the Getty Trust, who were dumbfounded by the whole idea and considered Kiley something of a lunatic. His feisty personality, the enormous expense of the plan, and the fact that it was contrary to both conventional ideas of naturalism and any tradition in California estate gardening led to conflict. Within a year of the commencement of construction, Harold Williams, the president of the Getty Trust, fired Kiley against Meier's wishes, but the contract for the planting of the forest of oaks was under way. Subsequent landscape architects defended the scheme, and it survived Kiley's dismissal.

Following Kiley's departure, Emmet Wemple was asked to take over the landscape and work with Meier on design of the gardens. Besides being the landscape designer of the gardens and grounds of the original Getty Villa in Malibu, Wemple was a beloved figure in the profession of landscape architecture who had taught several generations of students at USC.

For the new Getty, this highly esteemed Southern California landscape architect produced a report that proposed a palette of plants and formal strategies derived from the traditions of the Mediterranean—especially Spain, Italy, and the Middle East—that incorporated a rich mix of colorful vines and shrubs, citrus, and evergreens, as well as a variety of water features, to animate the evolving series of courts and outdoor spaces of the campus. It was responsive to the client and the place.

Unfortunately, the strong personalities of a number of the architects and project managers, combined with the continuously evolving set of buildings, budgets, clients, and demands, were not a good match for Wemple's personality or method of working. His office would draw something, and the architects would change or delete it, so that little headway in designing the outdoor spaces was being made. Repeatedly left out of meetings or pushed aside, he became frustrated, while the senior leadership of the Getty Trust became increasingly disturbed by the lack of a strong landscape presence.

As the years went by and the Getty's board and management team were besieged by criticism for letting Meier design all the structures, the need for a suitable foil to the architecture became increasingly pressing. Having fired Kiley and concluded that the most prominent local landscape architect was not equal to the task, the Getty approached a number of other California artists who had recently created large outdoor works of art; site-specific land art was, at that moment, a worldwide phenomenon. But this gambit proved equally problematic. James Turrell and Dan Flavin proposed sunken rooms with light effects, another artist asked to work inside of a building rather than outdoors, and another, Robert Irwin, seized the largest open space on the site—a sloping area between two groups of buildings—and almost immediately got into a dramatic, multiyear, public fight with Meier over the design of what is now a totally anomalous garden within the context of the rest of the ground plan. As for solving the problems of the many other spaces and integrating the whole, the Getty's director and trustees were pretty much back where they had been when Kiley departed.

At this point, with the project eight years behind schedule, Richard Meier asked me to come to Los Angeles to meet with the vice president of the Getty Trust and consider taking over the landscape design.

On the one hand, I had serious trepidations about entering the scene, given the situation. A lot of controversy surrounded the project already. Meier was under siege and so was the board. Kiley had been fired, Wemple treated poorly. And the artist Robert Irwin had been given a prime portion of the site. My partners and I were also reluctant to open an office in California, and clearly this job would require a local base.

On the other hand, I knew and admired Richard Meier and his work, and after examining the project site and model I decided that most of the criticism and backbiting was a result of envy or ignorance. The Getty Center was in fact a good project and had a chance to turn into something quite special. At the same time, the architect and client really needed help. I'd taken on worthy yet controversial projects in New York and London and brought them to a successful resolution—why not the Getty? Plus, we'd worked in Los Angeles previously and enjoyed it. I decided to take the job; we prepared a proposal that included a local landscape architect, Allan Fong & Associates, and the Getty accepted it.

Gardeners and horticulturalists occasionally remark that landscape architects don't know much about plants. Conversely, landscape architects have been heard to say that gardeners and horticulturalists by and large don't know much about design. Like many clichés, there is something behind both remarks. For the first half of the last century, most landscape architects learned horticulture in undergraduate curricula in colleges that had originated as agricultural schools, and they tended to know their plants well: a number of leading twentieth-century designers, such as Kiley, Lawrence Halprin, Hideo Sasaki, and Garrett Eckbo were in this group. After the Korean War, however, many leading landscape programs migrated to graduate schools with architecture and planning programs. This resulted in a shift to curricula that downplayed plants, biology, and horticulture, while emphasizing spatial composition, social use, construction, and materials.

Still, even the landscape architects in my generation knew something about trees, simply because trees could be used in architectural ways to shape and modulate space. In the case of the Getty, it was clear from the start that while our design for the center and its gardens would include a diverse palette of colorful shrubs, vines, and herbaceous and perennial plants, trees would be the essential and central element—both to provide relief from the ubiquitous marble-clad architecture and to act as a foil for it.

Although I had been steeped in modernist art rather than in horticulture while at university and had only drifted into my present field after exploring both civil engineering and architecture, I was confident about my own understanding of trees. I had grown up in the wilderness of Alaska, and the first watercolor I ever made, at age twelve, was of a landscape with trees. Later, in high school, I painted a luminous birch standing in the snow of our front yard. Like early paintings of trees by Mondrian or those used in films by Ingmar Bergman, this tree filled the entire page as well as my mind. And when I began to contemplate dropping out of civil engineering, I found myself painting nearby spruce trees in the winter ice fog. Although I never studied the botany of trees, I always paid attention to them. The associations that particular species conjure up can be quite powerful; the delicate birches and skinny black spruces that manage to survive in Alaska, for example, have a special meaning for me, even though they are rarely of any use in my work. My journey from such beginnings in the far north through the rest of America and its cities and into Europe and Asia has been filled with an extraordinary diversity of trees.

My education in California's trees, however, had been much more recent. Since 1986 some members of my office and I had been working in Los Angeles and learning our way around downtown and the west side of the city. During a project in the Hancock Park complex on one of the earlier versions of the Los Angeles County Museum of Art, I had asked the landscape architect Joseph Linesch to assist us with plant procurement and contractors, and he had introduced us to the extraordinary horticulturalist and landscape designer Morgan "Bill" Evans. Evans's family had owned the historic Evans & Reeves Nursery on Wilshire Boulevard, which had imported plants from all over the world prior to World War II, and Morgan and his brother had planted the now-famous South African coral trees (*Erythrina caffra*) on San Vincente Boulevard with cuttings from their nursery during the war. Later Evans had been hired by Walt Disney—to help first with Disney's own garden and its miniature train, and then with the planting of Disneyland.

While we were working on Hancock Park, Evans took me and two of my partners—Dennis McGlade and Bob Bedell—under his wing. A large, rangy man in cowboy boots and a big Cadillac, he began driving us around the city, teaching us about its trees. Evans had supplied horticultural specimens to landscape architects, agencies, and institutions throughout Los Angeles, in both posh and marginal neighborhoods, and he showed us particular specimens and handsome stands of all sorts of trees, from those in private gardens to others on the UCLA campus in Westwood—parts of which Wemple, along with Ralph Cornell, an early-modern landscape designer in the city, had made into a kind of arboretum that was planted and maintained by Evans. As we went, Evans explained, drilled, and quizzed us. This education, combined with the fact that Dennis had been working with me in Los Angeles for a number of years and had a strong horticultural background, contributed to my belief that we could collaborate with Meier. When I returned to Philadelphia after agreeing to do the project, my partners, staff, and I dove right in.

Designers often talk about their projects as if they are pure products of invention, but so much is fueled by powerful memories of one sort or another. Design is often analogous to recombinant DNA, assembling bits and pieces of various elements and experiences. I had spent years in the Mediterranean, storing up memories of plants, materials, light, particular situations and elements—especially of trees and architecture, gardens, historic sites, and agricultural landscapes. I had spent days and weeks drawing outdoors in Italy, Greece, Spain, and southern France, often sketching many of the very sites that the Getty trustees and Meier were intent on recalling and emulating. I had also considered the particular plants essential to life in ancient times that recur throughout the classical environment, such as olives, figs, pines, cedars, cypress, oaks, laurel, pomegranates, sycamores, and plane trees. In addition to being mesmerized by the remarkable spatial attributes of these ancient sites, I had scrutinized the elements that shape one's sense of movement through them: paths and stones, basins, water, hills, even the sky. As it happened, I had also first met Meier in Italy, when we were both at the American Academy in Rome. As we began work together on the Getty, a flood of useful memories inevitably came to mind.

The project seemed somewhat chaotic at the point my firm came on board. Some areas of the site had rough grading and foundations in construction; some were in the final stages of design; some had barely been designed at all. The challenge, which felt very daunting, was to develop a landscape scheme that might integrate the site into a unified plan. We studied Meier's models and drawings, noting the numerous levels, shapes, and the orientation of the spaces; many of these, adjacent to the museum, research library, and other facilities, were intended to be outdoor rooms for staff and visitors. It would have been better to be involved earlier; nevertheless, we developed a number of ideas for how to move forward. Agreeing with Wemple's preference for Mediterranean precedents when considering the planting palette and potential uses of water, we developed a plan to provide a simple series of formal responses to the architecture.

In addition to the familiar question of how to help an ensemble of formally disparate structures seem at home rather than alien and imposed on the site, there were basically two choices possible for each space: attempting harmony or generating contrast. I was particularly interested in whether we could play with the concept of a gradient in the design from wilder to more cultivated and sophisticated planting. Borrowing Cicero's notion of "second nature" (*altera natura*), which referred to agriculture and its infrastructure as opposed to "wild" nature, and incorporating the notion of pleasure gardens as a "third nature" (as was understood and expressed by Jacopo Bonfadio and others in sixteenth-century Italy), we proceeded with our design.

After several weeks of drawing, we headed back to Los Angeles with such an extensive set of plans, cross sections, and perspective sketches that they completely covered the walls of Meier's conference room. Because of the complexity of the scheme, I was concerned about how best to illuminate our proposal's underlying concept and principles for Meier and the Getty Trust's project leadership. On the plane out to California, I had asked a flight attendant for a glass of water in order to make a monochromatic wash drawing in a sketchbook of two cross sections, one above the other. The upper drawing was of the Villa Gamberaia in the hills outside Florence, and was based on a rendered cross section in Shepherd and Jellicoe's *Italian Gardens of the Renaissance,* a facsimile of which I had brought along. The lower sketch presented a summary from memory of our proposal for the Getty Center, depicting it as analogous to such a villa—in particular with regard to the scale and the devices of planting above, between, and below the structure. Implied in both sketches was a gradient of increasing artifice—from nature to culture as one approached the buildings themselves. At the initial presentation the following day, being able to pass the sketchbook around to those in attendance proved enormously helpful.

I proposed that the first task was to complete the work begun by Kiley and Wemple, the terracing and planting of the hills, which was to continue for several years. Another fundamental idea was to have the color of foliage and blossoms move from cooler in the lower and northern portions of the site to warmer and hotter on higher portions and the south and west. The next idea was to create two ribbons of trees, one from the north and one from the south, to tie the building complex to the greater site. One of the ribbons would be a row of umbrella pines (*Pinus pinea,* also called Italian stone pine) extending all the way up the access drive on the north, parallel to the train that brings people from the entry and parking garage near the highway to an arrival plaza at the top of the hill.

This skyline tree, which has been employed to line lanes and roads throughout Italy for centuries, needs pruning periodically to encourage upward growth. In the Mediterranean it has in this way served as a renewable source of wood for thousands of years while simultaneously producing stately trees evocative of classical porticos and temples. Thus began the practice at the Getty Center of patiently removing a whorl of branches from each tree on this entire plantation every few years. This row of trees concludes with a bouquet of four enormous umbrella pines in the arrival plaza—the dot at the end of an exclamation point. (Unbeknownst to visitors, these trees, which were found and purchased from the Irvine Ranch south of Los Angeles, are planted in a giant planter that sits above a loading dock and service entry to storerooms below.)

An equal and opposite gesture occurs to the southwest, where I had decided early on to bring a row of native California sycamores (*Platanus racemosa*) up the valley of the central garden, accompanying a watercourse. These trees are among the most characteristic of native California trees and are normally associated with the rivers, creeks, and arroyos of the region's coastal hills. In the midst of a deepening conflict between Meier and Irwin over this garden, I made a trip to San Diego to try to bring the two sides together. Irwin had engaged another landscape architectural firm, Spurlock Poirier, to assist him. Fortunately Marty Poirier had been a student at Harvard when I was the chairman of the department there, and we had a mutual regard for each other. Our shared idea of sycamores and a stream survived the various pressures and schemes that led to the final version of the central garden. This gesture culminates in a tall group of sycamores on the uppermost terrace at the museum entry.

Nearby, at the café entry, we planted London plane trees (*Platanus* × *acerifolia*). Seen all across Europe lining city streets, rivers, canals, and country roads, this tree happens to be a natural cross between the eastern American sycamor (*Platanus occidentalis*) and the Asian sycamore (*Platanus orientalis*) which occurred in London in the seventeenth century. At the Getty we planted them in a regular bosque, pollarded to form a terrace canopy above the tables and chairs set out by the restaurant. Such pruning is traditional throughout the Mediterranean and Middle East. These pollarded trees were prepared under the direction of McGlade and Rolla Wilhite at Berylwood Tree Farm—carefully thinned and pruned, with selected branches bent horizontally and weighted—for several years prior to coming to the site.

Plane trees and sycamores produce a generous and much appreciated shade; their leaves are not glossy or shiny, which would be hard on the eyes in the often overly bright Southern California sun, and their dappled bark is a source of endless visual stimulus. The native species is wild and rangy, leaning, bending, often branching and twiggy in picturesque ways, while the European hybrid is graceful, tall, and more open. Thus the California native sycamore (*Platanus racemosa*) is planted along the stream in the valley in Irwin's garden as I'd proposed, and ascends the stair to the uppermost terrace, where the cultivated London plane tree appears in its tall natural form (representing second nature) at the museum entry and in a pollarded form on the café entry terrace (embodying third nature).

Another area that called for shade in the form of a tree canopy was a series of terraces intended for the use of the Getty staff, administrators, and guests. These terraces extend north, stepping down to a circular lawn that serves as an emergency helicopter landing spot; beneath it is a large water reservoir, maintained for the purpose of fighting forest fires in the area. I chose umbrella pines for the task, partly because they were adjacent to the pines that we had planted along the entry road, and partly for their association with hilltop terraces, parks, and cafés in Rome and elsewhere.

In contrast to such generalized memories of the Mediterranean, memories of American, and specifically Los Angeles, gardens also played a part. The Getty's management team had been concerned about a narrow, multistory space resulting from Meier's arrangement of two of the buildings used for housing the foundation's executive and management offices and several of the grant program offices. It was a tall, awkward canyon that could leave employees in each building staring uncomfortably at one another across the narrow space. What to do? Recalling one of my outings with Morgan Evans, I realized that here was an opportunity for surprise and delight. Several years earlier, Evans had taken Dennis and me to the Virginia Robinson Garden in nearby Beverly Hills, which Evans had restored. There we had seen a shady stand of king palms growing in a steep, narrow canyon, an unusual and unforgettable sight. By planting palm trees between the two Getty buildings, we could create a similar effect.

Although palm trees are not native, they are strongly associated with Los Angeles and Southern California—so much so, in fact, that they were being shunned by designers and clients because they were deemed a common and banal cliché. But here they would be tucked into a deep and tight architectural space—away from the skyline, which is their normal situation visually. We decided to use feathery, tall, Mexican fan palms (*Washingtonia robusta*) for our screen between the two buildings. The palm also worked well with Meier's architecture, which clearly evokes the sun-blanched, Art Deco work of an earlier era that continues to be featured prominently in books and films set among the palms in L.A. This was a case of going with the architecture in terms of ethos and mood: the palms' elongated multiple trunks rising from the dim light below, and the color and texture of their spiky, shaggy heads in the light above.

Another device we decided to use to help unify the disparate parts of the complex was the repetition of white crepe myrtles (*Lagerstroemia* spp.) which had been part of the horticultural palette suggested earlier by Wemple—first alongside the lower train platform and then again above, on a walkway linking the auditorium and foundation offices to the museum and library/research center. In both cases they are planted in a line and pruned into an aerial hedge: an ancient trope. Here they reinforce the forms of the architecture. Their stretched rectangular mass of foliage and the rows of mottled trunks repeat and support the linearity, direction, and order of the buildings and walkways rather than play against them as do some of the other plantings.

There is a great deal of vegetation other than trees at the Getty: bougainvillea, wisteria, lavender, rosemary, even masses of bird of paradise (the official flower of Los Angeles), euphorbias and cacti, various ground covers, and flowers and herbs in pots. And yet it is the trees that interact most with the buildings, that modulate and give particular character to each space. A good example is the museum courtyard, where there are two quite different rows of trees: Montezuma cypress (*Taxodium mucronatum*) and sweetgums (*Liquidambar styraciflua*). Both are trees associated with water. The cypresses reinforce the direction of the space and align with the buildings that frame it. The sweetgums, however, are placed at a slight angle opposing the space at one end, so that they align with a different aspect of the composition across the central garden and with the scholars' study center beyond. These rows of trees are planted adjacent to tall travertine walls, partially screening them; the trees' color, form, and texture are especially vivid against the white stone. The sweetgums and cypresses also exhibit strong color in the fall—the former a dark scarlet, the latter a warm terra-cotta—maintaining harmony despite the difference in hue. One can climb or descend an exterior stairway beside the shorter row of sweetgums, which accents and points to a circular fountain. The tall, graceful line of cypresses accompanies a narrow, rectangular basin of water that stretches the length of the court.

Morgan Evans had first introduced us to *Taxodium* years before, in a ravine near UCLA. They were standing along a seasonal wash behind a school designed by Richard Neutra, which hid them from view. I found them majestic. A year or two later, I saw some larger ones along the Riverwalk in San Antonio, and then even older ones by a lake in Chapultepec Park in Mexico City. I thought that the Montezuma cypress had more presence than the more familiar bald cypress (*Taxodium distichum*) from our Gulf states. When we were developing the museum courtyard basin with Meier—with its thin, arching jets, reminiscent of those in the palace gardens of Spain—I recalled how such basins were originally derived from irrigation ditches, the *acequias* brought to California by Spanish missionaries. As with canals and aqueducts everywhere, especially in arid climates, these were often bordered with trees. This particular planting of *Taxodium* derives some of its potency from such an association.

Another tree that I became fond of while working in L.A. is the Peruvian peppertree (*Schinus molle*). When I first saw it, I was enchanted. Here was a medium-sized tree, as graceful as a weeping willow, birch, or cherry, that one could grow in an arid climate. I first used it for a garden in Brentwood and then again in a residential development near Playa del Rey. Fast growing, drought tolerant, it has a lovely weeping habit, providing not only good shade but also myriad pink peppercorns. At the Getty I first introduced them as a curtain at the train station at the bottom of the hill, in order to block the view of the highway and urban sprawl south of the platform. They also appear as a sculptural element on the uppermost level outside the library and again on a terrace below.

The first sketches I made for the project show olives in the central garden, drifting downhill in a meadow that I'd hoped people could wander and picnic in. The loss of this area to Irwin's garden-as-conceptual-artwork ended such a possibility, but a vestigial grove of olives was eventually installed in the area on the far side of his pond. One other missing item from the initial project is the Mexican palo verde tree or Jerusalem thorn (*Parkinsonia aculeata*) which we had originally intended to plant along a stairway and beyond to encircle a terrace at the southern end of the architectural axis that extends through the museum court to the northern terraces with their pines. This terrace was hot and almost always in the sun. On a clear day, from here one can see to the Channel Islands and Santa Catalina, glittering on the brilliant surface of the ocean. These lovely desert trees would have been ideal for the difficult microclimatic conditions of this area, but were vetoed by both the client and the architect, who couldn't imagine trees atop this terrace, which they had envisioned as completely open to the view. Switching gears, we turned it into the cactus terrace—a "look, don't touch" sort of place— and substituted large euphorbias, Peruvian cactus, and tree aloes (*Aloe barberae*) that have grown into striking Medusa-like presences.

Another tree type characteristic of California agricultural landscapes and cities alike is represented by members of the genus *Eucalyptus*. Although there are at least seven hundred varieties in nature in Australia and Southeast Asia, a particular handful introduced in the nineteenth century have become common from the Baja Peninsula to the San Francisco Bay. Originally used primarily for windbreaks in agricultural areas, today they are often considered hazardous, invasive, and an ecological problem because, under certain circumstances, they can suck large amounts of water out of the ground. They were planted in vast quantities at the Presidio in San Francisco by an early commandant, at Stanford in an arboretum begun by Olmsted, and throughout Los Angeles and San Diego in parks and on streets. Tall and graceful, with various forms and bark patterns, they are seen accompanying Mission Revival buildings in many dreamy, regional, Impressionist-style paintings from the end of the nineteenth century.

Morgan Evans had taught my partners and me to identify several of the more attractive ones on our drives about the region. Among them were puffy-topped *Eucalyptus camaldulensis*; *Corymbia maculata*, with its giraffelike bark patterns; and lemon-scented *Eucalyptus citriodora*. While puzzling over what to do in a space adjacent to a reference room in the study center that was contained by a very high curving wall, I realized that planting an array of eucalyptus in front of it would provide patterns and shadows against the wall without filling up the space and making it dark and oppressive. Like the narrow canyon where we located the fan palms, this was an instance of employing a skyline tree in a completely different context that would be as interesting as it was practical. Because of the isolated, mountaintop location, one could enjoy the virtues of its visual attractiveness with none of the conventional worries about flammability or threat to the water table.

There were also occasions where we used only one or two trees as sculptural objects to inhabit or enliven a defined and often more intimate space, such as a specimen strawberry tree (*Arbutus unedo*), set in a small garden adjacent to an office in the foundation grants building, and a pink trumpet tree (*Tabebuia rosea*) in a lower sunken garden where the tree's flowers are at eye level for people passing on an upper walkway nearby. For two spaces at different levels adjacent to the library and archive, it occurred to us that—given the inspiration underlying the original classical collection—it would be nice to have edible plants that have been associated with the Mediterranean since biblical times. And so today the library and archive look out on olive and citrus trees.

But while such singular gestures can give character or spice to particular spaces, overall it is the larger groupings and ensemble planting, the extended lines and ranks of trees, that provide the coherence and continuity of the Getty landscape.

From its conception through the lengthy period of design and construction, the Getty Center was wrapped in controversy. Local critics pronounced that it would be inaccessible and inhospitable—a botched artistic extravagance. As soon as it opened, however, people flocked to it, and they have continued to do so in droves—so many more than were anticipated, in fact, that services for them, such as toilets, bookstore, café, and places to sit, had to be expanded almost immediately.

At the same time, the Getty Center's panoply of trees, threaded through disparate spaces and levels, between and around the campus's numerous buildings, have continued to grow, many to handsome maturity. And in doing so, they have accomplished what the president and trustees were looking for two decades earlier, when there was so much Sturm und Drang over the landscape design: they have established a sense of calm and harmony, even though each of the spaces between and around the buildings has its own size, shape, and character. The ubiquitous presence of mature trees flowing around and through the campus has, in fact, knit it together, giving the whole a sense of unity and balance, of having settled comfortably into place. For the citizens of Los Angeles, the Getty Center is now part of the larger fabric of the city, and its outdoor spaces are treated as parks and squares, de facto extensions of the public realm.

In October 2017 the OLIN firm received the American Society of Landscape Architects Landmark Award, which is given to built works of landscape architecture between fifteen and fifty years old that have kept their design integrity and contributed to the cultural or civic realm. In the case of the Getty, however, one could argue that the landscape truly found its integrity only over time, as the trees grew up and filled in, and the rough edges in a vast compound designed by multiple and often competing professionals were smoothed or knit together. *Landscape Architecture* magazine quoted one of the jurors as saying, "I don't think we could do better than recognizing the Getty as a special, special place." A significant aspect of its perceived special nature is the array, selection, and disposition of its trees.

Garden, Villa Aurelia, American Academy in Rome, 2008

THE PROBLEM OF NATURE AND
AESTHETICS IN PLANTING DESIGN

(2020)

Near the beginning of the last century Gertrude Jekyll wrote in remi-
niscence, "I think of all [the] kinds of planting for pleasure, wild gardening needs the greatest caution and most restraint." Regarding her own
efforts at Munstead Wood, she reflected that "now, after forty years, it
has all grown into a state of satisfactory maturity." She went on to write,
"The fine green English turf has ever been a source of pride and pleasure in our gardens. The smooth level bowling-green, always a beautiful
thing near dressed grounds . . . , bounded by walls or by a hedge of Yew
or Hornbeam . . . , whether for summer play or for quiet saunter, must
always have been, as it ever will be, one of the most delightful of garden
spaces." Planting is one thing; surviving to maturity is another. In addition, restraint is often a virtue. "It would be well in these days," Jekyll
advised, "when gardening possibilities are so vast and the designer may
be tempted to run wild, that he should restrain himself and strive to
regain the older simplicity and charm, remembering that the first purpose of a garden is to be a place of quiet beauty such as will give delight
to the eye and repose and refreshment to the mind."[1]

While one may justifiably question whether the garden she designed
for the historic Hestercombe House meets today's ideas of simplicity
and restraint, these quotes from perhaps the greatest garden innovator

Originally delivered in 2018 at the conference "The Aesthetics of Planting Design" held at
Berkeley; a shorter, illustrated version appears in Marc Treib, ed., *The Aesthetics of Contemporary Planting Design* (ORO Editions). The text here was revised in 2020.

and polemicist of the past century introduce several subjects that are key when considering aesthetics in landscape design: nature and naturalism, time and the dynamics of change in the natural world, and the omnipresence of fashion and style in human culture.

In "Land and Beauty," an essay I presented to the Philosophical Society of Texas (yes, there is such a thing and it is a serious group), I noted:

> For Western philosophers prior to the twentieth century, *Nature* writ large and beyond us—whether of the *Arizona Highways* variety or stormy alpine scenes—*Nature* as vast, terrible, unknowable, wild and truly inhuman by definition, this was the *Sublime,* not the *Beautiful.* For them beauty had to do with human scale, such as one sees in paintings of the seventeenth century that characterize an emerging sensitivity to landscape as a subject for art, . . . works that depicted a portion of the world inhabited for several thousand years.

I continued,

> Beauty and the Sublime, especially as related to nature, landscape, and art, have been concerns of Western thought for centuries. Longinus wrote *On the Sublime* in the first century; in 1756 Edmund Burke published his *Philosophical Enquiry into the Origin of Our Ideas on the Sublime and Beautiful,* and Kant's *Observations on the Feeling of the Beautiful and the Sublime* followed soon after in 1763. Hegel's remarks about nature and beauty in *On Art, Religion, Philosophy: Introductory Lectures in the Realm of Absolute Spirit* were delivered in Berlin between 1818 and 1831; only five years later, beginning in 1836 and continuing through 1847, both Emerson and Thoreau assayed the topic in their quintessentially American way. Despite a bevy of twentieth-century European (and a handful of American) thinkers dismissing this entire skein of thought as outdated and hopeless, recently some of our own contemporaries, such as Stanley Cavell and Jeremy Gilbert-Rolfe, have written thoughtfully and persuasively about these dropped threads regarding our need for and methods of consideration of these twin topics: Beauty and the Sublime.[2]

One of the main debating points in recent times has been whether those things people find "beautiful" are subjective or objective—whether the phenomenon resides within the beholder or within the thing beheld. Notions that any feeling or perception could be universal or characteristic of all humans versus a belief that they must inevitably be culturally determined have contested violently through journals and institutions, a *paragone* (one might say) of sorts between nature and nurture. There is evidence on both sides in the debate between universality and culture.

Despite its recurring cycles of seasons, for as long as recorded thought humans have held nature to be wild and chaotic, violent and unpredictable. Especially in Western societies, wild nature has long been considered ugly and unknowable. The American continent and its vast natural landscape seemed as terrifying and malevolent to the first Europeans who arrived here as it was promising for physical and spiritual rewards. As people became more familiar with the landscapes of the New World, artists like Frederic Edwin Church began to see nature and its beauty as an expression of divinity, complementing physical experience with the spiritual realm. Today, however, many members of advanced societies consider nature neither unknowable nor chaotic, due to the new forms of mathematics and scientific discoveries in physics and chemistry. Yet the majority of the population probably still views nature and wilderness as foreign and confusing. The problem stems from a lack of intimate familiarity with nature and an inability to see and understand its processes, especially for those who spent their childhood in cities. In recent times, ecology and geology have provided the analytic tools for comprehending nature's complex forms and interactions. With the aid of computer science, we can understand and describe all manner of natural events and phenomena at varying scales, from subatomic particles and mitochondrial DNA to cyclonic storms. Nevertheless, a major earthquake or hurricane is still described as a "natural disaster," when in truth the resulting destruction is usually a "human disaster." Nature is really only releasing energy in the particular form of an event, whether as a storm or a tremor. The damage it inflicts is measured against buildings and infrastructure, both the product of human actions.

A number of contemporary writers have declared the end of nature in much the same manner as, in the nineteenth century, some authors declared the death of God. Discussions of an "Anthropocene" era are useful in acknowledging that through their activity humans have altered the geo-biophysical and chemical nature of the Earth. Thanks to the laws of thermodynamics and a few other mechanisms, however, nature and natural processes are still very much at work everywhere. We are creatures of nature. If we are to talk about planting and planting design, we are necessarily plunged into considerations of nature, as plants are among the most ubiquitous and familiar aspects of nature on earth. They are also a major part of the palette of landscape architecture, a factor that distinguishes the profession from other practical or fine arts. Plants are not only interesting complex structures, but also alive, changing in size and shape, only to eventually die. They blow and wiggle in the wind, produce a surfeit of twigs, seeds, and leaves, and generally make for a rich, but messy, place. They also instigate our thinking about what is "beautiful." Beauty is phenomenal. It is an attribute or result, an effect of events, things, and ideas that generate feeling. It is a property, like yellow or B-flat. It's not a thing, but truly in the eye, ear, or mind of the beholder; it occurs within an individual's sensibility influenced by a synthesis of animal sensations and cultural background. A slippery diversity and difference in categories of things considered beautiful have troubled many, especially considering that the experience of beauty seems tied to pleasure and the stimulus of the senses or intellectual delight.

There are fashions in everything human and cultural: food, clothes, body shape, weapons, transportation, architecture, furniture, medicine—and very much so in art, landscape, and garden design. Our ideas of what is beautiful—or merely attractive, acceptable, dull, vulgar, or ugly—are framed in part by our acquired ideas regarding nature and what we think is "natural." In the most effervescent years of the Enlightenment, theories of planetary movements, vision, and metaphysics supported the strict use of Euclidian geometry in design and planning. Along with other mathematicians and philosophers, René Descartes contributed to the conception of the cosmos and the natural world for figures like André Le Nôtre, who used grids, lines, and planes to organize and plant vast territories considered beautiful from his day to our own. More recently, landscape architects such as Daniel Urban Kiley and Peter Walker have employed related geometries to design landscapes also perceived to be attractive and on occasion truly beautiful—although not subscribing to the theology, cosmology, or politics of the seventeenth century.

Changes in sensibility, politics, and philosophy in eighteenth-century England produced a remarkably different rhetoric about nature and the perception of what is beautiful in gardens. The so-called informal planting of their grounds, along with undulating landforms, water bodies, and curving paths, comprised schemes as vast as those of Le Nôtre and similarly screened out their context, commonly agriculture, with a different functional order and geometry. The differences between the way masses of trees were used in these two bodies of work is their most obvious distinguishing feature. Le Nôtre's ranks of trees often lead off into the distance with a suggestion of endless extension, and by implication the possession and control of the territory beyond. In contrast, Capability Brown and his contemporaries habitually encircled estates with thick shelter belts and forest plantations that limited their ultimate territory while masking what lay beyond.

Brown's and William Kent's landscapes were as laborious and expensive to create from the chalk and clay terrain of southern Britain as Le Nôtre's had been in France. Although employing vast quantities of nursery-grown plants, they were nonetheless referred to as "natural" by contemporaries. These landscapes began as artistic contrivances but over time have evolved into habitats for diverse communities of plants and animals, and today play an important role in the ecology of their regions. Some at the time considered them to be beautiful, while others found them too simple, empty, and socially destructive to the villagers who were displaced by their construction. Nevertheless, what they share with wild nature that leads people to consider them beautiful is of interest, especially because it is intimately connected to their planting. This has to do with their scale, generosity of diverse foliage, ample meadows, and accompanying surfaces that reflect and refract light and engage the broad sky in a manner similar to those of natural situations.

Until relatively recently, many historians believed that eighteenth-century English parks were monochromatic symphonies of green; in fact, they were enriched with a wealth of showy flowering plants. Brown and his assistants planted masses of flowering shrubs, fruit trees, and perennials set within the broad parklands. By the eighteenth century, international ambitions of England and France created colonies around the globe that were home to interesting and useful plants, which were brought back, propagated, exchanged, and widely planted with enthusiasm, generating profit for the colonizing countries of Europe. Nearly all of this colorful planting was located within close proximity of the villas and along favorite walks and drives of estates. Most examples have disappeared in subsequent centuries, although in gardens such as Stourhead and Longleat in England, remnants or re-creations of the cornucopia of multicolored herbaceous and flowering shrubs remain from the time of Brown and Humphry Repton.

Traces of this fashion for imported plants can be found throughout the parks of Europe and Britain. A stunning allée of American bald cypress, brought as seedlings to France from the bayous of Louisiana, was planted by Auguste Famin in 1809 at the chateau de Rambouillet in northern France. Equally unknown is a superb allée of giant sequoias lining the entry drive to Dunmore Park at Airth in Scotland, built for John Murray, the former governor of colonial Virginia and the Bahamas. Given the role of Scottish botanists and plant hunters in America and Asia, it is no surprise that one can find fine examples of these once fashionable trees on a number of estates in England and Scotland. Pine, larch, ash, oak, and cypress, paired with masses of rhododendrons, azaleas, and a wealth of flowering trees from Asia and America, were planted widely.

Frederick Law Olmsted's plantings are also mistakenly believed to have been limited to pastoral efforts that relied almost solely on acres of greensward, trees in great plantations, a handful of heroic specimens, and background drifts of monotonous shrubs. This is certainly what time, erosion, and municipal budgets have worn them down to, but their original composition and appearance were rather different. In fact, Olmsted senior was quite knowledgeable about plants installed in his parks and gardens, many of which had completely disappeared by the 1950s. It is undeniable that he adapted aspects of the pastoral English park to American use, and that he decried excessive horticultural display, arguing against imported plants he felt inappropriate in American landscape design. On numerous occasions he suggested instead that humble natives were adequate and more desirable, species such as "nannyberry, hazel, shadbush, dogwood, even elder, or if an evergreen (conifer) will benefit the place, a stout, short, shock-headed mountain-pine, with two or three savins and a prostrate juniper at their feet."[3] He noted that landscape design is an art: "Landscape moves us in a manner more nearly analogous to the action of music than anything else."[4]

He bristled at what he saw as inappropriate uses, remarking that "planting . . . without system or design is a waste of money,"[5] and he asserted that naturalism was not really natural. What did he mean by that? The next year, in an essay on landscape gardening (for a time the name he preferred to landscape architecture), Olmsted set out his attitude toward the composition and differences between landscape design and natural scenery:

> This brings us to the consideration that from the point of view of art or of the science of the imagination we may ask for something more in a landscape than breadth, depth, composition, and consistency. . . . In the possibility, not of making a perfect copy of any charming natural landscape, or of any parts or elements of it, but of leading to the production, where it does not exist, . . . of some degree of the poetic beauty of all natural landscapes, we shall thus find not only the special function and the justification of the term landscape gardening, but also the first object of study for the landscape gardener, and the standard by which alone his work is to be fully judged. There are those who will question the propriety of regarding the production of the poetic beauty of natural landscape as the end of landscape gardening, on the ground that the very term "natural beauty" means beauty not of man's design, and that the best results of man's labor will be but a poor counterfeit, in which it is vain to look for the poetry of nature.[6]

And in 1874, discussing his design ideas for a park in Montreal, he wrote, "It will be desirable to plant trees and bushes . . . not by any means in rows and at regular intervals but *naturally,* in groups and clusters and thickets, with frequent glades and openings where under favorable circumstances distant views can best be commanded."[7]

He wrote on several occasions that an over-interest in horticulture and the production of exotic varieties (whether from importation or nursery cultivation and breeding) was antithetical to the sensibility needed to produce successful garden and park design. In his view, it produced sensibilities that might be deep in particular knowledge but were too narrow to be able to produce works of artistic coherence or social success. Consider his eye and interest in the following remarks he made in a draft of his 1865 preliminary report on Yosemite and the Mariposa Grove, describing parts of the valley floor and the Merced River floodplain:

> Banks of heartsease and beds of cowslips and daisies are fre-quent, and thickets of alder, dogwood and willow often fringe the shores. . . . Flowering shrubs of sweet fragrance and balmy herbs abound in the meadows, and there is everywhere a deli-cate odor of the prevailing foliage in the pines and cedars. . . . If we analyze the operation of scenes of beauty upon the mind, and consider the intimate relation of the mind upon the nervous system and the whole physical economy, the action and reac-tion which constantly occurs between bodily and mental condi-tions, the reinvigoration which results from such scenes is readily comprehended. . . . The enjoyment of scenery employs the mind without fatigue, and yet exercises it, tranquilizes it and yet enliv-ens it; and thus, through the influence of the mind over the body, gives the effect of refreshing rest and reinvigoration to the entire system.[8]

In his 1878 essay "Landscape Gardening," Olmsted described a pro-posed design for a front yard, and in lieu of an ordinary straight hedge he suggested that

> its bushes shall not all be of one sort, and in good time they shall be bushes in earnest, leaping up with loose and feathery tops, six, eight, and sometimes ten feet high. And they shall leap out also toward us. Yet from the house half their height shall be lost behind an under- and out-growth of brake and bindweed, dog-rose and golden-rod, asters, gentians, buttercups, poppies, and irises. . . . There will be coves and capes and islands of chick-weed, catnip, cinquefoil, wild strawberry, hepatica, forget-me-not, and lilies-of-the-valley, and, still farther out, shoals under

the turf, where crocuses and daffodils are waiting to gladden the children and welcome the bluebird in spring.[9]

Olmsted had his ideas about nature, and we have ours—which, depending on your age, region, and education, may vary considerably. They will certainly influence your view of what is beautiful in terms of planting.

Sixty years later, Jens Jensen summed up many of his thoughts on the use of native vegetation in landscape design in an essay for an international garden congress held in Berlin in 1938. Jensen, whose work openly derived from an appreciation of the native plants of the American Midwest, clarified that he was not sympathetic to the ideas of his German contemporary Willy Lange or the National Socialists then in power—both strong advocates for indigenous planting. But like them, Jensen found the natural plant associations—in this case of the Midwest prairie—to be beautiful, and he was deeply interested in developing an American landscape as a true cultural expression. While aware that a garden isn't a prairie, he wrote, "A garden of variety and novelty, flowers packed in like sardines in a box, discarded when they are through blooming, has no spiritual worth."[10]

The major shifts in theoretical concepts of nature, the world, and its order from the late eighteenth through the nineteenth century affected Western society's sense of aesthetics and beauty in art—and in turn, planting design. A number of revolutions, wars, and the discrediting of rationalism, the rise of modern physics, and the world wars of the twentieth century all exerted their influence. Landscape design wasn't immune to trends sweeping through art and architecture, although until very recently not much had been said since Christopher Tunnard voiced his thoughts about planting design in 1938.[11] Shapes of planted areas and masses of color, paired with a tendency to position lone or groups of specimen trees in striking asymmetrical situations, echoed the compositional strategies of earlier practitioners such as Olmsted, or Asian prints and brush drawings. This tendency is especially evident in the work of the leading landscape designers of their times, such as Hideo Sasaki, Daniel Kiley, and even Garrett Eckbo, who embraced a modernist pastoral combined with a dash of De Stijl or Mondrian in his disposition of plants.[12]

As I've noted elsewhere, prior to the early 1950s most landscape architecture curricula stressed horticulture; in subsequent decades less emphasis was placed on a wide knowledge of plants, but trees were still valued for the architectural or sculptural element they contributed to landscape design. Leading designers such as Sasaki, Eckbo, Kiley, and Lawrence Halprin, who had learned their plants in an earlier era, nevertheless eschewed diverse herbaceous and understory plants in their work, instead favoring more "architectural" schemes that emphasized spatial arrangements and contemporary materials such as concrete.

Following the Vietnam War, a significant intellectual and ideological paradigm shift had a distinct impact on plant use in landscape architecture. The environmental movement, which followed on the heels of efforts for civil rights and against war, coincided with a distrust of authority, governance, industry, and planning control. Just as modernist architects and landscape architects had rejected neoclassical and Beaux-Arts aesthetic traditions, so too, many in the field of landscape architecture now turned away from a modernist pastoral or more architectural compositions in favor of planting schemes based on ecological ideas, often employing what were considered native plants. Among other beliefs, this profound shift in sensibility expressed a disdain for gardens and plants used in orderly geometric compositions, whether as a stately row of a single species of tree or as bold and colorful planting arrangements.

Wild nature was lauded as the "ideal," and "native plants" in various stages of succession and association were the means to achieve it. Traditional lawns that had graced village greens and residential neighborhoods throughout America—a sight that had calmed and delighted its citizens for centuries—were now seen as aesthetically passé, and even aesthetically and morally corrupt. A "born free" attitude spread across the country and through the profession, advocating the removal of lawns and replacing them with wilder grasses, ground covers, and shrubs, purportedly to provide habitat for myriad creatures. Some states went so far as to pass laws that only "native species" could be planted on state property and in public parks.

Some landscape architects went whole hog and couldn't bring themselves to plant two or three trees of the same species, much less in a row. Perhaps the most dramatic result of this attitude was the replanting of Jacques Gréber's handsome allées along the Benjamin Franklin

Parkway in Philadelphia with a mélange of species, because the designers believed the practice to be environmentally beneficial. In fact, the result was not appreciably beneficial, and was certainly less graceful and beautiful. Such ideas in the hands of skilled designers, however, when employed in other more appropriate settings, did produce handsome results. Examples include the large park plantings by Andropogon Associates, a prominent ecologically driven firm in Philadelphia, in its scheme for the Crosby Arboretum in Mississippi and their rehabilitation of the University of Pennsylvania's Morris Arboretum in Philadelphia.

To say that all art or landscape design comes from nature in some way is one thing, but to trace all its varieties from direct imitation to abstraction is another. So too is designing to evoke the memory of a place distant in time or space. Design employing "natural" processes may be the most difficult—for example, using fire to maintain a particular landscape character as it does in the wild. A variety of concepts in regard to the natural world often coexist at any one time. The professional concerns and daily activities of scientists today are noticeably different from those of landscape architects and artists, although each group appreciates and often believes and respects the ideas of the other. The cultural geographer J. B. Jackson has argued that to attempt to imitate nature is both a bad idea and impossible to achieve.[13] Without question we need to bring nature into our cities and lives, particularly those aspects that stimulate our senses, such as the qualities presented by vegetation: color, light, pattern, texture, variable and rich forms, sound, and movement. While I agree there is a need for adopting natural processes into the making of our cultural environment, I am also interested in the potential for representation and purposeful meaning deriving from an artful expression. How can one do so?

Some of the more beautiful landscapes created in the last century have abstracted one or several properties found in natural situations and deployed them skillfully. At times this has been accomplished with a remarkably minimalist touch; at other times and in a broader manner, it has taken a more sweeping and fulsome form. Among the most rarified abstract representations of natural landscapes is the sculpture garden called *California Scenario,* created by the artist Isamu Noguchi in an office park set within the sprawl of Costa Mesa, California. There he produced what might almost be called "landscape dioramas" that recall the now-historic thematic displays of natural history museums a generation ago. In his design, Noguchi abstracted several distinct landscapes from locations in California and reshaped them as sculpture: a circular mound peppered with desert plants evokes the sere landscape of gravel desert regions such as the Mojave Desert or Joshua Tree National Monument. He also points the visitor to the coastal redwood groves that fill the valleys of the Pacific coast ranges; riparian plants that line the streams and arroyos of the foothills; and the wandering rivers and alluvial plains that underlie the vast agricultural enterprise of the Central Valley. *California Scenario* is skillful, witty, and markedly modernist in its formal composition—a piazza-sized version of a tabletop still-life painting by Cézanne, Braque, or Giorgio Morandi.

A more recent work by Michael Van Valkenburgh, for the Isabella Stewart Gardner Museum in Boston, purposefully directs our thoughts and feelings toward the second-growth forests of New England by featuring a twisting stone path leading through thickets of thin gray birches, paperbark maples, shadbush (*Amelanchier*), ferns, and kinnikinnick (*Arctostaphylos*). With its regional plants and obvious references to the second-growth forests that once ranged from Pennsylvania to the Mississippi, this garden pits reference against verisimilitude: a work of art that is made from the very stuff, the actual material, that it is representing, but is neither a copy nor an imitation. While many visitors, whether lay or professional, may mistake the garden as "natural," it is not a literal copy, nor could it ever be. One reason that it is not natural relates to scope. Real prairies, old fields, and young (or old) forests are more extensive spatially, often vastly so. Also, old fields are dynamic: some evolve into woodland, some are transformed by fire or are beset by plagues and destroyed. In contrast, this is a garden arrested in time; through maintenance and weeding it will remain. It is a work of artifice, not nature, even as it loses its youth and becomes in truth an older landscape.

The Gardner Museum garden embodies a taste and aesthetic different from those of earlier eras that took pleasure in the beds of massed ornamentals that so pathetically filled municipal gardens, railroad stations, and Victorian estates at the end of the nineteenth century. It also departs from 1960s modernism, dependent as it was on Christopher Tunnard's tepid orientalism and vague employment of elements drawn from surrealism. With the rare exception of Roberto Burle Marx in Brazil, who was a superb horticulturalist and plantsman, such ideas haven't had many proponents until recently.

Two exemplary projects employing highly controlled abstractions of natural landscapes, while not natural in and of themselves, are the Soros residence garden at Southampton, Long Island, completed in 1965, and the Lurie Garden in Millennium Park in Chicago, opened in 2004. The Soros garden, designed by A. E. Bye, is an evocation of the regional Atlantic coast seaside landscape of dunes, their forms, and their vegetation. Subtle grading of the land presents a set of undulating forms that welcome the daily and seasonal movement of light and shade. Bye's plant choices were consistently minimalist, schemes that disposed masses of shrubs in drifts that highlighted the landform. This approach to planting represents restraint in its palette with generosity in the quantum of plants used. Regrettably, the current owner has littered the original and unique graceful spaces with large modern sculptures, transforming a superb work of landscape art into an inert backcloth for more common objects.

At the very same time that Bye was creating his gardens, a countervailing aesthetic strategy could be seen in the work of Daniel Kiley and later Peter Walker and myself. Inspired by André Le Nôtre's employment of trees, we have taken pleasure in the geometric order of ranks, allées, and bosques—sometimes in urban contexts, sometimes in rural ones. In projects like the Novartis headquarters in Basel, Switzerland, the IBM campus in Solana, Texas, and the 9/11 Memorial in Manhattan, Walker's return to geometric order is evident.[14] It is also evident in my design for the Wexner estate in New Albany, Ohio, and portions of the Getty Center in Los Angeles. At times reductive, these projects often represent an exercise in formal composition with little or no particular reference to nature, except for their use of natural elements. Rather than from variety, their pleasure derives from the texture, color, pattern, and spatial repetition that recall the minimalist music of the period by Philip Glass, Steve Reich, and Terry Riley.

The realization of the Lurie Garden in Chicago coincided with a renewed American interest in meadows. Several sources fed this trend. The first was the strengthening of an ecological vision that saw turf lawns as polluting and unecological; the second regarded meadows

as more advantageous in terms of landscape maintenance, stormwater treatment, and habitat for beneficial insects and small animals. A
third factor was the resurrected interest in native plants once used by a
handful of late nineteenth-century designers and landscape architects
in America and in northern Europe shortly thereafter, such as Jens Jensen, the Olmsted brothers, and Beatrix Farrand, who had collected,
propagated, and employed native plants in her work. In the Netherlands, Scandinavia, and Germany, grasses, aquatics, shrubs, and alpine
species had all become popular in gardens and parks prior to World
War II. Meadows, per se, have been appreciated for centuries, whether
described as flowery leas in poetry and song or depicted in paintings
and tapestries. Unbeknownst to most Americans who were besotted
with lawns composed of cool-climate northern European turf grasses,
this love of meadows with their diversity of plants persisted abroad.

Few landscape architects in America shared this view when Wolf-
gang Oehme emigrated from Germany to the United States in 1957.
With a deep horticultural knowledge, Oehme had worked in nurseries
and gardens in Germany and England before his arrival here. He was
an admirer of Willy Lange and other prewar plantsmen who had advocated the use of native plants and grasses mixed with selected species
of flowers and shrubs. By the 1970s, when his colleagues and the press
took notice of the stunning gardens that he and his partner James van
Sweden had been making in the mid-Atlantic region, others had also
begun to experiment with meadow and so-called natural planting.

At almost the exact same time that Oehme's and van Sweden's work
was on the rise, in 1972 Peter Walker completed the Weyerhaeuser
headquarters south of Seattle, with its stunning wildflower meadow.
Considerable differences distinguish Weyerhaeuser from Oehme's and
van Sweden's work and the Lurie Garden, however. The Weyerhaeuser
landscape was grounded in the mountain meadows of the West, with
their broad sweeps of lupines, grasses, and carexes (sedges). Although
composed of only a few species, it too changes continuously like more
natural meadows, appearing dramatically different as seasons progress
from one to another.

The Lurie Garden, by the Dutch plantsman Piet Oudolf and the
landscape architect Kathryn Gustafson, realized thirty years after Weyerhaeuser, falls within the tradition of such representation. Spectacular

and surprising to many as it was, it possessed a substantial pedigree. Oehme and van Sweden had been at work in the mid-Atlantic for several decades. For many landscape architects, this aesthetic appeared new and fresh, however, and also vaguely "ecological" in its seeming opposition to the lawns and shrub beds of conventional gardens. That this planting required extensive horticultural literacy and gardening experience, and nonetheless required considerable maintenance, also made it difficult to imitate—as many discovered.

The recent work of Piet Oudolf has furthered this aesthetic and attitude. In essence he introduced a variety of American prairie plants to Europe so successfully that this "look," this aesthetic, has now become common throughout England, Germany, the Netherlands, and France. Just as a fashion for the English landscape park had spread across these same countries at the end of the eighteenth and early nineteenth centuries, one can now find wild meadows and great swathes of prairie grasses on historic estates in Britain and on the Continent.

The public success of the Lurie Garden is in large part attributable to the aesthetic appreciation of tens of thousands of people who are captivated by the extent and diversity of the garden's plants and their varying colors, textures, seed heads, and stems. The seemingly unplanned and disordered but pleasing combination of species has resulted in forms and juxtapositions that belie the calculation and planning underlying it all. As in the work of Jekyll and Farrand, plants carry the day when arranged effectively, for example, the pinks and lemony colors that play off a range of blues and mauves, or the burnished ochers and bronzes of twigs against the grays and pale greens of other twigs.

A few years after the popular success of the Lurie Garden, the High Line in New York City opened to remarkable public acclaim. On an abandoned elevated railroad track in the former meatpacking district on Manhattan's West Side, James Corner Field Operations, in collaboration with Piet Oudolf and the architecture firm Diller Scofidio + Renfro, adopted the conceit of using plants that grow in the poor soils along the margins of railroads and old abandoned fields to produce a remarkable work. Like all ambitious gardens, its seeming simplicity is deceptive. In actuality, extensive care is required for the vegetation to remain robust and diverse. Patrons and agencies with the means to do so have decided the effects are well worth the cost. It must also be said, however, that thirty years ago the look of dead, desiccated, mashed grasses and herbaceous plants for several months of the year would have been considered completely unacceptable in a public landscape of high aesthetic ambition. Its acceptance involved changes in class and taste, maintenance and appearance, and attitudes toward nature and order in the human environment.

My personal use of the presentation and representation of nature in planting design might be characterized as "all of the above." I have embraced each of these modes at certain times and in certain projects. I grew up in Alaska, and my contact with wild nature was immersive, constant, and palpable. Despite being a dropout from civil engineering and architecture and having had no studies in horticulture or biology, I had spent years carefully looking at the world around me. Using painting I studied and recorded my environment—the trees, hills, mountains, flora, and fauna—while somewhat aimlessly drifting through high school in Fairbanks. And I have continued to document trees, flowers, ground cover, even ferns in the Pacific Northwest, New England, Europe, and the Southwest ever since. In recent years I have pondered the possibility of introducing beauty into our projects through the use of several devices: abstraction and concentration; the revelation of the interest and beauty of something commonly considered ugly or chaotic; and representation that invokes aspects of memories of particular places.

Our office's very first project, the 1976 landscape for Johnson & Johnson's baby products division headquarters, near Princeton, New Jersey, featured a meadow that mixed grasses and native wildflowers. Preserving a lonely existing old hedgerow, we started with bare ground; it took about three years to defeat the invasive species and coax the grasses and wildflowers to settle down into a handsome meadow. At that time it didn't dawn on me that this was an unusual ambition, or that it would become an issue with the client—a few years after the meadow had matured and was doing well, the client plowed it under and turned the site into a vast green desert of mown lawn. I suspect the reason was that they thought it was too messy, especially in the late winter when it didn't have the manicured feel of a country club lawn. A dozen or so years later, working with the architect Frank Gehry on a social housing project in Frankfurt, Germany, I was more aware of what

I was doing, and the trope I was working. For that project I proposed to sweep fragments of orchards and meadows through the parking areas and introduce a heavily planted wild edge for stormwater runoff. Our German client understood and implemented the design.

After some years in practice and teaching I became interested in representation and issues of meaning in the construction of landscape. In 1983 I collaborated with the architect Peter Eisenman on a competition—the first of many we worked on together—for an arts center at Ohio State University, today known as the Wexner Center. With an interest in memory, I purposefully set out to invoke a sense of the prairie that had once existed on the site. There was no intention to make some "real" scrap of actual prairie as a setting for the building. Instead, various horticultural species were mixed into a semi-random composition, accompanied by two rows of viburnum shrubs to stand in for the scaled-down effect of the trees we see further in the distance—and also as an echo of the windbreaks that were widely planted by farmers across the midwestern prairies and the Great Plains. The project also embodied another memory of a landscape separated from Ohio in time and distance. Employing the geometry of a grid, with the architect I created a series of boxes or plinths rimmed with red sandstone that were given varying heights; from the tops of these, the grasses and shrubs emerged. It was homage of sorts to a memory of the Etruscan necropolis at Cerveteri, north of Rome, a gridded complex of tombs cut from red volcanic tufa, most of which were essentially rectangular earth-covered vaults planted with an assortment of native grasses, shrubs, and cypress. These plinths with their grasses also resembled giant blocks of cut turf. It was an unforgettable and powerful landscape of stone and earthen architecture and vegetation. In all, the Wexner Center landscape combined references to these two different landscapes, each with its own particular beauty.

For me it was a clear example of landscape representation. Although I loved this project, the landscape, like the building itself, created something of a scandal in Ohio. In Columbus grass had always been supine, like a well-behaved carpet or mat for buildings to sit on. Our landscape was regarded as too active, too assertive, and it was hated by many on campus, as well as by the donor. Time passes, taste changes. Soon this landscape will be destroyed, as many have wished since we made it.

More buildings are to be erected on the site. Once again, a landscape full of content is regarded as an empty space that would make a good building site.

A somewhat more abstract experiment was the cactus garden at the Getty Center in Los Angeles, although not in terms of directly evoking a particular place. There is something about cacti and other succulents that both fascinates and repels people. These plants often have beautiful, colorful, fragile flowers, but they can also really hurt you. Their forms can be droll, elegant, amusing, and charming, or frightening, monster- or Medusa-like. A number of botanical gardens and collections around the world have attempted to create public cactus gardens with mixed success; in California these include Lotusland in Montecito and the Desert Garden at the Huntington Library in San Marino. One of the most extensive is on the south coast of Majorca. Following the normal manner of garden composition, they have attempted to combine conventional strolling gardens with a taxonomically organized botanical collection, rarely coming off as successful artistic compositions, let alone beautiful ones. The pleasure to be had is one of fascination paired with suspended horror or anxiety.

My partner Dennis McGlade and I regarded the cactus garden at the Getty as an exercise in form, color, and texture, while exposing the true nature of a site in arid Los Angeles. The garden was also a practical response to architect Richard Meier's intention to create a long masonry arm to balance the composition of his museum. Doing so produced an area where no one could venture—the result of an agreement between the Getty's attorneys and the neighboring community of Brentwood. In the distance was the glare of the sun from the ocean and the reflective surfaces of the roofs and streets of Santa Monica. Just below lay the lush gardens and tree-lined streets of Brentwood and Beverly Hills, maintained with the assistance of a massive water supply brought from the north by the California Aqueduct. I suggested that we pull back this verdant curtain to reveal just how dry the place really is.

To reveal the beauty in these cacti and other succulents—their strange beautiful/horrible quality—we presented them in isolation to emphasize their formal properties, but also the peculiar energy and harmoniousness gained when they were seen in large masses. We planted a series of trays beside a stairway, augmented by several large euphorbias, that can be experienced from afar and on occasion dramatically close and within them. By any stretch of the imagination this did not constitute a representation of local nature or, for that matter, of any particular place. The plants, which derive from North and South America as well as Africa, aren't to be found in California. The garden was a pure and simple composition relying on harmony and contrast of form, texture, and color.

In contrast to this exercise at the Getty, I have experimented for a number of years with landscape designs that directly refer to the region in which they are located, using a select number of elements to represent particular aspects of that environment. These are not to be construed as pretending to re-create wild nature, however. The first is a conference center facility for the Church of Latter-day Saints in Salt Lake City, designed in collaboration with the architect Robert Frasca and his firm, ZGF. In this case the landscape was draped over a giant building nearly ten acres in floor area, and a 21,000-seat auditorium. Treating the landscape/building as a mesa or mountain, we clad the blank sides of the auditorium with the vegetation that grows in the canyons of Utah and on the steep slopes of the nearby Wasatch Range. The trees are mostly firs and maples, but they have been heavily planted to bring into the city an odd recollection of the nearby canyons. I will repeat that this was no attempt at any form of re-creation. For example, Douglas firs are the most common conifer in the cool and shady mountain valleys; they would have been uncomfortable growing in urban conditions and quite likely end up too tall and leggy if planted on the rooftop. Instead, slow-growing Serbian spruces were substituted for the Douglas firs. On a different portion of the rooftop, small bristlecone pines—a native of lands hundreds of miles farther south and to the west—were chosen for their dwarfish scale and to create a sense of distance and sweep when looking off toward the Great Salt Lake. The project was complete artifice; it was not nature.

In turn, the inspiration for a four-acre meadow on the central portion of the roof was the alpine meadows found along the length of the Rocky Mountains. No commercial nursery could provide such a diversity of native species in the quantity we needed, so the growing was contracted out, and members of the church pitched in to plant the thousands of plugs, seedlings, and small pots. To our happy surprise, meadow mice, lemmings, and apparently some rabbits have found their way up the stairs and now live there—only to be hunted by hawks and owls, as they are in the wild. In addition to offering habitat, this scheme has resulted in utilitarian environmental benefits regarding heat, energy, water, and longevity for the building's roofing. But none of that was the instigating motive. I simply wanted to present an aspect of the local environment that I considered beautiful to people for their pleasure.

Elsewhere, a client for a private estate in France desired a pond. In the past I had designed a number of ponds and small lakes, in part inspired by my youthful summers in the interior of Alaska. One such lake was about thirty miles south of Fairbanks, where I helped build a Boy Scout camp in the woods. The lake was filled with life: spatterdock, lilies, irises, and reeds, with birches, willows, and spruce, as well as fish and beaver—all in all, a powerful source of reverie, form, and plant palette.

The French estate plan we developed combined existing elements of the site with the proposed interventions. Among these were a forest with paths, two small private walled gardens, a meadow, a buffer plantation around the perimeter—and a pond. While I was working on this scheme in the valley of the Seine north of Paris, it was hard not to think of Monet's garden in nearby Giverny. Copying was not the answer; but on the other hand, I felt that although it would be almost impossible not to echo in some way Monet's magnificent pond—the inspiration for many of his greatest paintings—there was no reason for not making another composition utilizing much of the same palette to achieve many of the same pleasurable effects.

Today, the meadow that resulted from transforming a banal horse paddock originally covered with a German fescue features a mixture of American and European grasses and perennials. Fortunately, we have learned how to establish grasses in a shorter period of time, but even so, it takes a few years for them to settle down, and the meadow requires careful maintenance, mostly mowing, several times a year. The pond also needs fairly rigorous cutting and harvesting of the water plants to keep the water open. The trees nearby will take time to shed their adolescent character, but time is part of our medium and maturity occurs within a few years. This landscape is not natural, but it is made of natural organisms and materials. It has already joined the local ecology of plants, animals, pests, and diseases as it operates under the laws of nature despite its origin in artifice. Its prime purpose is to provide pleasure through sensory delight, just as is offered by more famous antecedents both wild and domestic.

A recent experiment at another scale is the design for Apple Park in Cupertino, California, nearing completion at the time of writing. For me it has been a direct meditation on the nearly vanished natural and cultural landscapes of the immediate region. This landscape, comprising some 150 acres, is a complete fabrication. There is nothing natural about it. It's all artifice, although its subject is nature and the cultural landscape. The buildings on the site measure over 3 million square feet of office, research, and development space, and will be used daily by twelve thousand people as the setting for their waking, working lives. In the design of the landscape I purposefully set out to recall the lost orchards of the Santa Clara Valley that had once covered the site, as well as the natural plant communities that the orchards had replaced, which were composed largely of oak forest, oak savannah, and chaparral. To me orchards, like most of the agricultural and ranchland of the California coast, are quite beautiful, as are the hills and ravines and the combination of pasture and native vegetation. How to evoke the properties and qualities of this former landscape without copying or imitating any particular thing or place within it?

Landform and planting offered the two most effective devices for realizing such an aspiration. Therefore, we constructed a series of hills and small valleys on what was originally a totally flat site formerly composed of parking lots and two-story Hewlett Packard buildings. On these hills we've planted a wide selection of native plants along with a number of other American and Mediterranean species that are, considering climate change, appropriate to the slope and solar aspect. Over eight thousand trees have been planted, including over two dozen species of oaks, accompanied by a variety of conifers, manzanitas, sycamores, a wide variety of shrubs, perennials such as California lilac (*Ceanothus*), native salvias, and dozens and dozens of other species.

We've also planted over eight hundred fruit trees, which include thirteen varieties of heirloom stone fruits such as apricots, plums, nectarines, pluots, and cherries, and eleven varieties of apples. Like most people in our field, we are concerned about climate change and the vulnerability of a number of native species in this location to extinction in the very near future. In response we introduced a number of trees, shrubs, herbaceous plants, and bulbs from other regions that we suspect will survive in the future in the altered climate of the Bay Area. To assist with solving this problem, our client also built a pipeline to bring recycled water from a Santa Clara water treatment plant to ensure the plants' establishment and address extended droughts.

Given Apple Park's urban location and restrictions against air-polluting techniques such as using fire to manage the meadow and grassland, we embarked on a research project with two grass and seed suppliers to experiment with various mixtures of native grasses and wildflowers. Learning that some of the grasses that give the characteristic golden look of the California hills were actually of European origin and introduced by early settlers, we felt secure in exploring what combination might give us the effect we were after. We eventually settled on a group of mixes for different places on the site, chosen for the ability to thrive in different microclimates and for social use as well as symbolic or artistic relevance.

Ultimately, to many people the trees, shrubs, grasses, and bulbs of Apple Park will look "natural." The plants will behave naturally, responding as they must to biophysical laws, because they are de facto natural organisms—adding to the conceptual confusion. As the meadow-covered south hills at Apple Park slope gently toward the main building, everyone arriving will notice that they are in fact supported on one side by a four-and-a-half-story structural wall that runs for nearly a quarter mile. The artifice could not be more blatant, although recently installed portions of the hills and a jogging trail are clearly intended to emulate the character of the nearby terrain. As with all planting, these areas are inevitably going to evolve and change over time. The central problem regarding nature and its representation in making landscapes with any aspiration beyond utility or safety lies in the fundamental difference between the nature of art and the nature of nature. Nature and the natural world are in constant flux: things move, live, die, grow, decline, deposit, erode, are reborn, metamorphose, shift about, are unstable. In all, nature is dynamic, nature is constant, nature is infinite—it starts anywhere and goes in all directions. It is cyclical, and yet time goes in only one direction: the phenomena of time and entropy. This energy and absence of human control is part of our perception of its power, its profligacy, its evanescence, and its beauty.

The arts, on the other hand—whether so-called fine arts such as painting or sculpture, or "practical" arts such as architecture, landscape architecture, and gardening—have as their normal goal the creation of something that is largely fixed and intentionally stable, in the hope of achieving some long-lasting value for an audience or public. Beauty as a phenomenon of nature is transient, impermanent, whether fleeting or lasting days or years, but ultimately evanescent. A garden or landscape takes time to create, time to mature, and from its initiation entropy begins to alter its condition. Knowing that time is part of one's tools and limits, designers employ planting plans that rely on landform, masonry structures, slower-growing plants such as trees, and cyclically self-renewing plants such as bulbs and perennials to assist in stability and long-term reward. Ultimately one must accept that any landscape design will change through time, eventually disappearing or evolving into something else; or it will be necessary to renew, replant, and even rebuild the landscape. It is also true that in landscape design one is never truly free of earlier sources of form, particularly those of nature, and our sense of its elements and attributes contribute to its beauty.

I feel compelled to conclude with the belief that beauty is a serious matter; it is deep and has great value for humans. While beauty has many manifestations, one of the most accessible has been—and remains to be—found in plants in both natural and designed settings. A loss or diminution of our interest or comprehension of beauty regarding either would indeed be a great loss. As Sigmund Freud once remarked, "Beauty has no obvious use: nor is there any clear cultural necessity for it. Yet civilization could not do without it."[15]

NOTES

INTRODUCTION

1. Ian McHarg's seminal *Design with Nature* (1969) is the most well known of these, but other publications that engaged me included Joachim Toby Tourbier and Richard Noble Westmacott's *Lakes and Ponds* (1976); articles by Robert Giegengack on geological topics, especially pertaining to the Sahara; and books by the anthropologists Yehudi Cohen, *Man in Adaption: The Cultural Present* (1971), Setha Low, *Culture, Politics, and Medicine in Costa Rica* (1985), and Dan Rose, *Black American Street Life: South Philadelphia, 1969–1971* (1987).

FORM, MEANING, AND EXPRESSION IN LANDSCAPE ARCHITECTURE

1. The author first heard Fuller say this in a public lecture at Columbia University in the spring of 1965. The concept pervades much of Fuller's work and writing.
2. In Arthur Danto, *The Transfiguration of the Commonplace* (Cambridge, MA: Harvard University Press, 1981), 1–32.
3. Alan Colquhoun, "Form and Figure," *Oppositions* 12 (Spring 1978): 28–37, quotations on 29.
4. Edmund Husserl, *Logical Investigations,* trans. J. N. Findlay (New York: Humanities Press, 1970), 267. See also J. N. Mohanty, "Husserl's Theory of Meaning," in Frederick Elliston and Peter McCormick, eds., *Husserl: Expositions and Appraisals* (South Bend, IN: University of Notre Dame Press, 1977), 18.
5. Nelson Goodman, *Ways of Worldmaking* (Cambridge, MA: Hackett, 1978), 23.
6. See David Coffin, ed., *The Italian Garden* (Washington, DC: Dumbarton Oaks, 1972), especially Elisabeth MacDougall, "*Ars Hortulorum:* Sixteenth-Century Garden Iconography and Literary Theory in Italy" (37–59); or Coffin's own study of the Villa Lante, *The Villa in the Life of Renaissance Rome* (Princeton: Princeton University Press, 1979), 347–51. There are numerous books that discuss Japanese gardens. One of the best remains Masao Hayakawa, *The Garden Art of Japan* (New York: Weatherhill; Tokyo: Heibonsha, 1973).
7. Frederick Law Olmsted, "Montreal: A Mountain Top Park and Some Thoughts on Art and Nature," in S. B. Sutton, ed., *Civilizing American Cities: A Selection*

of Frederick Law Olmsted's Writings on City Landscapes (Cambridge: MIT Press, 1971), 204–6.

8. Danto, "Metaphor, Expression, and Style," in *Transfiguration of the Commonplace,* 169.

9. Ibid., 163–208.

10. Clement Greenberg, "'American-Type' Painting," in *Art and Culture: Critical Essays* (Boston: Beacon Press, 1961), 208–29. This remarkable essay explores the notion that American abstract expressionists managed to make explicit matters that were left implicit in previous European painting and vice versa.

11. Quoted in Frederick Law Olmsted, *Mount Royal, Montreal* (New York: Putnam, 1881), 43.

REGIONALISM AND THE PRACTICE OF HANNA/OLIN, LTD.

1. Victor E. Shelford, *The Ecology of North America* (Urbana: University of Illinois Press, 1963), 17.

2. Ibid., 18.

3. Henry Glassie, *Pattern in the Material Folk Culture of the Eastern United States* (Philadelphia: University of Pennsylvania Press, 1968), 33.

4. François Burkhardt, Claude Eveno, and Boris Podrecca, eds., *Jože Plečnik, Architect: 1872–1957* (Cambridge: MIT Press, 1989).

5. For discussions of the Ahwahnee Hotel and KiMo Theatre, see Carla Breeze, *Pueblo Deco* (New York: Rizzoli, 1990). For a discussion of the Ahwahnee Hotel in considering the career of Stanley Underwood, who designed it, see Joyce Zaitlin, *Gilbert Stanley Underwood: His Rustic, Art Deco, and Federal Architecture* (Malibu, CA: Pangloss Press, 1989). See Bill Bradley, *The Last of the Great Stations: 50 Years of the Los Angeles Union Passenger Terminal* (Burbank, CA: Interurban Press, 1989), for a discussion of Union Station.

6. Phoebe Cutler, *The Public Landscape of the New Deal* (New Haven: Yale University Press, 1985). The entire book advances this argument; see particularly 64–82.

7. The KiMo Theatre's name is possibly derived from a Native American phrase meaning "mountain lion"; see "Six Letters or Less: KiMo Theatre Naming Process Utilized the Power of Community," *Albuquerque Journal,* October 6, 2019.

8. Ian L. McHarg, *Design with Nature* (Garden City, NY: Doubleday / Natural History Press, 1969); see especially "A Response to Values," 79–93, and "The Naturalists," 117–26.

9. See Pietro Maria Bardi, *The Tropical Gardens of Burle Marx* (New York: Reinhold, 1964), and the exhibition catalog *Roberto Burle Marx: The Unnatural Art of the Garden,* by William Howard Adams (New York: Museum of Modern Art, 1991); Emilio Ambasz, *The Architecture of Luis Barragan* (New York: Museum of Modern Art, 1976); Dimitris Antonakakis, Agnis Pikionis, Thalis Argyropoulos, and Hélène Binet, "Landscaping the Athens Acropolis," in *Dimitris Pikionis, Architect, 1887–1968: A Sentimental Topography* (London: Architectural Association, 1990), 70–97; Lawrence Kreisman, *The Bloedel Reserve: Gardens in the Forest* (Bainbridge Island, WA: Arbor Fund, Bloedel Reserve, 1988), for discussion of Church's work (49–70) and for that of Haag (63–75).

10. The best presentations of these works to date are "Portland and Open Space Sequence" and "Seattle Freeway Park," in *Process: Architecture,* no. 4: *Lawrence Halprin* (Tokyo: Process Architecture Publishing, 1978), 159–84 and 227–37, respectively.

11. See Adolf Loos, "Ornament and Crime" (1908/1929), in *Ornament and Crime: Selected Essays,* ed. Adolf Opel, trans. Michael Mitchell (Riverside, CA: Ariadne, 1998), 167–76; Louis Sullivan, "Plastic and Color Decoration of the Auditorium," "Ornament in Architecture," and "The Tall Office Building Artistically Considered," in Robert Twombly, ed., *Louis Sullivan: The Public Papers* (Chicago: University of Chicago Press, 1988), 73–79, 79–85, 103–13, respectively; Christopher Alexander et al., *A Pattern Language* (Oxford: Oxford University Press, 1977), x–xix, lay out the premise; and Thomas Beeby, "The Grammar of Ornament / Ornament as Grammar," *Via* 3 (1977): 10–29.

12. Steen Eiler Rasmussen, *London: The Unique City* (London: Jonathan Cape, 1934); Donald J. Olsen, *The City as a Work of Art: London, Paris, Vienna* (New Haven: Yale University Press, 1986); Carl E. Schorske, *Fin-de-Siècle Vienna: Politics and Culture* (New York: Knopf, 1980).

13. See Edward Relph, *Place and Placelessness* (London: Pion, 1976).

14. Many designers have had their work mangled or destroyed by the process of construction. I am currently working on an article concerning Manhattan's Riverside Drive and Riverside Park, designed by Olmsted, Vaux, and John Bogart. An account of its terrible history is outlined in "The New York 'Riverside Drive,'" *Engineering News* 6.1 (January 4, 1879): 3–5, wherein the author writes: "Without ever having had, so far as known, a single day's experience in the designing or construction of park or road-work, they have changed at will the width, location and arrangements of roads, walks and drives, and the plans of walls and other structures; they have permitted nearly every tree on the drive and many in the park to be cut down, and have leveled off the natural knolls, making a barren waste out of what should be a picturesque scene, and, worse than all, they have permitted the construction of work to be done in a negligent and faulty manner, and have paid the contractor some $7,000 for material taken from the park outside of the lines of the avenue, endangering the validity of the assessment which should be laid upon the adjacent property. . . . The present Park Commission, in placing in incompetent hands the power of mutilating the work of art designed by Olmsted & Bogart, should be judged by the same standard that we would apply to a person who, having ordered a landscape from Kensett, should turn it over, when half finished, to be completed by a journeyman house-painter." The Olmsted correspondence in the Library of Congress sheds more light on the subsequent saga of despoliation and transmogrification as monuments are added that destroyed both the form and meaning of the design. See the letters between Florence Kellogg and Olmsted in July 1885, Olmsted's response of August 6, 1885, as well as John Haven's letter to him of August 12, 1885. The results of this and twentieth-century encroachments are there for everyone to see.

15. See Kenneth Frampton, "The Millennialistic Impulse in European Art and Architecture: Russia and Holland 1913–1922," in *Modern Architecture, 1851–1945* (New York: Rizzoli, 1983), especially 306–16; and the recent collection of essays by Bernard Tschumi, *Questions of Space* (London: Architectural Association, 1990), especially "Episodes of Geometry and Lust," 38–59, "Architecture and Its Double," 62–77, and "The Architecture of Dissidence," 80–85.

16. See Peter Eisenman, "The End of the Classical: The End of the Beginning, the End of the End," *Perspecta* 21 (1984): 155–72, and Eisenman, "The Futility of Objects: Decomposition and the Processes of Difference," *Harvard Architectural Review* 3 (Winter 1984): 64–81; Alan Colquhoun, *Modernity and the Classical*

Tradition (Cambridge: MIT Press, 1989), especially "Regionalism and Technology," 207–11.

17. See Jürgen Habermas, "Modernity—An Incomplete Project," in Hal Foster, ed., *The Anti-Aesthetic: Essays on Postmodern Culture* (Port Townsend, WA: Bay Press, 1983), 3–15; Kenneth Frampton, "Towards a Critical Regionalism: Six Points for an Architecture of Resistance," ibid., 16–30; and Frampton, *Modern Architecture and the Critical Present* (London: Architectural Design, 1982).

WILLIAM KENT, THE VIGNA MADAMA, AND LANDSCAPE PARKS

1. Vigne were agricultural lands associated with estates, especially country estates with villas. As the name suggests, these often included vineyards, but also more often than not pastures or meadows and trees, or cereal grains amid the fruit and trees. Woodland was referred to as *selva* or *bosco* or *boschetto.*

2. Nikolaus Pevsner, *The Englishness of English Art* (London: Praeger, 1964), 162–64 (originally given as Reith Lectures on the BBC in 1955 and published in 1956 by the Architectural Press).

3. Such remarks consistently appear throughout popular and scholarly writing. Nan Fairbrother, writing for *Horizon* magazine shortly after her popular garden history *Men and Gardens,* proclaimed, "England's original contribution to garden art is the landscape park. William Kent was among the first to see that 'all nature is a garden' and his famous dictum was 'Nature abhors a straight line,' a pronouncement which dismissed in five words all the magnificent acres of Renaissance gardens." Fairbrother, "Gardens since Eden," *Horizon* 1.5 (May 1959): 47. H. W. Janson in his widely used undergraduate text, *History of Art,* generalizes in the same vein: "Lord Burlington and his circle . . . invented what became known all over Europe as 'the English landscape garden.' Carefully planned to look unplanned, with winding paths, irregularly spaced clumps of trees and little lakes and rivers instead of symmetrical basins and canals, the 'reasonable' garden must seem as unbounded, as full of surprise and variety, as nature itself. It must in a word be 'picturesque,' like the landscapes of Claude Lorrain (which English landscape architects now took as their inspiration)." Janson, *History of Art,* 1st ed. (New York: Prentice Hall / Harry N. Abrams, 1962), 454–59. Another example: "Claude's poetic re-creation of classical legends . . . appealed strongly to the English gentry on the Grand Tour, who began to see landscape through his eyes." Geoffrey and Susan Jellicoe, *The Landscape of Man* (New York: Viking, 1975), 240. Kent's recent biographer, Michael Wilson, is careful to distance himself from such views and matter-of-factly states: "Much has been made in the past of the supposed connection between the Kentian landscape garden and the idealized Classical landscapes painted by Claude Lorrain, Salvator Rosa, and Gaspard Poussin. It is misleading to suggest that Kent set out deliberately to re-create their vision of a timeless Elysium in terms of actual landscape. . . . The misconception of Kent as basically a landscape painter who set out deliberately to project preconceived subject matter onto the natural canvas of real landscape perhaps derives from a superficial reading of Walpole's essay 'On Modern Gardening,' which contains such misleading phrases as 'He realized the compositions of the greatest masters in painting.'" *William Kent: Architect, Designer, Painter, Gardener (1685–1748)* (London: Routledge & Kegan Paul, 1984), 138, 198–99.

4. H. F. Clark, *The English Landscape Garden* (London: Pleiades, 1948), 4.

5. Ibid., 15.

6. Ibid., 36.

7. Kenneth Woodbridge, *Landscape and Antiquity: Aspects of English Culture at Stourhead, 1718 to 1838* (Oxford: Clarendon Press, 1970), 8, 23, 30, etc.; Christopher Hussey, *English Gardens and Landscapes, 1700–1750* (New York: Funk & Wagnalls, 1967), 48, 158.

8. Susan Lang, "The Genesis of the English Landscape Garden," in Nikolaus Pevsner, ed., *The Picturesque Garden and Its Influence outside the British Isles* (Washington, DC: Dumbarton Oaks, 1974), 3–29.

9. Ibid., 3.

10. Ibid., 6; see also Woodbridge, *Landscape and Antiquity*, 30–37.

11. Lang, "Genesis of the English Landscape Garden," 27. This also accords with a point made by John Dixon Hunt in several of his essays, namely that gardens in their artifice have a transforming nature on their surroundings. In their distinct abstract and often somewhat alien or "other" quality, gardens both stand out in contradistinction to what surrounds them and become entwined with it through an exchange of energy sparked by their difference. John Dixon Hunt, "The Garden as Cultural Object," in Stuart Wrede and William Howard Adams, eds., *Denatured Visions: Landscape and Culture in the Twentieth Century* (New York: Museum of Modern Art, 1989), 19–31.

12. Lang, "Genesis of the English Landscape Garden," 27. She also footnotes Elisabeth MacDougall's earlier article "*Ars Hortulorum*: Sixteenth-Century Garden Iconography and Literary Theory in Italy," in David Coffin, ed., *The Italian Garden* (Washington, DC: Dumbarton Oaks, 1972), 37–59.

13. I pointed this out in an as yet unpublished essay written in Rome in 1974 that I used for lecture notes for years at the University of Pennsylvania and Harvard. So too, John Dixon Hunt makes this point in *William Kent, Landscape Garden Designer* (London: Zwemmer, 1987), 30–32. Kent had studied the theater design sketches of Inigo Jones, one of his heroes, in the collection of his patron, Lord Burlington. Later he produced some of the most theatrical of drawings for his illustrations of Spenser's *Faerie Queene* and for landscape tableaus, such as Merlin's Cave for the Queen at Richmond and the various scenes and Gothicized follies at Rousham.

14. John Dixon Hunt, *Garden and Grove: The Italian Renaissance Garden in the English Imagination, 1600–1750* (London: J. M. Dent, 1986); see especially "The Way of Italian Gardens" and "Palladian Gardening." Sir Roy Strong, *The Renaissance Garden in England* (London: Thames & Hudson, 1979).

15. Although Wilson gives an account of Kent's decorative work in England, he doesn't seem familiar with the sources of the work nor does he develop an analysis of it. See Wilson, *William Kent: Architect, Designer, Painter, Gardener*, 39–63 and 88–123. That Kent feels free to mix genres and ideas seen in the Veneto (especially by Veronese) with those from the Piedmont, especially from Turin, as well as Emilia (Mantegna), Tuscany (Correggio), and Rome, most notably the work of the Carracci and Raphael's shop, reveals his deep and broad knowledge of the field. For example, Kent single-handedly introduces into England the exquisite grotesque style developed by Raphael and Ligorio (from the antique decorations of the Domus Aurea), laying the groundwork for Robert Adam a few years later. The complete revolution of taste and style that he initiates underlies the attacks on his methods and talent by George Vertue and others, which in turn has led to several generations of critics and historians repeating the untruth that his painted dec-

orations were not very successful. Based on the ceiling of the presence chamber and other work done at Kensington Palace in 1724 and afterward, it is impossible to conceive that he did not know the loggia of the Villa Madama or the rooms and curved arcade of the Villa Giulia.

16. Michel de Montaigne, *Travel Journal,* trans. Donald M. Frame (San Francisco: Northpoint Press, 1983), 96, italics added.

17. The number of scholars who have acknowledged this fact has grown steadily, while little material has been developed to explain and support the position. Those who have done so include Lang, "Genesis of the English Landscape Garden," 27; Claudia Lazzaro, "Nature without Geometry: Vineyards, Parks, and Woods," in *The Italian Renaissance Garden* (New Haven: Yale University Press, 1990), 109–30; David Coffin in his latest work, "Garden Parks," in *Gardens and Gardening in Papal Rome* (Princeton: Princeton University Press, 1991), 139–58; Elisabeth MacDougall in one of her earliest unpublished studies regarding the Villa Venarea Reale in the Piedmont; and John Dixon Hunt in "Villa and Vigna," in *Garden and Grove,* 30–40.

18. This sports complex, built by the Accademia Fascista della Farnesina in 1931, is an interesting ensemble that has attracted favorable architectural interest since its initiation. The 1930 Baedeker guide describes the Foro Mussolini then under construction with enthusiasm (475). More recently, historians and critics interested in Italian modernist architecture and its planning, such as Spiro Kostof, have written on this development; see Kostof, *The Third Rome, 1870–1950: Traffic and Glory* (Berkeley: University Art Museum, 1973), 37–38, 49, 72–73.

19. Martial, *Epigrams* 10.45.5; Juvenal, *Satires* 6.344. The nineteenth-century traveler Augustus Hare remarked that "the wine of the Vatican hill has had a bad reputation even from classical times"; this is largely due to the clay soils. Augustus J. C. Hare, *Walks in Rome* (New York: George Routledge & Sons, 1882), 649.

20. Mary Taliaferro Boatwright, *Hadrian and the City of Rome* (Princeton: Princeton University Press, 1987), 165–66, 398. The Via Flaminia runs almost due north through Umbria to the Adriatic, where it reaches the coast at Fano, and thence continues to Rimini. It is named for C. Flaminius, censor and twice consul, who was killed at the battle of Lake Trasimene in 217 BCE. The Via Cassia runs northwest through Tuscany to Florence, and has been redirected in recent times to connect with the Via Flaminia just north of the Ponte Molle.

21. Hare, *Walks in Rome,* 643. The Pons Milvius or Ponte Molle was built by the censor M. Aemilius Scaurus in 109 BCE. It was here that Cicero captured the emissaries of the Allobrogi in 63 BCE and thus brought the Catilinian conspiracy to an end. The structure was remodeled by Pope Nicholas V, who added the watchtowers to its northern end. It was restored in 1805 by Pius VII, who commissioned Giuseppe Valadier to erect a triumphal arch at its northern entrance. Blown up by Garibaldi while trying to hold Rome and repulse the French (Papal) army, it was again restored in 1850 by Pius IX. Closed to automobile traffic (which now uses an adjacent bridge), it was reopened to pedestrians after restoration in 1985. Among the more famous views is that by Piranesi, which emphasizes its fortified character.

22. Richard Krautheimer, *Rome: Profile of a City, 312–1308* (Princeton: Princeton University Press, 1980), 264. Note the photograph c. 1880 (fig. 203), which shows the area still empty except for the ancient road, fields, and brickworks.

23. Richard Krautheimer, *The Rome of Alexander VII, 1655–1667* (Princeton: Prince-

ton University Press, 1985), 110; see also the prints of Lieven Cruyl, fig. 74 (Piazza S. Pietro showing these trees extending north past the Villa Madama), and fig. 100 (Cruyl's map of 1665, which also clearly shows this allée amid the farm fields of the Prati).

24. Maerten van Heemskerck drawing (now in the Kupferstichkabinett, Berlin), reproduced in Krautheimer, *Rome: Profile of a City*, 276–77 (figs. 212, 213); the "Small Cartaro Map" of Rome of 1575, 68 (fig. 59); and Ugo Pinardo's 1555 view of Rome, which includes the Prati and most of Monte Mario, 238 (fig. 183). See also the "Veduta di Roma" of Hendrick van Cleve, c. 1588, in the exhibition catalog *Il paesaggio nel disegno del Cinquecento europeo* (Rome: DeLuca, 1972). Here one sees one of the earliest clear depictions of the situation of the Villa Madama, with the road from Porta Angelica leading across the vigne of the Prati to the winding allée of the entry drive up to the villa. Heavy trees and forest are seen on the slope above and also beside the villa. Below is shown a meadow at the base of the hill, extending to the river. No other structures are shown in the Prati.

25. Recent considerations of the building's history, design, and impact include David Coffin, *The Villa in the Life of Renaissance Rome* (Princeton: Princeton University Press, 1979), 245–57, and *Gardens and Gardening in Papal Rome,* 35, 39, 51, 61–63; Lazzaro, *The Italian Renaissance Garden,* 22, 93; Paolo Portoghesi, *Rome of the Renaissance* (New York: Phaidon, 1972), 76–79, figs. 55–59; and Guy Dewez, *Villa Madama: A Memoir Relating to Raphael's Project* (London: Lund Humphries, 1993). The often reproduced and discussed drawings for this work now in the Uffizi by Raphael date from 1518, two years before his death. There are also drawings by Francesco da Sangallo from 1525, and records of payments to Antonio da Sangallo in 1524 and 1525 for waterworks.

26. Fountains and stucco decoration by Giovanni da Udine, sculpture by Bandinelli, architecture by Giulio Romano, fresco by Romano, hydraulics by Sangallo the Younger and da Udine. This work has been much discussed; see Coffin, *The Villa in the Life of Renaissance Rome,* 245–47, and *Gardens and Gardening in Papal Rome,* 61–63; Luigi Dami, *The Italian Garden* (Milan: Bestetti & Tumminelli, 1925), 14–15, 34–35; Dewez, *Villa Madama: A Memoir,* 9–31; Lazzaro, *The Italian Renaissance Garden,* 93–95; Georgina Masson, *Italian Gardens* (London: Thames & Hudson, 1961), 129–31, and *Italian Villas and Palaces* (London: Thames & Hudson, 1959), 237; Portoghesi, *Rome of the Renaissance,* 76–79; J. C. Shepherd and Geoffrey A. Jellicoe, *Italian Gardens of the Renaissance* (1925; repr., London: Alec Tiranti, 1966), 9, 59–60; and Paul van der Ree, Gerrit Smienk, and Clemens Steenbergen, *Italian Villas and Gardens* (Munich: Prestel, 1992), 123, 164–65.

27. See Coffin, *The Villa in the Life of Renaissance Rome* and *Gardens and Gardening in Papal Rome;* Lazzaro, *The Italian Renaissance Garden;* and Masson, *Italian Gardens* and *Italian Villas and Palaces.* All discuss the loggia, theater, and terrace, plus miscellaneous details. With the exception of the nymphaeum discussed by Coffin, there is no discussion of the park at all.

28. Maerten van Heemskerck (1498–1574), a Dutchman who resided in Rome from 1532 to 1536, produced hundreds of sketches and drawings of antiquities, buildings, and topography in and around Rome. Most of these drawings reside in the Kupferstichkabinett, Staatliche Museen, Berlin, and have proved invaluable to scholars for the wealth of precise information they contain. See Christian Hülsen and Hermann Egger, *Die römischen Skizzenbücher von Marten van Heemskerck* (Berlin: Bard, 1913).

29. See Michael Kitson, *Claude Lorrain: Liber Veritatis* (London: British Museum Publications, 1978), 8. Claude Gellée, known as Claude Lorrain, was born in Champagne, in the province of Lorraine, in 1600. He moved to Rome sometime between 1613 and 1623 and was apprenticed to a painter of landscape and illusionist material named Agostino Tassi. He is known to have visited Naples during his apprenticeship with Gottfried Wals, another from Tassi's shop. In 1625 he returned briefly to Nancy, the capital of Lorraine, but in 1626 he returned to Rome permanently, where he worked and lived until his death in 1682. There have been three biographies of Claude. The earliest is that of Joachim von Sandrart of 1675, which, although written and published before Claude died, is not considered to be altogether reliable by recent scholars. This is partly because it is unknown how much actual contact he had with Claude, and the fact that it was apparently written after his return to the Netherlands. The next, that of Filippo Baldinucci, although published in 1728 was written before 1696. Baldinucci had come to Rome in 1681 to do a biography of Bernini and is generally regarded as having been closer to the sources and facts. A third biography, that of Lione Pascoli, appeared in 1730, and is largely a rewrite of Baldinucci. At the beginning of the twentieth century, the leading scholar of Claude's work was Arthur Hind, who began cataloguing and collating his drawings and prints. Hind gives more credence to some of Sandrart's statements than recent scholars. More recently, the definitive studies have been Marcel Roethlisberger, *Claude Lorrain: The Drawings*, 2 vols. (Berkeley: University of California Press, 1968), and *Claude Lorrain: The Paintings*, 2 vols. (New Haven: Yale University Press, 1961); Kitson, *Claude Lorrain: Liber Veritatis*; Pamela Askew, ed. *Claude Lorrain, 1600–1682: A Symposium* (Washington, DC: National Gallery of Art, 1984); and Diane Russell, *Claude Lorrain, 1600–1682* (Washington, DC: National Gallery of Art, 1982).

30. From 1626 Claude lived in the Via Babuino; from 1627 to 1650 in the parallel Via Margutta; and from 1650 again in the Via Babuino. Arthur M. Hind, *The Drawings of Claude Lorrain* (London: Halton & Truscott Smith, 1923), 9.

31. Hind, *Drawings of Claude Lorrain*, 8. All of his biographers—Sandrart, Baldinucci, Hind—attest to his sketching from nature and discuss various expeditions. Numerous sketches are inscribed with notations of their location. Hind (*Drawings of Claude Lorrain*, 2) accepts Baldinucci's assertion regarding his painting in the Villa Madama grounds. Numerous paintings are derived from the view to the north from the Vigna Madama, or possess major elements found in his studies made there. These are recorded in his *Liber Veritatis* as follows (RC = Marcel Roethlisberger and Doretta Cecchi, *L'opera completa di Claude Lorrain* [Milan: Rizzoli, 1975]):
    LV 8: Landscape with figures, 1636. Landscape with peasants crossing a ford. Metropolitan Museum of Art, NY; RC 59, p. 91.
    LV 15: Landscape with a goat herd, 1637. Two paintings seem to relate to this record, one in Rome in the Rospigliosi-Pallavicini collection, 1637, RC 70, p. 93, and another in London in the National Gallery, 1637, RC 69, p. 93. Some think that Constable made a copy of this latter one, and that it is the one mentioned by Baldinucci as the painting made in the Vigna Madama; see Roethlisberger and Cecchi, *L'opera completa*. Kitson disagrees, thinking that this is another studio work. In my view, considering its small size, vertical format, and view of the small ravine at Claude's favorite spot in the Vigna Madama, it well could have been begun out of doors and finished in the studio.

LV 21: Landscape with a river and men building a boat, 1637–38. This is a view along the Tiber looking north toward Mount Soracte; the Ponte Molle is out of sight around the corner. Kitson, *Claude Lorrain: Liber Veritatis*, 64–65.

LV 22: Landscape with river and peasant milking a goat; ferry and mill in background, 1637. Opposite hand to previous painting. Appears to be in the Prati, also looking north, i.e., further downstream and on the opposite bank. The painting is in the Boston Museum of Fine Arts; RC 81, p. 95.

LV 68: Landscape with a river, recasting of same material as LV 8. This lovely painting is lost.

LV 83: Idealized view of Tiber below the Ponte Molle, showing the Vigna Madama in lower area on the left, 1644. "Pastoral Landscape," Windsor Castle; RC 146, p. 104.

LV 85: Partially idealized view of the right bank and the Ponte Molle on the right of the painting, looking north, 1644. "Pastoral Landscape," Madrid, Prado; RC 148, p. 104.

LV 90: Idealized working over of material from LV 83, 85, 1645. "Pastoral Landscape with Ponte Molle," Birmingham, City Museum; RC 153, p. 105.

32. British Museum (hereafter BM), Roethlisberger, *Claude Lorrain: The Drawings* (hereafter R) 356; Kitson, *Claude Lorrain: Liber Veritatis*, 109–10.

33. Sketches of the ravine: BM, R 4, 5, 6, 7, 293, 295, 386, 387, 419, 420, 587; Morgan, R 592; Haarlem, R 675; the lower end where it broadens out: BM, R 291r, 292, 540, 297; floodplain meadow: BM, R 540; Wildenstein, R 539; BM, R 299; bosque or woods: Haarlem, R 62r; BM, R 103; Haarlem, R 415; Haarlem, R 4r6; BM, R 298; riverbank: Boston, R 294; BM, R 422r; hippodrome terrace: Oxford, R 357; Haarlem, R 296.

34. Haarlem, R 145r; Ottawa, R 426; private collection, R 427; R 736. There are numerous portraits of trees that could easily have been done here and that certainly look like further study of particular trees depicted in other drawings that are clearly from here, just as there are many variations of a couple of particular groups and clumps of trees in the pine wood and along the ravine. One obvious example of this is the oak depicted in BM, R 290r. It is almost certainly the same tree as the central one in BM, R 291r, one of those inscribed by Claude as being executed in the Vigna Madama.

35. BM, R 26; Louvre, R 423; Wildenstein, R 875; Christ Church, Oxford, R 486.

36. BM, R 619r. This is one of the few drawings where Claude actually inscribed a date, albeit on the verso—here, 1646.

37. There were several painters from Utrecht in this family; this particular painting was made between 1640 and 1660 by Cornelius Bloemart II, b. Utrecht 1603, d. Rome 1684. The Poussin sketches date from 1635–40. The view of the Tiber and banks looking north from the walk later known as Poussin's walk is in the Musée Fabre, Montpellier; see Peter Galassi, *Corot in Italy: Open-Air Painting and the Classical-Landscape Tradition* (New Haven: Yale University Press, 1991), pl. 192, p. 162. The study of five trees done in the vigna depicting several of the same ones as Claude is in the Louvre; see Walter Friedlander, *Nicolas Poussin: A New Approach* (New York: Harry N. Abrams, 1964), fig. 70, p. 72. The view of the Ponte Molle from the Vigna Madama is in the Albertina, Vienna; see Jean Leymarie, Genevieve Monnier, and Bernice Rose, *Drawing: History of an Art* (New York: Skira/Rizzoli, 1979), 170. His sketch of the Aventine, c. 1642, is in the Uffizi; see Curtis O. Baer, *Landscape Drawing* (New York: Harry N. Abrams, 1977), pl. 58, p. 150.

38. The most obvious are those done at the Villa Crescenzi, around the Forum, Colosseum, and Tivoli. He drew antique and contemporary structures in their setting rather carefully. The first few years of sketches reproduced in Roethlisberger, *Claude Lorrain: The Drawings,* abound with examples.

39. Both are now in the Museum of San Martino, Naples (inv. nos. 1136/18 and 3333, respectively) and are reproduced in Walter Vitzthum, *Drawings by Gaspar Van Wittel (1652/53–1736) from Neapolitan Collections* (Ottawa: National Gallery of Canada, 1977), plates 30 and 40.

40. This is one of a series done by Ingres after arriving at the French Academy, now in the Ingres Museum, Mountauban; reproduced in Hans Naef, *Ingres in Rome* (exh. cat., International Exhibitions Foundation, 1971), plate 25, p. 20.

41. "Group of young pines near Ponte Molle," Kunstmuseum, Bern; reproduced in Galassi, *Corot in Italy,* pl. 210, p. 173.

42. Corot's pencil-and-ink drawing and oil sketch on paper (both now in the Louvre) of "La Promenade du Poussin," as well as Poussin's similar study and that of François-Marius Granet (considerably inferior), can be seen in Galassi, *Corot in Italy,* 162–65.

43. John Robert Cozens, *Rome from the Villa Madana*, appeared at Sotheby's London sales in 1997 and 2017; see www.sothebys.com/en/auctions/ecatalogue/lot.139 .html/2017/old-master-british-works-paper-l17040. Cozens (1752–1797) accompanied Payne Knight to Italy in 1776 and was in Rome by November. He remained sketching through 1777 and returned to England in 1779.

44. This handsome drawing, now in the Albertina Collection, Vienna, and frequently reproduced, can be seen in *Old Master Drawings from the Albertina* (exh. cat., International Exhibitions Foundation, 1984), pl. 74 and pp. 253–54.

45. Collection of the Los Angeles County Museum of Art, seventeenth-century Roman.

46. Giuseppe Vasi (1710–1782), *Prospetto Città di Roma, MDCCLXV.* Similar to the large multiple prints of his protégé Piranesi, this view is very particular about topography and artifacts.

47. This is a painting now in the Kunstsammlungen zu Weimer. It is reproduced as plate 21 in Nicholas Boyle, *Goethe: The Poet and the Age* (Oxford: Clarendon Press, 1991), vol. 1, *The Poetry of Desire.* Jacob Philipp Hackert (1737–1807) came to Italy in 1768 and met Goethe in Naples in 1787, where he had moved to become a court painter.

48. See Raymond Keaveney, *Views of Rome: From the Thomas Ashby Collection in the Vatican Library* (London: Scala Books with Biblioteca Apostolica Vaticana and the Smithsonian Institution, 1988); the Percy drawing is reproduced as pl. 47, p. 189; Gimelly, pl. 49, p. 195; Wilson, pl. 61, p. 229. There are several other drawings of the area around the Ponte Molle and the Acqua Acetosa by different people during this period that also confirm the drawings of Claude.

49. Hunt, *William Kent, Landscape Garden Designer,* 51–53, 55, 69, 85, 89; also Wilson, *William Kent: Architect, Designer, Painter, Gardener,* 198.

50. Wilson, *William Kent: Architect, Designer, Painter, Gardener,* 25–38.

51. Hunt, *William Kent, Landscape Garden Designer,* 41–42; John Harris, "William Kent's Drawings at Yale and Some Imperfect Ideas upon the Subject of His Drawing Style," in John Wilmerding, ed., *Essays in Honor of Paul Mellon: Collector and Benefactor* (Washington, DC: The National Gallery of Art, 1986), 143–44.

52. Striking examples of Kentian borrowing from Roman or other Italian sources for

which no particular mention of knowing the source, sketch, or reference is made by Kent are given by Margaret Jourdain, *The Work of William Kent, Artist, Painter, Designer and Landscape Gardener* (London: Country Life, 1948); Hunt, *William Kent, Landscape Garden Designer*; and Wilson, *William Kent: Architect, Designer, Painter, Gardener*. He simply knew this material, had absorbed it and drew on it at will. Hunt alludes to such a situation in his consideration of Kent's theatrical qualities, his borrowings and methods, by mentioning Cardinal Pietro Ottoboni's opera productions in Rome during the years Kent was in the city. Several scholars have noted that the scenery executed by Filippo Juvarra for *Iphigenia in Tauris* bears a striking resemblance to the principal ensemble in the pleasure ground of Stourhead executed largely by Henry Flitcroft, the draftsman employed by Burlington and Kent throughout their long association. While Kent's own masque-like scenes for book illustrations, parties, and gardens are heavily derived from the masque design sketches and studies of Inigo Jones that were in the possession of Burlington, which he obviously studied assiduously, again his own direct experience of theater in Rome, and of design for the theater by people as skilled as Juvarra, played a key role in the formation of his imagination and resources.

53. See MacDougall, "*Ars Hortulorum*"; Wilson, *William Kent: Architect, Designer, Painter, Gardener*; and Hunt, *William Kent, Landscape Garden Designer*.

54. For a catalogue raisonné of Jones's designs and sketches for the theater, see Stephen Orgel and Sir Roy Strong, *Inigo Jones and the Theater of the Stuart Court,* 2 vols. (Berkeley and London: University of California Press and Sotheby Parke Bernet, 1973). Kent clearly knew these drawings well, as he quotes and borrows both content and manner of representation from them. The most relevant sketches are those for *Luminalia,* Scene 1: Night (plates 383 and 384).

55. Hussey and Hunt have written at some length on this topic. Elisabeth MacDougall has pointed out that the original proposal by Kent for a pyramid and curved masonry exedra at the end of the cedar allée facing the Rotunda was based on the circus of Ciriaco Mattei at his villa on the Caelian as designed by Giacomo del Duca. Kent eventually uses this motif at Stowe as the Temple of British Worthies. His use of the Pantheon motif occurs several times in his own work and singularly in that of his protégé, Flitcroft, at Stourhead. At Stowe, Kent used a columnated round temple surmounted by a dome to represent what became known as the "Temple of Ancient Virtue." It is based on several ancient Roman prototypes, notable the Temple of Vesta in the Forum and the Temple of Vesta at Tivoli, known as the "Sibyl's Temple." These were tended by cloistered virgins (precursors to Christian nuns) and were symbols of piety and virtue. The cascades in the Venus Vale at Rousham are a recapitulation of his many studies for cascades, the first of which is at Chiswick; all of them appear to be based on the series of cascades in the upper axial garden at the Villa Aldobrandini, Frascati.

56. All of the known drawings by Kent for garden designs are reproduced in Hunt, *William Kent, Landscape Garden Designer*. The obelisk and arch for Chiswick can be seen in plates 8, 27, 30; the aviary at Chiswick with berms as columns, plates 7, 14, 44; the canal transformed to a river, plates 26, 29, 31, 41, 44; trees trimmed up to act as a screen and evoke Italian park planting at Chiswick, plates 26, 31, 32, 33, 34, 36, 38, 41, 44; the uneven or sloping grading at Chiswick, plates 8, 13 (this appears to be the area near the entry and cascade), 26, 31, 34, 41.

57. During what were to prove to be his last years, while working at Rousham, Kent also executed several projects at Stowe. Hunt, Peter Willis, MacDougall, and

Hussey have written at length about this garden and some of Kent's sources. The two most obvious additional sources for his work here were the theatrical drawings of Inigo Jones and the topography of various Roman vigne, including the Vigna Madama. The most important designs of Jones in this regard are those for the masques *Luminalia* (performed at Whitehall in 1638) and *Florimène* (1635). One scene and its back cloth of a lawn leading down to a lake with an island in the moonlight, flanked by groups of tall deciduous trees, must have haunted Kent as much as it has everyone who has ever seen it, whether onstage or in his drawing or its reproduction. While working on Chiswick in the late 1720s and early 1730s he cribbed directly from this set design. As in other elements such as the Temple of British Worthies, initially developed for Chiswick and later worked into his designs for Stowe, so too he reuses this particular vision. The softening of the great south lawn and groves flanking it, the loosening of the lakes and their margins, the positioning of the bridges and pavilions as executed during the period of his influence at Stowe bear a striking resemblance to sketches of both Jones and Kent. It must be said also that the theatrical drawings of Jones, while not influenced by Claude, who was his contemporary, were also in part inspired by a sojourn to Italy and fond memories of the Roman Campagna, its villas and vigne, and emerging contemporary techniques of representation. Another feature of the Stowe landscape relates more directly to Kent's utilization of the Madama imagery: the Grecian Valley, which leads away from the Temple of Concord and Victory northeast of the house. In some ways this may well be thought of as Kent's last work, certainly at Stowe, although created shortly after his death by Cobham and Brown. Originally known as the Grecian Temple, its most prominent feature is a dog-leg valley, created by excavation at considerable effort and framed by a continuous plantation of forest trees, fronted and softened by clumps and trees along its edges—notably cedars, larch, Scotch fir, beech, sycamore, and yew. Here, emptied of fountains and architectural features, was constructed a pure landscape scene based on the schemata of the vale of the Vigna Madama. In one direction (southeast), the vale leads down to his Elysian Fields with its temples, grottoes, cascades, and shrine. In the other (northeast), it stretches out to the countryside, its end veiled in groves of trees. Today, mowed awkwardly, overgrown, and hemmed in on the sides with a monotonous solid crush of trees, it scarcely resembles the artful vale it once was.

58. Hunt, *William Kent, Landscape Garden Designer,* reproduces these drawings: Claremont, plates 60, 61, 63, 69; Esher, plates 68, 83, 84, 87; Rousham, plate 105.

59. Ibid., plate 69. This is the same sort of shallow-draft boat that appears in Claude's sketch and painting of the Tiber and Mill, and which is memorialized in the fountain of Bernini at the foot of the Spanish Steps in the district where Kent and Claude resided. Other instances of compositions in English landscape parks of the eighteenth century that bear an uncanny resemblance to this portion of the Vigna Madama can be offered. The most notable is the view out to the river and bridge from the peripheral walk of Wray Wood at Castle Howard. The subsequent addition of the mausoleum (yet another version of the Sibyl's Temple at Tivoli) by Nicholas Hawksmoor only renders the scene more Claudian, and oddly enough does for that landscape what Claude himself did to the Tiber and Campagna view from Madama in numerous paintings—that is, transformed it into a mythical and literary landscape. A study of the subliminal infusion of this particular composition or view into other gardens and parks would undoubtedly yield more

examples—Buscot House, Prior Park, etc. How many people were aware of the source is doubtful, however.

THE MUSEUM OF MODERN ART GARDEN

1. Philip Johnson, "Built to Live In" (MOMA pamphlet, 1931), in Robert A. M. Stern, ed., *Philip Johnson: Writings* (New York: Oxford University Press, 1979), 30.
2. See Kenneth Frampton, *Modern Architecture, 1851–1945* (New York: Rizzoli, 1983), 317–24, for a discussion of the De Stijl movement and especially of Van Doesburg's impact at the Bauhaus in 1921–22.
3. Philip Johnson, *Mies van der Rohe* (New York: Museum of Modern Art, 1947), 59–60.
4. Ibid., 3rd ed. (New York: Museum of Modern Art, 1978), 210; see the discussion with Ludwig Glaeser, printed as an epilogue, 205–11. All subsequent citations of Johnson's *Mies van der Rohe* refer to this edition.
5. Philip Johnson, "Whence and Whither: The Processional Element in Architecture," *Perspecta* 9/10 (1965): 170.
6. Johnson, *Mies van der Rohe,* 96–121.
7. Elizabeth Kassler, *Modern Gardens and the Landscape* (1964), rev. ed. (New York: Museum of Modern Art, 1984). Kassler never says so in so many words, but the images, quotes, and captions establish their convergence from different points of view: 12, 15, 21, 27, 58, 59.
8. Peter Eisenman, introduction to Stern, *Philip Johnson: Writings,* 16.
9. Stern, *Philip Johnson: Writings,* 194–95, from a bright and irritating talk Johnson gave in Seattle in 1957.
10. Especially the House with Three Courts (unbuilt; 1934), the Lange House (Krefeld, Germany; 1935), and the Hubbe House (Magdeburg, Germany; 1935).
11. See Mirka Beneš, "Inventing a Modern Sculpture Garden in 1939 at the Museum of Modern Art, New York," *Landscape Journal* 13.1 (Spring 1994): 1–20, for a discussion of the earlier history of this garden; and Robert A. M. Stern, *New York, 1930: Architecture and Urbanism between the Two World Wars* (New York: Rizzoli, 1987), 141–45, for the history and nature of this building.
12. Johnson, *Mies van der Rohe,* 205.
13. Ibid., 167–69.
14. Ibid., 154, italics added.
15. Mildred Schmertz, "The New MOMA: Expansion and Renovation of the Museum of Modern Art, New York City," *Architectural Record,* October 1984, 164–77.
16. See *Process: Architecture,* no. 94: *Robert Zion: A Profile in Landscape Architecture* (Tokyo: Process Architecture Publishing, 1991), 70–71.
17. Robert Zion, *Trees for Architecture and the Landscape* (New York: Van Nostrand Reinhold, 1968), with the MOMA garden, 163. This book was to become a standard reference for a generation of architects and landscape architects regarding rooftop planting, drainage, irrigation, nutrition, hardy street trees, and so on.
18. For example, Paley Park, one block away on 53rd Street, also designed by Zion, was built four years later.
19. This author remembers a particular misty night in the summer of 1966, leaning on the parapet of the upper garden, with the long haunting phrases of Sonny Rollins's tenor saxophone climbing up from the lower garden terraces where his band was set up near Maillol's colossal nymph, with the lights of midtown Manhattan shimmering on the wet stainless steel of Rickey's blades moving in the breeze.

20. Johnson, "Whence and Whither," 171.

21. Ibid., 172.

22. That Johnson was on the move intellectually, searching for new directions away from the precedents of Mies and his beginnings, is revealed by the neoclassically inspired design work and by the things he wrote and was recorded to have said in the late 1950s and early 1960s.

23. Philip Johnson, "Johnson," *Perspecta* 7 (1961): 3.

24. Ibid., 5–6.

25. Johnson discusses this interest and particular aspects of Schinkel's work in a lecture delivered in 1961 in Berlin prior to the garden addition: "Schinkel and Mies," in Stern, *Philip Johnson: Writings,* 165–77; see also his earlier remarks about Schinkel and others in the article he wrote on his own house for *Architectural Review:* "House at New Canaan, Connecticut," *Architectural Review* 108 (September 1950): 152–59.

26. Quoted by Walter Hopps, director of the Menil Collection, in the *New Yorker,* July 29, 1991, 49.

27. Robertson was a partner of Richard Llewelyn-Davies at the time with the New York office. The author personally followed these studies with great interest as they were developed in 1976–77 in their 58th Street office.

28. See Schmertz, "The New MOMA."

29. Eisenman, introduction to Stern, *Philip Johnson: Writings,* 18.

30. Ibid., 22; Johnson, "Whence and Whither," 171.

31. Schmertz, "The New MOMA," 166.

32. From Mies van der Rohe's "Über Kunstkritik" (1930), translated in Johnson, *Mies van der Rohe,* 196.

33. Stern, ed., *Philip Johnson: Writings.*

34. I say the United States, not America, on purpose, for by this time the Mexican Luis Barragán had already begun his series of remarkable landscape and architectural experiments that also pursued some of these same formal strategies, but with a very different vocabulary of materials, color, and cultural reference.

35. Kiley, Eckbo, and Rose also acted on Christopher Tunnard's teaching regarding modernist form, but almost exclusively in suburban settings prior to this date. Halprin had also been experimenting with compositional ideas derived from modern art, but largely in suburban shopping centers and suburban residential work in California, Texas, and Illinois. The lesson of Johnson's MOMA scheme appears to have been clear and immediately absorbed by designers interested in this problem.

WHAT I DO WHEN I CAN DO IT

1. The work of the Olin partnership and its predecessor firm, Hanna/Olin, has been published extensively: Laurie Olin, Peter Rowe, and John Dixon Hunt, *Transforming the Common/Place: Selections from Laurie Olin's Sketchbooks* (Cambridge, MA: Harvard Graduate School of Design, 1996); Jane Gillette, "Western Civ: The J. P. Getty Center," *Landscape Architecture* 87 (December 1997): 52–61, 72, 77; Peter Rowe, *Civic Realism* (Cambridge: MIT Press, 1997), 151, 193–95; Laurie Olin, "Landscape Design and Nature," in George Thompson and Frederick Steiner, eds., *Ecological Design and Planning* (Chichester, UK: John Wiley, 1997), 109–39; Clifford Pearson, "Wagner Park," *Architectural Record,* February 1997, 64–69; Michael Maynard, "A Park with a View," *Landscape Architecture* 87 (Jan-

uary 1997): 26–31; Laurie Olin, "Regionalism and the Practice of Hanna/Olin, Ltd.," in Therese O'Malley and Marc Treib, eds., *Regional Garden Design in the United States* (Washington, DC: Dumbarton Oaks Research Library and Collection, 1995), 243–70 (also included in the present volume); Frederick Steiner and Todd Johnson, "Perfecting the Ordinary" (profile of Hanna and Olin), *Landscape Architecture* 82 (March 1992): 68–77; Peter Rowe, *Making a Middle Landscape* (Cambridge: MIT Press, 1991), 156, 158, 161, 162, 165, 172, 173; Jory Johnson, "Pastures of Plenty: Thirty Years of Corporate Villas in America," *Landscape Architecture* 80 (March 1990): 54–56.

2. Georgina Masson pointed this out to me in Rome when she was working on one of her last books on Republican Rome. Lanuvium lay between Albano and Anzio, about ten miles south of Rome. Like many of his peers, Brutus owned more than one villa. Another favorite of his was near Cicero's in Campania; see John D'Arms, *Romans on the Bay of Naples: A Social and Cultural Study of the Villas and Their Owners from 150 B.C. to A.D. 400* (Cambridge, MA: Harvard University Press, 1970), 184. William MacDonald and John Pinto, in *Hadrian's Villa and Its Legacy* (New Haven: Yale University Press, 1995), also discuss his garden and its allusions (269).

3. Cicero, *Epistulae ad Atticum* 15.9.

4. For Sperlonga, see Giulio Jacopi, *L'antro di Tiberio a Sperlonga* (Rome: Istituto di Studi Romani, 1963) and *I ritrovamenti dell'antro cosiddetto "di Tiberio" a Sperlonga* (Rome: Istituto di Studi Romani, 1958); Roland Hampe, *Sperlonga und Vergil* (Mainz am Rhein: P. von Zabern, 1972); and Ariel Hermann, "Sperlonga Notes," *Acta ad Archaeologiam et Artium Historiam Pertinentia* (Institutum Romanum Norvegiae) 4 (1969): 27–32. Hampe gives a bibliography on the topic on pp. ix–xi. For Hadrian's grand entourage of architecture, tableau, and landscape, see MacDonald and Pinto, *Hadrian's Villa and Its Legacy*: discussion of literary themes expressed through art and furnishings, 146–51; landscape of allusion, 6–7, 182, 268–69; extensive bibliography, 375–80. For Pliny's Tuscan villas, see his letter to Domitius Apollinaris (5.6) in Pliny the Younger, *Letters and Panegyricus*, vol. 1, trans. Betty Radice (London: Loeb, 1969), 339–53.

5. James Longenbach makes this remark in a discussion of the poems that deal with ambiguity, order, human effort, fate, and nature in the two volumes that followed *Harmonium*, namely *Ideas of Order* and *Owl's Clover*. Longenbach, *Wallace Stevens: The Plain Sense of Things* (Oxford: Oxford University Press, 1991), 165.

6. In a letter of December 10, 1935, to Ronald Lane Latimer, the publisher of a limited edition of *Ideas of Order*, the volume containing "The Idea of Order at Key West," Stevens wrote, "You know, the truth is that I had hardly interested myself in this (perhaps as another version of the pastoral) when I came across some such phrase as this: 'man's passionate disorder,' and I have since been very much interested in disorder." Holly Stevens, ed., *Letters of Wallace Stevens* (New York: Knopf, 1981), 300. Earlier in the same letter he remarks that "poetry will always be a phenomenal thing." For a discussion of this and his assessment of Stevens's political and aesthetic views as presented in the poems of this period, see Longenbach, *Wallace Stevens*, 148–75.

7. Helen Vendler, *Wallace Stevens: Words Chosen Out of Desire* (Knoxville: University of Tennessee Press, 1984), 45. In a later lecture from the same series she discusses ideas of order and the discontinuity between the voices of nature and the singer (67–73).

MORE THAN WRIGGLING YOUR WRIST (OR YOUR MOUSE)

1. Michael Graves, "The Necessity for Drawing: Tangible Speculation" (1977), in Brian M. Ambroziak, *Michael Graves: Images of a Grand Tour* (New York: Princeton Architectural Press, 2005), 235–36.

THE LESS SAID . . .

1. "Evelyn Waugh: The Art of Fiction" (interview, 1962), in *The Paris Review Interviews, III* (New York: Picador, 2008), 71.
2. John Dixon Hunt, *Greater Perfections: The Practice of Garden Theory* (Philadelphia: University of Pennsylvania Press, 2000); see particularly chapter 5, "Word and Image in the Garden," 116–28.
3. John Dixon Hunt, *Nature Over Again: The Garden Art of Ian Hamilton Finlay* (London: Reaktion Books, 2008), and *The Afterlife of Gardens* (London: Reaktion Books, 2004). A particularly useful set of essays on Finlay, his writing, sculpture, and landscape installations can be found in "From Book to Garden and Back: Ian Hamilton Finlay—Four Essays and an Exhibition Catalogue," a special issue of *Word and Image,* 21.4 (October–December 2005), largely the work of Hunt with Michael Baridon, Harry Gilonis, and other contributors.
4. See Lawrence Halprin, *The Franklin Delano Roosevelt Memorial* (San Francisco: Chronicle Books, 1997), and Phyllis Tuchman, "The Franklin Delano Roosevelt Memorial," in *Lawrence Halprin: Changing Places* (exh. cat., San Francisco Museum of Art, 1986), 90–103; *Report to the President and Congress by the Franklin Delano Roosevelt Memorial Commission* (Washington, DC, 1978).
5. Hunt, *The Afterlife of Gardens,* 110, 111.
6. Among the many discussions of the Woodland Cemetery and Crematorium, the following provide a good sampling: Stuart Wrede, *The Architecture of Erik Gunnar Asplund* (Cambridge: MIT Press, 1980); Elizabeth B. Kassler, *Modern Gardens and the Landscape,* rev. ed. (New York: Museum of Modern Art, 1984), 76–79; Colin St. John Wilson, "The Dilemma of Classicism," in *Gunnar Asplund, 1885–1940: The Dilemma of Classicism* (London: Architectural Association, 1989), 14–19; Colin St. John Wilson, "The Dilemma of Classicism," in *Sigurd Lewerentz 1885–1975: The Dilemma of Classicism* (London: Architectural Association, 1989), 14–20. Marc Treib has frequently referred to the Woodland Cemetery in numerous essays on landscape, as does Anne Whiston Spirn throughout *The Language of Landscape* (New Haven: Yale University Press, 1998), and Caroline Constant has produced a monograph, *The Woodland Cemetery: Toward a Spiritual Landscape: Erik Gunnar Asplund and Sigurd Lewerentz, 1915–61* (Stockholm: Byggförlaget, 1994).
7. For discussion of Haag's work at Bloedel, see Lawrence Kreisman, *The Bloedel Reserve: Gardens in the Forest* (Bainbridge Island, WA: Arbor Fund, Bloedel Reserve, 1988); Susan Rademacher Frey, "A Series of Gardens," *Landscape Architecture* 76 (September–October 1986): 54–61; William Saunders, ed., *Richard Haag: Bloedel Reserve and Gas Works Park* (New York: Princeton Architectural Press, 1998); Laurie D. Olin, "Richard Haag," in Charles A. Birnbaum and Stephanie S. Foell, eds., *Shaping the American Landscape: New Profiles from the Pioneers of American Landscape Design Project* (Charlottesville: University of Virginia Press, 2009), 121–23.
8. Although Hunt has shown the aircraft sculpture/birdfeeder in lectures to students, it doesn't appear in any of his books. Other works, including *Nuclear Sail*

(and Halprin's use of inscriptions), appear in *The Afterlife of Gardens,* 95–112; in *Greater Perfections,* 112–35; and in *Nature Over Again,* especially 88–99.

9. Nelson Goodman, *Ways of Worldmaking* (Cambridge, MA: Hackett, 1978), 23.

10. Susanne K. Langer, "The Cultural Importance of the Arts," *Journal of Aesthetic Education* 1.1 (Spring 1966): 11–12, quoted in John N. Serio, introduction to *Wallace Stevens: Selected Poems* (New York: Knopf, 2009), xiv, xxi.

11. Wallace Stevens, "The Noble Rider and the Sound of Words" (1942), in *The Necessary Angel: Essays on Reality and the Imagination* (New York: Knopf, 1951), 31, quoted in Serio, introduction to *Wallace Stevens: Selected Poems,* xiv.

12. "What Did I Mean Then or Now?" was published two years later and appears elsewhere in this volume. The original essay, "Form, Meaning, and Expression in Landscape Architecture," appeared in *Landscape Journal* 7.2 (Fall 1988): 149–68; a slightly revised version is also included in this volume.

13. Hunt, *Greater Perfections,* 128.

14. John Dixon Hunt, *Historical Ground: The Role of History in Contemporary Landscape Architecture* (New York: Routledge, 2014), 160.

15. Jane Gillette, "Can Gardens Mean?" *Landscape Journal* 24.1 (2005): 85–97. Her essay is reprinted in Marc Treib, ed., *Meaning in Landscape Architecture and Gardens: Four Essays / Four Commentaries* (Oxford and New York: Routledge, 2011), 134–65, along with her comments on it (166–73). The essay of mine Gillette addresses is "Stourhead," in *Across the Open Field: Essays Drawn from English Landscapes* (Philadelphia: University of Pennsylvania Press, 2000), 257–76.

16. John Dixon Hunt, "Stourhead Revisited and the Pursuit of Meaning in Gardens," in *Site, Sight, Insight: Essays on Landscape Architecture* (Philadelphia: University of Pennsylvania Press, 2016), 58.

17. After I delivered this talk at the University of Pennsylvania, a woman approached me to say she believed that—ironically—the *Tannenbaum* was introduced into the winter holiday life of Germans in the eighteenth or nineteenth century by Jews. Whether that was really the case, the worship of trees, especially evergreen ones, and their inclusion in part as boughs or in whole in winter ceremonies have roots in classical-era antiquity, whether Druids from the north or pantheistic Greeks and Romans in the south.

WHAT DID I MEAN THEN OR NOW?

1. *The Random House Dictionary of the English Language* (New York: Random House, 1966), 888.

2. Laurie Olin, "Form, Meaning, and Expression in Landscape Architecture," *Landscape Journal* 7.2 (Fall 1988): 149–68. A slightly revised version of the essay is included elsewhere in this volume.

3. This statement was written by my partner, Robert Hanna, ten years earlier, in 1977. Later, philosophical difference became a deep source of tension between us, contributing in part to our eventual breakup.

4. Steven Krog, "Is It Art?" *Landscape Architecture* 71 (May 1981): 373–76, and "Creative Risk-Taking," *Landscape Architecture* 73 (May–June 1983): 70–76.

5. Simon Swaffield, ed., *Theory in Landscape Architecture: A Reader* (Philadelphia: University of Pennsylvania Press, 2002), 74–75; Marc Treib, "Must Landscapes Mean? Approaches to Significance in Recent Landscape Architecture," in Treib, ed., *Meaning in Landscape Architecture and Gardening: Four Essays / Four Commentaries* (London and New York: Routledge, 2011), 82–125.

6. Laurie Olin, *Across the Open Field: Essays Drawn from English Landscapes* (Philadelphia: University of Pennsylvania Press, 2000); the essay discussed here is "Stourhead," 257–76.

7. Most notably Malcolm Kelsall, who in "The Iconography of Stourhead" (*Journal of the Warburg and Courtauld Institutes* 46 [1983]: 133–43) dismisses aspects of Kenneth Woodbridge's thought that had influenced me considerably. See John Dixon Hunt, "Stourhead Revisited and the Pursuit of Meaning in Gardens," *Studies in the History of Gardens & Designed Landscapes* 26.4 (October–December 2006): 328–41.

8. Jane Gillette, "Can Gardens Mean?" *Landscape Journal* 24.1 (2005): 85–97, reprinted in Treib, *Meaning in Landscape Architecture and Gardens,* 134–65.

9. Nelson Goodman, *Ways of Worldmaking* (Cambridge, MA: Hackett, 1978), 23.

10. Olin, "Form, Meaning, and Expression," 158.

11. *Random House Dictionary of the English Language,* 888.

CIVIC REALISM AND LANDSCAPE

1. See Peter Rowe, *Civic Realism* (Cambridge: MIT Press, 1997), 84. For this sequence of thought and the topic in general I am indebted to Rowe, whose *Civic Realism* initiated my interest and understanding of what it turned out I was doing. I will draw heavily for a time in this essay on some of his work in this book written what seems now like a long time ago.

2. Isaiah Berlin, "Realism in Politics" (1954), in Berlin, *The Power of Ideas,* ed. Henry Hardy, 2nd ed. (Princeton: Princeton University Press, 2013), 163. Berlin goes on to note that at times and for some people it has a sinister or disagreeable connotation, as when they say that "they (fear that they) are 'realists'—usually to explain away some unusually mean or brutal decision" (163). This he identifies as largely the result of Hegel and his followers, both conservative and radical, and their attack on Enlightenment optimism and an insistence that humanity needs to face unpleasant historical forces and various constructs of history that propose draconian laws and inevitable conflicts and determinist outcomes.

3. Linda Nochlin, *Realism* (London: Penguin, 1971), 13, quoted in Rowe, *Civic Realism,* 85.

4. Rowe, *Civic Realism,* 83.

5. J. B. Jackson, "The Imitation of Nature" (1959), in *Landscapes: Selected Writings of J. B. Jackson,* ed. Ervin H. Zube (Amherst: University of Massachusetts Press, 1970), 87.

6. Henri Lefebvre, *The Production of Space* (1974), trans. Donald Nicholson-Smith (Oxford: Blackwell, 1991), 31; Rowe, *Civic Realism,* 130.

7. Rowe, *Civic Realism,* 139–40.

8. Stanley Cavell has attempted to summarize the discourse of this period and its topics in his essay "The Incessance and the Absence of the Political," in Andrew Norris, ed., *The Claim to Community: Essays on Stanley Cavell and Political Philosophy* (Stanford: Stanford University Press, 2006), 262–317.

9. This section is heavily dependent on and drawn from a discussion found in Rowe, *Civic Realism,* 192–93, which he in turn derived from sessions and discussion with me at the time. I have put some of it back into diction more like my own voice and quoted directly other portions in his voice. It also reflects a number of discussions and readings that Nelson Goodman, John Whiteman, and I shared at Harvard from 1984 to 1986.

10. Richard Louv, *Last Child in the Woods: Saving Our Children from Nature-Deficit Disorder* (Chapel Hill, NC: Algonquin Books, 2005).

11. See discussion of this study in "Brain Fatigue Goes Green," *New York Times,* April 2, 2013.

12. Rowe, *Civic Realism,* 193; and "Natural Appreciation and Pursuit of Ordinary Perfection: Recent Work of Hanna/Olin," in Laurie Olin, Peter Rowe, and John Dixon Hunt, *Transforming the Common/Place: Selections from Laurie Olin's Sketchbooks* (Cambridge, MA: Harvard Graduate School of Design, 1996), 60–67.

13. Jackson, "The Imitation of Nature," 87.

14. Stanley Cavell, "An Emerson Mood," in *The Senses of Walden: An Expanded Edition* (San Francisco: North Point Press, 1981), 145–46.

15. Ibid., 148.

GLOBAL, REGIONAL, LOCAL

1. Laurie Olin, "Regionalism and the Practice of Hanna/Olin, Ltd.," in Therese O'Malley and Marc Treib, eds., *Regional Garden Design in the United States* (Washington, DC: Dumbarton Oaks Research Library and Collection, 1995), 243–70. A slightly revised version is included in this volume.

2. Ibid., 243; see also Victor E. Shelford, *The Ecology of North America* (Urbana: University of Illinois Press, 1963), 17ff.

3. For further details see, in this volume, "Regionalism and the Practice of Hanna/Olin, Ltd.," 50–51; see also Henry Glassie, *Pattern in the Material Folk Culture of the Eastern United States* (Philadelphia: University of Pennsylvania Press, 1968), 33.

4. For examinations dealing with architecture, see François Burkhardt, Claude Eveno, and Boris Podrecca, eds., *Jože Plečnik, Architect: 1872–1957* (Cambridge: MIT Press, 1989); *Living in a Modern Way: California Design, 1930–1965* (exh. cat., Los Angeles County Museum of Art, 2011); and *Overdrive: L.A. Constructs the Future, 1940–1990* (exh. cat., Getty Research Institute, 2013).

5. Kenneth Frampton, "Towards a Critical Regionalism: Six Points for an Architecture of Resistance," in Hal Foster, ed., *The Anti-Aesthetic: Essays on Postmodern Culture* (Port Townsend, WA: Bay Press, 1983), 13–30, quotation on 22; see also Frampton, *Modern Architecture and the Critical Present* (London: Architectural Design, 1982).

6. Frampton, "Towards a Critical Regionalism," 21.

7. Alexander Tzonis and Liane Lefaivre, "The Grid and the Pathway: An Introduction to the Work of Dimitris and Suzana Antonakakis," *Architecture in Greece* 15 (1981): 15.

8. See, for example, Liane Lefaivre and Alexander Tzonis, *Critical Regionalism: Architecture and Identity in a Globalizing World* (Munich: Prestel, 2003).

9. Quoted in Frampton, "Towards a Critical Regionalism," 22.

10. These notes from my sketchbook were made at a lecture by Harries at the Graduate School of Fine Arts, University of Pennsylvania, on February 11, 1994. All subsequent Harries quotations are from the same source.

11. For a more detailed discussion of the Salt Lake City project see, in this volume, "Water, Urban Nature, and the Art of Landscape Design," 257–58.

12. For detailed discussions of the Sixteenth Street Transitway Mall design see, in this volume, "Regionalism and the Practice of Hanna/Olin, Ltd.," 64–65, and "Civic Realism and Landscape," 211–12.

13. John Dixon Hunt, *Historical Ground: The Role of History in Contemporary Landscape Architecture* (New York: Routledge, 2014), 3. He uses a project of mine, Robert Wagner Jr. Park in New York City, and my discussion of it in the essay "What I Do When I Can Do It" (included elsewhere in this volume) to make his point.
14. Matthew Hutson, "Quenching Consumers' Thirst for 'Authentic' Brands," *New York Times,* December 28, 2014.
15. Ibid.
16. J. B. Jackson, "The Imitation of Nature" (1959), in *Landscapes: Selected Writings of J. B. Jackson,* ed. Ervin H. Zube (Amherst: University of Massachusetts Press, 1970), 87.

WATER, URBAN NATURE, AND THE ART OF LANDSCAPE DESIGN

1. Laurie Olin, "Landscape Design and Nature," in George F. Thompson and Frederick R. Steiner, eds., *Ecological Design and Planning* (New York: Wiley, 1997), 109–39.
2. Ian L. McHarg, *Design with Nature* (Garden City, NY: Doubleday / Natural History Press, 1969). A twenty-fifth anniversary edition was published in 1995.
3. A number of such projects are presented in whole or part in Susan Weiler and Katrin Sholtz-Barth, *Green Roof Systems: A Guide to the Planning, Design, and Construction of Landscapes over Structure* (New York: Wiley, 2009).
4. Isaiah Berlin, *The Hedgehog and the Fox: An Essay on Tolstoy's View of History* (London: Weidenfeld & Nicolson, 1953).
5. For further discussion of Director Park, see, in this volume, "Civic Realism and Landscape," 212–15.
6. "Rainwater System to Save Half-Million Gallons of Water a Year," *Yale Alumni Magazine,* January–February 2008, 19.
7. For a discussion of the ecological analogies suggested and employed in this project, see Laurie Olin, "Landscape Ecology and Cities," in Tony Atkin and Joseph Rykwert, eds., *Structure and Meaning in Human Settlements* (Philadelphia: University of Pennsylvania Museum of Archaeology and Anthropology, 2005), 307–22.
8. Justin Gillis, "U.S. Climate Has Already Changed, Study Finds, Citing Heat and Floods," *New York Times,* May 7, 2014. Gillis's front-page article, accompanied by a four-color map showing the degrees of temperature change throughout the United States, documented the third report of the National Climate Assessment initiative, prepared by a large scientific panel overseen by a federal advisory committee. Gillis quotes the report's conclusion that "climate change, once considered an issue for the distant future, has moved firmly into the present."
9. Several major deserts, including the Sahara and that of western China, have been growing significantly during the past decade, encroaching on formerly temperate green regions. The situation in the American Southwest has evolved rapidly in recent decades to one of continuing drought that, as of this writing, has all seven states that draw water from the Colorado River struggling for alternative and additional sources. California's Central Valley currently produces half of the nation's fruit and vegetables, but in 2015 it is anticipated to leave more than 600,000 acres of land unplanted, with a loss of $11 billion in income and jobs in our most populous state. In early 2014 the *New York Times* reported that California's State Water Project, the main municipal water distribution system, was unable to provide allocations to local agencies and farmers, and more than a dozen municipalities were projected to run out of water in a few months.

"Obama, in Drought-Stricken California, Announces Aid Package," *New York Times,* February 15, 2014.

10. There is an extensive and growing bibliography of articles and books on the topic of climate change, which range from scientific to academic and the general popular press. Even before hurricanes Katrina (2005) and Sandy (2012), the *New York Times,* for example, in a steady stream of articles and editorials has attempted to keep the public informed of the growing body of facts and evolving situation. A sample of articles from early 2014 includes, in addition to the one mentioned in note 8 above, Michael Wines, "Colorado River Drought Forces a Painful Reckoning for States," January 6; Justin Gillis, "The Flood Next Time," January 14; Porter Fox, "The End of Snow?" February 6; and Jennifer Medina, "California Seeing Brown on Water-Starved Farms Where Green Used to Be," February 15. Articles on the rise in sea levels have been well researched and written. The *New York Review of Books* has had a continuing sequence of extensive essays on the topic by Bill McKibben and others documenting the facts regarding melting glaciers; ozone in the atmosphere; transformations, crashes, and explosions in ocean and terrestrial plant and animal populations; and the effects on human global population, as well as economic and political conflict resulting from climate change. My own recent memoir, "From Sundogs to the Midnight Sun" (*Hudson Review* 66.1 [Spring 2013]: 50–93), regarding my youth in Alaska, ends with a consideration of circumpolar changes currently taking place.

11. *Our Common Future,* also known as the Brundtland Report, was issued in October 1987 by the World Commission on Environment and Development of the United Nations, often called the Brundtland Commission after its chair, Gro Harlem Brundtland, who served three terms as Norway's prime minister and later became director-general of the World Health Organization.

12. Elizabeth Kolbert, author of *Field Notes from a Catastrophe: Man, Nature, and Climate Change* (New York: Bloomsbury, 2006), an account of the current ongoing assault on the ecosphere, has recently published *The Sixth Extinction: An Unnatural History* (New York: Henry Holt, 2014), in which she presents the case that we are about to witness one of the greatest calamities in world history as a result of damage done to the environment in myriad ways: that between a quarter to half of the extant species on the planet will disappear within the current century, since it is unlikely we humans will make significant changes in our behavior and reverse a large number of current globally common practices and behaviors that makes this level of extinction likely.

13. This phenomenon has been the subject of study and enormous concern for decades. Rachel Carson, in *Silent Spring* (Boston: Houghton Mifflin, 1962), first published as a series of articles in the *New Yorker* and subsequently in book form despite the efforts of the American chemical industry to prevent it, raised the topic of the plummeting population of birds in New England. This resulted in immediate concern and debate on a national and public level, leading to the eventual banning of the use of the pesticide DDT. A considerable aspect in the creation and direction of the EPA and its work has been to address the fragility of natural communities and to prevent their decline and extinction. The most recent discussion of the topic that surveys species extinction throughout the history of the planet, with particular focus on the current situation worldwide, is Kolbert's *The Sixth Extinction.*

14. John Onions, *Art and Thought in the Hellenistic Age: The Greek World View, 350–50 BC* (London: Thames & Hudson, 1979), 38–52.

15. McLuhan quoted in Denis Donoghue, *Words Alone: The Poet T. S. Eliot* (New Haven: Yale University Press, 2000), 103 and 139.

16. Paul Fréart de Chantelou, *Diary of the Cavaliere Bernini's Visit to France,* trans. Margery Corbett, ed. Anthony Blunt (Princeton: Princeton University Press, 1985), 94; originally published as *Journal du voyage du cavalier Bernin en France,* ed. Ludovic Lalanne (Paris, 1885).

17. See Richard Louv, *Last Child in the Woods: Saving Our Children from Nature-Deficit Disorder* (Chapel Hill, NC: Algonquin Books, 2005); Peter H. Kahn and Stephen R. Kellert, *Children and Nature: Psychological, Sociocultural, and Evolutionary Investigations* (Cambridge: MIT Press, 2002); and Edward O. Wilson, *Biophilia* (Cambridge: MIT Press, 1984). Recent concerns regarding our dependence on nature for health are anticipated in earlier eras. See, for example, Clarence J. Glacken, *Traces on the Rhodian Shore: Nature and Culture in Western Thought from Ancient Times to the End of the Eighteenth Century* (Berkeley: University of California Press, 1990), which presents an exhaustive record of human attitudes to the natural environment through Western history.

18. Peter Aspinall, Panagiotis Mavros, Richard Coyne, and Jenny Roe, "The Urban Brain: Analysing Outdoor Physical Activity with Mobile EEG," *British Journal of Sports Medicine,* first published online, March 6, 2013; Clare Cooper Marcus and Marni Barnes, eds., *Healing Gardens: Therapeutic Benefits and Design Recommendations* (New York: Wiley, 1999); and Roger S. Ulrich, "Natural versus Urban Scenes: Some Psychological Effects," *Environment and Behavior* 13.5 (1981): 523–56. See also the websites of Therapeutic Landscapes Network, healinglandscapes.org, and the Landscape and Human Health Laboratory at the University of Illinois Urbana-Champaign, lhhl.illinois.edu, for descriptions of current academic programs in this area of study and publications.

19. Étienne Gilson, *The Arts of the Beautiful* (1965; repr., Champaign, IL: Dalkey Archive Press, 2000), 21.

20. Ibid., 22–23.

21. G. W. F. Hegel, *The Phenomenology of Mind* (1807), ed. and trans. J. B. Baillie, 2nd ed. (London: Macmillan, 1931), 5.

22. Denis Donoghue, *Speaking of Beauty* (New Haven: Yale University Press, 2003), 107.

23. Laurie Olin, "The Unstated Goal," in Laurie Olin et al., *OLIN: Placemaking* (New York: Monacelli Press, 2008), 14–15. This topic is also dealt with at length in my essay "Land and Beauty," *Proceedings of the Annual Meeting at Houston, December 5–7, 2008* (Austin: Philosophical Society of Texas, 2012), 64–75.

24. Donaghue, *Speaking of Beauty,* 125.

25. T. S. Eliot, "Burnt Norton," in *Collected Poems, 1909–1935* (New York: Harcourt Brace, 1936), 219. Donoghue takes up some of the implications of this passage in "The Force of Form," in *Speaking of Beauty,* 125–26.

26. Donoghue, *Speaking of Beauty,* 121, italics added.

27. Charles Baudelaire, "The Painter of Modern Life" ("Le peintre de la vie moderne," 1863), in *The Painter of Modern Life and Other Essays,* ed. and trans. Jonathan Mayne, 2nd ed. (London: Phaidon, 1995), 3.

28. See, for example, Randolph T. Hester Jr. and Amber D. Nelson, *Inhabiting the Sacred in Everyday Life* (Staunton, VA: George Thompson Publishing in association with the American Land Project, 2016).

29. J. B. Jackson, *Landscapes: Selected Writings of J. B. Jackson,* ed. Ervin H. Zube

(Amherst: University of Massachusetts Press, 1970), 87. See also Janet Mendelsohn and Christopher Wilson, eds., *Drawn to Landscape: The Pioneering Work of J. B. Jackson* (Staunton, VA: George Thompson Publishing, 2015).

30. William Shenstone, "Unconnected Thoughts on Gardening," in *The Works in Verse and Prose of W. Shenstone, Esq.,* 2nd ed., 2 vols. (London: R. Dodsley, 1765), 2:106. I wrote this statement on a card and pinned it on the wall above my desk at work many years ago. I don't know where I first saw it, but I was doing a lot of reading on eighteenth-century English landscape parks, gardens, and theory at the time. Shenstone was an amateur gardener and poet who wrote passionately about gardens and impoverished himself building his remarkable estate, Leasowes, in Shropshire. A contemporary description of Leasowes, likely written by Robert Dodsley, is in the same volume, i–xxx.

TREES AND THE GETTY

1. From Ashbery's collection *Some Trees* (1956). I heard Ashbery read the title poem from his first book at the YMHA in New York in 1966. Several friends and I had gone to hear him because of our interest in his recent book, *The Tennis Court Oath* (1962), which contained the most radically modern, difficult, and abstract verse he would ever write.

THE PROBLEM OF NATURE AND AESTHETICS IN PLANTING DESIGN

1. Gertrude Jekyll, *A Gardener's Testament* (1937; repr., Woodbridge, UK: Antique Collectors' Club, 1982), 14, 35, 58.
2. Laurie Olin, "Land and Beauty," *Proceedings of the Annual Meeting at Houston, December 5–7, 2008* (Austin: Philosophical Society of Texas, 2012), 66.
3. Frederick Law Olmsted, "Landscape Gardening" (1878), in *Frederick Law Olmsted: Essential Texts,* ed. Robert Twombly (New York: Norton, 2010), 157.
4. Quoted in Charles Beveridge, *Frederick Law Olmsted: Designing the American Landscape,* rev. ed. (New York: Rizzoli, 1998), 31.
5. Frederick Law Olmsted to Horatio Admiral Nelson, March 26, 1877, in Charles E. Beveridge, Carolyn F. Hoffman, and Kenneth Hawkins, eds., *Parks, Politics, and Patronage, 1874–1882,* vol. 7 of *The Papers of Fredrick Law Olmsted* (Baltimore: Johns Hopkins University Press, 2007), 314.
6. Olmsted, "Landscape Gardening," 157–59.
7. Olmsted to Horatio Admiral Nelson, 314, italics added.
8. Frederick Law Olmsted, *Yosemite and the Mariposa Grove: A Preliminary Report* (1865; Yosemite National Park, CA: Yosemite Association, 1995), 4, 13, 17.
9. Olmsted, "Landscape Gardening," 156.
10. Jens Jensen, "Garden Design: Special Lecture," in *Jens Jensen: Writings Inspired by Nature,* ed. William H. Tishler (Madison: Wisconsin Historical Society Press, 2012), 106.
11. Christopher Tunnard, *Gardens in the Modern Landscape* (1938, rev. 1948; repr., Philadelphia: University of Pennsylvania Press, 2018).
12. There is by now a huge literature on this subject; useful references include, in addition to Tunnard's *Gardens in the Modern Landscape,* Peter Walker and Melanie Simo, *Invisible Gardens: The Search for Modernism in the American Landscape* (Cambridge: MIT Press, 1996); Marc Treib, ed., *Modern Landscape Architecture: A Critical Review* (Cambridge: MIT Press, 1993); Kenneth Helphand, *Lawrence*

Halprin (Athens: University of Georgia Press in association with Library of American Landscape History, 2017); Alison Hirsch, *City Choreographer: Lawrence Halprin in Urban Renewal America* (Minneapolis: University of Minnesota Press, 2014); Lawrence Halprin, *A Life Spent Changing Places* (Philadelphia: University of Pennsylvania Press, 2011); Marc Treib and Dorothée Imbert, *Garrett Eckbo: Modern Landscapes for Living* (Berkeley: University of California Press, 1997); Dan Kiley and Jane Amidon, *Dan Kiley: The Complete Works of America's Master Landscape Architect* (Boston: Bulfinch Press, 1999); William Saunders, ed., *Daniel Urban Kiley: The Early Gardens* (New York: Princeton Architectural Press, 1999).

13. J. B. Jackson, "The Imitation of Nature" (1959), in *Landscapes: Selected Writings of J. B. Jackson,* ed. Ervin H. Zube (Amherst: University of Massachusetts Press, 1970).

14. Peter Walker and Leah Levy, *Peter Walker: Minimalist Gardens* (Washington, DC: Spacemaker Press, 1997).

15. From Freud's seminal work *Civilization and Its Discontents* (1930), in *The Standard Edition of the Complete Psychological Works of Sigmund Freud,* vol. 21 (London: Hogarth Press, 1961), 82; quoted in Jeremy Gilbert-Rolfe, *Beauty and the Contemporary Sublime* (New York: Allworth Press, 1999), 41.

INDEX

211; paving design and materials, 64, 210–11, 234; and regionalism, 64–65

Siza, Álvaro, 226

Skidmore, Owings & Merrill, 19

Skillman, NJ: Johnson & Johnson baby products division project, 73, 250, 324

Sloane, John, 201

Smirke, Robert, 125

social spaces. *See* civic spaces

Socrates, 219, 277

Somers, NY: IBM office complex project, 67–68, 72

"Some Trees" (Ashbery), 291

Soros garden, Southampton, NY (Bye), 44, 321

Sparta, 140

Speaking of Beauty (Donoghue), 286–87

species extinction, 243, 276, 353nn12–13

Speer, Albert, 183

Spirn, Anne Whiston, 11

Spurlock Poirier landscape architecture firm, 301

stairs and ascending paths, in architecture and landscape design, 123–26

Stamford, CT: Mill River Park and Greenway master plan project (OLIN: Sanders), 261; Pitney Bowes headquarters project, 59, 73

Standing Woman (Lachaise sculpture), 118

Stata Center for Computer, Information, and Intelligence Sciences, MIT (Gehry), 259

Stebbins, Emma, 36

Steele, Fletcher, 45, 172

Steiner, Frederick R., 247

Stella Garden, Philadelphia (Schwartz), 17

Stern, Henry, 208–9

Stern, Robert A. M., 131, 142

Stevens, Wallace, 146–47, 152, 178, 347n6; "Anecdote of the Jar," 147; "The Idea of Order at Key West," 146–47; and order/disorder, 146, 156, 347nn6–7; and "thingness," 164, 202

Stickley, Gustav, 52

Stiles College. *See* Yale University, Stiles and Morse Colleges project

Stoicism, 140, 175

Stone, Edward Durell, 116, 129

stormwater management, 250–52, 256–61, 265–68

Stourhead, Wiltshire, England (Hoare and Flitcroft): circuit, 123; and Claude's paintings, 81; Elysium park, 27, 182, 230; Flitcroft and, 343n52, 343n55; Gillette on, 182, 191; Hunt on, 181–82; influence of, 175; and Juvarra's scenery paintings, 343n52; Kent and, 107; and meaning, 35, 182, 190–91; Pantheon, 27, 35, 343n55; plantings, 314; pleasure garden, 157; Temple of Apollo, 35, 123; and sense of place, 230

"Stourhead" (Olin; from *Across the Open Field*), 181–82, 190–91

"Stourhead Revisited and the Pursuit of Meaning in Gardens" (Hunt), 11, 181–82

Stowe House, Buckinghamshire, England (Kent): Bridgeman and, 103; Brown and, 103, 343–44n57; Elysian Fields, 103, 175; Grecian Valley, 103, 343–44n57; influence of, 79, 175; Kent and, 79, 103, 105, 175, 343n55, 343–44n57; lake, 28; and meaning, 35; and Rousham, 103; Temple of Ancient Virtue, 175, 343n55; Temple of British Worthies, 82, 343n55, 343–44n57; and theatrical designs, 343–44n57; Vanbrugh and, 103

Stravinsky, Igor, 165; Place Igor Stravinsky, Paris, *196*

streams. *See* lakes and other water bodies

Strong, Roy, 82

structuralism, 76, 193

sublime, the, 284; and nature, 310–11; philosophers' writings on, 310

Sullivan, Louis, 38, 58

surrealism: and Harlequin Plaza, Denver (SWA/Hargreaves), 20, 22; and modernist landscape designs, 134, 321; and regionalism, 76; and Robert Wagner Jr. Park project, 151

sustainability, 206, 218, 260, 269–70